Data Management
and File Processing

PRENTICE-HALL SOFTWARE SERIES
Brian W. Kernighan, advisor

Data Management and File Processing

MARY E. S. LOOMIS

Department of Management Information Systems
University of Arizona

PRENTICE-HALL, INC., Englewood Cliffs, New Jersey 07632

Library of Congress Cataloging in Publication Data

Loomis, Mary E. S. (date)
  Data management and file processing.

  Includes index.
  1. File organization (Computer science) 2. Data
base management. I. Title.
QA76.9.F5L66 1983   001.64   82-23084
ISBN 0-13-196477-1

Editorial/production supervision
  and interior design: *Lynn S. Frankel*
Cover design: *Miriam Recio*
Manufacturing buyer: *Gordon Osbourne*

*Cover graphic adapted from the corporation logo
of D. Appleton Company, Inc., Manhattan Beach, California 90266.
Reprinted by permission.*

Printed in the United States of America

10 9 8 7 6 5 4 3

ISBN 0-13-196477-1

Prentice-Hall International, Inc., *London*
Prentice-Hall of Australia Pty. Limited, *Sydney*
Editora Prentice-Hall do Brasil, Ltda., *Rio de Janeiro*
Prentice-Hall Canada Inc., *Toronto*
Prentice-Hall of India Private Limited, *New Delhi*
Prentice-Hall of Japan, Inc., *Tokyo*
Prentice-Hall of Southeast Asia Pte. Ltd., *Singapore*
Whitehall Books Limited, *Wellington, New Zealand*

To Igor, the ultimate constant . . .

Contents

CHAPTER 14. INTRODUCTION TO FILE ORGANIZATION
AND MANAGEMENT   264

CHAPTER 15. FILE STORAGE DEVICES   276

CHAPTER 18. SORTING AND MERGING FILES 338

CHAPTER 19. RELATIVE FILE ORGANIZATION 360

Preface

This book is written for people who are concerned about the proper management of data resources. Data, after all, are the driving forces of all information systems; it is the data that give all other components of a computer system their reasons for being. Data resources play an integral role in the decision-making processes of all types of organizations, be they in the public or the private sectors, the competitive or regulated markets, large or small. Additionally, data are expensive; they must be collected, validated, organized, stored, maintained, aggregated and summarized, disseminated, and protected. This book addresses the problems of structuring, organizing, and processing collections of data so that they are available and responsive to users' information needs.

There are two main parts of the text: the first (Chapters 1 to 13) deals with the area traditionally known as data structures; the second (Chapters 14 to 21) focuses on management and processing of files. Chapter 22 is an introduction to database management systems. The reader is guided from the most basic aspects of data management (including stacks, queues, and linked lists) through more complex data structures (trees, B-trees, graphs) into processing of files (sequential, relative, indexed sequential, and multi-key organizations) and the elements of complex database management systems.

The book will be most meaningful to readers who have at least an introductory knowledge of computer systems and programming. A good deal of the book concerns algorithms for building and manipulating data structures and file organizations. These procedures generally are presented in either COBOL or Pascal. COBOL was selected because of its prevalence in today's data management environments. Pascal represents the family of increasingly popular block-structured languages, has nice data-typing features, and conveniently exhibits the logical structure of algorithms. You need not know both (or even either) of these languages to find the book quite readable. If you are beginning with knowledge only of FORTRAN (or Basic or PL/I or an assembler language or . . .) and you spend a little time with the code presented in the text, you will be able to finish the book with not only an understanding of the principles of data management and file processing, but also reasonable introductory knowledge of COBOL and Pascal. Only standard COBOL (ANSI X3.23-1974, ISO 1989–1978, also known as COBOL74) and fundamental Pascal constructs have been used. The appendix includes documentation of the meta-language used to describe the COBOL syntax. It is not necessary for you to have a mathematical background, but a basically logical approach to problem-solving certainly would be helpful.

Each chapter ends with a brief summary (which also masquerades as an introductory overview if read prior to the chapter), a list of terms, and a set of review exercises. The terms include words that were introduced in the chapter or were especially important to understanding of the text material. You will benefit from testing yourself on the meanings of these terms and perusal of the definitions in the Glossary at the end of the book.

Some of the review exercises require only short answers. Others suggest programs and projects to assist you in strengthening your understanding of the material. In general, the simpler, recall exercises appear first, followed by the more interesting, "action" exercises. Answers to selected questions are included after the Glossary.

The text is appropriate to support Course CS5 (Introduction to File Processing) and the less mathematical aspects of Course CS7 (Data Structures and Algorithm Analysis) from the ACM Curriculum Committee on Computer Sciences "Recommendations for the Undergraduate Program in Computer Science" (*Comm. ACM*, 22(3), March 1979). At the graduate level it supports Course CS32 (Information Storage and Access) from the same committee's "Recommendations for Master's Level Programs in Computer Science" (*Comm. ACM*, 24(3), March 1981). It also is appropriate to support Course C1 (Information Structures) and aspects of Course C3 (File and Communications Systems) from the ACM Curriculum Committee on Computer Education for Management's "Recommendations for Graduate Professional Programs in Information Systems" (*Comm. ACM*, 15(5), May 1972), as well as the corresponding courses from the same committee's "Curriculum Recommendations for Undergraduate Programs in Information Systems" (*Comm. ACM*, 16(2), December 1973).

I use the book in a one-semester graduate course and a two-semester undergraduate course sequence in a Management Information Systems program in a College of Business and Public Administration. The graduate course also has been cross-listed with the Computer Science program in the College of Liberal Arts.

My fundamental objective in writing this book has been to structure and draw together the principles of data management and file processing in a readable presentation. The intent has been to preserve the essence of more rigorous mathematical treatments of the subject matter, while not bogging down the unsuspecting reader with too many details. A blend of theoretical concepts and practical applications guides the orientation of the text.

Upon completion of the book, the reasonably motivated reader prepared with programming skills will be able to analyze the trade-offs of the data-handling needs of a particular problem situation, select the appropriate data structure or file organization, build the structure, retrieve selected data, update and maintain the structure, *and understand* what is going on. The book will give you a firm foundation for growing with the evolving technology of the complex information-handling field. You will be well prepared for follow-up study in database management techniques.

ACKNOWLEDGMENTS

This book has benefited from the feedback of many students in the Department of Management Information Systems at The University of Arizona. The comments of Clayton Curtis and Fred K. Nelson have been especially constructive. I thank the Prentice-Hall staff and editors, especially Lynn Frankel, for their fine work. Lynn's joyousness has made my job a real pleasure. The reviewers commissioned by Prentice-Hall, Inc., have led to considerable improvements in the text, notably in its early chapters. The project was materialized through the patient support of Ms. Kathy Todd, whose expertise at the keyboard is music to my ears.

The work would never have even gotten off the ground, let alone been given a chance to fly, without the encouragement of my husband, Tim. He has provided the constancy and perspective necessary to enable me nearly simultaneously to complete this manuscript and *Data Communications* (Englewood Cliffs, N.J.: Prentice-Hall, 1983), while maintaining some semblance of sanity. Allison's levity has contributed immeasurably.

MARY E. S. LOOMIS

Data Management and File Processing

CHAPTER 1

Introduction to Data Structures

The first part of this book discusses the major types of data structures and tells how they are managed by computer programs. This introductory chapter should give you an understanding of what a data structure is and why data structures are important in the world of information systems, as well as general knowledge of several simple data structures.

DATA

Before starting our discussion of data structures, let us first consider what data are and how they support information systems. Fig. 1 illustrates the roles that data play in the events of any organization. The large circle labeled "data" represents the overall data resource of the organization. This resource is an active participant in the organization's operations and planning. The small circles represent individual elements or items of data. These elements can be considered to be raw facts. They are aggregated and summarized in various meaningful ways to form information. Decisions are made on the basis of this information; we hope that the decisions we make *are* informed ones. Implementation of the results of decisions yields actions, which in turn generate more data. These data then can be incorporated into another cycle of the decision-making process.

Note that any given data element may participate in the generation of multiple "pieces" of information. It is important that there be flexi-

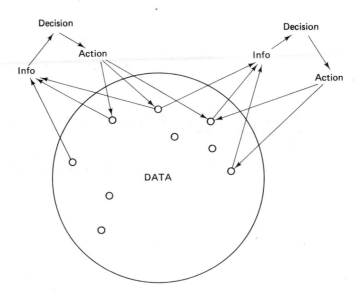

FIGURE 1   The use of data by events in an organization.

bility in the ways that data items are aggregated and summarized, so that meaningful information can be produced to support the decision at hand. Note also that some data elements in an organization's data resource may have resulted from actions taken by forces or bodies external to the organization. The actions of competitors, the behavior of customers or clients, and the forces of legal requirements all enter into an organization's decision-making process.

The data resource must support several types of decision-making. It is convenient to recognize three levels of decisions:

> *Operational* decisions, which govern the daily operations of the organization. These decisions are made by low-level management.
>
> *Control* decisions, which determine the way the organization executes its designated "mission." These decisions are sometimes called *tactical* decisions and are made by middle-level management.
>
> *Planning* decisions, which develop and define the organization's "mission." These decisions are sometimes termed *strategic* decisions and are made by top levels of management.

The same element of data may participate in the production of information to support all three levels of decision-making. For example, one data element, the number of green telephone handsets produced by plastic-stamping machine #12345-78, could be used in answering each of the following questions:

1. How many green telephone handsets should machine #12345-78 be set up to produce today? (Operational)
2. Based upon production, failure, and repair data, should we purchase three more plastic-stamping machines for making telephone handsets? (Control)
3. Should the firm acquire a subsidiary company that produces plastic-stamping machines, thus increasing its ability to respond to changing market forces? (Planning)

Each of these decisions must be based upon valid data.

DATA MANAGEMENT

Data are expensive. They must be managed in such a way that they are correct and are available to produce needed information. Aspects of data handling include:

- Measurement
- Collection
- Transcription
- Validation
- Organization
- Storage
- Aggregation
- Update
- Retrieval
- Protection

Data management systems are concerned with doing these things to data. Their ultimate objective is to make the data resource resilient, flexible, and adaptable to supporting an organization's decision-making processes. Four useful guidelines for a data management system are:

1. Data must be **represented** and **stored** so that they can be *accessed* later.
2. Data must be **organized** so that they can be *selectively* and *efficiently* accessed.
3. Data must be **processed** and **presented** so that they *support the user environment effectively*.
4. Data must be **protected** and **managed** so that they retain their *value*.

These guidelines are the motivation for much of the material covered in this book. A major reason for the importance of data structures is that they can help us to achieve guidelines (1) and (2).

We will be discussing the representation, storage, and organization of data on both primary and secondary storage devices. With *primary storage*, the time required to access the data stored in one location is the same as the time needed to access the data stored in any other location on the device. Primary storage also is commonly called *main memory*. With *secondary storage*, the time required to access the data stored in one location may be different from the time required to access the data stored in another location on the same device. Secondary storage is also called *auxiliary memory* and includes movable-head disks, fixed-head disks, magnetic tape, punched cards, and so forth.

Data management concerns are different for data stored in primary and secondary storage. We will be considering management of data in primary storage in the first part of this book, on data structures, and management of data in secondary storage in the second part, on file organization and processing.

DATA STRUCTURES

We approach the study of data representation, organization, and processing from the viewpoint of data structures. A *data structure* is a class of data that can be characterized by its organization and the operations that are defined on it.

Data structures are very important in computer systems. In a program, every variable is of some explicitly or implicitly defined data structure, which determines the set of operations that are legal upon that variable. The data structures that we discuss here are termed *logical data structures* in the sense that there may be several different physical representations on storage possible for any given logical data structure. For each data structure that we consider, several possible mappings to storage will be introduced.

Table 1 categorizes the various data structures that are discussed in this book. Some are primitive, that is, they are not composed of other data structures. These are commonly called *primitive data types*. We will consider briefly three examples of primitive data types: integers, booleans, and characters. A *compound data type* is constructed from one or more primitive data types. The compound data type that we will use as an example is the string. Many programming languages provide support for these data types.

Data types can be organized in various ways to form data structures. The dividing line between data types and simple data structures is fuzzy, and the terminology has evolved to call some organizations of data types "data structures" and to call others "compound data types." The two *simple data structures* that we will consider are arrays and records. These structures can be combined in various ways to form more complex data structures, which are sometimes called *compound data*

TABLE 1 Categorization of Data Structures Discussed in This Book.

DATA TYPES			DATA STRUCTURES			FILE STRUCTURES
Primitive	*Compound*		*Simple*	*Linear*	*Nonlinear*	
Integer	String		Array	Stack	Binary tree	Sequential organization
Boolean			Record	Queue	Binary search tree	Relative organization
Character				Linear linked list	*M*-way search tree	Indexed sequential organization
					B-tree, B*-tree, B+-tree	Multi-key organization
					Trie	
					General tree	
					Graph	

5

structures. Most of the first part of this book deals with compound data structures.

There are two fundamental types of compound data structures: linear and nonlinear, depending on the complexity of the logical relationships they represent. The linear data structures that we will discuss include stacks, queues, and linear linked lists. The nonlinear data structures include trees and graphs. We will find that there are many types of tree structures that are useful in data management.

The data structures applied to collections of data in secondary storage are called *file organizations.* The four basic types of file organization that we will discuss are sequential, relative, indexed sequential, and multi-key file organizations. Understanding of these techniques can lead directly into study of methods for managing full-scale database systems.

EXAMPLES: DATA TYPES

You are probably already familiar with a number of data types, and we will use some of those familiar data structures as examples in this chapter. One simple data type is the *integer.* An integer is a member of the following set of numbers:

$$[\ldots, -(n + 1), -n, \ldots, -2, -1, 0, 1, 2, \ldots, n, n + 1, \ldots].$$

The fundamental operations on integers are familiar: addition, subtraction, multiplication, division, exponentiation, and so forth. These operations all work on pairs of numbers; they are binary operators. A unary operator has only one operand. Negation, which changes a number's sign, is a familiar example of a unary operator.

A second example of a simple data structure is the *boolean* data type, which is also called the *logical* data type. A data element of this type can have one of two values: *true* or *false*. The defined set of operations on this data structure is different from the legal set of operations for integers. The three basic boolean operators are *not, and,* and *or*. Table 2 shows the results of applying each of these operators to each of the valid boolean values. Note that *or* and *and* are both binary operators, while *not* is a unary operator. *Not* has precedence over *or* and *and*; that is, in the absence of parentheses which change the order of evaluation, *not* is evaluated before *and* or *or*. For example, in evaluation of the expression

     A and not B,

B is first negated, and the result is *and*ed with *A*.

TABLE 2 Boolean Operators.

Value of First Operand	Value Second Operand	Operator		
		and	*or*	*not**
true	true	true	true	false
true	false	false	true	false
false	true	false	true	true
false	false	false	false	true

*Applied to first operand.

The values *true* and *false* can also result from what are known as *relational operators*. Relational operators do not have boolean operands; rather they are operators with results of type boolean. These operators include $<, >, =, \leqslant, \geqslant, \nless, \ngtr, \neq$. For example, $<$ may operate on two integers, with the result being a boolean data value: $6 < 12$ is *true*.

A third primitive data type with which you are probably already familiar is *characters*. A character is an element taken from a set of symbols. One possible set of symbols is:

[0,1,2,3,4,5,6,7,8,9,A,B,C,D, . . . ,X,Y,Z, ,?,.,*,+,-,/]

which includes the numeric digits, the alphabetic characters, and some special characters. Various compilers offer different character sets, which usually differ in the special characters that they include.

A compound data type that is constructed from the character data type is the *string*. A string is a finite sequence of symbols taken from a character set. The character set used to generate strings is called an *alphabet*. The set of strings that can be derived from the alphabet A = [C,D,1] includes the following: 'CD1', 'CD', 'DDC', '1D111', and so forth, including the null or empty string. We delineate the beginning and the end of a string by the quote marker.

The string is a very important data type, partly because it is so widely used. For instance, strings are the basic medium in which programs are written and transmitted to the computer. They are the principal medium of exchange of information with users. Strings are used in fields of records within files to store information. They are used in programming languages to name variables, labels, and procedures. In a more general context, it is via strings that humans communicate with each other.

The set of all possible strings that can be derived from an alphabet is called a *vocabulary*. The vocabulary V which is derived from alphabet A is sometimes denoted: $V_A = A*$. An alphabet need not contain only characters from our familiar alphabet [A,B,C,...,Y,Z]; it may contain any valid symbols. If the alphabet is [0,1], then the obtainable strings are commonly called *bit strings*.

More formally, let us denote a string S which is derived from the alphabet A by:

$S := `a_1 a_2 \ldots a_N`$
where each character $a_i \epsilon A$, for $1 \leqslant i \leqslant N$. (eq. 1-1)

Every string has an attribute called its *length*, which is the number of characters in the string.

The operations that are legally defined upon strings are different from those that are legally defined for integers. The three major operations on strings are:

1. Length
2. Concatenation
3. Substring

Denote by LENGTH the length operator, which gives the value of the string's length attribute. It has one operand, of type *string*, and produces a result of type *integer*. We can apply LENGTH to the string S defined by eq. 1-1, giving result N by writing:

$N :=$ LENGTH(S).

Concatenation operates on two strings, placing them end to end to produce a resultant string. Denote by CONCAT the concatenation operator. It has two operands, both of type *string*, and produces a result of type *string*. If S is defined by eq. 1-1 and S^0 is defined by

$S^0 := `b_1 b_2 \ldots b_M`$
where each character $b_i \epsilon B$, for $1 \leqslant i \leqslant M$

on alphabet B, then

CONCAT(S,S^0) is $`a_1 a_2 \ldots a_N b_1 b_2 \ldots b_M`$

The length of the resultant string is the sum of the lengths of the component strings:

LENGTH (CONCAT(S,S^0))=LENGTH(S)+LENGTH(S^0).

The concatenation of the string with value 'STOVE' and the string with value 'PIPE' results in the string 'STOVEPIPE'.

Substring has a single string as one of its operands and generates a new string as its result. In order fully to specify the substring operation, one must specify not only the operand string, but also the starting point within that string and how many characters are to be taken from that string to form a new one. Denote by SUBSTR the substring operator.

It has one operand of type *string*, has two operands of type *integer*, and produces a result of type *string*. If S is defined by eq. 1-1, then

SUBSTR(S,i,j) is '$a_i, a_{i+1}, \ldots a_{i+j-1}$'
where i is the starting point, $0 \leqslant i \leqslant$ LENGTH(S)
j is the number of characters to take, $0 \leqslant j \leqslant$ LENGTH(S)
and $0 \leqslant i + j - 1 \leqslant$ LENGTH(S),
for i, j of type *integer*.

The LENGTH (SUBSTR(S,i,j)) is j.

The SUBSTR operator can be used to undo the effects of the CONCAT operator:

SUBSTR(CONCAT$(S, S^0), 1,$ LENGTH$(S))$ is S
and SUBSTR(CONCAT$(S, S^0),$ LENGTH$(S)+1,$ LENGTH$(S^0))$ is S^0.

These three string operators—length, concatenation, and substring—cannot meaningfully be applied to variables that are of the integer data type. If we want to put the integer 12 together with the integer 34, we probably are not referring to concatenation with result 1234, but rather to addition with result 46. However, it is certainly valid to concatenate string '12' and string '34' with result a third string '1234' of length 4. Integers are sometimes converted to strings and manipulated as strings, then converted back to integers.

There are other composite operations that are legal upon strings. For example, denote by INSERT the insertion operator. It has two operands of type *string*, one operand of type *integer*, and produces a result of type *string*. INSERT(S, S^0, i) inserts the string S^0 into the string S, such that the first character of S^0 is the ith character of the result.

INSERT(S, S^0, i) is CONCAT(CONCAT(SUBSTR$(S,1,i-1), S^0),$
SUBSTR$(S, i,$ LENGTH$(S)-(i-1)))$
where $1 \leqslant i \leqslant$ LENGTH$(S)+1$.

Denote by DELETE the deletion operator. It has one operand of type *string*, has two operands of type *integer*, and produces a result of type *string*. DELETE(S,i,j) deletes from S the substring of length j that starts at the ith character.

DELETE(S, i, j) is CONCAT(SUBSTR$(S, 1, i-1),$
SUBSTR$(S, i+j,$ LENGTH$(S)-(i+j-1)))$
where $1 \leqslant i \leqslant$ LENGTH(S)
$0 \leqslant j \leqslant$ LENGTH(S)
$0 \leqslant i+j-1 \leqslant$ LENGTH(S)
for i, j of type *integer*.

We have distinguished between an integer value and a string value by delimiting the latter with the quote markers. In order to distinguish between integer and string values, programming languages commonly use the same convention. If 1234 is an *integer*, it is written 1234. If 1234 is a *string*, it is written either '1234' or "1234". In the same way, programming languages distinguish between string values and names of variables. For instance, ELMER may be ELMER the name of a variable, or ELMER the string. The string ELMER is written 'ELMER' or "ELMER"; the variable name ELMER is written ELMER.

DECLARATION OF DATA STRUCTURES
IN PROGRAMMING LANGUAGES

Programming languages give the programmer the means to assign data structure types to variables. A variable must have values taken from the set of defined values for its data type and only those operations that are defined as being legal for that data type should be performed upon the variable. Various programming languages have different ways of assigning types to variables; some compilers take more seriously than do others the responsibility of verifying adherence to the rules that characterize a particular data structure. For example, some compilers really do not care whether or not a program moves an alphabetic character like 'Q' to an integer field; they will even let the program go ahead and add 'Q' to something else, with no warning or notice of possibly meaningless results. Other compilers would generate a compile-time error or execution-time error depending upon when the event occurred.

Some languages, such as Pascal and COBOL, require that the programmer explicitly declare the type of every variable used in the program. Other languages, for example FORTRAN, have some implicit data typing. For instance, variables whose names start with *I, J, K, L, M,* or *N* are integer data types unless explicitly declared otherwise.

In some languages, such as COBOL, there is a special division of a program whose primary purpose is definition of data types. In some other languages, for example Pascal, the type of a variable merely has to be declared prior to the first use of the variable. PL/I has the *DECLARE* statement for data definition; Pascal offers the *var* statement; FORTRAN programmers use *INTEGER*, *REAL*, and *DIMENSION* statements.

Most programming languages now in use offer the programmer a predefined set of data types for use in characterizing variables. Others, perhaps most notably Pascal with its *type* statement, actually enable the programmer to define and name data structures. Sometimes this feature is used to give a programmer-defined name to a composite of system-defined types, but more creative data typing by the programmer is also supported.

Following are the ways in which a programmer would define variables that are integer, boolean, and character data structures in COBOL and Pascal. Assume the integer variable is to be named *COUNT* and to have a maximum of three digits; the boolean variable is to be named *SWITCH*; the character variable is to be named *BETA*.

```
COBOL:  DATA DIVISION.
        01  COUNT PICTURE S999.
        01  FLDA PICTURE X.
            88 SWITCH VALUE 'Y'.
        01  BETA PICTURE X.
```

The *S* in *COUNT*'s *PICTURE* clause represents a signed value and is needed to allow negative values to be stored in a numeric variable. COBOL does not have a data type called boolean; instead the condition-name feature can be used to associate words with the values that a data item can assume. Those condition-names can then be used in conditional statements. For example, here, the 88-level condition-name *SWITCH* is defined to have the boolean value *true* when *FLDA* equals 'Y' and the boolean value *false* for all other values of *FLDA*. The programmer then can code

```
IF SWITCH THEN...
   ELSE...
```

instead of

```
IF FLDA = 'Y' THEN...
   ELSE...
```

The *X* pictures on *FLDA* and *BETA* indicate that values are to be taken from the full character set; the *9* picture on *COUNT* indicates that values are to be taken from the numerics.

```
Pascal:
   var count : integer;
       switch : boolean;
       beta : char;
```

The number of digits in *count* could be controlled by format in read and write commands; variable *switch* can be assigned the value *true* or *false*.

Strings can be defined easily in COBOL. To declare a variable named *ADDRESS* to be a string with length of 25 characters:

```
01   ADDRESS   PICTURE X(25).
```

The alphabet for deriving strings is the full character set supported by the compiler.

Declaration of string variables in Pascal is somewhat more cumbersome:

var address : packed array [1..25] of char;

Here each element of the array called *address* holds one character of the string. The array must be packed if it is desirable to refer to the string as a whole; otherwise only the component characters of the string could be referenced. We consider arrays in detail in the next chapter.

The programmer-defined typing facility of Pascal allows the programmer to give a name to a new composite data structure, then to assign that new type to variables. For example, the composite data structure formed from the elementary data type *char* could be given the name *string25*:

type string25 = packed array [1..25] of char;

Then the programmer could specify that variables *name* and *address* both are of this type:

var name, address : string25;

Some languages have built-in operators for manipulation of variables of type *string*. PL/I has *LENGTH*, *SUBSTR*, and ‖ (concatenation). COBOL has *STRING* and *UNSTRING*. Pascal does not have these fundamental operators. The programmer who needs to perform string operations must write the corresponding routines or extract them from a library of codes. Some languages, notably SNOBOL and UCSD Pascal, are specialized to enable the programmer to handle string data easily.

MAPPINGS TO STORAGE: INTEGERS

One characteristic of a logical data structure is that each may have several possible storage mappings or physical representations. In this section, some alternatives for mapping integers to storage are discussed.

One possible storage mapping for integers is called the *sign-and-magnitude* form. This is the conventional form for number representation by humans. Positive integers are identified by a plus sign and a string of digits which represent the magnitude; negative integers are identified by a minus sign and a string of digits which represent the magnitude. The plus sign is frequently omitted in our everyday use of numbers. However, it must be retained with the number for processing by the computer. The magnitude of a number is the natural value of the string of digits. In everyday usage by humans, a number's magnitude is represented in its base 10 form. In computer memory, we represent magnitude in its base 2 (binary) form.

Humans nearly exclusively use the sign-and-magnitude form. If we were to develop computer algorithms for adding numbers in sign-and-magnitude form, we would find that when the operands have unlike signs, addition actually requires subtraction, which becomes complicated. To circumvent this problem, another storage mapping called *complement* representation was developed.

Given the nonnegative integers X, X', and R, we define X' to be the *complement of* X *with respect to* R or *the* R*'s complement of* X when $X + X' = R$. In complement representation, the integers X are called *true forms* and the integers $X' = R - X$ are called the *complement forms*.

In a binary computer, one practical choice of the complementation constant R is as a power of 2;

$$R = 2^N.$$

The choice of N determines the range of integers that can be represented. The largest value representable in 2^N's complement form is 2^{N-1}. Mapping systems that use $R = 2^N$ are referred to as *two's-complement* systems. Table 3 illustrates the binary sign-and-magnitude representation and a two's-complement representation (using $R = 2^4$) of the integers in the range –7 to +7. The complement form $X' = R - X$ represents the negative integer $-X$; the true form X represents the positive integer X.

The algorithms used to perform arithmetic on integers represented

TABLE 3 Two Methods for Representation of Integer Values:
Binary Sign-and-Magnitude and Two's-Complement

Integer	Binary Sign-and-Magnitude	Two's-Complement	
–7	–111	1001	
–6	–110	1010	
–5	–101	1011	complement
–4	–100	1100	forms
–3	–011	1101	
–2	–010	1110	
–1	–001	1111	
+0	+000	0000	
+1	+001	0001	
+2	+010	0010	
+3	+011	0011	true forms
+4	+100	0100	
+5	+101	0101	
+6	+110	0110	
+7	+111	0111	

in complement form are more convenient for the computer than are the algorithms to manipulate integers represented in sign-and-magnitude form. Thus, if much computation is to be performed on an integer variable, it may be advisable to represent it in storage using a complement form.

A second practical choice of the complementation constant R is:

$R = 2^N - 1.$

These mapping systems are commonly referred to as *one's-complement* systems. One of the exercises at the end of the chapter suggests that you construct the one's-complement representation (using $R = 2^4 - 1$) of the integers in the range –7 to +7. The one's-complement systems provide the same advantages over the sign-and-magnitude form as do the two's-complement systems. Some arithmetic algorithms are more complex for two's-complement form than for one's-complement form; others are more complex for one's-complement form.

Basically, both the sign-and-magnitude and complement forms represent integers by theme and variation on the number's magnitude. An alternative is to map integers to storage using a digit-by-digit approach, treating each digit as a character.

MAPPINGS TO STORAGE: CHARACTERS

There are many schemes in use today for the representation of character data. The two most prevalent encoding schemes are the Extended Binary Coded Decimal Interchange Code (EBCDIC) and the American Standard Code for Information Interchange (ASCII).

EBCDIC is an 8-bit code; 8 bits are required to represent any character in the character set. With 8 bits there are 2^8 (i.e., 256) possible combinations, and the EBCDIC code is thus quite rich. The character set that the EBCDIC code can generate includes both upper- and lower-case alphabet letters, the numeric digits, and many special characters.

ASCII is a 7-bit code. There are 2^7 possible combinations, which is half the number of characters offered by EBCDIC. The trade-off is that each character consumes less storage and can be transmitted more quickly.

Among the other encoding schemes available are some special-purpose codes, such as the family of Huffman codes. In this type of code, characters are represented by a variable number of bits depending upon the relative frequency of occurrence of the character in the vocabulary of the application. It is desirable to represent the most frequently occurring characters with the shorter bit patterns and less frequent characters with the longer bit patterns. For the example shown in Table 4,

Charac- ter	Frequency of occurrence (%)	Code	Number of bits	
0	55.5	0	1	
1	6.7	1000	4	
2	4.5	1100	4	
8	3.5	10010	5	
3	3.3	10100	5	
A	3.2	10101	5	
5	3.0	10110	5	
6	2.7	11100	5	
4	2.7	11101	5	
9	2.2	11110	5	
7	1.9	100110	6	
F	1.5	101110	6	
B	1.2	111110	6	
Blank	1.1	110110	6	
D	1.0	110100	6	
E	0.9	110101	6	
Z	0.7	1011110	7	
P	0.6	1111110	7	
N	0.5	1101110	7	
u	0.4	10011110	8	
C	0.4	10011100	8	
H	0.4	10011101	8	
R	0.3	10111110	8	
M	0.3	11111110	8	
L	0.3	11111111	8	
S	0.25	11011110	8	Average character length =
I	0.20	100111110	9	$0.555 \times 1 + 0.112 \times 4$
T	0.15	110111110	9	$+ 0.206 \times 5 + 0.76 \times 6$
K	0.15	110111111	9	$+ 0.018 \times 7 + 0.24 \times 8$
Y	0.13	1001111110	10	$+ 0.005 \times 9 + 0.0045 \times 10$
X	0.12	1001111111	10	$+ 0.0017 \times 11 + 0.0003 \times 12$
G	0.10	1011111100	10	$+ 0.0001 \times 16$
J	0.10	1011111101	10	= 2.91 bits per character
O	0.06	10111111100	11	
Q	0.03	10111111101	11	
V	0.03	10111111110	11	
W	0.03	101111111110	12	
.	0.01	1011111111110000	16	
–		1011111111110001	16	
?		1011111111110010	16	
&		1011111111110011	16	
/		1011111111110100	16	
+		1011111111110101	16	
<	below	1011111111110110	16	
)	0.001	1011111111110111	16	
(		1011111111111000	16	
%		1011111111111001	16	
=		1011111111111010	16	
#		1011111111111011	16	
?		1011111111111100	16	
,		1011111111111101	16	
@		1011111111111110	16	
		1011111111111111	16	

the character 0 is represented by a single bit 0; the character A is represented by a 5-bit pattern 10101; the character % is represented by a 16-bit pattern 1011111111111001. A trade-off to the resultant compressed storage requirement is the processing necessary to encode and to recognize characters.

Many compilers will allow a programmer to specify a multiplicity of codes for use within a single program. For example, a COBOL program might read or write some data to files using EBCDIC, perhaps for tape drive compatibility. Other data might be read or written in ASCII, probably for input/output on terminal devices. Other data might be represented using an internal display code, if they are not to be shared with processes on any other equipment. Any particular data element can be encoded using only one scheme.

When a character-encoding scheme is used to represent integers, a plus or minus sign must be stored with the representation to indicate whether the integer is positive or negative. Generally this sign is stored to the right of the low-order digit of the number.

Many compilers also offer other options and variations on these codes for integer representation. Perhaps the most widely used alternative is the *packed-decimal* format. This scheme represents numeric data more concisely by storing two digits per 8 bits, rather than one digit per 8 bits (EBCDIC). The right-most 8 bits contain not only the low-order digit of the number, but also the sign of the number. Table 5 illustrates the representations of the integers +903 and −903 using various character-oriented schemes.

TABLE 5 Examples of Character-Oriented Numeric Representations.

Code	+903			
EBCDIC	11111001	11110000	11110011	01001110
ASCII	0111001	0110000	0110011	0101011
Packed-decimal	10010000	00111100		

Code	−903			
EBCDIC	11111001	11110000	11110011	00100000
ASCII	0111001	0110000	0110011	0101101
Packed-decimal	10010000	00111101		

MAPPINGS TO STORAGE: STRINGS

Now that we have discussed how individual characters are represented, let us consider alternatives for representing strings of characters. The discussion in this section is limited to representation of strings in contiguous space; storage of a string of length N will require physically adjacent space for N characters.

In order to describe the contiguous storage mapping of a string, it is necessary to indicate both where the string's space starts and where it terminates. In each of the following conventions, at least one auxiliary variable of data type *pointer* is required. More will be said about the *pointer* data type later; for now suffice it to say that the value of a variable of data type *pointer* is an address; i.e., the pointer identifies a storage location.

There are at least three simple ways to describe string variables stored in contiguous space. We use as our examples two strings: STRING1 = 'ABCDEFG' and STRING2 = 'BCD'.

1. Keep a table of the following information for each string variable: its name, its starting address, its length. For example,

NAME	START	LENGTH
STRING1	PTR1S	7
STRING2	PTR2S	3

The corresponding storage format could be:

```
A B C D E F G B C D
↑             ↖
PTR1S         PTR2S
```

or (overlaying the strings):

```
A B C D E F G
↑   ↖
PTR1S  PTR2S
```

2. Keep a table of the following information for each string variable: its name, its starting address, its terminating address. For example,

NAME	START	TERM
STRING1	PTR1S	PTR1T
STRING2	PTR2S	PTR2T

The corresponding storage format could be:

```
A B C D E F G B C D
↑       ↗   ↖   ↖
PTR1S  PTR1T  PTR2S  PTR2T
```

or (overlaying the strings):

```
A B C D E F G
↑   ↖   ↗   ↖
PTR1S  PTR2S  PTR2T  PTR1T
```

3. Keep a table of the following information for each string variable: its name and its starting address. Use an end-of-string marker (e.g., ξ) in storage to delimit the string. For example,

NAME	START
STRING1	PTR1S
STRING2	PTR2S

The corresponding storage format could be:

Another consideration in the representation of strings in storage is whether that representation is to be packed or unpacked. Given a particular encoding scheme, and assuming a word-oriented machine, the *packed representation* of a string consists of placing each of the successive codes for the characters in the string in successive storage words, with as many of the characters as possible in any given word. The string 'BINDERSTWINE' with four character-per-word packing is given in Fig. 2.

FIGURE 2

Generalizing, with K characters per word, the number of words required to store string S is $\left\lceil \dfrac{\text{LENGTH(S)}}{K} \right\rceil$, where $\lceil \; \rceil$ is the ceiling function.* Sometimes the character codes fit evenly in a word; if there are 32 bits per word or 16 bits per word, then EBCDIC with 8 bits per character fits very well. However, ASCII, with 7 bits per character, will allow two characters in a 16-bit word with two unusable bits remaining, or four characters in a 32-bit word with four unusable bits remaining.

The *unpacked representation* for a string consists of storing one to a word the character codes for each of the successive characters. Each character is generally placed in the high-order bits of its word. The string 'BINDERSTWINE' stored in unpacked format is given in Fig. 3.

---

*The ceiling function yields the first integer value greater than or equal to the operand. For example $\lceil 3.16 \rceil$ is 4; $\lceil 3 \rceil$ is 3.

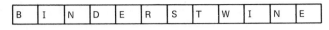

B	I	N	D	E	R	S	T	W	I	N	E

FIGURE 3

The number of words required to store string S in unpacked format is LENGTH(S).

Which of the two types of string representation is better? It all depends upon the objectives at hand. Packed representation is ideal for situations where minimizing storage utilization is paramount; however, operations are generally slower upon the packed representation than upon the unpacked representation. The unpacked representation requires no shifting, masking, or conversion when the contents of the words are manipulated.

SELECTION OF APPROPRIATE MAPPINGS

The previous sections should have convinced you that there are indeed several possible mappings of the example data structures to storage. The determination of which option is the most appropriate mapping to use is based upon (1) how the variable will be manipulated, (2) the range of values that the variable will have, (3) the characteristics of the computer and memory that will process and store the variable.

The choice of one's- and two's-complement form implies that the arithmetic algorithms used are less complex for the computer than if a sign-and-magnitude representation were used. Algorithms to compute with integers represented in a digit-by-digit code are even more complex than are the sign-and-magnitude algorithms. In fact, many compilers convert numbers from a digit-by-digit form to either sign-and-magnitude or complement representation prior to performing arithmetic.

If calculations are so much less efficient with the digit-by-digit representations, why do they exist? The basic reason for the importance of coding schemes such as EBCDIC and ASCII is their capability to represent nonnumeric characters. Additionally, if numeric data are to be displayed on a terminal screen or written on a report intended for human consumption, they must be represented in a displayable code.

Why are there so many coding schemes? The primary reason is that they have been developed by different groups for various purposes. Some machines, such as many IBM computers, use 32-bit words. An 8-bit/character code (e.g., EBCDIC) is very convenient for representing data with that word size. The DEC System 10 has 36-bit words. A 7-bit/character code (e.g., ASCII) conveniently represents five characters per word, with room for 1 sign bit. Large CDC computers, like the CYBER 175 and CDC 7600, have 60-bit words. These machines are well suited for scientific computing because of the greater precision made possible by the relatively long word length. A 6-bit/character code (e.g., BCD) conveniently represents ten characters per word. Some space-saving codes are used when memory space is tight or communications capacities are quite limited.

The most widely used codes today for data exchange between machines are EBCDIC and ASCII. Many compiler vendors offer both these options in their compilers. Additionally, nearly all the terminal vendors supply equipment with processors that accept one or both of these codes.

SUMMARY

This chapter began with a review of the importance of data to organizations' decision-making processes. Four guidelines for data management systems were proposed. The concept of data structure was then introduced and the various data structures that will be discussed in this book were categorized.

Integers, booleans, and characters were introduced as examples of primitive data types. These data types were probably already familiar to some readers. The compound data type called string and its fundamental operators (length, concatenation, and substring) were introduced.

The facilities for declaration of integers, booleans, characters, and strings in COBOL and Pascal were reviewed. These two languages will be used throughout the book to illustrate the types of support provided to programmers for data structure definition and manipulation.

There are several alternative ways to map any logical data structure to physical computer storage. Sign-and-magnitude and complement representations of integers were discussed. EBCDIC and ASCII were introduced as techniques for mapping character data to storage, then were extended to use for character-oriented mapping of integers to storage. Finally, the packed-decimal representation of integers was introduced.

The mapping of a string to storage involves both (1) the representation of each character of the string, and (2) the representation of the combination of characters to form the string. Alternatives for storing information needed to find the beginning and ending symbols of a string were proposed, then the distinction between packed- and unpacked-string representation was made.

The selection of the most appropriate mapping scheme for any particular data structure should be based on the manipulations to be performed on that data, the characteristics of the values that the data structure will have, and the characteristics of the computer and the memory that will process and store the data structure. Some of the elementary trade-offs among mappings were introduced.

Data structures are essential to information systems. In order to be able to design efficient support for the data resources of an information system, one must have an understanding of how data are represented and manipulated. The data types that are used in a program help determine what the storage requirements are of that program, what its processing requirements are, what the input–output requirements are, what the response time will be, and so forth. A multiplicity of data structures is available primarily because different types of data are used in different ways. The data structures used actually define the access paths that are supported between data elements. The orientation of this book is toward understanding how the various data structures can be used in solving problems efficiently and effectively.

Terms

alphabet
ASCII
auxiliary memory
bit string
boolean data type
boolean operator
character data type
complement representation
concatenation
EBCDIC
integer data type

main memory
packed-decimal representation
packed-string representation
primary storage device
secondary storage device
sign-and-magnitude representation
string
string length
unpacked string representation
vocabulary

Review Exercises

1. List the various aspects of data handling that are required in an information system. Of these functions, which are likely to be the most expensive? Why?

2. Give five examples of integer values.

3. Give as many examples as you can of boolean values.

4. What is the result of each of the following operations, where boolean variable

FIRST has value *true*, variable SECOND has value *false*, and variable THIRD has value *true*?

(a) *not* FIRST

(b) FIRST *and* SECOND

(c) FIRST *and* THIRD

(d) FIRST *or* SECOND

(e) FIRST *or* THIRD

(f) *not* FIRST *or* THIRD

(g) *not* (FIRST *or* THIRD)

(h) *not* FIRST *and* SECOND

(i) *not* (FIRST *and* SECOND)

(j) FIRST *and not* SECOND

(k) *not* (FIRST *and not* SECOND)

5. What is the result of each of the following operations, where string variable *S1* has value 'PIE', variable *S2* has value 'MAGIC', and variable *S3* has value 'WHEEL'?

(a) LENGTH($S2$)

(b) LENGTH($S3$)

(c) CONCAT($S2,S1$)

(d) SUBSTR($S3$,4,3)

(e) CONCAT(SUBSTR($S2$,1,3),$S1$)

(f) CONCAT(SUBSTR($S2$,1,3),$S3$)

(g) SUBSTR(CONCAT($S1,S2$),1,LENGTH($S1$))

(h) SUBSTR(CONCAT($S2,S1$),LENGTH($S2$)+1,LENGTH($S1$))

(i) INSERT($S1$,SUBSTR($S3$,6,1),3)

(j) DELETE($S2$,2,2)

(k) INSERT($S1$,DELETE($S3$,1,3),1)

6. Construct the one's-complement representation (with $R = 2^4 - 1$) of the integers in the range –7 to +7.

7. What is the minimum value of R needed to represent the R's complement of values between (a) –10 and +10? (b) –100 and +100?

8. What is the minimum value of R needed to represent the two's-complement of values between (a) –10 and +10? (b) –100 and +100?

9. How many bits are required to represent values in two's-complement form with $R = 2^N$?

10. How many bits are required to represent values in one's-complement form with $R = 2^N-1$?

11. What are the largest and smallest values that can be represented in two's-complement form with (a) $R = 32$? (b) $R = 256$? (c) $R = 2^N$?

12. What are the largest and smallest values that can be represented in one's-complement form with (a) $R = 31$? (b) $R = 255$? (c) $R = 2^N-1$?

13. What techniques are used to map integers to storage by the compilers available to you?

14. What techniques are used to map characters to storage by the compilers available to you?

15. Find charts that give the EBCDIC and ASCII character codes.

16. Give the EBCDIC representation of your name and address.

17. Give the ASCII representation of your name and address.

18. Represent your social security number or some other identification number using EBCDIC, ASCII, and packed decimal.

19. Give at least three possible storage representations of the three string values: 'MAGPIE', 'PIE', and 'MAGENTA'.

20. What are the basic trade-offs to be considered in overlaying string representations in storage?

21. What are the basic trade-offs to be considered in packing string representations in storage?

22. What are the basic trade-offs to be considered in using (A) a length indicator to terminate a string representation, (B) a pointer to terminate a string representation, and (C) an end-of-string marker to terminate a string representation?

23. Determine what types of primary and secondary storage devices are available at your computer facility. What are their capacities? What are the relative costs of their usage?

24. What is the full character set used by your Pascal (or COBOL or FORTRAN or PL/I or . . .) compiler?

25. Find out how to format character string input for your local Pascal compiler.

26. Write a program that reads and writes five character strings, each of length 10.

27. Modify your program to read and write N character strings, each of some unknown length. What are the required inputs to the program?

28. Write a program that implements the LENGTH, CONCAT, and SUBSTR operators.

29. Augment your program from 28 to implement the INSERT and DELETE operators.

CHAPTER 2

Arrays

This chapter discusses the very common data structure known as the array. Arrays are basic building blocks for more complex data structures. Nearly every kind of complex structure can be represented logically by an array. We first define simple and multi-dimensional arrays. Then the facilities for declaring array variables in COBOL and Pascal are reviewed. Much of the chapter is devoted to discussion of how one- and multi-dimensional arrays are mapped to storage. Finally, a discussion of techniques for representing triangular and sparse arrays closes the chapter. We will find that arrays are used extensively in both file structuring and data management, which will be discussed throughout this text.

DEFINITIONS: ONE-DIMENSIONAL ARRAYS

An *array* is a finite, ordered set of homogeneous elements. The ordering property means that the first, second, third, . . . , nth element of an array can be identified. The elements of an array are homogeneous, i.e., of the same data type. One array might be comprised of elements that are all of data type string; another might be comprised of elements that are all of data type integer; the elements of an array may each themselves be of the data type array. Arrays are also referred to as *tables*.

The simplest form of array is a *one-dimensional array*, or *vector*. A one-dimensional array named *VICTOR*, which consists of N elements, can be depicted as in Fig. 4.

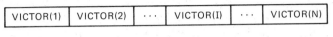

| VICTOR(1) | VICTOR(2) | ⋯ | VICTOR(I) | ⋯ | VICTOR(N) |

FIGURE 4

The *subscript*, or *index*, of an element designates its position in the array's ordering. In the notation used here, a particular element is identified by the name of the array followed by the element's subscript enclosed in parentheses, i.e., *VICTOR(I)*. Other possible notations to designate the element of array *VICTOR* with subscript I include *VICTOR[I]*, $VICTOR_I$, and $VICTOR^I$.

Note that only the array itself is given a name. Elements of an array are referred to by their subscripts, i.e., by their relative positions in the array. This naming convention enables the programmer to write algorithms that loop through the elements of an array, rather than having to name each of the elements distinctly.

More formally, the one-dimensional array A with elements of data type T having subscripts extending from L through U is:

$$A(L:U) = \{A(I)\}$$
$$\text{for } I = L, L+1, \ldots, U-1, U$$
where each element $A(I)$ is of data type T.

The notation $A(L:U)$ indicates that A's subscript value ranges from L through U.

As an example, a one-dimensional array might contain the temperatures recorded in a city for every hour during a 24-hour period. These elements are ordered by their corresponding time of the day.

The minimum allowable value of an array's subscript is called its *lower bound*; the maximum allowable value is called its *upper bound*. In our formal definition of an array, L is the lower-bound and U is the upper-bound of A's subscript. In the temperature-record example, a natural lower bound is 1 and upper bound is 24. Call the array *TEMP*. Then *TEMP(I)* is the temperature recorded at hour I, for $1 \leqslant I \leqslant 24$.

Another example of a one-dimensional array is a table of average state incomes. Name the array *AVG-INCOME*. The element *AVG-INCOME(I)* then is the average income of the Ith state, where the states are ordered sequentially, say alphabetically. Thus *AVG-INCOME(1)* is the average income of Alabama and *AVG-INCOME(50)* is the average income of Wyoming.

For some applications it is more natural to use a lower bound that is not equal to 1. For example, temperatures of an experiment that are recorded every ten seconds from time zero might more conveniently be stored in an array with lower bound 0. The lower bound may even be negative. This is commonly the case for arrays that store data to be displayed graphically, such as on an axis of points ranging from -100 to +100.

The number of elements in an array is called its *range*. The range of array $A(L:U)$ is $U-L+1$. The range of array $B(1:N)$ is N.

DEFINITIONS: MULTI-DIMENSIONAL ARRAYS

A two-dimensional array is an array in which each element is of data type array. An array named B which consists of M elements, each of which is an array of N elements can be depicted as an M-by-N table, as shown in Fig. 5.

FIGURE 5

It is necessary to specify two subscript values in order to identify an individual element of a two-dimensional array. By convention, the first subscript refers to a *row* of the array, while the second subscript refers to a *column* of the array. That is, $B(I,J)$ is the element of B that is in the Ith row and Jth column of array B, as indicated in Fig. 6.

FIGURE 6

More formally, the two-dimensional array B with individual elements of type T having row subscripts extending from 1 to M and column subscripts ranging from 1 to N is:

$$B(1:M,1:N) = \{B(I,J)\}$$
$$\text{for } I = 1, \ldots, M \text{ and } J = 1, \ldots, N$$
$$\text{where each } B(I,J) \text{ is of data type } T.$$

Array B is said to be of dimensions M by N. There are N elements in each row and M elements in each column of B; thus the total number of elements in array B is $M*N$.

Two-dimensional arrays are quite common. For example, the Chamber of Commerce of your city might keep track of the number of hours of fair weather in each day of the year. These data can be stored in an array with dimensions 365 by 24. Call the array W. Values of W could be determined by

$$W(I,J) = 1 \text{ if it is fair during the } J^{\text{th}} \text{ hour of the } I^{\text{th}} \text{ day of the year}$$
$$0 \text{ otherwise, i.e., if it snows, rains, sleets, drizzles, etc. during}$$
$$\text{the } J^{\text{th}} \text{ hour of the } I^{\text{th}} \text{ day of the year.}$$

Another example of a two-dimensional array is one that contains data about the grades of students in a class on the four semester-exams. This array, called $GRADE$, would have dimensions M by 4, where M is the number of students. Then $GRADE(I,J)$ is the grade achieved by the Ith student on the Jth exam. The value of I must be between 1 and M inclusive; J must be between 1 and 4 inclusive.

In general, a two-dimensional array B with its first subscript having lower bound L_1 and upper bound U_1 and its second subscript having lower bound L_2 and upper bound U_2 is defined as

$$B(L_1:U_1,L_2:U_2) = \{B(I,J)\} \text{ for } L_1 \leqslant I \leqslant U_1$$
$$\text{and } L_2 \leqslant J \leqslant U_2$$
$$\text{where each } B(I,J) \text{ is of data type } T.$$

The number of elements in a row of B is U_2-L_2+1 and the number of elements in a column of B is U_1-L_1+1. Thus the total number of elements in array B is $(U_2-L_2+1)*(U_1-L_1+1)$.

A *cross-section* of a two-dimensional array is obtained by holding one of the subscripts constant while varying the other through its entire range of values. The notation that is commonly used to denote a cross-section is an asterisk (*) for the subscript value that is to be allowed to take on its entire range of values. For example,

$$B(*,4)$$

refers to the fourth column of the array B pictured at the beginning of this section. That is,

$$B(*,4) = \{B(1,4), B(2,4), B(3,4), \ldots, B(M,4)\}.$$

Similarly,

$$B(I,*)$$

is the Ith row of the array B;

$$W(47,*)$$

is the row of W values recording the weather conditions on the 47th day of the year;

$$GRADE(*,3)$$

is the column of $GRADE$ values recording exam grades for all students on the third exam. A cross-section of a two-dimensional array is essentially a slice taken from the array.

The *transpose* of a two-dimensional array is obtained by reversing the subscript positions. The transpose of an M-by-N array is an N-by-M array. The transpose of array B is commonly denoted B^T. The transpose of the array B pictured at the beginning of this section is shown in Fig. 7.

FIGURE 7

By definition,

$$B(I,J) = B^T(J,I).$$

For example,

$$B(3,8) = B^T(8,3).$$

The element in row 3, column 8 of array B is the same as the element in row 8, column 3 of the transpose of array B.

An array can be defined to be three-dimensional, four-dimensional, up to N-dimensional. The concepts of subscript range and number of elements can be directly extended from one- and two-dimensional arrays to these higher-order arrays. In general, an N-dimensional array requires that the values of N subscripts be specified in order to identify an individual element of the array. An N-dimensional array A could be identified as

$$A(L_1:U_1,L_2:U_2,\ldots,L_N:U_N).$$

An individual element of array A could then be specified by $A(I_1,I_2,\ldots,I_N)$ where each subscript I_k is within the appropriate bounds $L_k \leqslant I_k \leqslant U_k$, for each $k = 1,2,\ldots,N$. The total number of elements in array A is:

$$\prod_{k=1}^{N}(U_k-L_k+1)$$

which could alternatively be written:

$$(U_1-L_1+1) * (U_2-L_2+1) * \ldots * (U_N-L_N+1).$$

An example of a three-dimensional array is one containing data about the number of students in each of a university's six classifications of students (freshman, sophomore, junior, senior, graduate, unclassified), by sex, for all of a university's ten colleges. Such an array might be called *COLLEGE-CT* and could be of dimensions 6 by 2 by 10. (Alternatively, it could be of dimensions 10 by 6 by 2, or 10 by 2 by 6, or 2 by 6 by 10, etc., as long as the reader knows what the meaning of each dimension is.) Array *COLLEGE-CT* could be drawn as shown in Fig. 8.

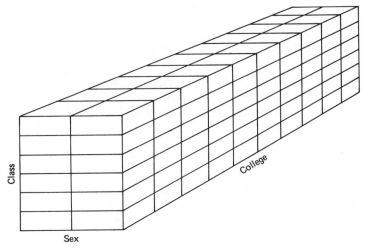

FIGURE 8

The value of element *COLLEGE-CT(I,J,K)*, then, is the number of students in class I of sex J for college K. To be valid, I must be 1,2,3, 4,5, or 6; J must be 1 or 2; K must be between 1 and 10 inclusive.

It is difficult to draw pictures of arrays with more than three dimensions.

A cross-section of a multi-dimensional array is formed by holding one or more subscript values constant and varying the other subscripts through their entire range of values. For example,

$$COLLEGE\text{-}CT(5,*,3)$$

is the "row" of *COLLEGE-CT* containing the number of students in the fifth class (graduate) of college 3, for both sexes. *COLLEGE-CT* (*,*,3) is the "plane" of *COLLEGE-CT* containing the number of students in college 3, for each class and both sexes.

DECLARATION OF ARRAYS IN COBOL AND PASCAL

The most common programming languages all use the same approach to declaration of variables of data type array. Consider first declaration of a one-dimensional array named TEMP with subscripts ranging from 1 to 24. Assume each element of the array is of data type integer, with range of values 0 degrees to 99 degrees.

In COBOL:

```
01  TEMP-TABLE.
    02  TEMP   OCCURS 24 TIMES
        PICTURE 99.
```

In Pascal:

```
var temp: array [1 . . 24] of integer.
```

Three things must be specified to declare an array: (1) the array name, (2) the subscript range, and (3) the data type of array elements.

Pascal allows a subscript's lower bound to be other than 1. For example,

```
var graphpts: array [-100 . . 100] of integer.
```

In COBOL arrays, a subscript must start from 1.

To refer to the Ith element of the array above, COBOL uses the notation: *TEMP(I)*. Pascal uses square brackets rather than parentheses about the subscript: *temp[i]* .

The declaration of an array to contain scores of 40 students on 4 exams would be as follows.

In COBOL:

```
01  GRADE-TABLE.
    02  STUDENT OCCURS 40 TIMES.
```

03   GRADE OCCURS 4 TIMES
               PICTURE 99V9.

In Pascal:

var grade: array [1 .. 40, 1 .. 4] of real.

In COBOL, the grade for the Ith student on the Jth exam is *GRADE (I,J)*. Pascal uses square brackets instead of parentheses: *grade [i,j]* . The subscript values must be within their valid bounds.

The maximum number of dimensions that can be declared for a COBOL array is three. For example,

01   COLLEGE-CT-TABLE.
  02   CLASSF OCCURS 6 TIMES.
    03   SEX OCCURS 2 TIMES.
      04   COLLEGE-CT OCCURS 10 TIMES
               PICTURE 9(5).

In Pascal this array would be defined by

var collegect: array [1 .. 6,1 .. 2,1 ..10] of integer.

In some languages, such as FORTRAN and COBOL, storage space is allocated to arrays at compile time. Thus the bounds must be specified when an array is defined. In other languages, such as PL/I, space can be allocated dynamically at execution time.

COBOL and Pascal (and other languages that allow programmers to declare arrays) have facilities for manipulation of individual elements of an array. The set of legal operations is defined by the data type of the elements. For example, substring and concatenation operations may be performed on elements of an array defined to be of data type string. Arithmetic calculations may be performed on individual elements of an array of integers or of decimals. For example, in COBOL,

COMPUTE TOTAL-PAY (I) = HRLY-RATE (I) * HRS-WORKED (I)

where each of the three variables is actually an array element.

Some programming languages also have array operations. For example, if A were declared to be an array in PL/I, then $A = A + 2$; would add 2 to each element of A. If A and B were declared to be arrays with the same dimensions, then in PL/I, $A = A * B$; would multiply each element of A by the corresponding element of B (i.e., by the element with the same subscripts), placing the result in A. This array multiplication is *not* matrix multiplication.

In PL/I, operations can be performed on cross-sections of arrays. For example,

GRADE(20,*) = 0;

sets each of the *GRADE* elements in the twentieth row to have value zero.

$$VECTOR(*) = ARRAY1(I,*) * ARRAY2(*,J);$$

multiplies the elements of the Ith row of *ARRAY1* by the elements of the Jth column of *ARRAY2*. The arrays must be declared to have compatible subscript range values. For example, if the second subscript of *ARRAY1* ranges from value 0 through 25, then the first subscript of *ARRAY2* must also range from value 0 through 25, as must the subscript of *VECTOR*. The above multiplication then has the same effect as does the following loop:

```
DO K = 0 TO 25;
    VECTOR(K) = ARRAY(I,K) * ARRAY2(K,J);
END;
```

MAPPINGS TO STORAGE: ONE-DIMENSIONAL ARRAYS

As with other data structures, there are several ways to represent arrays in memory. These representation schemes can be evaluated on the basis of four characteristics: (1) the simplicity of element access, (2) ease of traversal along various paths, (3) storage utilization efficiency, and (4) ease of growth. It is not possible to optimize all four of these factors simultaneously.

Let us initially consider storage mappings for a one-dimensional array named *EMPNO* with subscript lower bound 1 and subscript upper bound *N*. One way to store this array is so that the physical order of elements is the same as the logical order of elements. Storage for element *EMPNO(I+1)* will be adjacent to storage for element *EMPNO(I)*, for $I = 1, \ldots, N\text{-}1$.

In order to calculate the starting address of element *EMPNO(I)*, it is necessary to know:

1. The starting address of the storage space allocated to the array.
2. The size of each element in the array.

Denote by *B* the array's starting address, also known as its *base location*. Assume that each element of the array occupies *S* bytes. Then the starting address of the Ith element of the array is:

$$B + (I\text{-}1) * S \tag{eq. 2-1}$$

because $I\text{-}1$ elements, each of size *S*, physically precede the Ith element.

Let us now extend eq. 2-1 to find the address of the Ith element of an array which has its subscript lower bound not equal to one. For instance, consider the array declared $Z1(4:10)$. Taking a specific case, the starting address of $Z1(6)$ is:

$$B + (6\text{-}4) * S$$

because 6 - 4 (i.e., 2) elements precede $Z1(6)$. For an array declared $Z2(-2:2)$, the starting address of $Z2(1)$ is:

$$B + (1\text{-}(-2)) * S$$

because 1 - (-2) elements ($Z2(-2)$, $Z2(-1)$, and $Z2(0)$) precede $Z2(1)$.

In general, the element $ARRAY(I)$ of the array defined as $ARRAY(L:U)$ has starting address

$$B + (I\text{-}L) * S. \qquad \text{(eq. 2-2)}$$

This formula is correct whether the lower-bound L is positive, negative, or zero.

MAPPINGS TO STORAGE: MULTI-DIMENSIONAL ARRAYS

Because computer memory is linear, a multi-dimensional array must be linearized as it is mapped to storage. One alternative for linearization is to store first the first row of the array, then the second row of the array, then the third row, and so forth. For example, the array defined by $RATE\ (1:4,1:6)$, which logically appears as shown in Fig. 9,

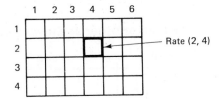

FIGURE 9

appears physically in *row-major order* as shown in Fig. 10.

FIGURE 10

This is the storage-allocation scheme used for arrays declared in most implementations of COBOL, Pascal, and PL/I.

Assuming that B is the array's base address and that each element of the array is of size S, the starting address of the element $RATE(I,J)$ is:

$$B + (I-1)*6*S + (J-1)*S$$

because there are $I-1$ rows, each of length $6 * S$, which precede the row that element $RATE(I,J)$ is in, and there are $J-1$ elements, each of length S, which precede element $RATE(I,J)$ in row I. Element $RATE$ $(2,4)$ is located at $B + 9*S$.

Generalizing, the element $ARRAY(I,J)$ of array defined by $ARRAY(L_1:U_1, L_2:U_2)$ has starting address:

$$B + (I-L_1)*(U_2-L_2+1)*S + (J-L_2)*S \qquad \text{(eq. 2-3)}$$

because there are $I-L_1$ rows, each of length $(U_2-L_2+1)*S$, which precede the row that element $ARRAY(I,J)$ is in, and there are $J-L_2$ elements, each of length S, which precede element $ARRAY(I,J)$ in row I.

Illustrating this, the array defined by $Z(-2:2, 4:6)$ can be depicted logically as shown in Fig. 11.

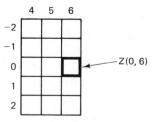

FIGURE 11

This array appears physically in row-major order as shown in Fig. 12.

FIGURE 12

There are two rows (row -2 and row -1), each of length $3 * S$, preceding row 0. In row 0, there are 2 (i.e., 6-4) elements, each of length S, preceding element $Z(0,6)$. That is, the starting location of $Z(0,6)$ is:

$$B + (0-(-2))*(6-4+1)*S + (6-4)*S,$$

which is $B+8*S$.

Another alternative for linearization of a two-dimensional array is to store the elements in *column-major order*, i.e., store first the first column, then the second column, then the third column, and so forth. The *RATE* array mentioned earlier in this section appears physically in column-major order as shown in Fig. 13.

Col 1   Col 2   Col 3   Col 4   Col 5   Col 6

Rate (2, 4)

FIGURE 13

This is the storage allocation scheme used for arrays declared in many implementations of FORTRAN.

Assuming that B is the array's base address and that each element of the array is of size S, the starting address of the element $RATE(I,J)$ is:

$$B + (J-1)*4*S + (I-1)*S$$

because there are $J-1$ columns, each of length $4*S$, which precede the column that element $RATE(I,J)$ is in, and there are $I-1$ elements, each of length S, which precede $RATE(I,J)$ in column J. Element $RATE(2,4)$ is located at $B + 13*S$.

When it is necessary to pass arrays between FORTRAN routines and routines written in other languages (e.g., COBOL, PL/I, Pascal), it is extremely important that the programmer be aware of the combination of linearization techniques used.

Generalizing, the element $ARRAY(I,J)$ of the array defined by $ARRAY(L_1:U_1,L_2:U_2)$, with column-major storage, has starting address:

$$B + (J-L_2)*(U_1-L_1+1)*S + (I-L_1)*S. \qquad \text{(eq. 2-4)}$$

Compare this equation to eq. 2–3.

In order to determine whether it is more advantageous to store an array in column-major order or in row-major order, it is necessary to know in what order the array elements are to be referenced. In fact, the available programming languages do not give the programmer a choice of array storage technique. Rather, especially in a virtual memory environment, the programmer should make a concerted effort to tailor the pattern of array element references to the storage pattern. For example, consider a procedure to calculate the average value of the elements in a 50-by-225 array named A. With column-major storage, the following reference pattern should be used:

In COBOL:

COMPUTE TOTAL = 0.
PERFORM SUM-UP VARYING J FROM 1 BY 1 UNTIL J > 225
                    AFTER I FROM 1 BY 1 UNTIL I > 50.

where

SUM-UP.
        TOTAL = TOTAL + A (I,J).

In Pascal:

```
total := 0;
for j := 1 to 225 do
    for i := 1 to 50 do
        total := total + a[i,j];
```

On the other hand, with row-major storage, which is more common with COBOL and Pascal, the following reference pattern is preferable: In COBOL:

COMPUTE TOTAL = 0.
PERFORM SUM-UP VARYING I FROM 1 BY 1 UNTIL I > 50
                    AFTER J FROM 1 BY 1 UNTIL J > 225.

where

SUM-UP.
        TOTAL = TOTAL + A (I,J).

In Pascal:

```
total := 0;
for i := 1 to 50 do
    for j := 1 to 225 do
        total := total + a[i,j];
```

TRIANGULAR ARRAYS

In the preceding section we discussed linearization of multi-dimensional arrays. In this section we consider some aspects of the linearization of a special type of array: triangular arrays.

A triangular array may be either *upper-triangular*, as shown in Fig. 14, or *lower-triangular*, as shown in Fig. 15, where all elements below (or above) the diagonal are zero. An array is called *strictly upper- (or lower-) triangular* if the elements of the diagonal are also zero.

In a lower-triangular array with N rows, the maximum number of

6 rows (handwritten)

$$\begin{bmatrix} X & X & X & X & X & X \\ 0 & X & X & X & X & X \\ 0 & 0 & X & X & X & X \\ 0 & 0 & 0 & X & X & X \\ 0 & 0 & 0 & 0 & X & X \\ 0 & 0 & 0 & 0 & 0 & X \end{bmatrix} \qquad \begin{bmatrix} X & 0 & 0 & 0 & 0 & 0 \\ X & X & 0 & 0 & 0 & 0 \\ X & X & X & 0 & 0 & 0 \\ X & X & X & X & 0 & 0 \\ X & X & X & X & X & 0 \\ X & X & X & X & X & X \end{bmatrix}$$

FIGURE 14 FIGURE 15

nonzero elements in the Ith row is I. The total number of nonzero elements thus is no more than

$$\sum_{I=1}^{N} I = \frac{N(N+1)}{2} .$$

(handwritten: $6\left(\dfrac{7}{\cancel{8}}\right) \dfrac{\cancel{40}\;21}{2}\;15$)

This expression is also true for an upper-triangular array with N rows. For large N, it would be desirable not to have to store all of the array's zero-valued elements.

One approach to this problem is to linearize the array and store only the elements of the nonzero triangular portion. Let us store the upper-triangular array T by rows in a one-dimensional array named S with subscript bounds 1 through $N(N+1)/2$. Element $T(1,1)$ is stored as element $S(1)$, element $T(1,2)$ is stored as element $S(2)$, and so forth up to element $T(1,N)$ which is stored as element $S(N)$. Then element $T(2,2)$ is stored as $S(N+1)$, because $T(2,1)$ is zero. Element $T(N,N)$ is stored as $S(N(N+1)/2)$. In general, where in S is $T(I,J)$ stored? Note that $I \leqslant J$ for all elements in the nonzero part of T.

Sometimes a program requires the use of more than one triangular array. If two of these arrays are of essentially the same dimensions, then it is a relatively straightforward task to store them in a manner that conserves space. Assume that array A is upper-triangular and N by N, and that array B is lower-triangular and N-1 by N-1. Then A and B can be stored together in an N-by-N array C as shown in Fig. 16. Elements $C(I,J)$ where $I \leqslant J$ are elements of A, and elements $C(I,J)$ where $I > J$ are elements of B. In fact, element $A(I,J)$ is stored as $C(I,J)$ for $I \leqslant J$, and element $B(I,J)$ is stored as $C(I+1,J)$ for $I \geqslant J$.

Let array A be upper-triangular, let array B be lower-triangular, and let both be N by N. Then array C must be N by N+1 in order to contain both A and B as shown in Fig. 17. Here element $A(I,J)$ is stored as $C(I,J+1)$ for $I \leqslant J$ and $B(I,J)$ is stored as $C(I,J)$ for $I \geqslant J$.

Consider now the case in which two upper-triangular arrays, say A and AA, both of which are N by N, are to share the same array space. One approach is to transpose one of the triangular arrays, say AA, such that instead of being upper-triangular, it appears to be lower-triangular.

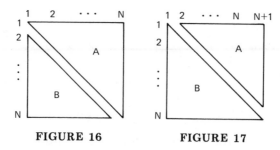

FIGURE 16   FIGURE 17

That is, array AA is transposed to form array AA^T, and element AA (I,J) becomes element $AA^T(J,I)$. Then A and AA^T can be stored together in an array C with dimensions N-by-$(N+1)$ as shown in the preceding paragraph. Element $A(I,J)$ is stored as $C(I,J+1)$, and element $AA(I,J)$ is stored as $C(J,I)$.

One problem with all of these linearization techniques arises when elements are made nonzero in the lower part of an upper-triangular array. The array then is no longer upper-triangular. If it shares the space of a square array with a lower-triangular array, there will be an obvious conflict. One solution is to not allow an upper-triangular array to be updated if that would cause the array no longer to be upper-triangular. Another approach is to recognize the change in array characteristics and move it to its own space.

SPARSE ARRAYS

Another special type of array which arises commonly in applications is a *sparse array*. It is actually difficult to draw the dividing line between those arrays that are sparse and those that are not; loosely, an array is called sparse if it has a relatively high density of zero elements. For instance, the array in Fig. 18, which has 8 nonzero elements out of 80, is sparse.

$$\begin{bmatrix} 0 & 0 & 0 & 0 & 1 & 0 & 0 & 2 & 0 & 0 \\ 0 & 1 & 0 & 0 & 0 & 0 & 0 & 0 & 0 & 0 \\ 1 & 0 & 0 & 0 & 0 & 0 & 0 & 0 & 0 & 0 \\ 0 & 0 & 0 & 0 & 0 & 0 & 0 & 0 & 0 & 0 \\ 0 & 0 & 0 & 4 & 0 & 0 & 0 & 0 & 0 & 0 \\ 0 & 0 & 0 & 0 & 0 & 0 & 0 & 2 & 0 & 0 \\ 0 & 0 & 0 & 0 & 0 & 0 & 0 & 0 & 0 & 0 \\ 2 & 1 & 0 & 0 & 0 & 0 & 0 & 0 & 0 & 0 \end{bmatrix}$$

FIGURE 18

Multi-dimensional sparse arrays can be linearized through the techniques presented earlier in this chapter; however there would be much wasted space. In some cases, such as a 1000-by-1000 array in which, say, 1500 elements of the million are nonzero, it is rare to be able to store the entire array in main memory at once. Let us now consider two alternative representations that will store explicitly only the non-zero elements.

Each nonzero element in a two-dimensional sparse array can be represented as a triple with the format (row-subscript, column-sub-script, value). These triples then can be ordered by increasing row-sub-script major and column-subscript minor, and can be stored as a vector. For example, using this approach, the 8-by-10 sparse array shown in Fig. 18 is represented by vector V, shown in Fig. 19.

		row	column	value
	V(1):	1,	5,	1
	V(2):	1,	8,	2
	V(3):	2,	2,	1
	V(4):	3,	1,	1
	V(5):	5,	4,	4
	V(6):	6,	8,	2
	V(7):	8,	1,	2
FIGURE 19	V(8):	8,	2,	1

This storage mapping uses more space to represent any particular non-zero element but avoids representing the zero elements.

If the sparse array were one-dimensional, each nonzero element would be represented by a pair. In general, each nonzero element of an N-dimensional array is represented by an entry with $N+1$ values.

Operations on the vector representation of the two-decimal sparse array must use the row and column information to determine where each value resides. One inconvenience with this form of representation is in handling addition of nonzero elements to the array or changing previously nonzero elements to have zero value. The problem is not in changing the element's value, but in maintaining the order of nonzero elements in the representation vector. For example, if the above array were updated so that the element with subscripts (1,8) were to have value zero, then vector elements $V(3)$ through $V(8)$ should be shifted to become elements $V(2)$ through $V(7)$. Similarly, if the element with subscripts (4,6) were to be updated to have value 9, then vector elements $V(5)$ through $V(8)$ would need to be shifted to become elements $V(6)$ through $V(9)$ and $V(5)$ would be the triple (4,6,9).

Another representation for sparse arrays is to use linked lists. We will defer consideration of that important alternative until Chapter 6, which discusses linked lists.

SUMMARY

An *array* is a finite, ordered set of homogeneous elements. The elements of an array are referred to by their positions, as specified by subscripts. The composition of arrays in which each element is of data type array results in multi-dimensional arrays. The chapter introduced the declaration of arrays in COBOL and Pascal programs.

One-dimensional arrays are mapped to storage in a straightforward linear way. In order to calculate the starting address of a particular element, it is necessary to know the base location of the array and the size of each preceding element in the array.

Multi-dimensional arrays must be linearized as they are mapped to storage. The most common linearization techniques for a two-dimensional array are to store the elements in row-major order (COBOL, Pascal, and PL/I) or in column-major order (FORTRAN).

The chapter terminated with a discussion of two special types of arrays: triangular arrays and sparse arrays. Use of the conventional array-linearization techniques generally results in excessive space requirements for these array types. Linearization techniques that are tailored to the characteristics of triangular and sparse arrays include storing two triangular arrays together in a single square array and representing only the nonzero elements of a sparse array.

The reader who is interested in more detailed information about arrays should consult the following references:

Hellerman, H. "Addressing multidimensional arrays," *Comm. ACM*, 5(4): 205–207, April 1962.

MacVeigh, D. T. "Effect of data representation on cost of sparse matrix operations," *Acta Informatica*, 7(4): 361–394, 1977.

Pooch, U. W., and A. Nieder. "A survey of indexing techniques for sparse matrices," *ACM Computing Surveys*, 5(2): 109–133, June 1973.

Rosenberg, A. L., and L. J. Stockmeyer. "Storage schemes for boundedly extendible arrays," *Acta Informatica*, 7(3): 289–303, 1977.

Standish, T. A. "Arrays," Chapter 8 in *Data Structure Techniques*, Reading, Mass.: Addison-Wesley Publishing Co., 1980, pp. 348–376.

Techniques for addressing into arrays are covered in Chapter 19 in the sections on address calculation techniques for relative files.

Terms

array	lower bound
cross-section	range
index	sparse array

strictly triangular array   triangular array
subscript   upper bound
transpose   vector

Review Exercises

1. In an array with columns numbered from 4 through 13 and rows from 6 through 12, what is the maximum number of elements that can be stored?

2. What is meant by the terms "row-major order" and "column-major order"?

3. How many elements are in the array $SPACE(A:B,C:D)$?

4. How many elements can be held by an array with dimension $A(1:N)$? $B(-N:0,3)$?

5. The array $TEST(1:10,1:5)$ is stored in memory by columns. If base location $B = 0$ and element size $S = 1$, what is the address of element $TEST(7,2)$?

6. Given: $ARRAY(10:30, 10:100)$, with base location = 50 and element size = 8 bits:
   (a) How many elements are in $ARRAY$?
   (b) What is the starting location of $ARRAY(21,75)$ if $ARRAY$ is stored by row?

7. Given array $A(50:100, 50:75)$, what is starting location of $A(62,56)$?

8. Write an algorithm to find the address of the jth element in the ith row of the array $IVAN\ (B:A,D:C)$, where each element in the array takes up n words of memory. Assume the starting location is 0.

9. Consider array $Q(A:B,C:D,E:F)$, base location = X, length of element = L.
   (a) Find the total number of elements of the array.
   (b) Find the starting location of $Q(I,J,K)$. What have you assumed about how the array is linearized and stored?

10. What is the maximum number of dimensions available for arrays in COBOL?

11. Given the COBOL array:

    01 TABLE.
        03 TABLE-ROW OCCURS 50 TIMES.
            05 TABLE-COL OCCURS 4 TIMES.
                07 TABLE-DEPTH OCCURS 6 TIMES PIC XX.

    How many elements does the table contain?

12. Illustrate and describe one method of representation for sparse arrays.

13. Write an algorithm to transpose a matrix.

14. Write a transpose algorithm for the following sparse matrix where you store the matrix as a vector of (row-subscript, column-subscript, value) triples.

$$\begin{bmatrix} 0 & 0 & 1 & 0 & 0 & 0 \\ 2 & 0 & 0 & 0 & 3 & 0 \\ 0 & 0 & 0 & 9 & 0 & 1 \\ 0 & 16 & 0 & 0 & 0 & 0 \end{bmatrix}$$

15. Write an algorithm to compute the product of two sparse matrices each represented as an array.

16. Show how two triangular arrays can be stored together.

17. How do you save space in storing two triangular arrays? What are the tradeoffs to be considered?

18. Show that an upper-triangular array with N rows has no more than $N(N+1)/2$ nonzero elements.

19. Consider storage of a lower-triangular N-by-N array T by rows in a one-dimensional array S with subscript bounds 1 through $N(N+1)/2$. What is the subscript in S of element $T(I,J)$? (Difficult!)

20. A regularly occurring type of sparse matrix is a "tridiagonal" matrix, where all elements except those on the main diagonal and the diagonals immediately above and below the main diagonal are zero. A 5-by-5 tridiagonal, for example, has the structure:

$$\begin{bmatrix} a_{11} & a_{12} & 0 & 0 & 0 \\ a_{21} & a_{22} & a_{23} & 0 & 0 \\ 0 & a_{32} & a_{33} & a_{34} & 0 \\ 0 & 0 & a_{43} & a_{44} & a_{45} \\ 0 & 0 & 0 & a_{54} & a_{55} \end{bmatrix}$$

Construct an algorithm to store a tridiagonal matrix in a singly subscripted array $B(I)$, with a_{11} in $B(1)$, a_{12} in $B(2)$, a_{21} in $B(3)$, a_{22} in $B(4)$, a_{23} in $B(5)$, etc. Give a direct formula for retrieving a_{ij} from B.

21. Write a program that traverses a maze. The maze is a two-dimensional 12-by-12 table with values of 1 indicating possible paths and 0s indicating walls. Here is an example maze:

0	0	0	0	0	0	0	0	0	0	0	0
0	0	0	0	0	0	1	1	0	0	0	0
0	1	0	0	0	0	1	1	1	0	0	0
0	1	0	0	0	0	1	0	1	0	1	0
1	1	0	0	1	1	1	0	1	1	1	1
0	1	1	1	0	0	1	0	0	0	1	0
0	1	0	1	0	0	1	0	0	0	0	0
0	0	0	1	0	1	1	1	1	0	0	0
0	1	1	1	1	0	1	0	0	0	1	0
0	1	0	0	0	0	1	0	0	0	1	0
0	1	0	0	0	0	1	0	0	0	1	0
0	1	1	1	1	1	1	1	1	1	1	0

There will be a single element in the first column with the value 1 and that will be the starting point. There will also be only a single value in the last column that is 1, which will be the ending point. The maze will be read in with one row per line. The row's values will be in the first 12 columns of the line.

Make up your own maze for testing purposes, then use the above example.

Output should consist of the path (excluding wrong turns), specified by row and column of the elements traversed, from the beginning to the end of the maze. You cannot traverse diagonals.

22. There is a data type known as a variable-length string, which has a length attribute that may take on different values over time. Consider an array of variable-length strings, for example the array $MONTH(1:12)$, where each element is a string of 0 to 9 characters, whose value is the name of the corresponding month. One way to store this array is to allocate space for 9 characters for each element, regardless of how much space is actually used. How could this array be stored so that the amount of empty space allocated to the array is minimized? Does your technique work if there will be modification of the values of the elements of the array?

CHAPTER 3

Records

This chapter introduces a simple data structure that is of major importance: the record. The record data structure is defined and compared with the other data types that have already been introduced, then facilities for declaring records in COBOL and Pascal are reviewed. The record data structure is a composite of other data types and this chapter is quite brief. The mapping of record variables to storage is straightforward and the operations on records should already be familiar.

The record type is fundamental to management of data on secondary storage devices such as magnetic tapes and disks. Records are the basic components of files and of databases. The record data structure introduced in this chapter will be an elementary construct used in the remainder of the text.

DEFINITIONS: RECORDS

A *record* is a finite, ordered collection of possibly heterogeneous elements that are treated as a unit. A record is distinguished from an array in that all elements in an array must have the same data type, but the component elements of a record may have different data types. A record is sometimes referred to simply as a *structure*. The elements of a record are commonly called fields. A *field* is a specified area of a record used for a particular category of information.

A unit of information derives at least some of its meaning from its relationship to other units of information. The record data structure enables a set of elements of logically related information to be explicitly grouped together. For example, the field named JOB-TITLE of data type *string* with value 'ANALYST' does not bear much information on its own. However, more information is conveyed when the JOB-TITLE field is coupled with other logically related fields, such as EMP-NO of data type *string* with value '123456789' and PAY-RATE of data type *decimal* with value 15.93. These heterogeneous elements cannot form an array because they are of different data types. They can, however, be grouped to form a record of employee information, as shown in Fig. 20.

FIGURE 20

JOB-TITLE	EMP-NO	PAY-RATE
ANALYST	123456789	15.93

An element of a record may be a composite data type, for instance another record structure or an array. For example, an employee's record might contain NAME and OFFICE-ADDR fields, as shown in Fig. 21.

JOB-TITLE	EMP-NO	PAY-RATE	NAME			OFFICE-ADDR	
			LAST	FIRST	INIT	BLDG	ROOM
ANALYST	123456789	15.93	MUD	JOE	N	CSC	403

FIGURE 21

It might also contain an array of PROJECT-CODES, as shown in Fig. 22.

JOB-TITLE	EMP-NO	PAY-RATE	NAME			OFFICE-ADDR		PROJECT-CODES				
			LAST	FIRST	INIT	BLDG	ROOM					
ANALYST	123456789	15.93	MUD	JOE	N	CSC	403	18	40	41	50	53

FIGURE 22

A field with no subordinate fields is called an *elementary item*; a field with subordinate fields is called a *group item*. OFFICE-ADDR and NAME are group items in the example above.

Composite records like this are quite common. It is also possible to have an array of elements of type record within a record. For example, an employee record might have an array of two TELEPHONE-NO group items, as shown in Fig. 23.

JOB-TITLE	EMP-NO	PAY-RATE	NAME			OFFICE-ADDR		PROJECT-CODES					TELEPHONE-NO			
			LAST	FIRST	INIT	BLDG	ROOM						AREA	LOCAL	AREA	LOCAL
ANALYST	123456789	15.93	MUD	JOE	N	CSC	403	18	40	41	50	53	202	2991673	301	6263116

FIGURE 23

It is useful to be able to define a variable to be of data type record. For example, the variable named EMPLOYEE can be a data structure of type record and be composed of the fields named JOB-TITLE, EMP-NO, PAY-RATE, NAME, OFFICE-ADDR, PROJECT-CODES, and TELEPHONE-NO, each, of course, with its own data type. The variable EMPLOYEE then can take on various sets of values over time. The example above illustrates an occurrence of the EMPLOYEE record variable.

A record generally contains an identifying field. Continuing the above example, a particular employee's EMPLOYEE record occurrence is identified by the value in its EMP-NO field. The identifying field of a record is called its *key* field. The key of a record may be either an elementary item or a group item. For example, a particular class's COURSE record might be identified by the value of its DEPARTMENT, NUMBER, and SECTION fields.

A collection of logically related record occurrences that are treated as a unit is called a *file*. Usually all of a file's record occurrences are of a single record format. Sometimes, however, there are several record formats on one file. For example, an EMPLOYEE record occurrence might be followed by several record occurrences of type PROJECT-RESPONSIBILITY, each detailing the employee's efforts on a particular project.

A major portion of this text is devoted to the topic of organizing files of records in such a way that they can effectively support applications processing. Although most files are stored on secondary-storage media, some relatively small, very commonly used files are stored in primary memory.

The operations that are legal upon records are those that are defined upon the contained fields, based upon their data types.

DECLARATION OF RECORDS IN COBOL AND PASCAL

Let us consider now the facilities that allow declaration of record variables in COBOL and Pascal.

COBOL uses a system of *level-numbers* to indicate the structures of records. A record description begins with the record name, which is always at the 01 level, and includes then the specifications for the fields contained in the record. For example, the EMPLOYEE record of the preceding section would be declared in the *DATA DIVISION* of a COBOL program as follows:

```
01  EMPLOYEE.
    02  JOB-TITLE        PICTURE X(7).
    02  EMP-NO           PICTURE X(9).
    02  PAY-RATE         PICTURE 9(2)V9(2).
```

```
02  NAME.
    03  L-NAME        PICTURE X(12).
    03  F-NAME        PICTURE X(8).
    03  INIT          PICTURE X.
02  OFFICE-ADDR.
    03  BLDG          PICTURE X(3).
    03  ROOM          PICTURE 9(3).
02  PROJECT-CODES OCCURS 5 TIMES PICTURE 9(2).
02  TELEPHONE-NO OCCURS 2 TIMES.
    03  AREA-CODE     PICTURE 9(3).
    03  LOCAL         PICTURE 9(7).
```

Each item description is preceded by a level-number taken from the set '01, 02, 03, ..., 49'*; the combination of these level-numbers describes the hierarchical structure of the fields in the record. An increase in level-numbers as from 01 to 02 between *EMPLOYEE* and *JOB-TITLE* and from 02 to 03 between *NAME* and *L-NAME*, between *OFFICE-ADDR* and *BLDG*, and between *TELEPHONE-NO* and *AREA-CODE*, indicates subdivision of a group item into its component fields. The group-item *EMPLOYEE* comprises *JOB-TITLE*, *EMP-NO*, *PAY-RATE*, *NAME*, *OFFICE-ADDR*, *PROJECT-CODES* and *TELEPHONE-NO*. The group-item *TELEPHONE-NO*, which is an array with two occurrences, comprises *AREA-CODE* and *LOCAL*.

Note that only the elementary items have *PICTURE* clauses. This data-typing information is not on group items.

A deeper hierarchy in COBOL would require use of greater level-numbers. For instance the *LOCAL* part of the telephone number could be subdivided into two elementary items named *EXCHANGE* and *NUMB*:

```
02  TELEPHONE-NO OCCURS 2 TIMES.
    03  AREA-CODE     PICTURE 9(3).
    03  LOCAL.
        04  EXCHANGE  PICTURE 9(3).
        04  NUMB      PICTURE 9(4).
```

Note that *LOCAL* no longer includes typing information because it is not an elementary item.

PL/I uses level-numbers in essentially the same way as does COBOL, except that PL/I uses level 1 instead of level 01, level 2 instead of level 02, and so forth.

Pascal uses a blocking facility rather than the level-number convention to define record structures. Each entry to be subdivided is bracketed by *record* and *end*, to indicate the grouping of data elements.

---

*Level-numbers from 01 to 09 can be written without the leading 0. Special meanings are given to the additional level-numbers 66, 77, 88.

```
type  name = record
                lname : packed array [ 1 . . 12] of char;
                fname : packed array [ 1 . . 8] of char;
                init : char
              end;
      addr = record
                bldg : packed array [ 1 . . 3] of char;
                room: integer
              end;
      localphone = record
                exchange : integer;
                numb : integer
              end;
      phoneno = record
                areacode : integer;
                local : localphone
              end;
      employeerec = record
                jobtitle : packed array [ 1 . . 7] of char;
                empno : packed array [ 1 . . 9] of char;
                payrate : real;
                empname : name;
                officeaddr : addr;
                projectcodes : array [ 1 . . 5] of integer;
                telephoneno : array [ 1 . . 2] of phoneno
              end;
```

This example shows use of the facility for definition of new data types, here *name*, *addr*, *localphone*, *phoneno*, and *employeerec*. This *type* statement could be followed by the definition of variables that have the defined structures. For example:

```
var employee : employeerec;
```

To refer to a particular element of a record structure, a uniquely identifying variable name must be used. If the simple field name is unique, then it suffices. If the field name is not unique, then some form of qualification must be used to make it unique. For example, consider the following COBOL record structure:

```
01  STUDENT.
    . . .
    02  BIRTH-DATE.
        03  MM              PICTURE 99.
        03  DD              PICTURE 99.
        03  YY              PICTURE 99.
    . . .
```

```
02  UNDERGRAD.
     03  MATRIC-DATE.
          04  MM          PICTURE 99.
          04  DD          PICTURE 99.
          04  YY          PICTURE 99.
     03  DEGREE-DATE.
          04  MM          PICTURE 99.
          04  DD          PICTURE 99.
          04  YY          PICTURE 99.
     . . .
02  GRAD.
     03  MATRIC-DATE.
          04  MM          PICTURE 99.
          04  DD          PICTURE 99.
          04  YY          PICTURE 99.
     03  DEGREE-DATE.
          04  MM          PICTURE 99.
          04  DD          PICTURE 99.
          04  YY          PICTURE 99.
     . . .
```

The data name *YY* is not unique, but it can be qualified to show which *YY* in the structure is referred to, for example *YY OF BIRTH-DATE*. However, *YY OF MATRIC-DATE* is not unique and further qualification is necessary: either *YY OF MATRIC-DATE OF UNDERGRAD* or *YY OF MATRIC-DATE OF GRAD*. A fully qualified variable name refers all the way back to the 01 level; for example *YY OF MATRIC-DATE OF GRAD OF STUDENT*.

Pascal uses a slightly different convention for qualification of variable names. The examples of the preceding paragraph would be:

```
birthdate.yy
undergrad.matricdate.yy
grad.matricdate.yy
student.grad.matricdate.yy
```

Fig. 24 is another example of a variable of data type *record* and its declaration in COBOL and Pascal. The record contains information about traffic flow at an intersection.

TRAFFIC

ID	LOC	SAMPLE-INFO						CORNER(1)			CORNER(2)				CORNER(4)		
		DATE			DAY	TIME		DIR(1)	DIR(2)	DIR(3)	DIR(1)	DIR(2)	DIR(3)	· · ·	DIR(1)	DIR(2)	DIR(3)
		MM	DD	YY		START	END										

FIGURE 24

COBOL:

```
01  TRAFFIC.
    02  ID                      PICTURE 99.
    02  LOC                     PICTURE X(5).
    02  SAMPLE-INFO.
        03  SAMPLE-DATE.
            04  MM              PICTURE 99.
            04  DD              PICTURE 99.
            04  YY              PICTURE 99.
        03  SAMPLE-DAY          PICTURE X(3).
        03  SAMPLE-TIME.
            04  START-TIME      PICTURE 9(4).
            04  END-TIME        PICTURE 9(4).
    02  CORNER OCCURS 4 TIMES.
        03  DIR OCCURS 3 TIMES  PICTURE 9(6).
```

Pascal:

```
type  date = record
                mm: integer;
                dd: integer;
                yy: integer
             end;
      time = record
                starttime: integer;
                endtime: integer
             end;
      sampleinfo = record
                sampledate: date;
                day: packed array [1 .. 3] of char;
                sampletime: time
                   end;
      trafficrec = record
                 id: integer;
                 loc: packed array [1 .. 5] of char;
                 trafficsample: sampleinfo;
                 dir: array [1 .. 4, 1 .. 3] of integer
               end;
var traffic: trafficrec;
```

FORTRAN does not have a facility for declaration of record variables. Rather, each of the component elementary items is defined separately; their grouping to form a record is only implicit. Program logic or documentation should indicate that a group of fields actually forms a record.

MAPPINGS TO STORAGE

Data of type *record* are nearly always mapped linearly to storage. Memory is allocated to each of the elementary items in the record, in order and contiguously by order of appearance in the declaration. For instance, in the above *TRAFFIC* record, the memory layout would be as shown in Fig. 24.

This linear mapping technique often causes data elements to begin off of word boundaries. On some machines, certain types of processing require that data be aligned on a certain type of boundary: halfword, fullword, or doubleword. In order to ensure correct alignment in these cases it may be necessary to insert space containing no meaningful data between data elements. This filler space is called *slack bytes* or *padding*.

Proper alignment of data elements and natural boundaries can result in more efficient execution of some arithmetic and subscripting operations. When data elements appear between word boundaries or if they cross word boundaries, they may need to be moved elsewhere in order to execute some machine operations. Synchronization can be accomplished by recognizing word boundaries and organizing data appropriately using padding in the data structure, or by using the COBOL *SYNCHRONIZED* clause. See a COBOL language manual for details of this clause.

SUMMARY

A *record* is a finite, ordered collection of possibly heterogeneous elements, which may themselves be composite structures (records or arrays). The primary purpose of the *record* data type is to group together for input/output purposes logically related fields. The elements of a record can be referred to individually within a program, and the entire group of elements in the record can be treated collectively for input/output operations.

The operations that can be performed on the elements of a data structure are defined by their individual data types.

The mapping of a record to storage is generally simple and linear. Sometimes padding space is inserted within a record for purposes of enhancing the efficiency of certain arithmetic operations. This space can be inserted explicitly or by use of a programming language feature such as the COBOL *SYNCHRONIZED* clause.

Records are important because they can preserve the natural logical structure of related items of information.

Terms

elementary item	key
field	padding
file	record
group item	slack bytes

Review Exercises

1. What is the difference between an array and a record? Can an array be part of a record? Can a record be part of an array?
2. Why might a programmer decompose a field into component pieces?
3. Two programs access the same file of records. One program treats *phoneno* as an elementary item, while the other program considers *phoneno* to be a group item. Why the discrepancy?
4. Just based on the contents of this chapter, why do you think FORTRAN has been considered not to be a business-oriented programming language?
5. What are the trade-offs to be considered in brute-force use of padding and use of the COBOL *SYNCHRONIZED* feature?
6. Find out what the structure of records is on your local student or employee file.
7. Study several examples of record declarations in COBOL or Pascal programs.
8. Write a program to read data into the structure of the EMPLOYEE record used as an example in this chapter.

CHAPTER 4

Stacks

One of the most commonly used linear data structures is the stack. The operations that define the stack data structure are introduced, then the facilities for declaring and manipulating stacks are discussed. Much of the chapter is devoted to examples of the use of stacks in solving problems.

DEFINITIONS: STACKS

A *linear list* is a general data structure comprised of an ordered set of elements; the number of elements in the list can vary. We will denote the linear list named A comprised of T elements at time t as

$$A = [A_1, A_2, \ldots, A_T].$$

If $T = 0$, then A is said to be an empty or null list. An element can be deleted from any position in the general linear list and a new element can be inserted into any position in the list.

A *stack* is a special case of linear list in which insertion and deletion operations are restricted to occur only at one end, which is referred to as the stack's *top*. We denote by TOP(S) the top element of the stack S. For stack S, where

$$S = [S_1, S_2, \ldots, S_T]$$

the TOP(S) is S_T.

We use NOEL(S) to denote the number of elements in stack S. NOEL(S) is an attribute of stack S and has an integer value. For the stack S above, NOEL(S) is T.

The stack insertion operator is called *push* and the deletion operator is called *pop*. For an example of the effects of these operators, let us start with an empty stack named S. $S = [\,]$ can be represented pictorially as Fig. 25(a).

NOEL(S) = 0, TOP(S) undefined.   FIGURE 25(a)

We first push on the element A, giving $S = [A]$, (Fig. 25(b)):

NOEL(S) = 1, TOP(S) = A,   FIGURE 25(b)

then push on the element B, giving $S = [A,B]$, (Fig. 25(c)):

NOEL(S) = 2, TOP(S) = B,   FIGURE 25(c)

then push on the element C, giving $S = [A,B,C]$, (Fig. 25(d)).

NOEL(S) = 3, TOP(S) = C.   FIGURE 25(d)

We could pop an element, giving $S = [A,B]$, (Fig. 25(e)):

NOEL(S) = 2, TOP(S) = B,   FIGURE 25(e)

then perhaps push on two more elements, say D then E, giving $S = [A,B,D,E]$, (Fig. 25(f)):

NOEL(S) = 4, TOP(S) = E.   FIGURE 25(f)

We might then want to pop an element off the stack, giving $S = [A,B,D]$, (Fig. 25(g)):

NOEL(S) = 3, TOP(S) = D,   FIGURE 25(g) and so forth. The stack is said to operate in a *last-in-first-out* (LIFO) manner. Elements are removed in the reverse of the order in which they were inserted into the stack.

If there are NOEL elements in a stack, then the NOELth element is the top element. We can draw logical pictures of stacks such that their tops are to the up or the down direction, (Fig. 26(a)):

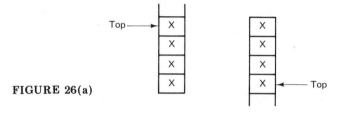

FIGURE 26(a)

or draw them horizontally such that their tops are to the left or the right direction, (Fig. 26(b)):

FIGURE 26(b)

It doesn't really matter, as long as we use a consistent approach for any particular stack. Here we generally use the convention of having the top in the up direction.

In any case, for stack

$$S = [S_1, S_2, \ldots S_{NOEL}]$$

we will say that element S_I is *on top of* element S_J, for $I > J$. S_I is more accessible than the elements that it is on top of, that is, S_I will be popped off the stack before any element that it is on top of. S_I has been in the stack for less time than any of the elements that it is on top of.

Any picture that we draw of a stack is really only a snapshot in time. The top element changes as the stack is pushed and popped; the bottom remains fixed.

A common example of a stack is a pile of trays in a cafeteria. The trays are supported by a spring mechanism in a casing such that only the top tray is visible and available for removal (Fig. 27). Adding another tray to the top of the stack compresses the spring; removing a tray

FIGURE 27

lightens the load on the spring such that the next tray appears at the counter level.

Another example of a stack is a railway system used to shunt cars from one position to another (Fig. 28).

FIGURE 28

The last railcar placed on the stack is the first one that can be taken off the stack. Investigate the use of the push and pop operations in various combinations to rearrange the order of cars in a train.

There are four basic operations that are legally defined for data type *stack*:

1. CREATE (stack)
2. ISEMPTY (stack)
3. PUSH (element, stack)
4. POP (stack)

We denote by CREATE(S) the operator that returns an empty stack with name S. By definition

$$\text{NOEL (CREATE}(S)) \text{ is } 0$$
$$\text{and} \quad \text{TOP (CREATE}(S)) \text{ is null.}$$

We denote by ISEMPTY(S) the operator that determines whether or not stack S is empty. The operand is of data type stack; the result is of data type boolean. ISEMPTY(S) is true if stack S is empty (that is, if NOEL(S)=0) and false otherwise. Note that ISEMPTY (CREATE(S)) is true.

We denote by PUSH(E,S) the operator that adds element E to the top of stack S. The result is the augmented stack. Note that

TOP(PUSH(E,S)) is E.

PUSH(E,S) also increments NOEL(S). The result of pushing an element onto any stack cannot be an empty stack:

ISEMPTY(PUSH(E,S)) is false.

We denote by POP(S) the operator that removes an element from the top of stack S. The result is the decreased stack. If it is desired to save the popped element, action to do so should be taken prior to the pop operation. Note that POP(S) decrements NOEL(S). It is an error to try to pop an element from an emp   stack:

POP(CREATE(S)) yields an error condition.

In the absence of such an error, POP(S) decrements NOEL(S) and changes TOP(S).

The pop operator undoes the results of the push operator:

POP(PUSH(E,S)) is S.

You might find it useful to derive other tautologies from combinations of the elementary stack operators.

DECLARATIONS OF STACKS IN COBOL AND PASCAL

Although stacks are widely used, most programming languages do not have a built-in data type *stack*. In order to program a solution for a problem that calls for use of a stack variable, the programmer must use the language's existing features in some way that enables the stack's operation to be simulated. There are several different ways to represent stacks. Perhaps the simplest way to represent stack variables is to house them in arrays. In this section we introduce this method of handling stacks in COBOL and Pascal.

A stack can be housed in an array, but it is essential to recognize that a stack and an array are two entirely different things. First, recall that there are no restrictions on where elements can be inserted into or deleted from an array. Thus it is the *programmer's* responsibility to enforce the LIFO rules for a stack that is housed in an array. Second, housing a stack in an array immediately constrains the stack to contain homogeneous elements. Another artificial constraint is imposed when the programmer must specify the upper bound on the array's subscript values. A stack variable has no constraint on the maximum number of elements that it may contain at any given time. (If we wanted, we could have an infinitely tall stack of cafeteria trays or poker chips.) However, a stack variable housed in an array is confined to the space allocated to that array. In fact, a stack grows and shrinks over time, but an array has a constant size.

Let's consider the declaration of a variable named S of data type *stack*. Assume that each element of S will be of data type *integer* and that S will have a maximum of 100 elements. In addition to declaring the array that will house S, we must declare a variable *TOP-PTR* whose value will be the subscript of the present top element of the stack. We name the combined array and top indicator the *STACK-STRUCT*. With this representation, NOEL(S) = *TOP-PTR*. ISEMPTY(S) is true when *TOP-PTR* = 0 and is false when *TOP-PTR* > 0.

In COBOL:

```
01  STACK-STRUCT.
    02  S                    OCCURS 100 TIMES
                             PICTURE 9(5).
    02  TOP-PTR              PICTURE 9(3).
```

In Pascal:

```
type stackstruct =
         record     stack : array [1..100] of integer;
                    topptr : integer
         end;
    var      s : stackstruct;
```

If there were several stacks used in the same program, each would have its own top indicator. (Note that we used *TOP-PTR* because *TOP* is a COBOL reserved word.)

The compilers will not detect violations to the LIFO rules of operation for stacks housed in arrays. The programmer must be careful not to index into S anywhere except using the value of *TOP-PTR*.

The operations of pushing and popping S can be programmed as follows. We use *EON* to be the element to be pushed onto S and *EOFF* to be the element popped off of S. Note that we save *EOFF*. We will use the variable *NOEL-MAX* to be the maximum number of elements that S's array can accommodate; here *NOEL-MAX* = 100. Throughout we indicate that the actions that a program takes upon detecting an overflow condition (attempt to push onto a full stack) or an underflow condition (attempt to pop an empty stack) are dependent upon the application.

In COBOL paragraphs:

```
PUSH.
        IF TOP-PTR < NOEL-MAX
        THEN COMPUTE TOP-PTR = TOP-PTR + 1
                MOVE EON TO S (TOP-PTR)
        ELSE overflow-condition.
POP.
        IF TOP-PTR > 0
        THEN MOVE S (TOP-PTR) TO EOFF
                COMPUTE TOP-PTR = TOP-PTR - 1
        ELSE underflow-condition.
```

In Pascal procedures:

```
procedure push (eon:integer);
begin if (s. topptr<noelmax)
        then begin s.topptr := s.topptr + 1;
                    s.stack [s.topptr] := eon
            end
        else OVERFLOW-CONDITION
end;
procedure pop (var eoff:integer);
begin if (s.topptr>0)
        then begin eoff := s.stack [s.topptr];
                    s.topptr := s.topptr - 1
            end
        else UNDERFLOW-CONDITION
end;
```

We have assumed that S is a globally known variable.

It is important to caution again that the integrity of a stack must be maintained by the programmer when the stack is housed in an array. It is the programmer's responsibility to ensure that only the top pointer is used as the point of reference into the stack.

There are other ways to represent a stack variable even when there is no built-in *stack* data type. We will discuss these representations later, as in the chapter on linked lists.

EXAMPLE APPLICATIONS OF STACKS

Stacks are used extensively in solving a wide variety of problems. They are used by compilers, by operating systems, and by applications programs. In this section we outline several uses of stacks; there are many others. We will look at three examples and will use one of our major languages (COBOL or Pascal) in each.

Example: Matching Parentheses

One task of a compiler is to verify that the programmer has adhered to the grammatical rules (syntax) of the programming language. Consider the syntax verification problem of ensuring that for each left-parenthesis there is a corresponding right parenthesis. A stack can be used to facilitate the matching procedure.

The algorithm is simple: we scan the string elements left to right. Whenever we encounter a left parenthesis, we push it onto a stack. Whenever we hit a right parenthesis, we check the state of the stack. If it is empty, then we have found a right parenthesis that does not close a left parenthesis and have an error. If the stack is not empty, we have found a pair and merely pop the stack. If the stack is not empty at the end of the string, then there is at least one unclosed left parenthesis. At any point in the scan, the number of elements in the stack is the nesting depth of the parenthesis. A given program statement has a parenthesis nesting depth that varies, depending upon how far through the statement the scan has proceeded.

We program this routine in COBOL. The string to be scanned is stored character-by-character in an array *STRING*. The stack is housed in an array *STACK*. Assume we know that 80 is the maximum number of characters in the string and that the actual string terminates with a semicolon (;). The data structures are defined by

```
01  STACK-STRUCT.
    02  STACK            OCCURS 80 TIMES
                         PICTURE X.
    02  TOP-PTR          PICTURE 99 VALUE 0.
01  STRING.
    02  CHAR             OCCURS 80 TIMES
                         PICTURE X.
01  NEXT-CHAR            PICTURE 99.
```

These structures are manipulated by the following code:

```
PERFORM SCAN-NEXT-CHAR
        VARYING NEXT-CHAR FROM 1 BY 1
        UNTIL NEXT-CHAR > 80
            OR CHAR(NEXT-CHAR) = ";".
IF TOP-PTR NOT = 0
    invalid-syntax-unclosed-left-parenthesis
```

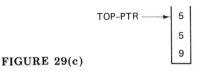

FIGURE 29(c)

After 25 calls to the procedure *compound*, the stack is as shown in Fig. 29(d).

FIGURE 29(d)

There have been 24 calls from statement 5, and *yr* finally has the value 0. Now the stack comes into play as the calls are unraveled. Each invocation of *compound* needs to be returned from in order (LIFO) until the original call is reached. Return from the last call to *compound* results in popping the stack such that it is as shown in Fig. 29(e).

FIGURE 29(e)

Eventually all of the addresses are popped off the control stack and we return to statement 9. The next statement writes the determined value of *nowhave*, which is the amount you need to deposit.

In this example, the Pascal compiler established the need for a stack and provided the instructions for properly pushing and popping the stack. In the prior example, the COBOL programmer carried all responsibility for handling the stack.

Some compilers are not able to handle recursive procedure calls because they do not have the needed stack mechanisms. Before programming one and expecting it to work (especially in COBOL or FORTRAN), check your local language manuals. Unfortunately, recursive procedures in these languages commonly compile apparently correctly but go haywire during execution.

Example: Postfix Notation

A third application of stacks is in the compilation of arithmetic expressions in high-level programming languages. The compiler needs to be able to translate from our usual form of representation of arithmetic statements such as the following:

$$((A+B)*C/D+E{\uparrow}F)/G$$

to a form that can more easily be used for generation of object code. The usual way in which we write arithmetic statements is in what is known as *infix notation*. For binary operators, such as addition, subtraction, multiplication, division, and exponentiation, the operator appears between the two operands, e.g., $A + B$, $E \uparrow F$. Stacks can be used to transform this notation to what is known as *postfix notation*, in which both operands appear before the operator, e.g., $A\ B\ +$, $E\ F\ \uparrow$. This form is easier for the compiler to handle, as we shall see.

Consider the following algorithm, which converts expressions from infix to postfix notation. A stack is used to retain infix operators until their operands have been scanned. The expression is scanned left to right. There are four basic rules.

1. If the symbol is "("
   it is pushed onto the operator stack.
2. If the symbol is ")"
   it pops everything from the operator stack down to the first "(." The operators go to output as they are popped off the stack. The "(" is popped off but does not go to output.
3. If the symbol is an operator,
   then if the operator on the top of the operator stack is of the same or higher precedence, that operator is popped off and goes to output, continuing in this fashion until the first left parenthesis or an operator of lower precedence is met in the operator stack. When that situation occurs, then the current operator is pushed onto the stack.
4. If the symbol is an operand,
   it goes directly to output.

The terminating symbol, here the semicolon, pops everything off the stack.

Let us first consider use of this algorithm with just three operator precedence levels.

Highest: Exponentiation (↑)
Middle: Multiplication (*), Division (/)
Lowest: Addition (+), Subtraction (−)

Figure 30 shows the operator stack and the output as each character of the infix arithmetic expression

$$((A+B)*C/D+E{\uparrow}F)/G;$$

is scanned.

Time point	1	2	3	4	5	6	7	8	9	10	11	12	13	14	15	16	17	18
Character scanned	(	(	A	+	B	)	*	C	/	D	+	E	↑	F	)	/	G	;
Operator TOP → stack	(	(	(	+	+	(	*	*	/	/	+	+	↑	↑		/		
		(	(	(	(		(	(	(	(	(	(	+	+				
				(	(								(	(				
Output			A		B	+		C	*	D	/	E		F	↑+		G	/

FIGURE 30

The resultant postfix expression is:

$$AB+C*D/EF{\uparrow}+G/.$$

Note that all parentheses have been removed from the expression. The parentheses were needed in infix notation to indicate the desired precedence of operators. In postfix notation, operator precedence is indicated solely by operator order. The postfix string can be scanned from left to right, setting up intermediate expressions which involve only binary operations as follows:

Step 1.	$T_1 = AB+$	String becomes: $T_1 C*D/EF{\uparrow}+G/$
Step 2.	$T_2 = T_1 C*$	String becomes: $T_2 D/EF{\uparrow}+G/$
Step 3.	$T_3 = T_2 D/$	String becomes: $T_3 EF{\uparrow}+G/$
Step 4.	$T_4 = EF{\uparrow}$	String becomes: $T_3 T_4 +G/$
Step 5.	$T_5 = T_3 T_4 +$	String becomes: $T_5 G/$
Step 6.	$T_6 = T_5 G/$	String becomes: T_6

You should note that no operator is scanned until after its two operands have been scanned. If you are familiar with an assembler-level language, it may be obvious the type of code the compiler would generate to implement the above six steps.

In the *DATA DIVISION*:

```
01  OP-STACK.
    02  STACK OCCURS 100 TIMES      PICTURE X.
    02  TOP-PTR                     PICTURE 9(3).
    02  NOEL-MAX                    PICTURE 9(3)
                                      VALUE 100.
01  IN-STRING.
    02  INFIX OCCURS 100 TIMES      PICTURE X.
01  HOUSEKEEPING.
    02  POSITION                    PICTURE 9(3).
    02  NEXT-CHAR                   PICTURE X.
    02  EOFF                        PICTURE X.
    02  OP-PRECEDENCE               PICTURE 9.
    02  TOP-PRECEDENCE              PICTURE 9.
01  PRECEDENCE-RULE.
    02  CHAR-CHECK                  PICTURE X.
        88  LEVEL-0                 VALUE '+', '-'.
        88  LEVEL-1                 VALUE '*', '/'.
        88  LEVEL-2                 VALUE '↑'.
        88  LEVEL-3                 VALUE '('.
    02  PRECEDENCE-LEVEL            PICTURE 9.
```

In the *PROCEDURE DIVISION* the driver is:

```
COMPUTE TOP-PTR = 0.
PERFORM SCAN-NEXT-CHAR
        VARYING POSITION FROM 1 BY 1
        UNTIL POSITION > NOEL-MAX OR INFIX (POSITION)
            = ';'.
PERFORM POP-STACK-TO-OUTPUT
        UNTIL TOP-PTR = 0.
```

and:

```
SCAN-NEXT-CHAR.
        MOVE INFIX (POSITION) TO NEXT-CHAR.
        IF NEXT-CHAR = '('
                PERFORM PUSH-STACK
        ELSE IF NEXT-CHAR = ')'
                PERFORM POP-STACK-TO-OUTPUT
                    UNTIL STACK (TOP-PTR) = '('
                PERFORM POP-STACK
        ELSE IF NEXT-CHAR = '↑' OR '*' OR '/' OR '+' OR '-'
                PERFORM FIND-OP-PRECEDENCE
                PERFORM FIND-TOP-PRECEDENCE
                PERFORM EMPTY-STACK-TO-LOWER-
                    PRECEDENCE  UNTIL  OP-PRECEDENCE >
                    TOP-PRECEDENCE
                PERFORM PUSH-STACK
```

```
                    ELSE DISPLAY NEXT-CHAR.
PUSH-STACK.
        COMPUTE TOP-PTR = TOP-PTR + 1.
        IF TOP-PTR > NOEL-MAX
                error-condition
        ELSE MOVE NEXT-CHAR TO STACK (TOP-PTR).
POP-STACK.
        IF TOP-PTR = 0
                error-condition
        ELSE MOVE STACK (TOP-PTR) TO EOFF
                COMPUTE TOP-PTR = TOP-PTR - 1.
POP-STACK-TO-OUTPUT.
        PERFORM POP-STACK.
        DISPLAY EOFF.
FIND-OP-PRECEDENCE.
        MOVE NEXT-CHAR TO CHAR-CHECK.
        PERFORM FIND-PRECEDENCE.
        MOVE PRECEDENCE-LEVEL TO OP-PRECEDENCE.
FIND-TOP-PRECEDENCE.
        IF TOP-PTR > 0
                MOVE STACK (TOP-PTR) TO CHAR-CHECK
                PERFORM FIND-PRECEDENCE
                MOVE PRECEDENCE-LEVEL TO TOP-PRECEDENCE
        ELSE MOVE 0 TO TOP-PRECEDENCE.
EMPTY-STACK-TO-LOWER-PRECEDENCE.
        PERFORM POP-STACK-TO-OUTPUT.
        PERFORM FIND-TOP-PRECEDENCE.
FIND-PRECEDENCE.
        IF LEVEL-0
                COMPUTE PRECEDENCE-LEVEL = 0
        ELSE IF LEVEL-1
                COMPUTE PRECEDENCE-LEVEL = 1
                ELSE IF LEVEL-2
                        COMPUTE PRECEDENCE-LEVEL = 2
                ELSE IF LEVEL-3
                        COMPUTE PRECEDENCE-LEVEL = 3
                ELSE error-condition.
```

An alternative mode of representation of an arithmetic expression is *prefix form*, in which the operator precedes its operands, e.g., $+AB$, $\uparrow EF$. One of the exercises at the end of the chapter asks you to consider what changes need to be made to the postfix algorithm above in order to generate strings that are in prefix form rather than postfix form.

The exercises also suggest that you consider enhancement of the conversion algorithms to incorporate treatment of the familiar relational operators ($<$, $<=$, $=$, $>=$, $>$), the boolean operators (*and, or, not*), and arithmetic unary operators (e.g., $-$, $+$). To assist your efforts, the operator precedences follow.

Level 6: unary −, unary +, *not*
Level 5: ↑
Level 4: *, /
Level 3: +, −
Level 2: <, <=, =, >=, >
Level 1: *and*
Level 0: *or*

Note that we also assigned to (a high priority in the above COBOL routine. This facilitated handling of the stack.

We will return to consideration of prefix, infix, and postfix notation when we discuss binary trees.

MAPPINGS TO STORAGE

We have already discussed the use of an array to house a stack. We have also seen that one-dimensional arrays are generally mapped to storage in a physically sequential manner. One contiguous set of addresses is allocated to array elements. The simplest mapping of a stack to storage uses the same approach. The stack is assigned a base location which remains fixed. The stack is then allowed to grow into adjacent locations.

So far we have considered allocating storage only to a single stack. Assume now that we have two stacks that need to co-exist in memory. If stack $S1$ will have a maximum of M elements and stack $S2$ will have a maximum of N elements, they could be allocated memory as depicted in Fig. 31.

FIGURE 31

This is not particularly efficient, especially if stacks $S1$ and $S2$ are never full at the same time.

Consider the case where we know that the number of elements in $S1$ and $S2$ *combined* will never exceed N.

$$\text{NOEL}(S1) + \text{NOEL}(S2) \leq N$$

One approach is to allocate room for each of them to grow to N elements, as above. At any given time there will be space allocated for at least N too many elements. An alternative approach will enable us to allocate room only for the combined maximum N. Face the two stacks such that they grow toward each other, as depicted in Fig. 32.

FIGURE 32

$S1$ and $S2$ will never run into each other, yet neither of them will ever overflow; together they can accommodate up to N elements. Stack $S1$ grows to the right and stack $S2$ grows to the left.

Consider now the problem of allocating memory to three or more stacks such that (1) overflow will occur only when the total size of all the stacks together exceeds the space available, and (2) each stack has a fixed base location. In fact it is not possible to adhere to both these conditions simultaneously for three or more stacks. When it is necessary to allocate memory to several stacks, one or both of the conditions has to be relaxed. Either more space has to be allocated or the stack bases may need to be moved around. One technique for efficient allocation of space when there are three or more stacks is called Garwick's technique, which periodically reallocates space to the stacks. At reallocation time, growth in each of the stacks is measured, and space is reapportioned so that each stack receives space proportional to its growth since the last reallocation. In this technique the stack bases move around; those stacks that tend to grow tend to get more of the space.

Later in the text we will discuss ways to allocate stacks to noncontiguous memory by using linked lists. It is generally not possible to predict the maximum size that a stack will obtain; thus dynamic storage allocation schemes (such as Garwick's technique) and noncontiguous storage schemes are quite commonly used.

SUMMARY

A *stack* is a special case of linear list in which insertion (push) and deletion (pop) operations are restricted to occur only at one end, which is
referred to as the stack's top. Stacks are commonly housed in arrays.
This approach imposes several constraints on stack use but is very commonly used. The integrity of a stack must be maintained by the programmer when the stack is housed in an array. It is the programmer's
responsibility to ensure that insertion and deletion operations occur
only at the stack's top. The chapter introduced the declaration and
manipulation of stacks in COBOL and Pascal.

An example was used to illustrate that a stack can be used in the
solution of problems that need a last-in-first-out data structure. Another
example of recursive calls to determine a desired investment amount
showed the need to return to where called from. A stack was used by
the compiler to keep track of these locations in order by call. The postfix example used both a LIFO pattern for which operands pertained to
a particular operator and a nesting pattern of parentheses.

The chapter terminated with a discussion of allocation of memory
to multiple stacks.

For further information regarding stack management, refer to:

Garwick, J. "Data storage in compilers," *BIT*, 4: 137–140, 1964.

Knuth, D. E. *The Art of Computer Programming, Vol. I, Fundamental Algorithms.*
Reading, Mass.: Addison-Wesley Publishing Co., 1973, pp. 234–251.

Standish, T. A. "Stacks and queues," Chapter 2 in *Data Structure Techniques.*
Reading, Mass.: Addison-Wesley Publishing Co., 1980, pp. 28–41.

Terms

infix notation	prefix notation
last-in-first-out (LIFO)	push
linear list	recursive procedure
pop	stack
postfix notation	syntax

Review Exercises

1. Draw a stack and indicate the direction of elements in and out.
2. Fill in the blanks:
   (a) If you pop an empty stack, you get a(n) _____ .

(b) If you correctly push element i onto a stack, Top = _____ .

(c) Top of an empty stack = _____ .

(d) If you pop and then push element i, Top = _____ .

(e) How many elements are in a newly created stack? _____ .

3. What are the results of the following assertions:

(a) ISEMPTY (CREATE (S)) is _____ .

(b) ISEMPTY (PUSH(i,S)) is _____ .

(c) POP(CREATE (S)) is _____ .

4. What is the result of TOP(PUSH(i,S))? _____ .

5. What is the result of POP(PUSH(i,S))? _____ .

6. How can a stack be implemented in FORTRAN?

7. Write an algorithm that adds elements to a stack.

8. Write an algorithm that deletes elements from a stack.

9. Write an algorithm that creates and loads a stack.

10. List three applications of stacks in a business operation; for each give reasons why stacks would be preferable to arrays.

11. The algorithm "PUSH" checks for an overflow condition, and algorithm "POP" checks for an underflow condition. What is meant by overflow and underflow, and why would we want to check for such conditions? What might be the appropriate action to take under each condition?

12. What is the postfix form for each of the following:

(a) $A * B - (C+D) - (E-F) + F/H \uparrow I$

(b) $((B * C) + C/D \uparrow F) + G$

(c) $A \uparrow B * C - D + E / F / (G+H)$

13. Write an algorithm for popping an item off a stack and assigning the value popped to variable x.

14. Write a program that uses a stack to check for matching left and right parentheses, left and right braces, and left and right brackets in a string of characters.

15. Write an algorithm that uses a stack to convert an arithmetic expression from infix to prefix notation.

16. Write a program to implement your infix-to-prefix conversion algorithm.

17. Write a Pascal program to convert an arithmetic expression from infix to postfix notation.

18. Write a program to convert an arithmetic expression from infix to postfix notation, where the arithmetic expression may contain the following operators: $<, <=, =, >=, >$, and, or, not, unary -, unary +, $\uparrow$, *, /, +, -.

19. STACK

    3
    4
    1
    8
    5
    6

Write an algorithm that will create a new stack containing the elements of STACK above in ascending order. Minimize the number of intermediary stacks used.

CHAPTER 5

Queues

Another special case of the data structure *linear list* which was defined in Chapter 4 is the queue. Whereas stacks are restricted such that elements are added to and deleted from only the top of the list, queues are restricted such that elements are added to the rear of the list and deleted from the head of the list. We are all familiar with queues as they commonly arise in our everyday lives. We stand in queues in supermarkets, banks, and post offices. Cars generally proceed in queues through intersections. Queues also commonly arise in computer-based information systems. Customer orders enter queues to be filled; products enter inventory queues; tasks enter queues in computers awaiting service from the CPU.

In this chapter the operations that define the queue data structure are introduced; then facilities for declaring and manipulating queues in COBOL and Pascal are covered. Several examples of applications that use queues are discussed at the end of the chapter.

DEFINITIONS: QUEUES

A *queue* is a special case of the general data structure linear list defined in the preceding chapter as

$$A = [A_1, A_2, \ldots, A_T].$$

In a queue, insertion is restricted to occur only at one end of the list, which we call the *rear*; deletion is restricted to occur only at the other end of the list, which we call the *front*. We denote by FRONT (Q) the front of the queue Q and by REAR (Q) the end of the queue Q. For queue Q where

$$Q = [Q_1, Q_2, \ldots, Q_T]$$

FRONT (Q) is Q_1 and REAR (Q) is Q_T.

We use NOEL (Q) to denote the number of elements in queue Q. NOEL (Q) is an attribute of queue Q and has an integer value. For queue Q above, NOEL (Q) is T.

The queue insertion operator is called *insert* and the deletion operator is called *remove*. For an example of the effects of these operators, let us start with an empty queue named Q. $Q = [\,]$ can be represented by Fig. 33(a).

```
  _____
  _____
```

NOEL(Q) = 0
FRONT(Q) undefined

FIGURE 33(a)   REAR(Q) undefined

We first insert element A, giving $Q = [A]$ (Fig. 33(b)):

```
  _____
  |   A   |
  _____
```

NOEL(Q)   = 1
FRONT(Q) = A

FIGURE 33(b)   REAR(Q)   = A

then the element B, giving $Q = [A,B]$, (Fig. 33(c)):

```
  _____
  |   A   |   B   |
  _____
```

NOEL(Q)   = 2
FRONT(Q) = A

FIGURE 33(c)   REAR(Q)   = B

then the element C, giving $Q = [A,B,C]$, (Fig. 33(d)):

```
  _____
  |   A   |   B   |   C   |
  _____
```

NOEL(Q)   = 3
FRONT(Q) = A

FIGURE 33(d)   REAR(Q)   = C

We could then remove an element from Q, giving $Q = [B,C]$ (Fig. 33(e)):

NOEL(Q) = 2
FRONT(Q) = B
REAR(Q) = C   **FIGURE 33(e)**

then perhaps insert two more elements, say D then E, giving $Q = [B,C,D,E]$ (Fig. 33(f)):

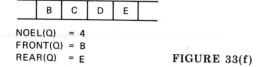

NOEL(Q) = 4
FRONT(Q) = B
REAR(Q) = E   **FIGURE 33(f)**

We might then want to delete an element from the queue, giving $Q = [C,D,E]$ (Fig. 33(g)):

NOEL(Q) = 3
FRONT(Q) = C   **FIGURE 33(g)**
REAR(Q) = E

and so forth. The queue operates in a first-in-first-out (FIFO) manner. Elements are removed in the order in which they were inserted into the queue. You should compare the activity of this example queue with that of the example stack in the preceding chapter. The same sequence of operations occurs in both cases, but the contents of the lists are quite different.

If there are NOEL elements in a queue, then the NOEL[th] element is at the rear of the queue; it is the element that has been in the queue the least amount of time. The first element of the queue is at the front of the queue; it is the element that has been in the queue the longest.

It doesn't really matter whether we draw a queue such that it grows from right to left (Fig. 34(a)):

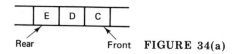

Rear   Front   **FIGURE 34(a)**

or from left to right (Fig. 34(b)):

Front   Rear   **FIGURE 34(b)**

or vertically, as long as we are consistent in keeping track of the queue's front and rear.

In any case, for queue

$$Q = [Q_1, Q_2, \ldots, Q_{NOEL}]$$

we will say that element Q_I is *in front of* element Q_J, for $I < J$. Q_I will be removed from the queue before any of the elements that it is in front of. Q_I has been in the queue longer than any of the elements that it is in front of. Clearly this is the way the people near the front of the post office line would like the order of service to be determined.

There are four basic operations that are legally defined for data type *queue*:

1. CREATE (queue)
2. ISEMPTY (queue)
3. INSERT (element, queue)
4. REMOVE (queue)

We denote by CREATE (Q) the operator that returns an empty queue with name Q. By definition:

NOEL (CREATE (Q)) is 0,
FRONT (CREATE (Q)) is undefined,
REAR (CREATE (Q)) is undefined.

We denote by ISEMPTY (Q) the operator that determines whether or not queue Q is empty. The operand is of type queue; the result is of type boolean. ISEMPTY (Q) is true if queue Q is empty (that is, if NOEL (Q) = 0) and false otherwise. Note that ISEMPTY (CREATE (Q)) is true.

INSERT (E, Q) is the operator that inserts element E into queue Q. By definition, E is placed at the rear of the queue. The result of the operation is the augmented queue.

REAR (INSERT (E, Q)) is E

NOEL (Q) is incremented by the INSERT operation, and

Q_{NOEL} is E.

The result of inserting an element into any queue cannot be an empty queue:

ISEMPTY (INSERT (E, Q)) is false.

In only one condition does inserting an element into a queue affect the front of the queue:

If ISEMPTY (Q)
then FRONT (INSERT (E,Q)) is E
else FRONT (INSERT (E,Q)) is FRONT (Q).

We use REMOVE (Q) to denote the operator that removes the front element from queue Q. The result is the decreased queue. If it is desired to save that first element, action to do so should be taken prior to the removal operation. NOEL (Q) is decremented by the REMOVE operation, and the previously second element of Q becomes the new front element.

It is an error to try to remove an element from an empty queue:

If NOEL $(Q) = 0$
then REMOVE (Q) yields an error condition.

Note that

REMOVE (CREATE (Q)) also yields an error condition.

In only one case does the removal of an element from a queue undo the immediately previous insertion of an element into the queue:

If ISEMPTY (Q)
then REMOVE (INSERT (E,Q)) is Q
else REMOVE (INSERT (E,Q))
        = INSERT $(E$, REMOVE (Q)).

If Q is not empty, then the insertion and removal operators act independently.

DECLARATION OF QUEUES IN COBOL AND PASCAL

Just as most programming languages do not have a built-in data type *stack*, so do they not have a built-in data type *queue*. In order to program a solution for a problem that calls for use of a queue variable, the programmer must use the language's existing features in a way that enables the queue's operation to be simulated. One of the simplest ways to represent a queue variable is to house it in an array. In this section we introduce this method of handling a queue in COBOL and Pascal.

Housing a queue in an array immediately imposes two artificial constraints on that queue. First, the elements that are inserted into the queue must be homogeneous, because that is part of the definition of an array. Second, the programmer must specify an upper bound on the number of elements in the queue when it is housed in an array. A queue variable has no logical constraint on the maximum number of elements that it may contain. (The queue for the Uptown Picture Show Emporium might wind around the block three and a half times on Saturday night.) However, a queue variable housed in an array is confined to the space allocated to that array. In fact, a queue grows and shrinks over time, but an array has constant size.

Housing a queue in an array has the additional difficulty that the integrity of the queue is the programmer's responsibility. It is up to the programmer to ensure that the queue operates on a FIFO basis. The programming language itself will not ensure that elements won't be inserted and removed willy-nilly from the middle of the data structure.

Let's consider the declaration of a variable named Q of data type queue. Assume that each element of Q will be an integer and that Q will have a maximum of 100 elements. In addition to declaring the array that will house Q, we must declare variables that point us to the front and rear elements of the queue. F and R will be integer variables whose values will be subscripts of the first and last elements of the queue, respectively. We name the combined array and its front and rear indicators the $QUEUE$-$STRUCT$.

In COBOL:

```
01  QUEUE-STRUCT.
    02  Q                    OCCURS 100 TIMES
                             PICTURE 9(5).
    02  F                    PICTURE 9(3).
    02  R                    PICTURE 9(3).
```

In Pascal:

```
type  queuestruct =
         record queue: array [1 .. 100] of integer;
                f,r: integer;
         end;
var q:  queuestruct;
```

Initially, we will set F and R equal to 0 for the empty queue. The insertion and removal operators are actually quite simply implemented in COBOL and Pascal. The main complication is in checking that F and R do not point outside of the bounds of the queue's array. We use the variable $NOEL$-MAX to be the maximum number of elements that the queue's array can accommodate; here $NOEL$-MAX = 100. Throughout we indicate that the actions that a program takes upon detecting an overflow condition (attempt to insert an element into a full queue) or an underflow condition (attempt to remove an element from an empty queue) are application-dependent.

Note that inserting an element into an empty queue requires moving both the F and R pointers. When removing an element from a queue makes the queue be empty, the F and R pointers are reset to 0 so that insertion into the queue will then proceed from the low end of the array. We use EON to be the element inserted onto the queue and $EOFF$ to be the element removed from the queue. Note that we save $EOFF$ and assume that q is a globally known variable in the Pascal examples.

In COBOL:

```
INSERT.
    IF  R = NOEL–MAX
            overflow-condition
    ELSE COMPUTE R = R + 1
        MOVE EON to Q (R)
        IF F = 0
                COMPUTE F = 1.
REMOVE.
    IF  F > 0
        MOVE Q (F) to EOFF
        IF  F = R
                COMPUTE F = 0
                COMPUTE R = 0
        ELSE COMPUTE F = F + 1
    ELSE underflow-condition.
```

In Pascal:

```
procedure insert (eon:integer);
begin if(q.r < noelmax)
        then begin q.r := q.r + 1;
                    q.queue[q.r] := eon;
                    if (q.f = 0)
                    then q.f := 1
                end
            else OVERFLOW–CONDITION
end;
procedure removeq(var eoff : integer)
begin if(q.f > 0)
        then begin eoff := q.queue[q.f];
                    if(q.f = q.r)
                    then begin q.f := 0;
                                q.r := 0
                        end
                    else q.f := q.f + 1
                end
            else UNDERFLOW–CONDITION
end;
```

Note that the number of elements in the queue at any given time can be calculated from the values of the front and rear pointers.

> If $F = 0$
> then NOEL (Q) is 0
> else NOEL (Q) is $R - F + 1$

Let us now examine a bit more carefully these algorithms and the use of an array to house a queue. Consider the successive insertion and removal of elements; for example, insert four elements (Fig. 35(a)),

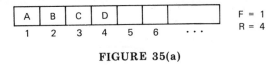

FIGURE 35(a)

remove two elements (Fig. 35(b)),

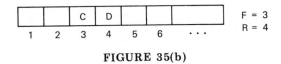

FIGURE 35(b)

insert three more elements (Fig. 35(c)),

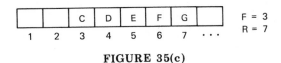

FIGURE 35(c)

remove two more elements (Fig. 35(d)),

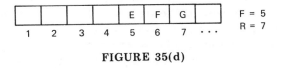

FIGURE 35(d)

and so forth. The queue is traveling left-to-right through the array. What happens when $R = 100$ and we need to insert more elements into the queue? We have hit the boundary of the array. The queue is full only if $F = 1$ and the maximum has been reached, i.e., NOEL $(Q) = 100$. However, it is probably more likely that the front of the queue has migrated "to the right" due to removal of one or more elements and $F > 1$. It may even be the case that $F = 100$ and there is only one element in Q yet it appears as if Q is full.

One approach to solving this problem is to house the queue in a larger array. This is not a terribly attractive solution unless we have an infinite amount of storage to devote to that array or can take advantage of *a priori* knowledge of the queue's behavior over time.

A better approach is to arrange Q in a circular fashion, considering $Q(1)$ as following $Q(NOEL\text{-}MAX)$, as in Fig. 36. (In the following we replace variable $NOEL\text{-}MAX$ by the variable N in order to make the diagrams easier to draw.)

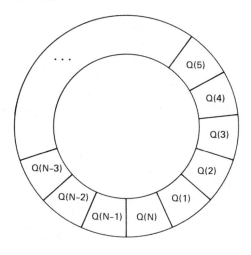

FIGURE 36

Now, depending upon how the insertion and removal operators are implemented, the queue will use the circular array differently. We present two alternatives here; other alternatives will be left as exercises.

First, let us continue with our convention of having variable F point to the first element in the queue and variable R point to the last element in the queue. Various configurations of the queue at several points in time are given in Fig. 37, where X marks a slot that is occupied by an element of the queue. Note that the queue's elements may span the boundary between $Q(1)$ and $Q(N)$, as shown in the third picture. The insertion and deletion operators must account for resetting of the F and R pointers when they cross the boundary from value N to value 1.

The condition for an empty queue is $R = F = 0$. A full queue is depicted in Fig. 38. Note that this queue "grows" in the counterclockwise direction. What does the queue look like when it contains just one element? Compare the positions of the F and R pointers when the queue

FIGURE 37

FIGURE 38

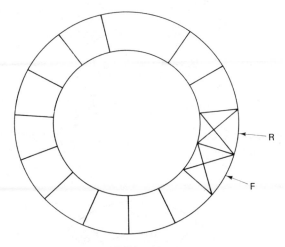

FIGURE 39

is full and when the queue contains just two elements, as shown in Fig. 39.

The INSERT and REMOVE operators for circular queues are implemented as follows:

In COBOL:

```
INSERT.
    IF  R = N
            COMPUTE R = 1
    ELSE COMPUTE R = R + 1.
    IF  R = F
            overflow-condition
    ELSE MOVE EON TO Q(R)
        IF F = 0
            COMPUTE F = 1.
REMOVE.
    IF F = 0
            underflow-condition
    ELSE MOVE Q (F) TO EOFF
        IF F = R
            COMPUTE F = 0
            COMPUTE R = 0
        ELSE IF F = N
                COMPUTE F = 1
            ELSE COMPUTE F = F + 1.
```

In Pascal:

```
procedure insert(eon:integer);
begin if(q.r = n)
    then q.r := 1
```

```
            else q.r := q.r + 1;
            if(q.r = q.f)
            then OVERFLOW-CONDITION
            else begin q.queue[q.r] := eon;
                        if(q.f = 0)
                        then q.f := 1
        end;
    end;


procedure remove(var eoff : integer);
begin if(q.f = 0)
        then UNDERFLOW-CONDITION
        else begin eoff := q.queue[q.f];
                    if(q.f = q.r)
                    then begin q.f := 0;
                                q.r := 0
                        end
                    else if(q.f = n)
                        then q.f := 1
                        else q.f := q.f + 1
        end;
    end;
```

Note that if we use the same algorithms but number the slots in a clockwise rather than counterclockwise direction, then the queue will appear to move in a clockwise direction. If we retain the counterclockwise numbering scheme but change the insertion and removal codes such that the R and F pointers are decremented rather than incremented, then the queue will appear to move in a clockwise direction.

Some programmers prefer to number the array slots from 0 to N-1, rather than from 1 to N (Fig. 40).

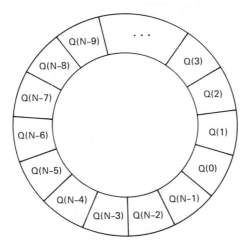

FIGURE 40

Now we can handle the transition over the $Q(N-1) - Q(0)$ boundary using modulo arithmetic, which is a built-in function in Pascal, FORTRAN, and PL/I. $A \underline{mod} B$ in Pascal is the integer remainder resulting when A is divided by B. $I := A \underline{mod} B$ in Pascal is equivalent in result to COBOL's

DIVIDE A BY B GIVING C REMAINDER I.

The insertion and removal operations then can be implemented in the Pascal program as follows. Replace the code

    if(q.r = n)
    then q.r := 1
    else q.r := q.r + 1

by

    q.r := (q.r+1) mod n;

in the *insert* procedure. Replace the code

    if(q.f = n)
    then q.f := 1
    else q.f := q.f + 1

by

    q.f := (q.f+1) mod n;

in the *remove* procedure.

Actually, this change to the scheme of numbering slots makes it somewhat more difficult to detect the condition of an empty queue. Note the $F = R = 0$ now is indicative of a queue with one element, in the slot 0 (Fig. 41).

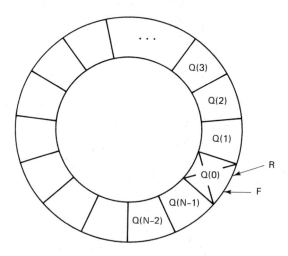

FIGURE 41

In order to alleviate this difficulty, a second technique for representing a queue in a circular array is commonly used. Rather than having F point *to* the front element of the queue, we use F to point to the slot *preceding* the one containing the front element of the queue. Examples are shown in Fig. 42. Now the queue is empty when $F = R$, and it is

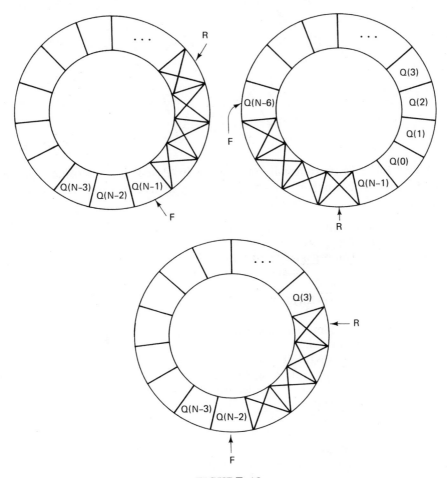

FIGURE 42

full when $R = (F+1)$ *mod* N (Fig. 43). Note that the maximum number of elements that can be contained in this queue is $N - 1$, even though there are N slots. If we were to allow N elements to enter the queue, then the condition for full $F = R$ would be the same as the condition for empty. This paradox could of course be handled by recognizing whether $F = R$ resulted from an insertion (queue is full) or a removal (queue is empty), or simply by maintaining the value of NOEL(Q).

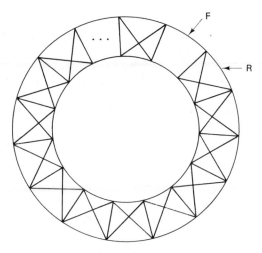

FIGURE 43

The insert and removal operations in Pascal for a circular queue with indices 0 through $n - 1$ and f pointing in front of the first element follow.

```
procedure insert (eon:integer);
begin if(q.f<>(q.r+1) mod n)
      then begin q.r := (q.r+1) mod n;
                 q.queue[q.r] := eon
           end
      else OVERFLOW
end;
procedure removeq(var eoff:integer);
begin if(q.r = q.f)
      then UNDERFLOW-CONDITION
      else begin q.f := (q.f+1) mod n;
                 eoff := q.queue[q.f]
           end;
end;
```

You should compare these algorithms with the algorithms presented earlier for f pointing to the queue's first element.

An alternative representation would have R point to the slot one behind the rear of the queue, with F pointing to the first element. You should develop the insertion and removal algorithms for this approach.

Thus we have proposed at least six approaches to representation of a queue in a circular array (Fig. 44). The representation mode is determined by the way that pointers are handled in the insertion and removal algorithms used. In all cases it must be possible to detect when the queue is empty and when it is full. The algorithms for handling these various approaches are all of essentially the same complexity. We have

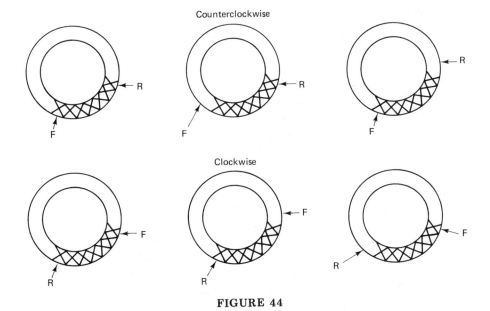

Counterclockwise

Clockwise

FIGURE 44

presented the variety of techniques here because *all* are in extensive use; the maintenance programmer may very well have to deal with any and all of the techniques.

There are other ways to represent a queue variable besides housing it in an array. We will discuss these representations later, primarily in the next chapter, on linked lists.

EXAMPLE APPLICATIONS OF QUEUES

Queues are extensively used in applications that simulate the behavior of real systems in which there is FIFO activity. Queues build up in many commonplace situations: cars enqueue at a traffic light; patrons wait in line at the post office; shoppers queue up at checkout counters in grocery stores; messages queue up in communications networks; files are spooled to be delivered in FIFO order to a line printer; and so on.

Designers are often interested in improving the performance of such systems, where performance can be measured by a variety of parameters:

- Average number of elements in the queue.
- Average time spent in the queue.
- Probability that queue length will be greater than some number.
- Probability that queued time will be greater than some number.

- Minimum and maximum queue length over a period of time.
- Minimum and maximum time in queue over a period of time.

There are three basic approaches to determining values for the above parameters: observation, simulation, and queueing theory. Observation can be applied to the study of an existing system. For instance, you may have seen people sitting at traffic lights counting the cars waiting and proceeding through the intersection. Observation is not appropriate to study systems that are still in the design phase or to study effects of changes to existing systems.

One of the most powerful tools that can be used to study the behavior of systems is simulation. A simulation program exercises a model of the system under study. For example, a simulator of a grocery store checkout system would generate arrivals to the checkout queues, would characterize each arrival by the amount of service it requires, would represent the rate of service rendered at each checkout stand, and so forth. The simulator would gather statistics during the operation of the model over some period of time. These statistics would characterize the behavior of the queues that develop.

In order to build a simulation model, it is necessary to have rather substantial statistics available to characterize the system under study. These statistics include arrival distributions, the means and standard deviations of service times, and so on. These data may be gathered by observation or may be hypothesized for a "paper" system that does not yet exist.

Once the simulation model is developed, its parameters can be adjusted and experimented with fairly easily. Effects of changes to the system can be investigated. For example, what happens to the system behavior if we set up an additional checkstand? What happens if we have two quick-check lines instead of one? What happens if we slightly slow down the rate of service, say by requiring that all customer checks be verified by the store manager?

Queueing theory is an analytic approach to studying behavior of systems that involve queues. A set of equations and curves has been developed with sound mathematical basis for estimating queue sizes, waiting times, probabilities of delay, and so forth. Just as is the case with simulation, assumptions regarding the characteristics of the system under study must be made in order to apply the results of queueing theory. For example, the arrival rate of entries to the queues must be established; the number of queues and the number of servers (who remove elements from queues) must be determined; the service discipline must be characterized (e.g., serve to completion—as in the grocery store—versus serve some quantum of time and then put the element at the end of the queue so it will be served again later—as in computer timesharing systems); and the distribution of service demands must be selected.

One of the interesting results of queueing theory shows that the queueing configuration of multiple servers, each with its own queue (Fig. 45)

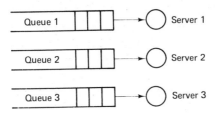

FIGURE 45

has a longer average waiting time than does the same system configured with a single queue (Fig. 46),

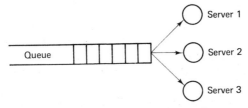

FIGURE 46

where the element at the front of the queue is serviced by whichever server happens to become available next. You may have seen this type of queue management implemented in your local post office or bank. Why is it not generally used in grocery stores?

SUMMARY

A *queue* is a special case of linear list in which insertions are restricted to occur only at one end of the queue, which is referred to as the queue's rear, and removals are restricted to occur only at the other end of the queue, which is referred to as the queue's front.

Queues are used extensively in computer operation; for instance, in selecting the next job to be serviced, in selecting the next file to be printed on the printer, in selecting the next card to read from the card reader. Additionally, queues are extensively used for modeling purposes, as in the simulation of traffic patterns in grocery stores, post offices, barber shops, and so forth. A queue can be used in the solution of problems that need a first-in-first-out data structure.

Queues can be represented in storage in much the same way as are stacks; by being housed in arrays. As with stacks, the integrity of a queue must be maintained by the programmer when the queue is housed in an array. It is the programmer's responsibility to ensure that insertion and deletion operations occur only at the queue's rear and front, respectively.

Because queues propagate through storage with successive insertions and removals, circular arrays are commonly used. The algorithms for managing queues are deceptively simple; the reader should be careful to build a sound understanding of them.

Terms

first-in-first-out (FIFO)
queue

queueing theory
simulation

Review Exercises

1. Describe the similarities and differences between queues and stacks.
2. At which end of a queue is an insertion made? A removal?
3. Why are queues that are housed in arrays usually represented in circular rather than linear fashion?
4. Can a stack be circular?
5. In looking at an algorithm to insert an element into a queue, how can one tell if the queue is moving clockwise or counterclockwise?
6. When is the *mod* function convenient to use in circular queues?
7. How do you test for an empty queue? Describe your placement of the front pointer.
8. Write a procedure to add an element to a circular queue when the first element is designated F and when R indicates the space just past the end of the queue.
9. Write an algorithm to count the number of items in a circular queue.
10. Write an algorithm for deleting an element from a circular queue when R points to the rear and F points to one space ahead of the front.
11. Write an algorithm for adding an element to a circular queue when R points to the rear and F points to the front.
12. Draw a queue of ten elements indicating the front and rear. Give the algorithm to check to see if a queue is full.
13. Write an algorithm to put two queues of varying lengths (but with a sum total length of N) into an array of N slots.
14. A CPU allows each transaction a maximum of 2 units of processing time; if that task is completed, then it is sent on for output to disk or to a terminal; if not, it is sent back to the rear of the queue that it came from for further proc-

essing. Given that all tasks are queued for the CPU and that 2 priorities exist—priority 1, which gets precedence, and priority 2, which is subordinate to priority 1—and given the following transactions:

Trans	Priority	Time of Entry	Req. Service
A	1	0	1
B	2	0	2
C	2	1	6
D	1	2	4
E	1	2	3
F	2	3	2
G	1	5	1

trace the history of the applicable queues and the CPU's processing in 1-unit intervals until all processing is completed.

15. (a) There is a bank with two tellers. One is experienced, one is new. The average transaction time for the new teller is twice as long as for the experienced teller. Write an algorithm to direct customers to the appropriate teller so that the average waiting time for both lines is equal.

(b) Now assume that the new teller "learns" after each transaction and his/her transaction time decreases by $\frac{1}{n}$ (where n = transaction time for the experienced teller) after each transaction. Write an algorithm to equate line waiting times for this situation.

CHAPTER 6

Linked Lists

In this chapter we consider the use of linked lists to represent linear data structures: general linear lists, stacks, and queues. Later in the book we will address the use of linked lists to represent nonlinear data structures: trees and graphs.

LINKED LIST REPRESENTATION

In preceding chapters we represented stacks and queues by housing them in arrays. A basic constraint imposed by this mode of representation is that the amount of storage allocated to the stack or queue is fixed. The space is allocated regardless of whether the stack or queue is empty, and there is the possibility of overflow if the stack or queue becomes larger than expected. This is also a problem when an array is used to house a general linear list.

However, there is an even more severe constraint imposed in the general case. What happens when the 43rd element, say 'IGOR,' is removed from a linear list of 2492 names? Elements 1 through 42 are not affected, but elements 44 'IVAN' through 2492 'ZELDA' logically should each be shifted in the array; element 44 becomes new element 43, element 45 becomes element 44, . . . , element 2492 becomes element 2491. Now, what happens when a new element, say 'HORATIO,' is to be inserted after element 41, 'HORACE'? Elements 42 'HOWARD' through 2491 'ZELDA' logically need to be shifted "down" in the array to make room for the new element 42. The new element cannot just be tacked onto the end of the array, because the logical ordering of elements in the linear list is conveyed by the physical ordering of elements in the array.

A solution to the data movement problems encountered in using sequential representation is to instead use nonsequential representation. Sequential representation mirrors the logical ordering of elements in a linear list in physical storage; the logical ordering and the physical ordering are the same. With nonsequential representation, the logical ordering of elements and the physical ordering of elements need *not* be the same. The logical ordering is represented by having each element point to the next element; the elements of the linear list are linked together. To access the elements in logical order, these links are followed.

Fig. 47 is a picture of a linear linked list that contains four elements.

FIGURE 47

There is a pointer named *FIRST* to the first element of the list. Each element (or node) has a link to the next element of the list. The last element has a *NULL* pointer, which indicates that there is no next element. Note that each element of the list actually has two parts: *INFO*, which is the data contents of the element, and the *NEXT* pointer field. Each element is a record data structure (see Chapter 3).

The linked elements do not have to be physically adjacent. Our list of four elements might be as shown in Fig. 48.

FIGURE 48

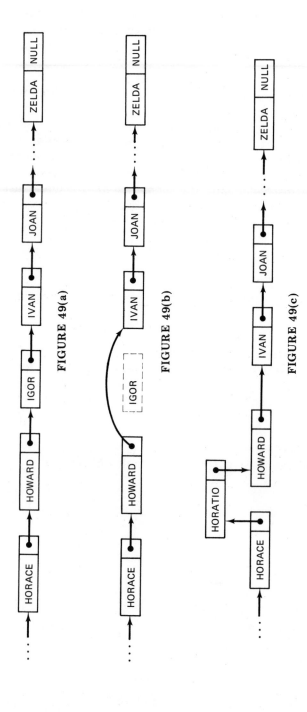

FIGURE 49(a)

FIGURE 49(b)

FIGURE 49(c)

A linear list with no elements is called an *empty list*. The linked list representation of an empty list is merely a null *FIRST* pointer. The operation of creating an empty list then is:

FIRST := NULL.

Recall that another constraint imposed by using an array to house a queue or stack is that the elements are required to be homogeneous. This constraint can be relieved by using the linked list representation scheme. Heterogeneous elements can be linked together.

The benefits of linked list representation become apparent when the insertion and removal operations are considered. To remove the 43rd element, say 'IGOR,' of a linear list with 2492 elements (Fig. 49(a)), it is necessary only to change the pointer in the prior (42nd) element to point to the next (44th) element (Fig. 49(b)).

To insert a new element, say 'HORATIO,' after the 41st element, it is necessary only to change the pointer of the 41st element to point to the new element and to have the new element point to the 42nd element (Fig. 49(c)). There is no shifting of data necessary.

Of course the new element must have the appropriate data structure to accommodate the link to the next element of the list. We assume that there are functions called GETNODE, that returns the location of an empty node of the proper format for the list in question, and FREENODE, that places newly emptied nodes back into the pool of available space. We will detail these two functions later.

The costs of using a linked list rather than sequential representation are basically two. First, space is required in the linked representation for the pointer fields. Second, it will usually take longer to search for an element in a linked representation than when the list.is housed in an array. Recall that there is a calculation that can be used to find the starting location of the Nth element in an array. In order to find the Nth element in a linked list (assuming no use of auxiliary pointers), the chain of the previous $N-1$ elements must be traversed.

BASIC OPERATIONS ON A LINKED LIST

We consider now the basic operations on a linked list. In the next sections we will see how linked lists are declared and manipulated in programs.

It is necessary to introduce some notation. Let P be a pointer variable. Its value is an address, i.e., the location of some other variable. The operations that are legal on pointer variables are the following:

1. Test for NULL.

2. Test for equality with another pointer variable.
3. Set to NULL.
4. Set to point to a node.

Denote by

> NODE(P)   the node pointed to by P;
> INFO(P)   the value in the information portion of the node pointed to
>   by P;
> NEXT(P)   the value in the link portion of the node pointed to by P.

Consider the linked list of Fig. 50(a).

FIGURE 50(a)

The algorithm to remove from the linked list the element following the one pointed to by P follows. We use Q as an auxiliary pointer variable and will first set it to point to the element to be removed.

> (a)   Q := NEXT(P)
> (b)   NEXT(P) := NEXT(Q)
> (c)   FREENODE(Q)

After step (a), we have the structure shown in Fig. 50(b).

FIGURE 50(b)

After step (b), we have the structure shown in Fig. 50(c).

FIGURE 50(c)

After step (c), we have the structure shown in Fig. 50(d). This sequence of operations returns the removed element to be reused, except if P

FIGURE 50(d)

points to the last element of the list. How should the algorithm be modified to accommodate that situation?

The algorithm to insert a variable *NAME* into the linked list such that it follows the element pointed to by *P* follows. Again we use the auxiliary pointer *Q*, as well as another, called *NEW*. The result of the GETNODE operation is the location of an empty node, into which we place the contents of *NAME* and an appropriate link.

(a)   NEW := GETNODE
(b)   INFO(NEW) := NAME
(c)   Q := NEXT(P)
(d)   NEXT(P) := NEW
(e)   NEXT(NEW) := Q

After steps (a) and (b), we have the structures shown in Fig. 51(a).

FIGURE 51(a)

After steps (c) and (d), we have the structures shown in Fig. 51(b).

FIGURE 51(b)

After step (e), we have the structures shown in Fig. 51(c).

FIGURE 51(c)

It is important to recognize that links such as *P*, *Q*, *NEW*, and the *NEXT* variables all point to *nodes*, not just to the *INFO* part of nodes. An arrow points to an entire box.

We will develop many other algorithms that operate on linked lists in our discussions of their manipulation in various programming languages.

MANAGEMENT OF AVAILABLE SPACE

We have already assumed the existence of two functions—GETNODE and FREENODE—which we used in our insertion and removal algorithms. Now let us look at these functions in more detail.

The storage pool contains all space that is not now in use. Let us assume that this space is formatted into units that correspond to the structure of nodes for our linked list. In fact a program may use several linked lists, each with nodes of a different format, in which case we would have several pools of empty nodes. For purposes of simplifying our explanation, we will assume for now that we have only one node type to worry about.

What is an appropriate structure for the storage pool? We probably do not want to use sequential representation, because nodes will be removed rather randomly from our linked list and we would like that space to be reusable. Therefore the storage pool will be represented using a linked structure. Logically, however, the storage pool is merely a linear list. The GETNODE function returns the location of the *next* free node in the storage pool; there is a logical ordering of these free nodes.

Initially, when all "user" lists are empty, the storage pool contains all the available space. We will use *AVAIL* as the pointer to the first node on the list of available space (Fig. 52).

FIGURE 52

When a node is needed for insertion to a list, it is obtained from this list of available space by invocation of the GETNODE function. Note that the exception condition of not having any more available space must be handled correctly.

```
         If AVAIL = NULL
         then out-of-free-space
(a)      else begin; GETNODE := AVAIL;
(b)                  AVAIL := NEXT(AVAIL);
(c)                  NEXT(GETNODE) := NULL;
         end;
```

After step (a), we have the structure shown in Fig. 53(a).

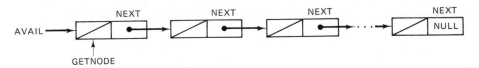

FIGURE 53(a)

After step (b), we have the structure shown in Fig. 53(b).

FIGURE 53(b)

After step (c) we have the structure shown in Fig. 53(c).

FIGURE 53(c)

The procedure FREENODE returns to the available space list a node that is no longer needed. This action makes that node's space re-usable. The argument of FREENODE is a pointer to the node that is to be placed into the storage pool. Quite simply, procedure FREENODE (Q) is:

(a)   NEXT(Q) := AVAIL
(b)   INFO(Q) := NULL
(c)   AVAIL := Q.

After step (a), we have the structure shown in Fig. 54(a).

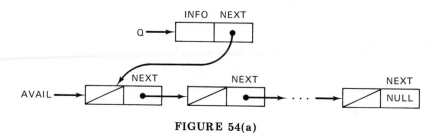

FIGURE 54(a)

After steps (b) and (c), we have the structure shown in Fig. 54(b).

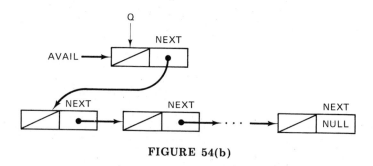

FIGURE 54(b)

Pointer Q will then be handled by the invoking routine in some appropriate manner. Q is probably an auxiliary pointer. The INFO portion of the newly freed node has been slashed, as have the INFO portions of other freed nodes in our diagrams, to indicate that it has been nulled and will be rewritten when eventually removed from the storage pool by a later GETNODE invocation.

These GETNODE and FREENODE algorithms structure the storage pool not just as a linear list, but as a stack. In fact, the storage pool is sometimes referred to as the *AVAIL stack*. How would the algorithms be different if the storage pool were structured as an *AVAIL queue*?

After a sequence of insertion and removal operations on a user list pointed to by *LIST*, it and the *AVAIL* list might be quite intertwined physically, although the proper management of links keeps them logically untangled. (Fig. 55).

FIGURE 55

In the remainder of our treatment of linked lists we will assume the existence of GETNODE and FREENODE.

DECLARATION OF LINKED LISTS IN PASCAL, USING POINTER VARIABLES

We now turn to techniques for declaring linked lists in programming languages. In the preceding sections we made rather extensive use of pointers. Pascal has a built-in pointer data type and facilities for controlling dynamic storage. A single node can be declared in Pascal by:

```
type nodeptr = ↑nodetype;
      nametype = packed array [1 .. 10] of char;
      nodetype = record
                       info:nametype;
                       next:nodeptr
                 end;
```

The notation ↑*nodetype* indicates that *nodeptr* is a data type that points to things that have *nodetype* type. In Pascal a variable that is declared to be a pointer is constrained to contain the address of a particular data type.

If we declare *p* to be of *nodeptr* type and *node* to be of *nodetype* type:

```
var p:nodeptr;
     node:nodetype;
```

then we represent by

```
        p↑.info
and     p↑.next
```

the *info* and *next* parts respectively of the *node* pointed to by *p*. The pointer *p* is given the NULL value by *p* := *nil*.

The following statements are used by the programmer to control space management:

$\underline{new}(p)$ Allocates space for one of whatever type p points to and sets p to the address.

$\underline{dispose}(p)$ Frees the object currently pointed to by p.

The Pascal run-time environment handles the free-space management.

The algorithm to remove from the linked list of nodes the element following the one pointed to by p is coded in Pascal as follows. We place the *info* contents of the removed *node* in variable *out*, and we assume that *node* has been globally declared.

```
procedure removaf(p:nodeptr,var out:nametype);
     var q:nodeptr;
     begin if(p↑.next = nil)
           then UNDERFLOW-CONDITION
           else begin q := p↑.next;
                      p↑.next := q↑.next;
                      out := q↑.info;
                      dispose (q)
                end;
     end;
```

The algorithm to insert a variable *in* into the linked list so that it follows the *node* pointed to by p is coded in Pascal as follows:

```
procedure inseraf(p:nodeptr,in:nametype);
     var q:nodeptr;
     begin new(q);
           q↑.info := in;
           q↑.next := p↑.next;
           p↑.next := q
     end;
```

Of course, prior to invoking these algorithms, a check should be made to ensure that there actually is a node pointed to by p. In Pascal, $p = \underline{nil}$ would indicate that there is no such node.

DECLARATION OF LINKED LISTS IN COBOL AND PASCAL, WITHOUT USING POINTER VARIABLES

When one is using a programming language that does not have a built-in *pointer* data type, the code for declaring and manipulating linked lists is a bit more complex. We will simulate pointer variables by housing a linked list in an array. The value of a pointer variable then becomes the value of a subscript.

Fig. 56 is a diagram of an array that houses a linked list of names.

	INFO	NEXT
1	IVAN	6
2	HOWARD	5
3		
4	HORACE	2
5	IGOR	1
6	JOAN	0
7		

FIRST = 4

FIGURE 56

	INFO	NEXT
1	IVAN	6
2	HOWARD	5
3		7
4	HORACE	2
5	IGOR	1
6	JOAN	0
7		0

FIRST = 4
AVAIL = 3

FIGURE 57

Note that each element of the array is a record with two fields: *INFO* and *NEXT*. We use the value 0 to represent NULL.

The *AVAIL* stack actually shares this same array of space (Fig. 57). Fig. 58(a) shows the linked list after removal of the element following the one pointed to by *P*, where *P* = 5, and after insertion of 'HORATIO' in the proper alphabetic sequence (Fig. 58(b)):

	INFO	NEXT
1	IVAN	6
2	HOWARD	1
3		7
4	HORACE	2
5		3
6	JOAN	0
7		0

FIRST = 4
AVAIL = 5

FIGURE 58(a)

	INFO	NEXT
1	IVAN	6
2	HOWARD	1
3		7
4	HORACE	5
5	HORATIO	2
6	JOAN	0
7		0

FIRST = 4
AVAIL = 3

FIGURE 58(b)

Because we are using arrays, we must establish an upper bound on the number of nodes that will be in the linked list; assume the maximum is 500.

The array can be defined as follows.
In COBOL:

```
01  SPACE-ARRAY.
    02  NODE OCCURS 500 TIMES.
        03  INFO         PIC X(10).
        03  NEXTNODE     PIC 9(3).
    02  FIRSTNODE        PIC 9(3).
    02  AVAIL            PIC 9(3).
```

We use *NEXTNODE* and *FIRSTNODE* here because *NEXT* and *FIRST* are reserved words in COBOL.

For purposes of comparison with the pointer-variable techniques of the previous section:

In Pascal:

```
type nodeptr = 0 . . 500;
     nametype = packed array [1 . . 10] of char;
     nodetype = record
                      info:nametype;
                      next:nodeptr
                end;
var node:array [1 . . 500] of nodetype;
    first,avail:nodeptr;
```

In all cases we will use the value 0 to represent null.

The algorithm to remove from the linked list the element following the one pointed to by *P* is coded as follows:

In COBOL:

```
REMOVAF.
     IF NEXTNODE (P) = 0
          underflow-condition
     ELSE COMPUTE Q = NEXTNODE (P)
          COMPUTE NEXTNODE (P) = NEXTNODE (Q)
          output INFO (Q)
          COMPUTE NEXTNODE (Q) = AVAIL
          COMPUTE AVAIL = Q.
```

In Pascal:

```
procedure removaf(p:nodeptr);
var q:nodeptr;
begin
     if(node[p].next = 0)
     then UNDERFLOW-CONDITION
     else begin q := node[p].next;
                node[p].next := node[q].next;
                writeln (node[q].info);
                node[q].next := avail;
                avail := q
          end;
end;
```

The algorithm to insert a variable *IN* into the linked list such that it follows the node pointed to by *P* is coded as follows:

In COBOL:

```
INSERAF.
     IF AVAIL = 0
     THEN overflow-condition
```

```
        ELSE COMPUTE Q = AVAIL
            COMPUTE AVAIL = NEXTNODE (AVAIL)
            MOVE IN TO INFO (Q)
            COMPUTE NEXTNODE (Q) = NEXTNODE (P)
            COMPUTE NEXTNODE (P) = Q.
```

In Pascal:

```
procedure inseraf(p:nodeptr,in:nametype);
var q:nodeptr;
begin if(avail = 0)
        then OVERFLOW-CONDITION
        else begin q := avail;
                    avail := node[avail].next;
                    node[q].info := in;
                    node[q].next := node[p].next;
                    node[p].next := q
            end;
end;
```

FURTHER MANIPULATIONS OF SINGLY LINKED LISTS

The basic operations of removing and inserting nodes in linked lists were detailed in the previous section. Here we develop algorithms to perform further manipulations on linked lists and lead into a discussion of common enhancements to singly linked lists. Each algorithm is encoded in either COBOL or Pascal. You should now be able to convert to the language of your choice.

First, how can you find the contents of the Ith node in a list? If the list were housed in an array, a calculation using base location of the array and node size would yield the address of the desired node. If the list is represented in a linked manner, then we must step through the elements of the list, counting until we find ourselves positioned on the Ith node. Of course, it is necessary to check that there actually are at least I elements in the list. We use the COBOL *SPACE-ARRAY* declaration from the preceding section.

```
        COMPUTE PTR = FIRSTNODE.
        PERFORM STEP-THRU-LIST
            VARYING J FROM 1 BY 1
                UNTIL J = 1 OR PTR = 0.
        IF PTR = 0
            list has fewer than I nodes
        ELSE output INFO (PTR).
```

where

```
        STEP-THRU-LIST.
            COMPUTE PTR = NEXTNODE (PTR).
```

The algorithm to determine the number of nodes presently in a linked list is related and is left to the reader.

The algorithm to insert an element at the beginning of a list has already been given in our discussions of the *AVAIL* stack. We have also seen the algorithm to remove an element from the beginning of a linked list, again in the discussion of the *AVAIL* stack. Let's consider now the algorithm to insert an element at the end of a linked list. We use the declarations from a previous section.

```
procedure inserend(first:nodeptr,in:nametype);
var newnode,q:nodeptr;
begin new(newnode);
      newnode↑.info := in;
      newnode↑.next := nil;
      q := first;
      do while(q↑.next<>nil)
         q := q↑.next;
      q↑.next := newnode
end;
```

We use *newnode* as the name of the pointer to the new node because *new* is a reserved word. This code works except in the case where the initial list pointed to by *first* is empty. Fix the procedure such that it works correctly for all cases.

We now have seen how linked lists can be used to implement not just stacks but also queues. It should be clear that if a linked list is used to represent a queue, there should be a pointer directly to the rear of that queue. Let's call that pointer *rear*. The insertion algorithm that we just coded then becomes:

```
procedure inserend(in:nametype,var rear:nodeptr);
var newnode:nodeptr;
begin new(newnode);
      newnode↑.info := in;
      newnode↑.next := nil;
      rear↑.next := newnode;
      rear := newnode
end;
```

An algorithm to reverse the elements in a linked list such that the last element becomes the new first element and the first element becomes the new last element involves stepping through the list to change all the pointers. In COBOL (again using the *SPACE-ARRAY*):

```
01  AUX-POINTERS.
    02  THISNODE        PIC 9(3).
    02  PRIORNODE       PIC 9(3).
    02  NEXTONE         PIC 9(3).
```

```
REVERSE-LIST.
    IF FIRSTNODE NOT = 0
    THEN COMPUTE THISNODE = FIRSTNODE
        COMPUTE NEXTONE = NEXTNODE (THISNODE)
        COMPUTE NEXTNODE (THISNODE) = 0
        PERFORM STEP-THRU-LIST UNTIL (NEXTONE = 0)
        COMPUTE FIRSTNODE = THISNODE.
STEP-THRU-LIST.
    COMPUTE PRIORNODE = THISNODE.
    COMPUTE THISNODE = NEXTONE.
    COMPUTE NEXTONE = NEXTNODE (THISNODE).
    COMPUTE NEXTNODE (THISNODE) = PRIORNODE.
```

Other algorithms that you may find useful to develop yourself are the following:

- Concatenate two linked lists into one linked list.
- Split a linked list into two linked lists such that the last element in the first one is the element pointed to by P (Fig. 59).

FIGURE 59

- Split a linked list into two linked lists such that the first list contains only elements where $INFO < M$ and the second list contains the elements where $INFO >= M$.

CIRCULARLY LINKED LISTS AND HEADER NODES

Now that you understand the fundamental operations on linked lists, we can investigate several enhancements that overcome various difficulties with the basic linked list.

One shortcoming that you probably have noticed already is that given a pointer P into a linked list, it is not possible to reach any of the elements that precede NODE(P). A simple change to the data structure will enable us to reach any node from any other node. Rather than storing a NULL pointer in the $NEXT$ field of the list's last element, have that last node point back to the beginning of the list (Fig. 60). This type of structure is called a *circularly linked list*.

You should investigate for yourself the changes that this

FIGURE 60

modification to the list structure implies for the algorithms that were presented in prior sections.

A famous problem that uses a circularly linked list is the Josephus problem. This problem has to do with selective deletion from a circularly linked list. There is a group of bandits in the Wild West who find themselves in a desperate predicament. The group is surrounded by the sheriff's posse and has no hope for mass escape. There is just one horse left. In order to select who shall take the horse and ride off with the booty, they (being a civilized group of bandits) do the following. Numbers are written on slips of paper and shuffled in a hat. The bandits stand in a circle. One is designated to be in the starting position (Fig. 61(a)).

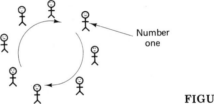

FIGURE 61(a)

A number, say n, is drawn from the hat and the count begins around the circle (clockwise); the nth person is eliminated. He steps out of the circle; the circle's boundary is tightened. The count begins again with the man to his left being number 1. Again the nth person is eliminated. The process continues until only one bandit remains. He grabs the goods, jumps on the horse, and rides off into the sunset.

Assume the initial circle of bandits is as shown in Fig. 61(b)

FIGURE 61(b)

and Jesse is selected number 1 (he's the biggest). The number 4 is drawn, and One-eye Sam is the first bandit to be eliminated. The count begins again with Slim, and Kit leaves the circle. Again the count begins with

Slim, and the number 4 falls on Slim. Jesse becomes first, and Big Mo loses as number 4. Jesse grabs the horse.

You should write a program that simulates this procedure. Inputs should be the list of names of bandits, ordered by their positions in the circle, and the drawn number n. Output the names of the bandits as they are eliminated and the name of the winner. The obvious choice of data structure for this problem is a circularly linked list.

In the future we assume that all linked lists are circular unless noted otherwise.

Now consider the problem of searching for a particular element, say the one that contains the name 'ELOISE,' in a circularly linked list. It's easy enough to get caught in an infinite loop while stepping through the list unless the programmer is very careful. Remember, the end of the list is no longer signaled by an element with NEXT(NODE) = NULL.

One commonly applied approach to this difficulty is to append a header node at the beginning or end of the list (Fig. 62).

FIGURE 62

The header node may be distinguished from the other nodes in one of two ways:

- It may have a special value in its *INFO* field which is invalid as data in the other elements (in this case we hash the *INFO* field as in the above diagram.)
- It may have a flag that marks it as a header node.

There may be meaningful data in a header. For instance, it could contain the number of nodes in the list, a user-oriented description of the list, a creation-date, or other information. /

When a circularly linked list with header is empty, it still has its header node as shown in Fig. 63.

FIGURE 63

That is, NEXT(HEAD) = HEAD.

The algorithm for insertion of a variable *NAME* at the head of this list then is:

```
NEW := GETNODE
INFO(NEW) := NAME
NEXT(NEW) := NEXT(HEAD)
NEXT(HEAD) := NEW
```

How does the existence of a header node affect the other algorithms presented in this chapter? You should note the indispensable value of drawing pictures to simulate pointer handling as you develop and analyze algorithms.

DOUBLY LINKED LISTS

You may have noted that our removal algorithms so far have all been specified such that the node *after* one pointed to is removed from the list. How can we remove the node pointed to by p? With only links to the *next* node, it is necessary that we step through the chain of nodes, comparing addresses until we are positioned on the one located at p, of course being careful not to fall off the end of a noncircular list. In Pascal, using pointer variables:

```
procedure removp(head:nodeptr,var p:nodeptr, out:nametype);
var prior, this:nodeptr;
    flag:0 .. 2;
begin
    prior := head;
    this := head↑.next;
    flag := 1; {search in progress}
    while flag = 1
        do begin
            if(this = head)
            then flag := 2; {have completed list, and not found node
                                   pointed to by p}
            if(this = p)
            then flag := 0 {have found node pointed to by p}
            else begin prior := this;
                        this := this↑.next {step to next node}
                    end;
        end;
    if(flag > 0)
    then NODE POINTED TO BY P IS NOT IN THE LIST
    else begin {removal of node pointed to by p}
                prior↑.next := p↑.next;
                out := p↑.info;
                dispose(p)
            end;
end;
```

This algorithm is considerably more complex than the removal algorithms that were presented previously. Here it is necessary not only to keep testing to see if the node pointed to by *this* is the node to be deleted, but also to keep track of what the *prior* node is so that it can be linked to the node after *this*, if *this* happens to be equal to *p* (Fig. 64).

FIGURE 64

You might find it a useful exercise to develop the above algorithm for a noncircularly linked list and/or a linked list without a header node.

When it is desirable to be able to traverse a linked list backwards or to delete particular nodes, there are advantages to using a doubly linked rather than singly linked list. In a *doubly linked list* each node has not only a pointer to the next node but also a pointer to the prior node (Fig. 65).

FIGURE 65

Variations on the above drawing are to not have a header node and/or to not be circularly linked.

We called the pointer to the next node *NEXT(NODE)*; we call the pointer to the prior node *PRIOR(NODE)*. These pointers could be named the *right* and *left* pointers, the *successor* and *predecessor* pointers, *s-link* and *p-link* pointers, and so forth.

As seen in Fig. 66, a fundamental property of doubly linked lists is that for any pointer *P* into the list,

$$NEXT(PRIOR(P)) = P$$

and
$$P = PRIOR(NEXT(P))$$ 　　　(Fig. 66)

An empty doubly linked list is as shown in Fig. 67.

That is,

PRIOR(HEAD) = HEAD

and　　NEXT(HEAD) = HEAD.

PRIOR(P)

NEXT(PRIOR(P))

PRIOR(NEXT(P))

NEXT(P)

FIGURE 66

FIGURE 67

A doubly linked list type can be declared as follows in Pascal using pointer variables:

```
type nodeptr = ↑nodetype;
     nodetype = record
                    prior:nodeptr;
                    info: nametype;
                    next:nodeptr
                end;
```

and as follows in COBOL without using pointer variables (assuming a maximum of 500 nodes):

```
01  SPACE-ARRAY.
    02  NODE OCCURS 500 TIMES.
        03  PRIOR        PICTURE 9(3).
        03  INFO         PICTURE X(10).
        03  NEXTNODE     PICTURE 9(3).
    02  HEAD             PICTURE 9(3).
    02  AVAIL            PICTURE 9(3).
```

We can now reconsider our algorithms for removal and insertion of elements in linked lists. First, for removal of the element pointed to by P from a doubly linked list, the pointers into that element need to be reset (Fig. 68(a)).

FIGURE 68(a)

In Pascal:

```
procedure removp(var p:nodeptr, out:nametype);
var pred,succ:nodeptr;
begin pred := p↑.prior;
      succ := p↑.next;
      pred↑.next := succ;
      succ↑.prior := pred;
      out := p↑.info;
      dispose(p)
end;
```

(a)

(b)

After step (a) we have the structure shown in Fig. 68(b),

FIGURE 68(b)

and after step (b) we have the structure shown in Fig. 68(c).

FIGURE 68(c)

Verify that this algorithm works even if p points to the only nonhead node in the circular doubly linked list.

In order to insert a variable *IN* into a doubly linked list such that it follows the node pointed to by P, we first establish the new node in the list, then reset the pointers appropriately. The key to this algorithm is to not destroy pointers that are needed later.

In COBOL:

```
INSERAF.
        COMPUTE NEW = AVAIL.
        COMPUTE AVAIL = NEXTNODE (AVAIL).
        MOVE IN TO INFO (NEW).
        COMPUTE NEXTNODE (NEW) = NEXTNODE (P).
```

    (a)   COMPUTE PRIOR (NEW) = P.
              COMPUTE NEXTNODE (P) = NEW.
              COMPUTE Q = NEXTNODE (NEW).
    (b)   COMPUTE PRIOR (Q) = NEW.

After step (a), we have the structure shown in Fig. 69(a).

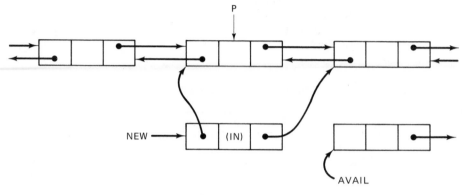

FIGURE 69(a)

After step (b), we have the structure shown in Fig. 69(b).

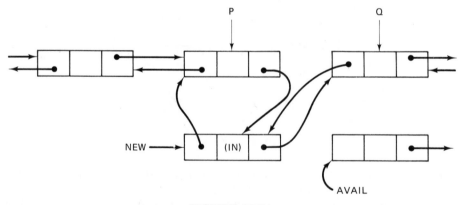

FIGURE 69(b)

Convince yourself that this algorithm works even when the list is initially empty.

    Try developing for doubly linked lists the algorithms suggested in the preceding sections. The algorithms should be as generally correct as possible. That is, it should not be necessary to have one algorithm to do something to an initially empty list and another to do the same thing to an initially populated list. The algorithm itself should handle the "extreme" cases.

The basic trade-off between use of singly linked and doubly linked lists is that of pointer storage and maintenance costs versus ease of list manipulation.

EXAMPLE APPLICATIONS OF LINKED LISTS

We now consider several applications that make good use of the linked list data structure. The first example uses linked lists to represent polynomials. The second example uses linked lists to represent alphabetically ordered string data. The third example shows how linked lists can be used to represent sparse arrays.

Polynomials

A polynomial is an algebraic expression of the form:

$$a_n x^n + a_{n-1} x^{n-1} + \ldots + a_2 x^2 + a_1 x + a_0$$

Each a_i is a coefficient of the corresponding power of the x variable. For example, in the polynomial

$$143x^4 + 201x^2 + 14x + 2$$

$a_4 = 143$, $a_3 = 0$, $a_2 = 201$, $a_1 = 14$, and $a_0 = 2$. Let's call this polynomial *POLY1*.

Polynomials are used in both scientific and business-oriented problems. General-purpose programming languages like Pascal, PL/I, COBOL, and FORTRAN do not have built-in data types or functions to manipulate polynomials directly. Rather, it is common to represent polynomials using arrays or linked lists. An appropriate node structure is (in Pascal):

```
type nodeptr = ↑nodetype;
     nodetype = record
                    exp : integer;
                    coef : integer;
                    next : nodeptr
               end;
```

where *exp* is the variable's exponent, *coef* is the corresponding coefficient, and *next* links this node to the next node in the polynomial representation. Only the terms with nonzero coefficients need to be represented.

It is convenient to link the nodes in order by decreasing *exp* values of the terms they represent (Fig. 70).

Addition (or subtraction) of two polynomials requires the addition

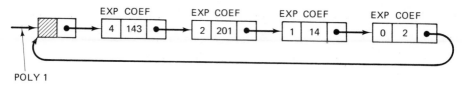

FIGURE 70

(or subtraction) of the coefficients of terms with matching exponents. For example:

$$143x^4 + \qquad\qquad 201x^2 + 14x + 2$$
$$+ \qquad\qquad 312x^3 - \quad 21x^2 \qquad\quad + 42$$
$$\overline{143x^4 + 312x^3 + 180x^2 + 14x + 44}$$

An algorithm to add polynomials POLY1 and POLY2 to form POLYSUM follows. Note that each of these polynomials is represented by its own singly linked, circular linked list with header node. The header nodes are passed to the procedure *polyadd*, which is written in Pascal. *Poly1* and *poly2* are pointers to the header nodes of polynomials POLY1 and POLY2, respectively. *Polysum* points to the header node of the polynomial POLYSUM, which is constructed by the procedure. Pointers $p1, p2$, and *psum* are the addresses of the terms presently being considered in POLY1, POLY2, and POLYSUM, respectively. The *match* indicator is used to signal the following conditions:

exp1high: There is a power of x in POLY1 that does not appear in POLY2.

expmatch: There is a power of x that appears in both POLY1 and POLY2.

exp2high: There is a power of x in POLY2 that does not appear in POLY1.

The *end1* and *end2* flags are used to signal that the last terms of POLY1 and POLY2, respectively, have been processed. If POLY1 terminates before POLY2, as in

(POLY1) $14x^4 + 3x^3$

+   (POLY2) $7x^3 + x^2 + 3$

then terms of POLYSUM from $exp = 2$ on can just be copied from POLY2, and vice versa if POLY2 terminates before POLY1.

The procedure *sumnode* is used to create the nodes of the resultant polynomial POLYSUM. The parameters passed to it indicate whether the term is being taken from POLY1 or POLY2 and enable the procedure to signal that the last term of that polynomial has been processed. *Nodeptr* is a globally known data type.

```
procedure polyadd(poly1,poly2:nodeptr;var polysum:nodeptr);
type match = (exp1high,expmatch,exp2high);
var p1,p2,psum:nodeptr;
    expflag:match;
    end1, end2: 0 .. 1;
procedure sumnode(poly:nodeptr;var p,psum:nodeptr, endflag:0 .. 1);
    {subprocedure declaration}
var pnew:nodeptr;
begin new(pnew); {add new node to sum list}
    psum↑.next := pnew;
    psum := pnew;
    psum↑.exp := p↑.exp;
    psum↑.coef := p↑.coef;
    p := p↑.next; {move p to next node on poly}
    if p=poly then endflag := 1 {check if at end of poly}
end; {sumnode}
begin end1 := 0; {main program block}
    end2 := 0;
    p1 := poly1↑.next;
    p2 := poly2↑.next;
    psum := polysum;
    if(p1=poly1)then end1 := 1; {have reached end of poly1}
    if(p2=poly2)then end2 := 1; {have reached end of poly2}
while (end1=0 and end2=0) {there are still terms to add}
do begin if(p1↑.exp>p2↑.exp) {pick term with greater exponent}
            then expflag := exp1high {as next term to add}
            else if(p1↑.exp=p2↑.exp)
                    then expflag := expmatch
                    else expflag := exp2high;
            case expflag of
            exp1high: sumnode(poly1,p1,psum,end1); {add poly1
                term}
            expmatch: begin sumnode(poly1,p1,psum,end1); {add
                poly1 term}
                            psum↑.coef := psum↑.coef+p2↑.coef;
                                {add poly2 term}
                            p2 := p2↑.next;
                            if p2=poly2 then end2 := 1 {end of
                                poly2}
                    end;
            exp2high : sumnode(poly2,p2,psum,end2) {add poly2
                term}
    end;
end;
{have reached end of at least one poly}
```

```
        while (end1=0) {have reached end of poly2}
        do sumnode(poly2,p2,psum,end2); {add rest of poly1 terms}
        while (end2=0) {have reached end of poly1}
        do sumnode(poly2,p2,psum,end2); {add rest of poly2 terms}
        psum↑.next := polysum
    end;
```

This program can be modified to handle instead the subtraction of two polynomials. A useful exercise is to write a program to add two polynomials that are represented by linked lists that are housed in arrays rather than implemented using pointer variables. How would the algorithm be different if the linked lists were not circular? If they did not have header nodes? If they were doubly linked? Why was the singly linked list chosen as the data structure here?

What are the algorithms for multiplication of polynomials? For division of polynomials?

Consider now the problem of manipulating polynomials in two variables, say in x and y. Again, a linked list is an appropriate data structure to represent this abstract data type. Each term can be represented by a node of the following type:

```
type nodeptr = ↑nodetype;
     nodetype = record
                      coef:integer;
                      xexp:integer;
                      yexp:integer;
                      next:nodeptr
                end;
```

Only the terms with nonzero coefficients need to be represented.

Algorithms to manipulate these polynomial representations can be simplified by requiring that the terms be linked in some specific order, say in sorted order by x exponent major, y exponent minor. For example:

$$14x^3 + 82x^2y - 47y^4 + 12y^2 + 6$$

would be as shown in Fig. 71.

FIGURE 71

Develop an algorithm to add two polynomials in two variables. How does it differ from the algorithm presented here to add two polynomials in one variable?

What is the appropriate node structure for terms of a polynomial in three variables? In *n* variables?

A Simple Multi-linked List

As we will discuss in more detail later, there are many cases where it is appropriate to use linked lists with more than two pointers per node. These data structures are called *multiply linked lists* or *multi-lists*.

One simple example of a data structure with three pointers per node is a doubly linked list of variable-length string data where each node contains a pointer to the actual data rather than the data value (Fig. 72).

FIGURE 72

The major benefit of using this data structure here is that the nodes of the primary doubly linked list can be fixed in length. Each contains three pointer values and one integer. Management of fixed-length chunks of memory is significantly less complex than is management of variable-length chunks of memory. Of course, here we still have to contend with the actual names of animals, which are variable length.

The real purpose of this example is to introduce multi-list structures. Each *NAME–PTR* field points to a singly linked, noncircular list that intersects with the primary doubly linked list. Our next application of linked lists uses a more fully developed multi-list structure.

Sparse Arrays

A common application of linked lists is to represent sparse arrays. Earlier we discussed sequential representations of sparse arrays. Linked representations of sparse arrays have the potential to significantly reduce storage requirements and to reduce the number of calculations performed in some array operations. Only the nonzero entries in an array will be represented.* The overhead introduced by the linked representation may outweigh the benefits if the array is not sparse enough.

One possible linked representation of a two-dimensional sparse array is the following. There is one linked list for each row and for each column of the array. Each of these linked lists has a header node and is circular, but is only singly linked. Each nonzero entry in the array is represented by an occurrence of a node of the form (in Pascal):

```
type nodeptr : ↑nodetype;
     nodeptr = record
                    row:integer;
                    column:integer;
                    value:integer;
                    nextincol:nodeptr;
                    nextinrow:nodeptr
               end;
```

Each node contains an indication of the row and column in which the nonzero entry appears, the value of the entry, and two pointers. One pointer is to the next node in the same row; one pointer is to the next node in the same column.

For example, the following 5-by-4 array:

```
1    0    0    0
0   -3    0    0
2    0    1    0
0    0   14    0
0    0    0    0
```

would have the representation shown in Fig. 73. Each nonheader node participates in two linked lists: one for its row and one for its column. In this example there are four nonzero rows and three nonzero columns; there are seven non-null lists. Here there are five nonzero entries in the array and nine header nodes. The fifteen zero entries have not taken up storage space.

This particular technique for representing a sparse array is quite satisfactory when there are frequent updates to the array. The linked structure makes it fairly easy to make changes in what is and is not a nonzero entry. For other approaches to representing sparse arrays, the interested reader should consult U. W. Pooch and A. Nieder, "A survey

---

*These "sparse" techniques can also be applied when most of the elements of the array take on a particular nonzero value, say 1.

FIGURE 73

of indexing techniques for sparse matrices," *ACM Computing Surveys*, 5(2):109–133, June 1973.

You might develop algorithms to add two sparse arrays (i.e., matrices) and to perform matrix multiplication on two sparse matrices.

What would be an appropriate structure to represent a sparse three-dimensional array? A sparse *n*-dimensional array?

SUMMARY

A linked list is a nonsequential way to represent a linear data type. Each node of a linked list contains at least one pointer, which links that node to the next node on the list. A linked list may be circular, in which case the last node points to the first node. Linked lists commonly are implemented with header nodes. In order to simplify algorithms to perform some insertions and removals from linked lists, pointers to prior as well as next nodes are often used. The resultant lists are called doubly linked lists.

When a given node can participate simultaneously in more than one linked list, the structure is said to be a multi-linked list. We will study these structures in more detail later.

We have seen how to use linked lists to represent not just general linear lists, but also special types of linear lists, notably stacks and queues. We have considered several representative applications that use linked lists. Singly linked lists are appropriate for representation of polynomials; a simple multi-list structure containing a doubly linked list can be used to represent sorted variable-length strings; a two-dimensional multi-list structure can be used to represent a sparse array.

The basic benefit of using a linked list is that it does not require sequential storage. Thus it can be quite advantageous to use linked lists when there is significant insertion and deletion activity in a logically ordered data structure. It is also appropriate to use a linked list when it is necessary to logically order elements that are not physically sequential, e.g., to implement a stack of available chunks of space. The basic costs of using a linked list are the space requirements for pointers and the overhead of manipulating and managing pointers.

We use linked lists extensively in the rest of this book. They are fundamental to data management techniques.

Terms

circularly linked list	null
doubly linked list	pointer variable
linked list	

Review Exercises

1. Fill in the NEXT pointers so that the following array representation of a linked list is in alphabetical order by INFO field contents. What does the AVAIL stack look like?

	INFO	NEXT
1	PEACH	
2	APPLE	
3		
4	CHERRY	
5	GRAPE	

2. A list of items appears in an array as follows:

	DATA	NEXT
1	ITEM G	
2	ITEM D	
3	ITEM J	
4	ITEM B	
5	ITEM E	
6	ITEM F	
7		
8		
9		

Show the contents of the NEXT fields to link the items alphabetically.

3. Insert items C, A, and Z to the above array such that the resultant linked list is still in alphabetic order.

4. Write an algorithm to find the jth element in a singly linked list.

5. Write an algorithm to return a circular linked list T to the pool of available nodes.

6. What is the result of NEXT(PRIOR(P)) in a doubly linked list?

7. Let X be a pointer to some arbitrary node in a singly linked list. Write an algorithm that will place '1234' in the *INFO* field of an additional node and insert this additional node after the node pointed to by X.

8. Write an algorithm that will insert a node S into a doubly linked list immediately before node X.

9. Write an algorithm that will invert a singly linked list. A doubly linked list.

10. Write the GETNODE and FREENODE algorithms for a storage pool that is structured as a queue.

11. How many links must be changed to delete an item from a doubly linked list?

12. Write the algorithms to add to and delete from a stack represented using a singly linked list.

13. Write the algorithms to add to and delete from a queue represented using a singly linked list.

14. Write a routine to concatenate two singly linked lists A and B.

15. How can the following sparse matrix be represented by linked lists?

$$\begin{matrix} 0 & 0 & 5 & 2 \\ 0 & 10 & 4 & 0 \\ 0 & 0 & 0 & 2 \\ 0 & 0 & 0 & 0 \end{matrix}$$

16. Write an algorithm to insert a value into a sparse matrix stored in circularly linked lists.

17. Write an algorithm to delete the element containing 'CAT' from the linked list below.

18. Write an algorithm to split the above linked list between 'BAT' and 'CAT' and attach header nodes from the list *AVAIL* to the new start of each list.

19. Why is a circular linked list appropriate for the Josephus problem? Write the algorithm to solve the Josephus problem.

20. Illustrate the use of linked lists to represent the polynomials $5x^3 + 7x^2 + 9$ and $3x^2 + 4x + 7$.

21. Show how linked lists can be used to represent and add the following polynomials.

$$7x^4 y - 3x^2 y^2 + 5y + 12y^2 - 2$$
$$9x^3 y^2 + 2x^2 y^2 - 11xy + 3y^3 + 15$$

22. Write an algorithm to count the number of nodes in a linked list.

23. Write an algorithm to count the number of nonzero elements in a polynomial represented using linked lists.

24. Consider the use of an array to store a linked list of book inventory information. The array is defined as follows in COBOL:

```
01  BOOK-ARRAY.
    02  BOOK-NODE OCCURS 15 TIMES.
        03  AUTHOR              PIC X.
        03  NEXT-AUTHOR         PIC 99.
        03  TITLE               PIC X.
        03  NEXT-TITLE          PIC 99.
        03  STOCK-NO            PIC 9(5).
        03  NEXT-STOCK-NO       PIC 99.
        03  PRIOR-STOCK-NO      PIC 99.
    02  HEADERS.
        03  FIRST-AUTHOR        PIC 99.
        03  FIRST-TITLE         PIC 99.
        03  FIRST-STOCK-NO      PIC 99.
        03  LAST-STOCK-NO       PIC 99.
        03  AVAIL               PIC 99.
```

Entries are linked alphabetically by author's last name, alphabetically by first word of title, and in ascending order by *STOCK-NO*. Show the contents of the *BOOK-ARRAY* after completion of each of the following transactions.

OPERATION	STOCK-NO	TITLE	AUTHOR
INSERT	53526	CREATIVE PHOTOGRAPHY	F. STOP FITZ-GERALD
INSERT	98374	NEWSPAPER ORIGAMI	LINUS TYPE
INSERT	14683	COOL HAND LUKE	HADDA DUWITT
INSERT	23764	THE LONGEST YARD	LOWEN MAUER
INSERT	49261	LA MARKE DE LA FRANCAISE	ASCENT AGU
INSERT	19822	BEER BASTED HOT DOGS	DR. FRANK ANN STEIN
INSERT	76482	FOUR-WAY ROMANCE	QUAD LAMOORE
INSERT	17760	COMPUTER SIMULATION	ARTIE ABACUS
INSERT	38641	BETSY WORE BLUE JEANS	DENN M. STRETCHER
INSERT	73920	FINGER LICKIN' GOOD	C. SANDERS
DELETE	14683		
DELETE	76482		

25. The GETNODE and FREENODE algorithms in the text assumed that all nodes were the same size. Write the GETNODE and FREENODE algorithms for management of a linked list when nodes are of various sizes.

CHAPTER 7

Sequential Searching and $\mathcal{O}(N^2)$ Sorting Techniques

In this chapter we take a breather from the process of learning about new data structures and instead devote our energies to studying further aspects of the linear data structures with which we are already familiar. We are going to consider several techniques for finding particular data values in linear structures and for sorting data values. Searching and sorting are quite closely related processes, as we shall see.

Consider a collection of records, each of which has a *key* that can be used to identify it. A key is composed of one or more fields of a record. Key values may be unique identifiers of records, or there may be duplicate values allowed. If duplicate key values are allowed, it may be desirable to differentiate between record occurrences with the same key value by their order of appearance in the collection. The concept of keys will extend throughout much of the rest of this book. *Searching* is the process of locating a record with a particular key value. *Sorting* is the process of arranging records so that they are in order by key value.

SEQUENTIAL SEARCHES

A search algorithm is a technique for finding a record (in some collection of records) that has some key value. We will call the key value, say k, the *argument* of the search. A search terminates either successfully when a record containing k is found or unsuccessfully when it is determined that there is no record containing k.

There are many search algorithms. In this section we cover the subset known as *sequential searches*, also known as *linear searches*. Later in the book we will consider nonlinear searches, which tend to perform considerably better than the techniques introduced here. However, sequential searches are quite simple and study of them is a good place to start our investigation of searching and sorting.

We assume that the collection of records that we are searching through has been organized as a linear list. We have seen that a linear list may be represented by an array or by a linked list. We will use the array representation here; you should determine how the use of linked representation would alter the algorithms.

Let $key(i)$ be the key value in the ith record of the list. The basic sequential search algorithm is to start at the beginning of the list and go through each record until the one with the desired key value (k) is found or the end of the list is reached. Assume there are n records in the list and that key, k, and n are global variables. In Pascal:

```
procedure findk;
var foundit: boolean; i:1 .. n;
begin
    foundit := false;
    i := 1;
    while(not foundit) and i ≤ n
    do if k = key[i]
        then foundit := true
        else i := i + 1;
    if(foundit)
    then writeln('Eureka!')
    else writeln('Rats')
end;
```

If the algorithm terminates with *foundit* = *true*, then the record with key value k is the ith one in the list. If the algorithm terminates with *foundit* = *false*, then the key value k does not appear in the list.

How efficient is this procedure? Let PROB(i) be the probability that the ith record is the one being sought. Then

$$\sum_{i=1}^{n} PROB(i) + Q = 1, \quad \text{where } Q = \text{probability that the key is not present.}$$

The optimal situation is for the record sought to be the first one looked at. The worst case is when keys of all n records are compared with k and either $key[n]$ = k or the sought record is not in the list.

The average, or expected, number of comparisons is:

$$\sum_{i=1}^{n} i*PROB(i) + Q*n$$

With probability PROB(1), 1 comparison is required; with probability PROB(2), 2 comparisons are required; . . .; with probability PROB(n) + Q, n comparisons are required. If all records are equally likely to be retrieved and every key sought is in the list, then

$$PROB(i) = \frac{1}{n} \text{ for all } i$$

and $$\sum_{i=1}^{n} i*PROB(i) \text{ is } \frac{n+1}{2.}$$

That is, on the average, about half of the keys will be compared with the argument k.

A sequential search algorithm is said to require "on the order of N" comparisons. That is, the expected number of comparisons is a linear function of the number of records in the collection. "On the order of N" is commonly denoted $o(N)$. Doubling the number of keys means that the process will take twice as long.

This is not a particularly good method of searching! For example, you probably have never used this technique to look up a name in the telephone directory, which is really just a linear list. How might we improve the situation?

Consider again the expression for the expected number of comparisons with a sequential search:

$$\sum_{i=1}^{n} i*PROB(i) + Q*n$$

If we have the freedom to arrange the records in the linear list in any order we choose, then the above expression is minimized when

$$PROB(1) \geqslant PROB(2) \geqslant \ldots \geqslant PROB(n)$$

That is:
$$PROB(I) \geqslant PROB(J)$$
$$\text{for } I < J.$$

By arranging the records by descending frequency of access, we improve the probability that fewer comparisons will be made. It may still be the case that n comparisons are needed (say we are looking for a key that is not in the list), but the *expected* number of comparisons will be minimized.

Consider now the more typical situation in which the relative frequency of access to the records is not known. There are several schemes to handle this problem. One is to observe requests to the list over a period of time, keeping count of the number of accesses to each record. When a representative sample of activity has been gathered, the records can be reordered according to the detected probabilities of access.

A second scheme is to let the list of records dynamically reorganize itself. With the "move-to-the-front" method, whenever there is a successful search for a key value, the corresponding record is moved to first position in the list. The record that was number one becomes number two, and so forth. In Pascal, assuming that there are n records in the list and that *rec* (which contains *key*), k, and n are globally known:

```
procedure movetofront;
var foundit:boolean;
     i:1 .. n;
     j:0 .. n;
     temprec:rectype;
begin
     foundit := false;
     i := 1;
     while (not foundit) and i ⩽ n
     do if k = key[i]
        then foundit := true
        else i := i + 1;
     if(foundit)
     then begin temprec := rec[i];
                j := i-1;
                while j > 0
                do begin rec[j+1] := rec[j];
                         j := j-1
                   end;
                rec[1] := temprec
          end;
end;
```

This method would perform better on a linear list represented by a linked list than by an array. Why?

Another dynamic reorganization scheme is the "transposition" method. Whenever there is a successful search for a key value, the corresponding record is interchanged with the immediately preceding record. In Pascal, making the same assumptions about variable declarations as in the *movetofront* procedure:

```
procedure transpose;
var foundit:boolean;
     i:1 .. n;
     temprec:rectype;
begin
     foundit := false;
     i := 1;
     while (not foundit) and i ⩽ n
     do if(k = key[i])
        then foundit = true
        else i := i + 1;
```

```
        if (foundit and i > 1)
        then begin temprec := rec[i];{transpose adjacent records}
                   rec[i] := rec[i-1];
                   rec[i-1] := temprec
              end;
    end;
```

The more frequently a record is retrieved, the more quickly it percolates to the number one position. Compared with the "move-to-the-front" method, the "transposition" method requires a longer period of activity to reorganize the collection of records. An advantage of the "transposition" method is that it does not allow an isolated request for a record to shift the entire collection of records. In effect, a record must earn its right to the top through a history of demand.

One way to reduce the expected number of comparisons when there is a significant frequency of unsuccessful searches is to order the records by key value. That is:

$$KEY(I) \leqslant KEY(J)$$
$$\text{for} \quad I < J$$

(or $KEY(I) \geqslant KEY(J)$ for $I < J$ in descending order.) This technique is useful when the list is a list of exceptions, such as bad credit card numbers, to be compared against. Most of the lookups are unsuccessful. Now an unsuccessful search terminates when the first key value greater than the argument is found, rather than at the end of the list:

```
        foundit := false;
        i := 1;
        while (not foundit) and key [i] ⩽ k
        do if(k = key[i])
              then foundit := true
              else i := i + 1;
```

We will consider other searching methods that take advantage of an ordered list in a later chapter.

INTRODUCTION TO INTERNAL SORTING METHODS

Sorting is the process of ordering a collection of records such that

$$KEY(I) \leqslant KEY(J)$$
$$\text{for} \quad I < J$$

(or $KEY(I) \geqslant KEY(J)$ for $I < J$ in descending order), where $KEY(I)$ is the key value of the Ith record.

There are two basic categories of sorting techniques: internal sorts and external sorts. *Internal sorting* methods are applied when the entire collection of data to be sorted is small enough that the sorting can take place within main memory. Several internal sorting methods are introduced in this chapter. *External sorting* methods are applied to larger collections of data where some (frequently most) of the collection resides on an auxiliary memory device such as a magnetic tape or disk. We will study external sorting methods in conjunction with the file processing part of this book.

Even though we are interested in obtaining sorted lists of records, we will routinely ignore the records and appear to be interested only in obtaining sorted lists of keys. Do not be confused by this sloppiness. If you prefer, when we indicate that "a key" should be inserted in a list or that "a key" should be selected from a list or that "two keys" in a list should exchange positions, interpret "a key" to mean "a key and its accompanying record" or "a key and the pointer to its corresponding record."

Throughout, we assume that the result of sorting is to be the keys in ascending order. You should be able to make whatever changes to the algorithms are necessary to result in a descending ordering of keys.

We will not require that key values be unique identifiers of records. A sorting algorithm is said to be *stable* if the original ordering of records with equal keys is preserved in the sorted ordering of those records. It is important to use a stable sort method if that original record ordering is meaningful. For example, that ordering may have been established by time of entry of the records in the original list. Not all sort methods are stable. As in our discussion of linear search techniques, we assume here that the linear list to be sorted is represented by an array. You should determine how the use of linked list representation would alter the algorithms.

A SELECTION SORT

One family of internal sorting algorithms is the group of *selection sorts*. The basic idea of a selection sort is to repeatedly select the smallest key remaining in the unsorted list of data as the next key in a growing sorted list of data (Fig. 74).

Remaining unsorted keys　　　　　　　　　Sorted keys

FIGURE 74

The entire list of unsorted keys must be available for us to be able to select the minimum key value in that list. The sorted list, however, can be output as we go along.

For example, consider the following unsorted list of keys:

14   3   22   9   10   14   2   7   25   6

The first selection pass identifies 2 as the minimum element and removes it from the unsorted list:

14   3   22   9   10   14   7   25   6   2

remaining unsorted keys   sorted list

The second selection pass identifies 3 as the minimum element and removes it from the unsorted list:

14   22   9   10   14   7   25   6   2   3

remaining unsorted keys   sorted list

After the sixth pass:

14   22   14   25   2   3   6   7   9   10

remaining unsorted keys   sorted list

In COBOL, the *straight selection sort* is:

```
01  UNSORTED-TABLE.
    02  UNSORTED-ENTRY    OCCURS N TIMES    PIC S99.

01  SORTED-TABLE.
    02  SORTED-ENTRY      OCCURS N TIMES    PIC S99.

02  AUX-ITEMS.
    02  CURR-MIN-KEY      PIC S99   VALUE HIGH-VALUES.
    02  NEXT-IN-SORT      PIC 9(3)  VALUE 1.
    02  I                 PIC 9(3).
    02  MIN-POS           PIC 9(3).
```

PERFORM SELECT-NEXT N TIMES.

where

```
SELECT-NEXT.
    PERFORM PICK-MIN VARYING I FROM 1 BY 1
            UNTIL I > N.
    MOVE UNSORTED-ENTRY (MIN-POS) TO
            SORTED-ENTRY (NEXT-IN-SORT).
    MOVE HIGH-VALUES TO UNSORTED-ENTRY (MIN-POS).
    MOVE HIGH-VALUES TO CURR-MIN-KEY.
```

and

> PICK-MIN.
>   IF UNSORTED-ENTRY (I) < CURR-MIN-KEY
>   MOVE I TO MIN-POS
>   MOVE UNSORTED-ENTRY (I) TO CURR-MIN-KEY.

This algorithm requires N passes over the unsorted list. In the Ith pass, $N{-}I$ comparisons of key values are made. The total number of comparisons then is:

$$\sum_{I=1}^{N} (N{-}I)$$

which is $N(N{-}1)/2$. This sort is said to require $\sigma(N^2)$ comparisons, because the N^2 term dominates the expression. The number of comparisons is proportional to the square of the number of keys in the collection. Doubling the number of keys means that the process will take four times as long.

The above program uses considerably more space than necessary. A modification of the straight selection sort is the *exchange selection sort*, in which the selected key value is moved into its final position by being exchanged with the key initially occupying that position. Consider again the unsorted list:

14	3	22	9	10	14	2	7	25	6

After the first pass, 2 is selected:

2		3	22	9	10	14	14	7	25	6
sorted		unsorted								

After the second pass,

2	3		22	9	10	14	14	7	25	6
sorted			unsorted							

After the sixth pass,

2	3	6	7	9	10		14	14	25	22
sorted							unsorted			

Note that this is not a stable sort. For example, here the first pass placed the first 14 after the second 14; in the seventh and eighth passes, the 14's will be appended to the sorted list in that reversed order.

In COBOL, the exchange selection sort is:

```
01  KEY-TABLE.
    02  KEY-ENTRY      OCCURS N TIMES      PIC S99.
```

```
01  AUX-ITEMS.
    02  CURR-MIN-KEY    PIC S99     VALUE HIGH-VALUES.
    02  NEXT-IN-SORT    PIC 9(3)    VALUE 1.
    02  I               PIC 9(3).
    02  MIN-POS         PIC 9(3).
    02  TEMP-KEY        PIC S99.

EXCHANGE-DRIVER.
    PERFORM SELECT-NEXT VARYING NEXT-IN-SORT FROM
                        1 BY 1 UNTIL NEXT-IN-SORT = N.
```

where

```
SELECT-NEXT.
    PERFORM PICK-MIN VARYING I FROM
                        NEXT-IN-SORT BY 1 UNTIL
                        I > N.
    MOVE KEY-ENTRY (NEXT-IN-SORT)
        TO TEMP-KEY.
    MOVE KEY-ENTRY (MIN-POS)
        TO KEY-ENTRY (NEXT-IN-SORT).
    MOVE TEMP-KEY
        TO KEY-ENTRY (MIN-POS).
    MOVE HIGH-VALUES
        TO CURR-MIN-KEY.
```

and

```
PICK-MIN.
    IF KEY-ENTRY (I) < CURR-MIN-KEY
        MOVE I TO MIN-POS
        MOVE KEY-ENTRY (I) TO CURR-MIN-KEY.
```

The exchange selection sort has essentially the same comparison requirements as does the straight selection sort; it is $o(N^2)$. In a later chapter we will consider other members of the family of selection sorts that perform better than this.

AN INSERTION SORT

Another family of internal sorting algorithms is the group of *insertion sorts*. The basic idea of an insertion sort is to take the next key of the unsorted list and insert it in its proper relative position in a growing sorted list of data (Fig. 75).

The entire list of sorted keys must be available throughout the process in order to be able to insert a key in its proper relative position.

Unsorted keys   Sorted keys

FIGURE 75

The unsorted list, however, can be input as we go along.

Compare this sorting technique with the selection sort method of the preceding section. When you sort a hand of playing cards, if you pick each card up as it is dealt to you and place it in its appropriate "slot" relative to the cards you already have, then you are using an insertion sort. On the other hand, if you wait until the entire hand is dealt, then pick out the card that should be leftmost and put it there, then pick out the card that should be second and put it there, and so forth, then you are using a selection sort.

Both are relatively poor techniques, as each is $\sigma(N^2)$, but each is relatively easy to understand and to program. Both are widely used.

Consider again our example unsorted list of keys:

| 14 | 3 | 22 | 9 | 10 | 14 | 2 | 7 | 25 | 6 |

The first pass considers the first key, which is 14, and results in:

3	22	9	10	14	2	7	25	6		14
unsorted list										sorted list

After the second pass:

22	9	10	14	2	7	25	9		3	14
unsorted list									sorted list	

After the sixth pass:

2	7	25	6		3	9	10	14	14	22
unsorted list					sorted list					

Like the exchange selection sort, the insertion sort can be programmed to sort in place.

In Pascal:

```pascal
procedure insertsort;
var key : array [1 .. n] of integer;
    tempkey : integer;
    i, j, jj : 1 .. n;
    foundpos : boolean;
begin
    for i := 2 to n
```

```
do begin j := 1;
        foundpos := false;
        while (not foundpos) and j < i
        do if(key [i] < key [j])
           then foundpos := true
           else j := j + 1;
        if (foundpos)
        then begin tempkey := key [i];
                   jj := i - 1;
                   while(jj > j - 1)
                   do begin key [jj+1] := key [jj];
                                           jj := jj - 1
                      end;
                   key[j] := tempkey;
             end;
     end;
end.
```

This sort as programmed here is stable. Why? What change to the code would make it an unstable sort?

A variation on the straight insertion sort is based on some prior knowledge of the distribution of key values represented in the list. In an attempt to reduce the extent of data movement, keys are inserted in their relative sorted positions leaving some empty slots between keys to accommodate keys to be inserted in following passes.

Later we will consider other members of the family of insertion sorts that exhibit better than $\sigma(N^2)$ behavior.

AN EXCHANGE SORT: THE BUBBLE SORT

A third family of internal sorting algorithms is the group of *exchange sorts*. The basic idea of an exchange sort is to compare pairs of key values and exchange them if they are not in the proper relative positions (Fig. 76).

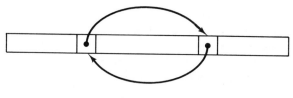

FIGURE 76

Very good sorting behavior can result from clever identification of the pairs to be compared. In this section, however, we consider a not-so-clever exchange sort: the *bubble sort*. Like the selection and insertion sorts presented in this chapter, the bubble sort requires $\sigma(N^2)$ comparisons. Nevertheless, the bubble sort is quite commonly used. We will investigate the better exchange sorts in later chapters.

The basic idea of the bubble sort is to allow each key to float to its proper position through a series of pairwise comparisons and exchanges with adjacent key values. Each pass results in bubbling one key to its final position in the sorted list.

Consider again our example unsorted list of keys:

```
 6
25
 7
 2
14
10
 9
22
 3
14
```

Because bubbles rise, we arrange the list vertically with the first key at the bottom. Each key is compared with the key above it and exchanged if the above key is smaller. When a key larger than the subject key is found, the subject key becomes the top one of the pair, and the process continues. After the pass, all keys above the last one to be exchanged must be in their final positions. They need not be examined in later passes.

The activity of the first pass bubbles up 14, 22, and 25:

		resulting in
25		25
6		6
22		22
7		7
2		2
14		14
10		10
9		9
14		14
3		3

We know 25 is in its final position.

The activity of the second pass bubbles up 14, 14, and 22:

		25

```
 6̸     22                            22
22 °°° 6                              6
 7̸       14                          14
 2̸   14 °°° 7      resulting in        7
14 °°° 2                              2
1̸0     14                           14
 9̸   14 °°° 10                       10
14 °°° 9                              9
 3                                   3
```

We know 22 is in its final position.

The activity of the third pass bubbles up 14 and 14:

25
22

```
 6̸     14                           14
14 °°° 6                              6
 7̸       14                          14
 2̸   14 °°° 7      resulting in        7
14 °°° 2                              2
10                                  10
 9                                   9
 3                                   3
```

We know that 14 is in its final position.

The activity of the fourth pass bubbles up 10 and 14:

25
22
14

```
 6̸     14                           14
14 °°° 6                              6
 7̸       10                          10
 2̸   10 °°° 7      resulting in        7
10 °°° 2                              2
 9                                   9
 3                                   3
```

and so forth.

The bubble sort really has very little to recommend it except that it is well known (probably because of its name) and unfortunately often used (probably because it is relatively easy to implement). It behaves a bit like the exchange selection sort, in which the small keys sink to the bottom of the list.

SUMMARY

This chapter has introduced our study of searching and sorting techniques. The methods presented here have all dealt with linear lists of data. All have had little to recommend them performance-wise; we will become acquainted with much better searching and sorting methods later when we consider techniques that structure data nonlinearly.

It was shown that a basic sequential search can be improved upon by ordering the keys in the list by decreasing frequency of access. A linear list may reorganize itself dynamically by (1) moving a key to the front of the list when it is requested, or by (2) exchanging a key with its front neighbor when it is requested, thus gradually moving it toward the front. The number of comparisons required for unsuccessful searches can be reduced by having the list sorted by key value.

Several basic internal sort methods were introduced. All required a number of comparisons approximately proportional to the square of the number of keys in the list; that is, all required $\sigma(N^2)$ comparisons. The straight selection sort repeatedly selected the smallest key remaining in the unsorted list as the next key in the sorted list. The exchange selection sort sorted the list in place. The straight insertion sort took the next key of the unsorted list and inserted it in its proper relative position in a growing sorted list. The bubble sort (an exchange sort) repeatedly compared neighboring pairs of key values and exchanged them if they were not in proper relative order.

Searching and sorting are exceedingly important activities in data processing. Understanding of the basic techniques presented here lays the foundation for understanding of the more complex and elegant searching and sorting techniques that support our file processing and data management needs. The outstanding attribute of the searching and sorting methods of this chapter is their simplicity.

Perhaps the best-known references for searching and sorting techniques are the excellent D. E. Knuth's *Vol. 3 Sorting and Searching: The Art of Computer Programming* (Reading, Mass.: Addison–Wesley Publishing Co., 1973), and H. Lorin's *Sorting and Sort Systems* (Reading, Mass.: Addison-Wesley Publishing Co., 1975).

Terms

bubble sort	$\sigma(n)$
exchange selection sort	$\sigma(n^2)$
exchange sort	search argument
external sort	searching
insertion sort	selection sort
internal sort	sequential search
key	sorting
linear search	stable sort

Review Exercises

1. Show by example the distinction between a stable sort and an unstable sort.
2. Consider the following probabilities of being search arguments:

key(i)	prob(i)
8	.05
2	.26
10	.21
4	.15
12	.32

   (a) What is the probability of an unsuccessful search?
   (b) If the keys are ordered as shown above, what is the expected number of comparisons for a sequential search?
   (c) Rearrange the keys to minimize the expected number of comparisons for a sequential search.
   (d) What is the expected number of comparisons for a sequential search for your answer to (c)?
3. Describe two techniques for dynamically rearranging a linear list to improve expected search times.
4. Compare use of the "move-to-the-front" method on a linear list housed in an array and housed in a linked list.
5. Compare use of the "transposition" method on a linear list housed in an array and housed in a linked list.
6. Why is it desirable to have a sort perform "in place"?
7. Using playing cards or other cards bearing key values, demonstrate the difference between an insertion sort, a selection sort, and an exchange sort.
8. Write a program to implement the bubble sort.

CHAPTER 8

General and Binary Trees

The data structures that have been discussed so far in this book have been linear structures. For each element, there has been a *next* element. This linearity is typical of strings, of elements along a single dimension of an array, of fields in a record, of entries in a stack, of entries in a queue, and of nodes in a simple linked list. In this chapter we begin our study of *nonlinear* data structures. In these structures each element may have several "next" elements, which introduces the concept of branching structures. These branching data types quite appropriately are called *trees*.

We discuss general and binary trees in this chapter, then examine special cases of these general data types in Chapters 9, 11, and 12. Chapter 10 discusses non-linear sorting techniques. Chapter 13 closes the section by considering a generalization of the tree structure.

DEFINITIONS: GRAPHS

One convenient way to discuss trees is first to introduce the more general data structure *graph* and then to constrain that data type to conform to the definition of a tree.

Intuitively, a graph is a set of points and a set of lines, with each line joining one point to another. The points are called the *nodes* of the graph, and the lines are called the *edges*. We denote the set of nodes of a given graph G by V_G and the set of edges by E_G. For example, in the graph G of Fig. 77,

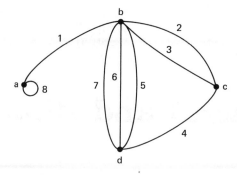

FIGURE 77

$V_G = \{a,b,c,d\}$ and $E_G = \{1,2,3,4,5,6,7,8\}$. The number of elements in V_G is called the *order* of graph G. A *null graph* is a graph with order zero.

An edge is determined by the nodes it connects. Edge 4, for example, connects nodes c and d and is said to be of *form (c,d)*. A graph is completely determined by its set of nodes and set of edges. The actual positioning of these elements on the page is unimportant. The graph of Fig. 77 is equivalent to the graph of Fig. 78.

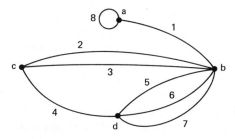

FIGURE 78

Note that there may be multiple edges connecting two nodes, e.g., edges 5, 6, and 7 are all of form (b,d). Some pairs of nodes may not be connected; for example, there is no edge here of form (a,c) or (a,d). Some edges may connect one node with itself; e.g., edge 8 is of form (a,a). These edges are called *loops*.

A graph G is called a *simple graph* if both of the following conditions are true:

1. It has no loops, that is, there does not exist an edge in E_G of form (v,v) where v is in V_G.
2. No more than one edge joins any pair of nodes, that is, there does not exist more than one edge in E_G of form (v_1, v_2) for any pair of elements v_1 and v_2 in V_G.

Fig. 79 depicts a simple graph derived from the example graph of Fig. 77.

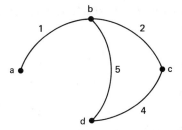

FIGURE 79

A graph that is not a simple graph is sometimes called a *multigraph*. You will find that edges are sometimes referred to as *arcs* and nodes are sometimes termed *vertices*.

A *connected graph* is a graph that cannot be partitioned into two graphs without removing at least one edge. The graph of Fig. 80 is *not* a connected graph.

FIGURE 80

A *path* in a graph is a sequence of one or more edges that connects two nodes. We denote by $P(v_i, v_j)$ a path connecting nodes v_i and v_j. For $P(v_i, v_j)$ to exist, there must be in E_G a sequence of edges of the following form:

$$P(v_i, v_j) = (v_i, x_1) (x_1, x_2) \ldots (x_{n-1}, x_n) (x_n, v_j)$$

The *length* of a path is the number of edges that it comprises. In the simple graph of Fig. 79, the following are paths between nodes b and d:

$p(b,d) = (b,c) (c,d)$	length = 2
$p(b,d) = (b,c) (c,b) (b,c) (c,d)$	length = 4
$p(b,d) = (b,d)$	length = 1
$p(b,d) = (b,c) (c,b) (b,d)$	length = 3

In general, we are interested only in paths in which a given node is "visited" no more than once. This restricts our interest to only the first and third paths above. The second path visits both nodes b and c twice; the fourth path visits node b twice. We will always be interested in *not* traversing the same edge more than once in a path.

A *cycle* is a path in which both of the following conditions are true:

1. No edge appears more than once in the sequence of edges.
2. The initial node of the path is the same as the terminal node of the path; i.e., $P(v, v)$.

In other words, a cycle returns to where it started. The graph of Fig. 78 has several cycles, for example:

$P(a,a) = (a,a)$
$P(b,b) = (b,c) (c,b)$
$P(b,b) = (b,c) (c,d) (d,b)$
$P(d,d) = (d,b) (b,c) (c,d)$
$P(d,d) = (d,b) (b,d)$

A graph with no cycles is said to be *acyclic*. Figs. 81(a) and (b) both represent acyclic graphs.

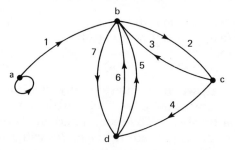

(a)

(b)   **FIGURE 81**

Another special case of the general graph data structure is a *directed graph*, in which directionality is assigned to the graph's edges. An example is shown in Fig. 82.

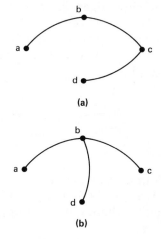

FIGURE 82

Each edge of a directed graph is represented by an arrow.

The *in-degree* of a node in a directed graph is the number of edges that terminate at that node; the *out-degree* of a node is the number of edges that emanate from that node. We denote by INDEG(v) and OUT-

DEG(v) the in- and out-degree, respectively, of node v. The *degree* of a node is the sum of its in- and out-degrees. For the example of Fig. 82:

INDEG(a) = 1	OUTDEG(a) = 2	DEG(a) = 3
INDEG(b) = 4	OUTDEG(b) = 2	DEG(b) = 6
INDEG(c) = 1	OUTDEG(c) = 2	DEG(c) = 3
INDEG(d) = 2	OUTDEG(d) = 2	DEG(d) = 4

Throughout this chapter we refer to the nodes of graphs by their labels. In reality, a node may contain any type of information. We will tend to ignore these node contents; you should not forget, however, that the ultimate purpose of graphs and trees is to impose a logical structure upon this information.

DEFINITIONS: GENERAL TREES

A very important class of graphs is those of data type *tree*. Intuitively, a tree is an acyclic simple, connected graph. A tree contains no loops and no cycles; there is no more than one edge between any pair of nodes. The graphs of Fig. 81 are trees; the graphs of the other figures in the preceding section are not trees.

Our attention will be restricted to the group of trees known as *rooted trees*. A tree is said to be rooted if it has one node (called the *root*) that is distinguished from the other nodes. The root of tree T is denoted ROOT(T).

More formally, a tree T is a finite set of zero or more nodes (v_1, v_2, ..., v_n) such that:

1. There is one specially designated node (say v_1) called ROOT(T).
2. The remaining nodes (v_2, ..., v_n) are partitioned into $m \geqslant 0$ *disjoint* sets named $T_1, T_2, ..., T_m$ such that each T_i is itself a tree.

The sets $T_1, ..., T_m$ are called the *subtrees* of ROOT(T). Note the recursive nature of this definition; we have defined trees in terms of trees. A tree with no nodes is a null tree; a null tree has no root.

Fig. 83 shows a tree in which we have labeled each node by a letter within a circle. This is the notation we will usually use in drawing trees. Here ROOT(T) = A. The three subtrees of root A are rooted at B, C, and D respectively. B is the root of a tree with one subtree, rooted at E. That subtree has no subtrees. The tree rooted at C has two subtrees, rooted at F and G respectively.

We sometimes apply directional characteristics to a tree's edges. An edge goes *from* a root node *to* a subtree's root, as shown in Fig. 84.

FIGURE 83

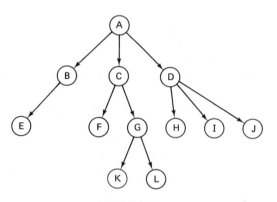

FIGURE 84

Here we have drawn the tree in the more typical fashion of data management texts: with its root on top and its edges (or *branches*) growing downward.

We have said that a tree has a specially designated node called its root. The root is not just randomly selected; rather it is a node distinguished by the property that

$$\text{INDEG}(v) = 0 \text{ for } v = \text{ROOT}(T).$$

Because a tree is a connected graph, there can be no more than one node with this property. Consider the subtrees of A from the tree of Fig. 84, as shown in Fig. 85. Note that the edges connecting A to B, C, and D do not appear in these subtrees, because A is not one of their nodes.

The terminology used in talking about general trees is similar to that used with genealogical trees and live trees. If there is an edge (A,B), then A is said to be the *parent* of B; B is said to be the *child* of A. A child thus has only one parent node. Two nodes with the same parent

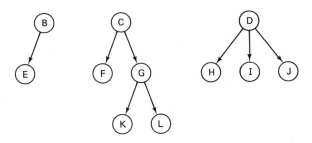

FIGURE 85

are called *brothers* (or *sisters*), and so forth in the vein of family trees. The nodes for which out-degree is zero are said to be *leaves* of the tree. The leaf nodes of the tree of Fig. 84 are E, F, K, L, H, I, and J.

The nodes of a tree are said to be on *levels*, where a node's level is determined by the length of the path from the root to that node. For example, in the tree of Fig. 84:

level 0	A
level 1	B, C, D
level 2	E, F, G, H, I, J
level 3	K, L.

The *height* of a tree is one plus the number of the highest level on which it has nodes. The *weight* of a tree is its number of leaf nodes. The height and weight of the tree of Fig. 84 are 4 and 7 respectively.

A collection of rooted trees is called a *forest*.

We have used one graphical notation to represent trees. Other graphical notations for tree structures include (1) nested sets (Fig. 86),

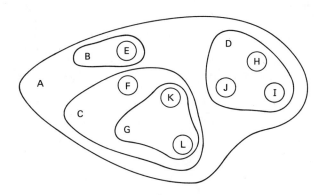

FIGURE 86

(2) nested parentheses:

$$(A(B(E))(C(F)(G(K)(L))) \ (D(H)(I)(J)))$$

```
A ------------
  B -----------
    E ----------
  C -----------
    F ----------
    G ----------
      K ---------
      L ---------
  D -----------
    H ---------
    I ---------
    J ---------
```
FIGURE 87

in which parentheses bracket the root and subtrees of each tree, and (3) indentation, as shown in Fig. 87.

DEFINITIONS: BINARY TREES

The most important class of general trees is binary trees. A *binary tree* is a finite set of nodes which either is empty or consists of two disjoint binary trees that are called the *left* and *right* subtrees. Note that in addition to the requirement that the maximum out-degree of any node of a binary tree is 2, there is the additional constraint that leftness and rightness are imposed upon subtrees. The binary trees of Fig. 88(a) are *not* the same; they are two different trees, one with a left subtree and one with a right subtree. The tree of Fig. 88(b) is not a binary tree, because its subtree does not have leftness or rightness (only downness).

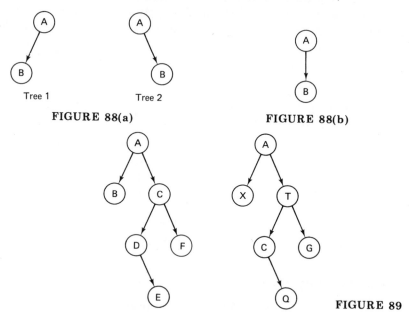

Tree 1   Tree 2

FIGURE 88(a)   **FIGURE 88(b)**

FIGURE 89

Two binary trees are said to be *similar* if they have the same structure, as exemplified in Fig. 89. Two binary trees are said to be *equivalent* if they are similar and contain the same information.

We now consider some properties of binary trees that further distinguish them from general trees. Consider a binary tree with K levels, as depicted in Fig. 90. Note that we now begin to omit the arrows on the tree's edges, as there is no question about where the root is.

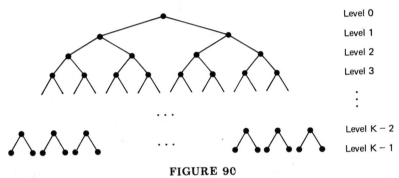

Level 0
Level 1
Level 2
Level 3
.
.
.
Level K − 2
Level K − 1

FIGURE 90

A binary tree is said to be *complete* if it contains the maximum number of nodes possible for its height. How many nodes does a complete binary tree with K levels contain? The number of edges coming into any level (except level 0) is twice as many as the number of nodes on the prior level. Thus the maximum number of nodes on the Ith level is 2^I. Therefore, a complete binary tree with K levels contains

$$\sum_{I=0}^{K-1} 2^I$$

nodes.

A binary tree with K levels is said to be *almost complete* if levels 0 through K-2 are full and level K-1 is being filled left to right, as shown in Fig. 91, for a 5-level tree.

FIGURE 91

The shortest maximum path length (denoted by PL_{max}) for a binary tree is achieved by making the tree as full (bushy) as possible. The minimum height (denoted by H_{min}) for a binary tree with N nodes is:

$$H_{\text{min}} = \lceil \log_2(N+1) \rceil$$

where $\lceil x \rceil$ denotes the ceiling function, i.e., the smallest integer $\geqslant x$. When $N = 1$, then $H_{\min} = 1$. When $N = 3$, level 1 is filled and $H_{\min} = 2$. When $N = 7$, level 2 is filled and $H_{\min} = 3$. (Recall that if $\log_2 X = y$, then $2^y = X$.)

The worst-case height is achieved when the binary tree is long and leggy, as demonstrated in Fig. 92.

FIGURE 92

Now the maximum height (denoted $H_{\max}$) for a binary tree with N nodes is:

$$H_{\max} = N$$

We will see that a major use of trees is to structure a collection of data in a manner that facilitates searching for a particular element. In general it will be desirable to arrange data in the tree in such a way that search path lengths are minimized.

REPRESENTATION OF BINARY TREES

Binary trees are most commonly represented by linked lists. Each node can be regarded as having three elementary fields: INFO(NODE) is the information stored in the node NODE; LEFT(NODE) and RIGHT

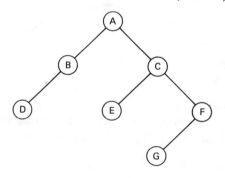

FIGURE 93(a)

(NODE) are pointers to the roots of NODE's left and right subtrees respectively. For example, the binary tree of Fig. 93(a) can be represented by linked lists as shown in Fig. 93(b).

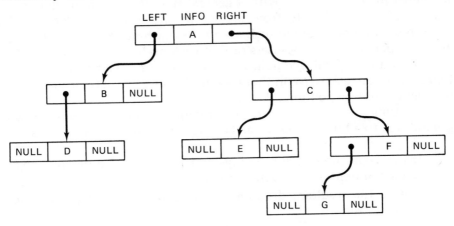

FIGURE 93(b)

The topological placement of the boxes of the linked lists on the page is of course meaningless; storage for the nodes could be scattered throughout memory.

In Pascal, a binary tree data type could be defined by the following:

```
type nodeptr = ↑ nodetype;
     nodetype = record
                    left : nodeptr;
                    info : integer;
                    right : nodeptr
                end;
```

In COBOL, a binary tree with a maximum of 500 nodes could be declared by the following:

```
01  BIN-TREE.
    02  NODE OCCURS 500 TIMES.
        03  LEFTN        PICTURE 9(3).
        03  INFO         PICTURE 9(5).
        03  RIGHTN       PICTURE 9(3).
```

Note that in the absence of built-in pointer variable support, the binary tree is housed in an array. We have used *LEFTN* and *RIGHTN* as names for the left and right pointers because *LEFT* and *RIGHT* are COBOL reserved words. To manage space in such an array would require use of an *AVAIL* list of empty (available) nodes, just as we discussed in the chapter on linked lists.

BINARY TREE REPRESENTATION OF GENERAL TREES

It is considerably easier to represent binary trees in programs than it is to represent general trees. With a general tree, it is unpredictable how many edges will emanate from a node at any given time. Thus node space has to be managed in such a way that each node is allowed a variable number of subtree pointers or that each node is allocated space for a fixed number of subtree pointers, whether they are all needed or not. Binary trees are attractive in that each node has a predictable maximum number of subtree pointers: 2.

Fortunately, there is a straightforward technique for converting a general tree to a binary tree form. The algorithm has two easy steps:

1. Insert edges connecting siblings and delete all of a parent's edges to its children except to its leftmost offspring.
2. Rotate the resultant diagram 45° to distinguish between left and right subtrees.

For example, consider the general tree of Fig. 84, which is reproduced here as Fig. 94(a).

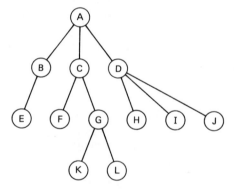

FIGURE 94(a)

Step 1 results in the structure depicted in Fig. 94(b).

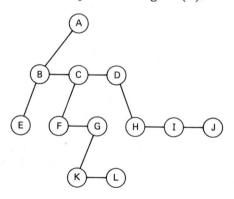

FIGURE 94(b)

Note that there is *not* an edge inserted to connect E and F; they are not siblings in the original tree because they have different parents (B and C). Step 2 results in the binary tree shown in Fig. 94(c).

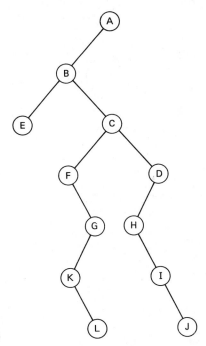

FIGURE 94(c)

In the resultant binary tree, left pointers are always from a parent node to its first (leftmost) child in the original general tree. Right pointers are always from a node to one of its siblings in the original tree.

Can the original general tree be reconstructed from the resultant binary tree? What happens when this transformation is applied to a general tree that is already a binary tree?

This transformation algorithm can also be applied to convert a forest of general trees to a single binary tree by considering the tree roots to be siblings. For example, the forest of Fig. 95(a) can be represented by the binary tree of Fig. 95(b).

Binary trees generated by this type of conversion tend to have fairly large heights for the number of nodes that they contain.

BINARY TREE TRAVERSAL

We will see that trees are commonly used to structure data to facilitate searches for particular nodes. Trees are also useful for representing collections of data that have branching logical structures. For example,

FIGURE 95(a)

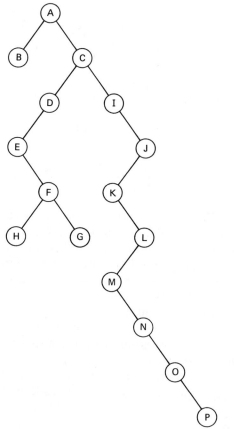

FIGURE 95(b)

binary trees 1 and 2 of Fig. 96 represent arithmetic statements. Each nonleaf node is an operator; its left and right subtrees are its operands. Tree 3 of the figure represents a collection of data elements that are positioned in the tree such that if K is the label of a node, then all labels of nodes in its left subtree are less than (or equal to) K and all labels of nodes in its right subtree are greater than K.

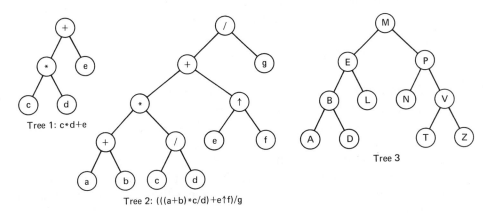

Tree 1: c*d+e

Tree 2: (((a+b)*c/d)+e↑f)/g

Tree 3

FIGURE 96

The process of going through a tree in such a way that each node is visited once and only once is called *tree traversal*. When a tree is traversed, its entire collection of nodes is looked at; tree traversal is the sequential opposite of searching for a particular node. There are several well-known methods of binary tree traversal. Each imposes a sequential, linear ordering upon the nodes of a tree. A node is said to be *visited* when it is encountered in the traversal; whatever processing is desirable on its contents is done at that time.

There are three types of activities in each of the binary tree traversal algorithms:

Visit the root.
Traverse the left subtree.
Traverse the right subtree.

The methods differ in the order in which these types of activities are performed.

Pre-order Traversal

1. Visit the root.
2. Traverse the left subtree in pre-order.
3. Traverse the right subtree in pre-order.

In-order Traversal

1. Traverse the left subtree in in-order.
2. Visit the root.
3. Traverse the right subtree in in-order.

Post-order Traversal

1. Traverse the left subtree in post-order.
2. Traverse the right subtree in post-order.
3. Visit the root.

Note the recursive nature of these definitions.

The nodes of the trees of Fig. 96 are visited in the following sequences when the trees are traversed according to the above-listed methods.

Tree 1:	Pre-order:	+*cde
	In-order:	c*d+e
	Post-order:	cd*e+
Tree 2:	Pre-order:	/+*+ab/cd↑efg
	In-order:	a+b*c/d+e↑f/g
	Post-order:	ab+cd/*ef↑+g/
Tree 3:	Pre-order:	MEBADLPNVTZ
	In-order:	ABDELMNPTVZ
	Post-order:	ADBLENTZVPM

The results of these traversals of trees 1 and 2 should remind you of the example application of stacks in Chapter 4 for notation of arithmetic expressions. Post-order traversal results in a string representation in postfix form; an operator is preceded by its two operands. Pre-order traversal results in a string representation in prefix form; an operator precedes its operands. In-order traversal results in a string representation in infix form; an operator appears between its operands. Note that the prefix and infix representations may lose proper operator precedence if the original arithmetic expression required use of parentheses to override natural precedence rules. In postfix notation, operator precedence is preserved and is indicated solely by operator order. For this type of example, post-order traversal appears to be the most useful.

By contrast, in-order traversal of tree 3 appears to yield the most useful results; the nodes are traversed in alphabetic sequence. Pre-order traversal is the most useful for other types of applications. One of the most important of these is traversal of the trees managed by hierarchical database management systems such as IBM's Information Management System (IMS). Pre-order traversal is equivalent to the IMS *hierarchic sequence* order.

Thus all three traversal techniques are important and have real application. The procedures that we present in the remainder of this chapter will use in-order traversal as the example technique. You should develop the corresponding pre-order and post-order procedures. Post-order is the most difficult in general.

A Pascal procedure to traverse a binary tree in in-order follows. Note that this procedure, like the definitions for traversals, is recursive.

```
procedure inorder(var rootptr:nodeptr);
begin if rootptr <> nil
        then begin inorder(rootptr↑.left);
                    writeln(rootptr↑.info);
                    inorder(rootptr↑.right)
        end;
end;
```

The data types *nodeptr* and *node* were defined earlier. It is relatively easy to write the corresponding recursive procedures to implement pre-order and post-order traversal.

In some implementations, nonrecursive routines that explicitly perform their own stacking and unstacking are more efficient than recursive routines. For example, a nonrecursive Pascal procedure to traverse a binary tree in in-order follows. This procedure uses the built-in pointer variable type to implement the binary tree and an array to implement the stack that is needed to keep track of node locations in the tree during traversal. *rootptr* is a pointer to the tree's root.

```
procedure inorder(rootptr:nodeptr);
type stackstruct = record stack:array [1 .. 500] of nodeptr;
                            topptr:0 .. 500
               end;
var next:nodeptr;
    goflag:boolean;
    s:stackstruct;
begin s.topptr := 0;
        next := rootptr; {start at root}
        goflag := true;
        while (goflag)
        do begin {build stack of pointers to nodes}
                {stop when encounter null left pointer}
            while (next<>nil)
            do begin s.topptr := s.topptr + 1;
                        s.stack[s.topptr] := next;
                        next := next↑.left
            end;
```

```
              {visit node on top of stack}
              if (s.topptr > 0)
              then begin next := s.stack [s.topptr];
                          s.topptr := s.topptr - 1;
                          writeln (next↑.info);
                          {traverse right subtree}
                          next := next↑.right
                   end;
              else goflag := false; {stack is empty}
      end;
end.
```

A nonrecursive COBOL procedure to traverse a binary tree in post-order follows next. This procedure houses the binary tree and the stack in arrays. We assume that the binary tree has a maximum of 500 nodes and that the value 0 is used to simulate a null pointer.

In the *DATA DIVISION*:

```
01  BIN-TREE.
    02  NODE                OCCURS 500 TIMES.
        03  LEFTN           PICTURE 9(3).
        03  INFO            PICTURE 9(5).
        03  RIGHTN          PICTURE 9(3).
01  AUX-PTRS.
    02  ROOT                PICTURE 9(3).
    02  NODEPTR             PICTURE 9(3).
01  STACK-STRUCT.
    02  STACK               OCCURS 500 TIMES
                            PICTURE 9(3).
    02  TOP-PTR             PICTURE 9(3)  VALUE 0.
```

In the *PROCEDURE DIVISION*:

```
POSTORDER.
    MOVE ROOT TO NODEPTR.
    PERFORM LOOP.
    PERFORM LOOP UNTIL TOP-PTR = 0.
```

where:

```
LOOP.
    PERFORM SAVENODE UNTIL NODEPTR = 0.
    MOVE STACK (TOP-PTR) TO NODEPTR.
    COMPUTE TOP-PTR = TOP-PTR - 1.
    DISPLAY INFO (NODEPTR).
    MOVE RIGHTN (NODEPTR) TO NODEPTR.
SAVENODE.
    COMPUTE TOP-PTR = TOP-PTR + 1.
    MOVE NODEPTR TO STACK (TOP-PTR).
    MOVE LEFTN (NODEPTR) TO NODEPTR.
```

THREADED BINARY TREES

The nonrecursive procedures for binary tree traversal given in the preceding section are not trivial. In fact, the use of stacks to keep track of
which nodes have and have not been visited (especially for post-order
traversal) is really quite messy. In order to facilitate the traversal of a
binary tree, we sometimes *thread* the tree with pointers that explicitly
show a traversal ordering. Intuitively, the threads link the tree's nodes
in the sequence of the traversal method.

There are two types of threads: a *right thread* links a node to its
successor node in the traversal ordering; a *left thread* links a node to its
predecessor node in the traversal ordering. From these definitions, it
should be clear that a tree can be threaded according to only *one* traversal method; it is threaded in pre-order *or* in-order *or* post-order. (Of
course auxiliary threads could be used to multi-thread a tree.)

We represent threads in our figures by dashed pointers. Fig. 97(a)
shows the three trees of Fig. 96 threaded in pre-order; Fig. 97(b) shows
them threaded in in-order; Fig. 97(c) shows them threaded in post-
order. Only right threads are illustrated.

One alternative for representing a threaded binary tree is simply to
have each node structured as follows:

```
type nodeptr=↑nodetype;
     nodetype=record
               left:nodeptr;
               info:integer;
               right:nodeptr;
               rightthread:nodeptr;
               leftthread:nodeptr
          end;
```

A nonrecursive procedure to traverse in in-order a binary tree which is
threaded in in-order follows. *firstin* points to the first node of the tree
in in-order.

```
procedure inorder(firstin:nodeptr);
var p:nodeptr;
begin p := firstin;
      while p <> nil
      do begin writeln (p↑.info);
               p := p↑.rightthread
         end;
end;
```

This is about as simple a traversal algorithm that can be obtained!

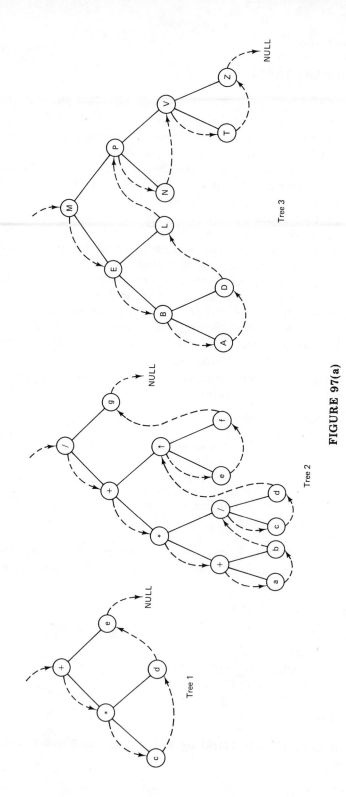

FIGURE 97(a)

Tree 1

Tree 2

Tree 3

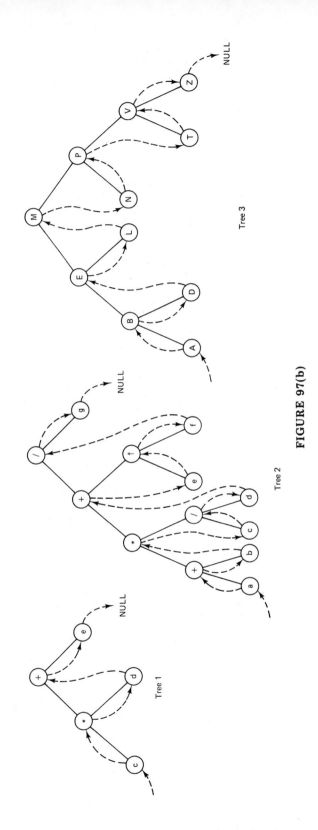

FIGURE 97(b)

Tree 1

Tree 2

Tree 3

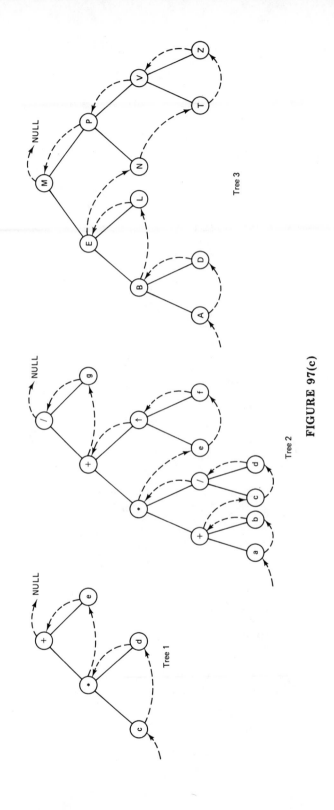

FIGURE 97(c)

Tree 1

Tree 2

Tree 3

A second alternative for representing a threaded binary tree requires less "overhead" storage for pointers but can make the tree management and traversal algorithms a little more complex. First, how many null pointers are there in an unthreaded binary tree with N nodes? Such a tree has a total of $2N$ (null and non-null) pointers: N pointers to left subtrees and N pointers to right subtrees. Of these, only $N-1$ are non-null, since each node except the root has only one pointer to it. Thus there are always $N+1$ null pointers. If you examine a tree that is threaded in pre-order, you will find that threads of nonleaf nodes parallel actual left pointers. There really is no need to duplicate these pointers. The leaf nodes, which need the threads, have null subtree pointers. We thus can represent a binary tree threaded in pre-order by having each node structured as follows.

```
type nodeptr=↑nodetype;
     nodetype=record
                  left:nodeptr;
                  threadflag:0 .. 1;
                  info:integer;
                  right:nodeptr
              end;
```

In order not to confuse threads and subtree pointers, *threadflag* can be set to value 0 when *left* represents a pointer to a left subtree and can be set to 1 when *left* represents a right thread. Alternatively, when a binary tree is housed in an array, left pointers can be represented by positive subscript values and right threads can be represented by negative subscript values, or vice versa.

The trees of Fig. 97 then appear as shown in Fig. 98.

The pre-order traversal procedure then is as follows:

```
procedure preordthr(root:nodeptr);
var p:nodeptr;
begin p := root;
      while p <> nil
      do begin writeln(p↑.info);
               p := p↑.left
         end;
end;
```

Note the similarity of this procedure to the one given for in-order traversal of a threaded tree.

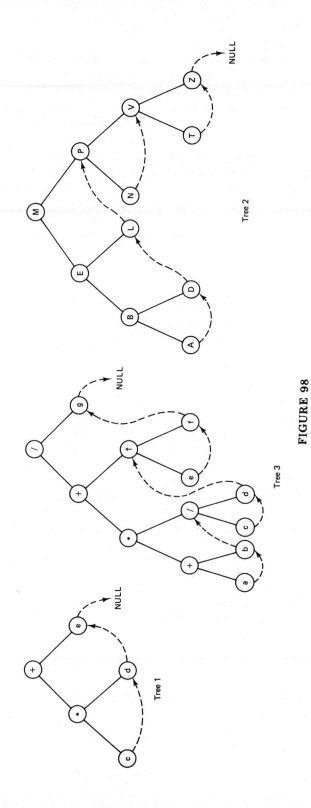

FIGURE 98

OPERATIONS ON BINARY TREES

The operations of inserting nodes into binary trees and removing nodes from binary trees are fairly straightforward. For example, consider the insertion of a node labeled *GNU* which is to become the root of the right subtree of some node *X* of a binary tree. There are two cases: either *GNU* will be a leaf or *GNU* will not be a leaf, depending upon whether or not *X*'s right subtree is initially empty. The possible results of inserting *GNU* are shown in Fig. 99(a).

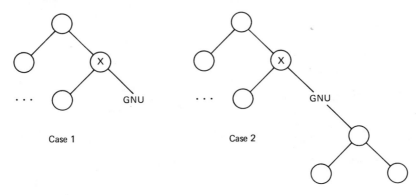

FIGURE 99(a)

If the tree is unthreaded, then a Pascal procedure to make these insertions in an unthreaded tree is as follows:

```
procedure insert(x:nodeptr;var gnu:nodeptr);
begin new(gnu);
      gnu↑.left := nil;
      gnu↑.right := x↑.right;
      x↑.right := gnu
end;
```

The more difficult aspect of inserting nodes in trees is determination of where they should go. We leave solution of this problem for later chapters.

If the tree is threaded, then the insertion procedure is a bit more complex. Fig. 99(b) shows the tree of Fig. 99(a) before and after insertion of *GNU* when the tree is threaded in in-order.

The insertion procedure then becomes:

```
procedure insert(x:nodeptr;var gnu:nodeptr);
begin new(gnu);
      gnu↑.left := nil;
      gnu↑.right := x↑.right;
      gnu↑.leftthread := x;
```

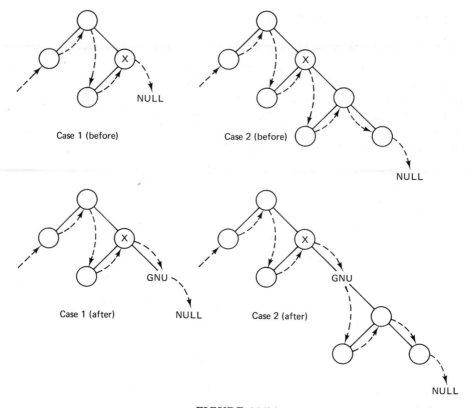

Case 1 (before)

Case 2 (before)

NULL

NULL

Case 1 (after)   NULL   Case 2 (after)

GNU

GNU

NULL

FIGURE 99(b)

```
        gnu↑.rightthread := x↑.rightthread;
        x↑.right := gnu;
        x↑.rightthread := gnu
end;
```

You should develop the insertion algorithm for binary trees threaded in pre-order and post-order. For the pre-order case, determine what differences (if any) are necessary when a *threadflag* is used to note that *left* is either a left subtree pointer or a rightthread.

The removal of nodes from a binary tree similarly involves "fixing up" the subtree pointers and the threads. Your experience with linked lists should make it clear that it is somewhat easier to remove nodes when the subtree linkages are bidirectional. For example:

```
type nodeptr=↑nodetype;
    nodetype=record
                left:nodeptr;
                info:integer;
                right:nodeptr;
```

```
        leftthread:nodeptr;
        rightthread:nodeptr;
        parent:nodeptr
end;
```

Note that to implement bidirectional subtree linkages requires just one additional pointer field per node: to the node's parent.

Removal of a node (call it X) from a binary tree becomes somewhat complex if that node is not a leaf. A decision must be made about the disposition of the removed node's children. It may be the case that these offspring nodes should also be removed from the tree. The difficulty in implementing this policy is in fixing up the threads. Another alternative is to move the root of X's left subtree or right subtree into X's position. This is easy (except for the threads) when only one of these nodes is non-null. If both are non-null, then a choice between them must be made. If the one selected has both its left and right subtrees non-null, then further difficulties arise. (Try it!) A reasonable alternative in some situations is to avoid these problems by not allowing a node to be removed unless it is a leaf.

APPLICATIONS OF TREES

Trees are very commonly used in information systems. In fact, we will devote the next several chapters to special cases of trees that are especially important to data management and file processing.

We have already taken glimpses at two applications of binary trees. (See Fig. 96.) A compiler commonly builds a binary tree in the process of scanning, parsing, and generating code for evaluation of arithmetic expressions. Collections of keyed data to which both rapid (direct) access to particular records and sequential access through the collection of records are required commonly are structured as binary trees. These types of trees are the focus of Chapters 9 and 10. More general trees are discussed in detail in Chapters 11 and 12. We return to applications of graphs in Chapter 13.

SUMMARY

This chapter introduced the *graph* data structure and constrained it to the structure *general tree*, which is an acyclic, connected, simple graph. Terminology pertaining to trees was introduced; then a special case of general tree, the *binary tree*, became the focus of attention. In a binary tree, each node has a maximum of two subtrees, which can be distinguished as a left and right subtree. Because it is easier to manage binary trees than general trees, it is useful to represent a general tree (or forest of general trees) by a binary tree form. An algorithm for this conversion was presented.

An important class of binary trees are those that are *almost complete*. Structuring a collection of nodes as an almost complete binary tree minimizes the maximum path length in the tree, thereby minimizing the longest search path through the tree to a particular node.

Sometimes instead of searching for a particular node, it is necessary to traverse a binary tree, that is, to visit all the tree's nodes. Several algorithms were presented for binary tree traversal: pre-order, in-order, and post-order. These algorithms differ in the order in which the root, left subtree, and right subtree are traversed. Each ordering is appropriate for a different type of application. To facilitate traversal, a tree may be threaded according to one of the traversal algorithms. Each node then points to its successor in the traversal path. Threads are commonly bidirectional, which makes node insertion and removal somewhat easier. Traversal of a general tree is accomplished by first converting the tree to its binary form.

Two interesting references to the use of trees to structure game-playing and decision theory problems are R. D. Luce and H. Raiffa, *Games and Decisions* (New York: John Wiley & Sons, Inc., 1958), and M. Newborn, *Computer Chess* (New York: Academic Press, 1975).

Terms

acyclic graph
almost complete binary tree
arc
binary tree
complete binary tree
connected graph
cycle
directed graph
edge
forest
graph
graph order
in-degree
in-order traversal
leaf node
left thread
loop

multigraph
node
out-degree
path
path length
post-order traversal
pre-order traversal
right thread
rooted tree
simple graph
threaded tree
tree
tree height
tree traversal
tree weight
vertex

Review Exercises

1. Can there be a cycle in a simple graph? If so, give an example. If not, why not?
2. Can there be a cycle in a tree?
3. Draw several graphs. For each graph answer the following questions. Is the graph: (a) acyclic? (b) connected? (c) directed? (d) simple? (e) What is the order of the graph? What is the (f) in-degree, (g) out-degree, (h) degree of each node?
4. Draw two binary trees that are similar.
5. Draw two binary trees that are equivalent.
6. Can there be two binary trees that are equivalent but not similar? If so, give an example. If not, why not?
7. What is the number of nodes on the Ith level of a complete binary tree with height K, where $I < K$?
8. What is the number of nodes on the Ith level of an almost complete binary tree with height K, where $I < K$?
9. Draw a complete binary tree with 10 nodes. Draw an almost complete binary tree with 10 nodes. What is the minimum maximum path length for a binary tree with 10 nodes? What is the maximum maximum path length for a binary tree with 10 nodes?
10. Why is it easier to represent binary trees in programs than it is to represent general trees?
11. Consider the binary tree:

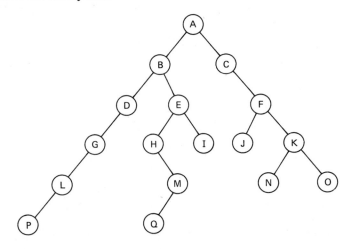

   List the nodes of the tree in (a) pre-order, (b) post-order, (c) in-order.
   Draw the tree as threaded in (d) pre-order, (e) post-order, (f) in-order, representing threads by dashed lines.
12. Is the following statement true or false? "The leaves of a binary tree occur in the same relative position in pre-order, post-order, and in-order."

13. Draw the binary tree corresponding to the forest:

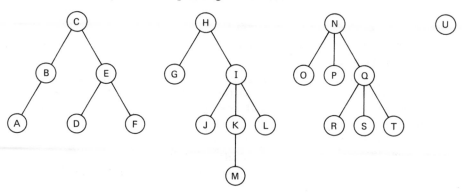

14. Transform the following general tree to a binary tree:

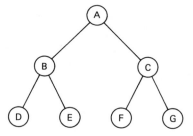

15. The following binary tree resulted from the transformation of a forest to a binary form. What was the forest?

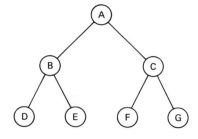

16. Represent the expression $((A+B)*C)/(D-E)$ as a binary tree. Traverse the tree in pre-order, post-order, and in-order. Why do you think post-order was chosen as the traversal order for expression evaluation, i.e., what can you see about the post-order traversal which makes computation easier than with the other orders?

17. Show the binary tree representation for the string ICDFEHABC produced:
(a) using pre-order, where the tree has structure:

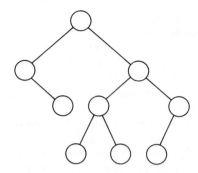

(b) using in-order, (c) using post-order.

18. Show the in-order threads in the following tree:

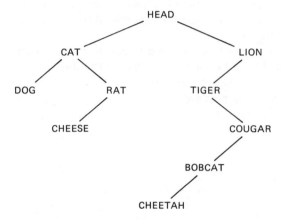

19. Give an example where post-order traversal is the most appropriate way to visit a tree. Do the same for in-order traversal and pre-order traversal.

20. Give the node structure for a binary tree that is threaded in both in-order and post-order.

21. Is is likely that a real binary tree would ever be threaded for more than one traversal type? Why or why not?

22. Consider a binary tree T with n nodes, $n \geq 0$. If T is not empty, the maximum level that any node of T can reach is n. If T is nonempty, then at least one node achieves some maximum level for that tree. What is the *minimum* value that this maximum level can be? For example, for $n = 1$ the answer is 1, while for $n = 2$ the answer is 2, and for $n = 3$ it is also 2. Express your answer as a formula in terms of n, $\log_2$ (logarithm to the base 2), and the ceiling function $\lceil \ \rceil$. Prove that your result is true.

23. Three basic orders for traversing a binary tree have been identified. Another alternative would be to proceed in three steps as follows:
(a) visit the root,

(b) traverse the right subtree,

(c) traverse the left subtree,

using the same rule recursively on all nonempty subtrees. Does this new order bear any simple relation to the three orders already discussed? What kind of threads should be defined to make traversal in this order easier?

24. Write a program that takes general trees as input and produces the corresponding binary trees as output.

25. Write iterative procedures to perform in-order traversal on a binary tree that is threaded in in-order; to perform pre-order traversal on a binary tree that is threaded in pre-order; to perform post-order traversal on a binary tree that is threaded in post-order. Write programs to implement the procedures.

26. Write recursive procedures to implement in-order, pre-order, and post-order traversal for unthreaded trees. Write a program to implement the procedures.

27. Write nonrecursive (i.e., iterative) procedures to implement in-order, pre-order, and post-order traversal for unthreaded trees. Write a program to implement the procedures.

28. What trade-offs are to be considered in deciding whether tree traversal should be implemented by a recursive or an iterative routine?

29. Write procedures to insert a new node in a binary tree that is threaded in in-order; in pre-order; in post-order.

30. Write procedures to remove a node from a binary tree; from a threaded binary tree.

CHAPTER 9

Binary Search Trees

In this chapter, attention turns to a special case of the binary tree data structure. The special case is called a binary search tree and is itself a data structure of major significance. Binary search trees are important for organizing large collections of data to which both direct and sequential access capabilities are required. After defining binary search trees, we investigate the basic operations on this data structure. We then introduce the issue of evaluating binary search trees and look at two subclasses of these trees which improve maintenance requirements while providing nearly optimal search lengths.

DEFINITIONS: BINARY SEARCH TREES

A fundamental requirement for use of a binary search tree to organize a collection of data is that each record in the collection must have an identifying key; these keys are commonly called "names," although their values could be alphanumeric or numeric. The use of a binary search tree to organize such a collection of records enables reasonable performance to be achieved both for access directly to a particular record based upon its name and for access sequentially to the entire collection in order by records' names.

A *binary search tree* over the collection of n records with names $N_1, N_2, \ldots, N_n$ is a binary tree each of whose nodes R_i bears one of the names N_i, for $i = 1, \ldots, n$. The nodes of the binary tree are arranged such that for each node R_i, the following properties hold:

1. All names of nodes in the left subtree of R_i precede the name labeling R_i:

> If $\quad R_j = \text{LEFT}(R_i)$
> then $N_j < N_i$.

2. The name labeling R_i precedes the names of all nodes in the right subtree of R_i:

> If $\quad R_j = \text{RIGHT}(R_i)$
> then $N_i < N_j$.

In general we require that the names in the collection be distinct, although this constraint sometimes is relaxed. The precedence of names is determined by their linear ordering according to a collating sequence.

For example, the binary tree of Fig. 100 conforms to the above properties and qualifies as a binary search tree over the names APE, BEE, COW, and DOG.

FIGURE 100

It is important to note that there are many possible ways to arrange the names of a record collection such that valid binary search trees result. For example, Fig. 101 shows four additional binary search trees over the names APE, BEE, COW, and DOG. Can you construct others?

(a)   (b)   (c)   (d)

FIGURE 101

As you construct binary search trees, you should notice that once you have started the tree and have decided which name should be inserted next, there is no choice about where to place that name. The properties that define a binary search tree dictate the relationships between nodes and determine where the next node should reside. The structure of a particular binary search tree is determined by the order in which the nodes are placed into the tree. Unless we allow the tree to be restructured during the insertion process, a new node is always inserted as a leaf.

The node structure for a binary search tree can be declared in Pascal as follows:

```
type nodeptr = ↑ nodetype;
     nodename = packed array [1 .. 10] of char;
     nodetype = record
                     left : nodeptr;
                     name : nodename;
                     info : integer;
                     right : nodeptr
                end;
```

for nodes with names of ten characters and integer information.

OPERATIONS ON BINARY SEARCH TREES

There are four basic operations on binary search trees: direct search, sequential search, node insertion, and node deletion. Let us consider each.

The properties of a binary search tree imply that there is a procedure for determining whether or not a node with a given name resides in the tree and for finding that node when it exists. To find the node with name n in the binary search tree rooted at R_i:

1. If the tree is empty, then the search terminates unsuccessfully.
2. If $n = N_i$, then the search terminates successfully; the sought node is R_i.
3. If $n < N_i$, then the left subtree of R_i is searched, i.e., $R_i :=$ LEFT(R_i).
4. If $n > N_i$, then the right subtree of R_i is searched, i.e., $R_i :=$ RIGHT(R_i).

This algorithm is programmed here as a Pascal recursive procedure, where r initially points to the tree's root:

```
procedure search(n:nodename,var r,foundnode:nodeptr);
begin if (r=nil)
        then foundnode := nil
        else if (n=r↑.name)
                then foundnode := r
                else if (n < r↑.name)
                        then search(n,r↑.left,foundnode)
                        else {n > r↑.name}
                                search(n,r↑.right,foundnode)
end;
```

The search terminates with *foundnode* either pointing to the sought node if it exists or with null value if name *n* is not in the tree.

Sequential search of a binary search tree is accomplished by traversing the nodes of the tree in such a way that the nodes are visited in order by their names. Which traversal algorithm should be used? A binary search tree may be threaded in order to facilitate sequential searching.

As discussed in the preceding section, insertion of a node in a binary search tree is really a simple matter. A new node always is placed in the position of a leaf; the structure of the tree is dictated completely by the properties of a binary search tree and by the node insertion order. The insertion algorithm is very similar to the direct search algorithm. To insert a new node with name *n* in the binary search tree rooted at R_i:

1. If the tree is empty, then node with name *n* becomes the root.
2. If $n = N_i$, then the insertion terminates unsuccessfully; the name is already in the tree.
3. If $n < N_i$, then the left subtree of R_i is searched until the appropriate position for the new node is found.
4. If $n > N_i$, then the right subtree of R_i is searched until the appropriate position for the new node is found.

This algorithm is programmed quite easily by using the same logic structure as did the previously written procedure to search a binary search tree. Let *newptr* be a pointer to a node which is to be inserted in the binary search tree rooted at *r*. In Pascal:

```
procedure insert(newptr,var r:nodeptr);
begin if (r=nil)
        then r := newptr
        else if (newptr↑.name = r↑.name)
                then DUPLICATE-ENTRY
                else if (newptr↑.name < r↑.name)
                        then insert(newptr,r↑.left)
```

else {newptr↑.name > r↑.name}

insert(newptr,r↑.right)

end;

The condition that causes the search procedure to terminate unsuccess-fully is the condition that causes the insertion procedure to terminate successfully; the condition that causes the search to terminate success-fully is the condition that causes the insertion to terminate unsuccess-fully.

Note that inserting names into a binary search tree in order results in a long tree with no branching (see tree (b) of Fig. 101).

The operation of deleting a node from a binary search tree is not quite so straightforward. If the node to be deleted is a leaf, then the process is simple; the leaf is pruned neatly from the tree. If the node to be deleted is not a leaf, then the process must do something to preserve that node's subtrees.

Consider first the deletion of the node with name PGMR from the binary search tree of Fig. 102.

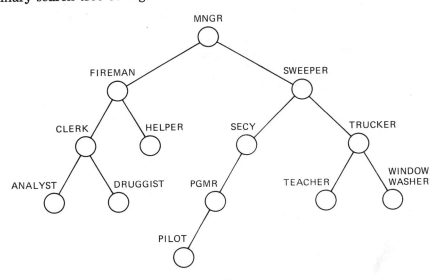

FIGURE 102

Removing the PGMR does not imply also removing the PILOT, rather PILOT can simply be moved into PGMR's vacated position, becoming the left subtree of SECY. Similarly, if instead SECY had been deleted, then PGMR could be moved into the vacated position; the tree rooted at PGMR would become the left subtree of SWEEPER. It appears that deleting a node with one null subtree implies moving the root of the node's non-null subtree into the node's vacated position.

Consider now the deletion of the node with name CLERK from

the tree of Fig. 102. Which of its two subtree roots should occupy its vacated position? Either can be moved in and not violate the rules of the binary search tree.

Deletion of a node like MNGR is more difficult. If FIREMAN takes MNGR's position, how are its subtrees, rooted at CLERK and HELPER, handled? You should develop an algorithm that will handle deletion of a node from any position in a binary search tree; first be sure that you understand the complexity of the problem.

Another approach to deletion is to avoid (at least temporarily) the complexity of the problem simply by marking the subject nodes as inactive. A later search or insertion needs to use a marked node's name to find its path through the tree. If the name looked for by the search or insertion procedure matches the name of a marked node, then the procedure must take different action than it normally would. You should modify the search and insert routines to accommodate marked nodes.

For more information about handling deletions, see J. Cohen's "Garbage collection of linked data structures," in *ACM Computing Surveys*, 13(3): 341–367, September 1981.

EVALUATION OF BINARY SEARCH TREES

We have seen that there are many possible binary search trees to organize a given collection of records. The effort required to find a particular record in a binary search tree depends upon the position of the record in the tree. The farther the sought record is from the tree's root, the greater is the effort required to find the record. The search effort is measured by the number of comparisons made before the search terminates, either successfully or unsuccessfully.

For example, to find the record with name DOG in the various binary search trees of Fig. 101 requires the following numbers of comparisons:

         tree (a)   1 comparison
              (b)   4 comparisons.
              (c)   3 comparisons.
              (d)   2 comparisons.

If it were necessary often to find DOG, then tree (a) would probably be considered to be a better binary search tree than would tree (b). In general, though, how does one determine whether one binary search tree is better than another? What is a good binary search tree? How are good binary search trees constructed?

A binary search tree cannot be evaluated well on the sole basis of the search path that it provides to just one record. Rather, the search paths through the entire tree should enter into the evaluation; thus the expected (i.e., weighted average) length of a search path in the tree is useful.

Let s_i be the probability that name N_i is sought, where N_i ($i=1, \ldots, n$) is one of the names in the tree, given that the search is a successful one. That is,

$$\sum_{i=1}^{n} s_i = 1.$$

Considering first just the successful searches, the expected search length for the binary search tree is

$$\sum_{i=1}^{n} s_i c_i$$

where c_i is the number of comparisons required to reach name N_i. c_i-1 is the number of the level upon which node R_i resides. For example, if the access probabilities for the names structured in the binary search trees of Fig. 101 were as follows:

APE	.2
BEE	.4
COW	.3
DOG	.1

then the expected search lengths for those trees would be:

	APE		BEE		COW		DOG		
(a)	.2*4	+	.4*3	+	.3*2	+	.1*1	=	2.7
(b)	.2*1	+	.4*2	+	.3*3	+	.1*4	=	2.3
(c)	.2*2	+	.4*1	+	.3*2	+	.1*3	=	1.7
(d)	.2*2	+	.4*1	+	.3*3	+	.1*2	=	1.9

Note that here in order to reduce the expected search length, the tree is structured so that the most frequently accessed names are placed as close as possible to the root. To accomplish this, the names must be inserted into the tree in the proper order. Clearly there are problems with this approach if the access probabilities are unknown! In these situations the designer sometimes can guess the relative frequencies of access, then restructure the tree after measures of actual usage have been gathered.

Note also that the expected path length of a binary search tree will change as names are inserted into the tree; what is today a good tree structure may tomorrow become a relatively poor tree structure because of name insertions and/or changes in the patterns of access to the tree's contents.

Before discussing how to accommodate these changes, we should also consider the effects of unsuccessful searches. Let u_i be the frequency with which an unsuccessful search terminates at node R_i. Note that $u_i = 0$ for any node R_i which has both its left and right subtrees non-null, because a search can never terminate unsuccessfully at such a node. Then the expected search length is:

$$p_s \sum_{i=1}^{n} s_i c_i + p_u \sum_{i=1}^{n} u_i c_i$$

where p_s is the probability of a successful search and p_u is the probability of an unsuccessful search, and

$$p_s + p_u = 1.$$

In some applications, the p_u may be much larger than p_s. For example, consider the use of a binary search tree to store numbers of stolen credit cards in an interactive credit-management system. Prior to making a sale, a store clerk keys in the number of the customer's credit card on a terminal and the system searches for that number in the tree. In nearly all cases, the search will be unsuccessful. The expected search length can be minimized by making these unsuccessful searches terminate with as few comparisons as possible. This implies that the tree should be as bushy as possible, that is, the expected search length here is minimized when the maximum path length in the tree is minimized. Note that here too there is the problem of handling unpredictable insertions into the tree in such a way that search performances do not deteriorate.

Actually achieving the *optimal* tree structure may require more work than it is worth; in fact it may be impossible because of lack of sufficient knowledge of access probabilities. Investigation has shown, however, that performance of binary search trees that are constructed by reasonable heuristic algorithms is competitive with that of optimal trees, while incurring much lower design costs. The two most obvious heuristics are those we have already introduced:

1. Put the frequently accessed names near the root of the tree.
2. Keep the tree balanced; that is, for each node, the left and right subtrees should have as nearly as possible an equal number of nodes, thereby minimizing the maximum path length.

If the access probabilities were known and no insertions were to be made in the tree, the binary search tree that yields optimal performance could be constructed (with some work) and would do better than a tree resulting from one of these heuristics. However, the heuristics are quite good and require considerably less effort to apply. It has been shown that, in general, binary search trees constructed from the second heuristic—balancing—give nearly optimal expected search lengths; balanced trees perform better in general than do trees constructed from the first heuristic. This result is somewhat comforting in that the access probabilities required by the first heuristic are commonly unavailable.

For details of analysis of various heuristic algorithms for constructing binary search trees, you are urged to consult the references at the end of the chapter.

Keeping a binary search tree in balance when there are node insertions and deletions is hard work. The difficulty is due to having to preserve the proper relationships between names in nodes and names in their subtrees. For example, consider the binary search tree of Fig. 103.

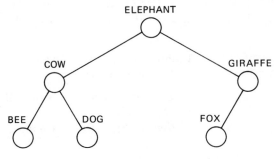

FIGURE 103

Inserting ZEBRA would be easy; it would be the right subtree of GIRAFFE and the tree would still be in balance. Instead, however, try to insert APE. The position of APE will be as the left subtree of BEE, which pulls the tree out of balance. The tree when balanced would be as shown in Fig. 104.

FIGURE 104

All of the nodes of the original tree had to be moved! A similar problem may occur upon deletion of a node from the tree.

In order to reduce the amount of work required to maintain a binary search tree while providing good search performance, we commonly relax the constraint and allow the trees to deviate from being balanced. However, the allowed deviation is small enough that the expected average search length is only slightly longer than that of completely balanced trees. In the next two sections we introduce two classes of binary search trees that allow relatively easy modification.

HEIGHT-BALANCED (AVL) TREES

One type of "almost completely" balanced trees is known as the *height-balanced tree*, or the *AVL tree*, after its Russian discoverers G. M. Adelson-Velskii and E. M. Landis (1962). A tree is height-balanced if its nodes are arranged such that for each node R_i, the following property holds:

> The height of the left subtree of R_i and the height
> of the right subtree of R_i differ by at most 1.

Recall from Chapter 8 that the height of a tree is one plus the number of the highest level on which it has nodes.

The binary search trees shown in Fig. 105(a) are all height-balanced.

FIGURE 105(a)

Note that although it is height-balanced, tree (c) is not completely balanced. The binary search trees of Fig. 105(b) are *not* height-balanced. The height constraint is violated at node APE in tree (a), at node COW in tree (b), and at node FOX in tree (c).

AVL trees provide good direct search performance. Although they

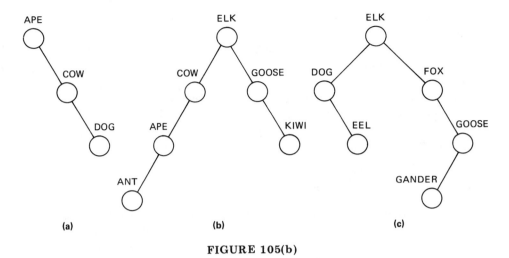

FIGURE 105(b)

tend to look somewhat more sparse than do completely balanced trees, the searches they require are only moderately longer. The worst possible search length for a completely balanced tree of n nodes is $\log_2 (n+1)$, while the worst possible search length for an AVL tree of n nodes is $1.44 \log_2 (n+1)$. The expected average search length for a completely balanced tree of n nodes is $\log_2 (n+1)-2$, and the expected average search length for an AVL tree of n nodes is $\log_2 (n+1)+\alpha$, where α is a constant which depends on the characteristics of the name distribution. (Consult Knuth [1973, pp. 453-454] for details of this analysis.) Thus AVL trees are nearly as good as completely balanced trees. The height constraint prevents an AVL tree from becoming too distant a cousin of a completely balanced tree.

If an insertion or deletion causes an AVL tree to become unbalanced, then the tree must be restructured to return to a balanced state. This restructuring process commonly is referred to as *rotation* and is not discussed further here. The interested reader could start investigation of tree-balancing techniques with perusal of Knuth (1973, pp. 453-463).

BOUNDED-BALANCED (BB) TREES

Another class of "almost completely" balanced trees is known as the *bounded-balanced trees*. These trees are also referred to as *BB trees* or *weight-balanced trees*. The basic idea of a bounded-balanced tree is to place a constraint on how far the tree can deviate from being completely balanced. This bound constrains the difference between the number of nodes in a left subtree and a right subtree. Although based on constraining subtree sizes rather than subtree heights, bounded-balance trees are similar in their properties to height-balanced trees. Both aim to reach a compromise between short search lengths and balancing requirements.

A bounded-balance tree carries a parameter β which controls this compromise. In a bounded-balance tree of balance β, where $0 < \beta \leq \frac{1}{2}$, for each node of the tree the fraction of the nodes in the node's left subtree lies between β and $1-\beta$. More formally, if SIZE(N) is the number of nodes in the tree rooted at node N, then the constraint is:

$$\beta \leq \frac{\text{SIZE(LEFT}(N)) + 1}{\text{SIZE}(N) + 1} \leq 1-\beta$$

If $\beta = \frac{1}{2}$, then the left subtree and right subree would have the same number of nodes, i.e., the tree would be completely balanced. If $\beta = \frac{1}{4}$, then one subtree could have up to three times as many nodes as the other. As the value of β approaches $\frac{1}{2}$, the bounding constraint becomes tighter. A tree designer selects the appropriate β value for the application.

The expected average search length for a bounded-balance tree is $\sigma(\log_2 n)$, where n is the number of nodes in the tree. If insertion or deletion causes a tree of this class to become unbalanced relative to its bound β, then the same types of rotations as are applied to the class of height-balanced trees are applied to return the tree to a balanced state.

The work required to keep an AVL or BB tree in conformance with its height- or size-ratio is considerably less than the work required to keep a tree *completely* balanced. If a transformation is required to keep a tree completely balanced after an insertion or deletion, that transformation requires movement of $\sigma(n)$ nodes, where n is the number of nodes in the tree. By contrast, if a transformation is needed to maintain height- or size-ratio conformance in an AVL or BB tree after an insertion or deletion, movement of $\sigma(\log_2 n)$ nodes is required. The reduction in work is accomplished by localizing movement to nodes along a single path from root to leaf in the AVL or BB tree, while movement in the completely balanced tree affects the entire tree.

SUMMARY

This chapter introduced the data structure *binary search tree*, which is applicable to organizing large collections of data records with identifying keys, where access directly to a particular record and sequential access to the entire set of records are both required. Algorithms were presented to perform the basic operations on binary search trees: direct search, sequential search, node insertion, and node deletion.

Understanding the nature of a binary search tree makes it obvious that some structures yield better search performance than do other structures. Two reasonable heuristics for building binary search trees were discussed; one of these heuristics—keeping the tree balanced—gives very nearly optimal search lengths without the work of actually constructing an optimal tree.

The difficulty of keeping a binary search tree completely balanced when there are node insertions and deletions was discussed, and two classes of "almost balanced" binary search trees were introduced that give good search performance yet require considerably less maintenance work than do completely balanced trees. *AVL-trees* (also known as *height-balanced trees*) constrain the height difference between each node's left and right subtrees to be at most 1. *Bounded-balance trees* (also known as *BB trees* or *weight-balanced trees*) constrain the difference between the size (i.e., number of nodes) of each node's left and right subtrees. The tree designer here specifies the parameter used in establishing the constraint.

Insertions and deletions of nodes in a balanced binary search tree may take that tree out of balance; the height or size constraint may be violated. In order to return the tree to a balanced condition, rotation may be applied to the tree.

The expected average search length for a balanced binary search tree is $o(\log_2 n)$.

For further details of binary search tree management, see:

Baer, J. L., and B. Schwab. "A comparison of tree-balancing algorithms," *Communications ACM*, 20(5): 322–330, May 1977.

Bruno, J., and E. G. Coffman. "Nearly optimal binary search trees," *Proc. IFIP Congress 1971*, North-Holland, pp. 99–103.

Foster, C. C. "Information storage and retrieval using AVL trees," *Proc. ACM 20th Natl. Conf.*, pp. 192–205, 1965.

Hibbard, T. "Some combinatorial properties of certain trees with applications to searching and sorting," *J. ACM*, 9(1): 13–28, January 1962.

Karlton, P. L., et al. "Performance of height-balanced trees," *Communications ACM*, 19(1): 23–28, January 1976.

Knuth, D. E. *The Art of Computer Programming: Vol. 3, Sorting and Searching*. Reading, Mass.: Addison-Wesley Publishing Co., 1973, pp. 422–471.

Nievergelt, J. "Binary search trees and file organization," *ACM Computing Surveys*, 6(3): 195–207, September 1974.

Standish, T. A. "Trees," Chapter 3 in *Data Structure Techniques*. Reading, Mass.: Addison-Wesley Publishing Co., 1980, pp. 44–129.

Terms

AVL tree
binary search tree
bounded-balance tree

height-balanced tree
rotation
weight-balanced tree

Review Exercises

1. Given a collection of names $N_1, N_2, \ldots, N_n$, in what sequence should those names be inserted to form a balanced binary search tree?

2. Do all of the compilers available at your installation use the same collating sequence? If not, how do they differ?

3. What type of threads should a binary search tree have in order to facilitate visitation of the nodes in sequence by their names?

4. Construct two additional binary search trees for the collection of keys structured in Fig. 102. Using the access probabilities

APE	.2
BEE	.4
COW	.3
DOG	.1

calculate the expected search lengths for your trees.

5. What is the difference between a balanced tree and a height-balanced tree?

6. Write nonrecursive (i.e., iterative) procedures to search a binary search tree and to insert a new node in a binary search tree.

7. Modify the procedures that search a binary search tree and insert a new node in a binary search tree so that they will recognize nodes that have been marked as deleted but that have not yet been removed from the tree.

8. Write a procedure to delete a given node from a binary search tree. Be sure to accommodate situations where the node to be deleted has 0, 1, or 2 non-null subtrees.

9. Read about techniques for keeping a tree in balance. Write a program to implement one of the techniques.

CHAPTER 10

Binary Searching and σ (Nlog$_2$N) Sorting Techniques

In Chapters 8 and 9 we began our study of nonlinear data structures. We discovered that through structuring of data in a binary tree, the search time to a particular record of the collection could be reduced significantly over structuring of that data in a linear data type; for a collection of n records, the expected average search length of a balanced binary tree is $\sigma(\log_2 n)$, whereas the average search length of a linear list is $\sigma(n/2)$. For large n, the binary tree exhibits much better performance.

Just as the branching structure of nonlinear data types helps to reduce search lengths, so also can nonlinear searching and sorting techniques improve performance over sequential searching and sorting methods. In Chapter 7 we considered several techniques for finding particular data values and for sorting collections of data values. These techniques all dealt with linear data structures and had little to recommend themselves performance-wise; the sort methods all required $\sigma(n^2)$ comparisons to reach completion. In this chapter we turn to better techniques for searching and sorting. These sorting techniques are all nonlinear and require $\sigma(n\log_2 n)$ comparisons on the average.

THE BINARY SEARCH

We have already covered a nonlinear tree-based search strategy in our discussion of binary search trees. When we were looking for the node with a particular key value, the comparison at each intermediate node directed us down the proper branch of the tree toward our destination. In a completely balanced tree, each comparison removes from further consideration one-half of the nodes remaining on the tree. Thus the expected average search length in a balanced binary search tree is $\sigma(\log_2 n)$. This is good performance compared with sequential searching methods.

However, sometimes it is necessary to search collections of data that are structured linearly. In the worst case, a linear search requires n comparisons; on the average, $n/2$ comparisons are needed. Linear searches are said to be $\sigma(n)$ searches. How can we improve upon this performance?

The binary search technique can be applied to data in a linear list as well as to data in a binary search tree. The major prerequisites are that records in the list must be in sorted order by the search key value and the number of records must be known. The binary search technique cannot be applied unless these prerequisites are met.

The search proceeds by successive probes into the list. The first probe compares the value of the key in the middle of the sorted list with the value sought. If the sought value is less, then the half of the list following the middle can be removed from further consideration. On the other hand, if the sought value is greater, then the half of the list preceding the middle need not be considered further. The second probe is to the key in the middle of the retained half of the original list. Again, if the sought value is less than this probed key's value, then the half of the (half-) list following the probe can be removed from further consideration. If the sought value is greater than this probed key's value, then the half of the (half-) list preceding the probe need not be considered further. And so the probing process continues until the sought key value is located or is determined not to reside in the list.

For example, Fig. 106 shows the sequence of probing activity involved in a binary search for the key value 72 in a sample linear list.

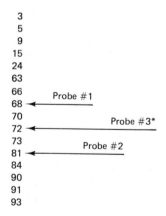

FIGURE 106

Initially there are 16 keys to consider. The first probe is to the 8th (16/2) key: 68. Because 68 < 72, further search needs only look at the second half of the list. The second probe is to the 12th ((8+16)/2) key: 81. Because 81 > 72, we now can discard the last quarter of the list. The third probe is to the 10th ((8+12)/2) key: 72, which is exactly the sought key value. Three probes were required here; a linear search would have required ten comparisons. For large lists, the performance improvement is even more dramatic.

The list is cut in half over and over again until either the middle key value is the desired value or the size of the remaining list is zero, implying that the sought key value is not in the list.

The binary search technique can be programmed as either an iterative algorithm or a recursive algorithm. An iterative binary search procedure written in COBOL follows. The linear list of N keys is housed in array *KEYLIST*; the sought key value is *SKEY*. *FOUNDIT* is set equal to the subscript of the array element with value *SKEY* if it exists or to 0 if *SKEY* is not found.

In the *DATA DIVISION*:

```
01  KEYLIST.
    02  KEYVALUE  OCCURS N TIMES      PICTURE S9(5).
01  AUX-VARIABLES.
    02  LOW         PICTURE 9(4).
    02  HIGH        PICTURE 9(4).
    02  MID         PICTURE 9(4).
    02  SKEY        PICTURE S9(5).
    02  FOUNDIT     PICTURE 9(4).


BINARY-SEARCH.
    COMPUTE FOUNDIT = 0.
    COMPUTE LOW = 1.
    COMPUTE HIGH = N.
    PERFORM PROBE UNTIL LOW > HIGH
                        OR FOUNDIT > 0.
```

where

```
PROBE.
    COMPUTE MID = (LOW + HIGH) / 2.
    IF SKEY = KEYVALUE (MID)
            COMPUTE FOUNDIT = MID
    ELSE IF SKEY < KEYVALUE (MID)
            COMPUTE HIGH = MID - 1
    ELSE COMPUTE LOW = MID + 1.
```

In this routine, the subscripts *LOW*, *MID*, and *HIGH* are prevented from taking on fractional values because they are declared to be integers.

A recursive binary search function written in Pascal follows next.

The variable names are the same as for the above COBOL procedure. The array *keylist* and the sought variable *skey* are global variables; the subscript range for *key* is from 1 to *n*.

```
procedure binsrch (var low,high,foundit : integer)
var mid : integer;
begin if (low > high) then foundit := 0
     else begin {probe}
            mid := (low+high) div 2;
            if (skey = key[mid])
            then foundit := mid
            else if (skey < key[mid])
                   then binsrch(low, mid–1,foundit)
                   else binsrch(mid+1, high,foundit)
        end {probe}
  end {binsrch};
```

This procedure would be invoked by a statement such as *binsrch*(1,*n*, *foundit*); the variable *foundit* would attain the value of the subscript of the entry in array with value *skey*, or would become zero if *skey* does not exist in the array.

The maximum number of comparisons required for a binary search of a sorted linear list of *n* elements is $\log_2 n$; the minimum number of comparisons required is 1. The expected number of comparisons is $1/2 \log_2 n$. Thus the binary search is said to be $o(\log_2 n)$.

A binary search should nearly always be used rather than a sequential search on a large collection of items ordered by the search key. In fact, commonly it is advantageous to build lists in sorted order to start with for purposes of being able to use the binary search technique. Actually, this dictate of always using a binary search should be modified somewhat to indicate its applicability to searching collections of data entirely resident in main memory. The binary search is an internal search method. The concept of nonlinear searching also can be applied to data collections resident on secondary storage; we consider such data organizations later in this book.

THE PARTITION-EXCHANGE SORT (QUICKSORT)

The family of exchange sorts was introduced in Chapter 7. Recall that in an exchange sort, pairs of key values were compared and exchanged if they were not in the proper relative positions. We suggested that very good behavior could result from an exchange sort if there were clever identification of the comparison pairs. The bubble sort was an example of a not-so-clever exchange sort. In this section we introduce a much better exchange sort: the *partition-exchange sort*, also known as *Hoare's quicksort*, or simply the *quicksort*. This method is attributed to C. A. R. Hoare (1962).

The basic idea behind the quicksort is to use the results of each comparison pass to guide the next comparison pass. During a comparison pass, keys are exchanged in such a manner that when the pass completes, the list has been partitioned so that key values in one partition (though unordered) are all less than a particular key value and key values in the other partition (though unordered) are all greater than that particular key value. The next comparison pass can then proceed with the two resultant partitions treated independently of each other. The comparison passes are localized successively to smaller and smaller partitions.

This sort technique is explained best perhaps by example. Consider the example unsorted list of keys from Chapter 7:

6
25
7
2
14
10
9
22
3
14

The first comparison pass has as its objective:

1. Identification of the final position of the first subject key (here 6) in the sorted list.
2. Partitioning of the list into two pieces, one of which contains only key values less than the first subject key, the other of which contains only key values greater than the first subject key.

To achieve this objective, the subject key value first is compared with the last element (here 14) of the list, then the next-to-last element (here 3) until a key value is found that should precede rather than follow the subject key value; such a key then exchanges positions with the subject key value (Fig. 107(a)). The comparison then proceeds *with the same subject* key value from the other direction; 6 is here compared with 25. Because the two are not in proper relative position, an exchange occurs (Fig. 107(b)). Now the comparison switches direction again to bottom up. 6 is compared with 22, with 9, with 10, with 14, then with 2, which is on the "wrong" side of 6. An exchange occurs (Fig. 107(c)). Comparison again switches direction to top down. 6 is compared with 7, which is on the wrong side of 6. An exchange occurs, resulting in a

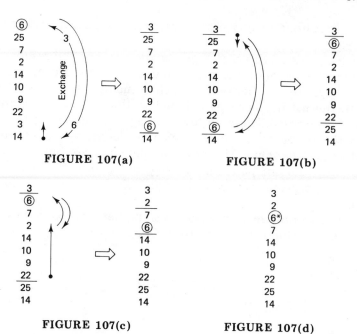

FIGURE 107(a)

FIGURE 107(b)

FIGURE 107(c)

FIGURE 107(d)

completed pass (Fig. 107(d)). At this point 6 is in its final position; everything before 6 is less than 6; everything after 6 is greater than 6. The two resultant partitions can now be sorted independently.

Let's consider the second partition.

```
 7
14
10
 9
22
25
14
```

The comparison pass over this partition shows that 7 is already in proper position. The next partition to consider is

```
14
10
 9
22
25
14
```

The pass proceeds with 14 the subject key (Fig. 107(e)).

As the sizes of the sublist partitions shrink, a simpler sort algorithm, e.g., straight insertion or selection, can be applied to reduce overhead.

FIGURE 107(e)

The analysis of the quicksort algorithm is rather straightforward. Consider first the average case. Assume that the proper final position for the first element K_i is in the middle of the unsorted list (Fig. 108).

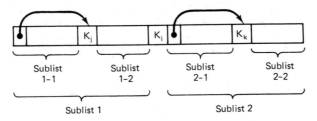

FIGURE 108

The first pass results in partitioning of the list into two sublists, each of approximately $n/2$ keys. Define a "superpass" to be one processing of the entire list. The first superpass requires $n-1$ compares.

The second superpass involves processing both sublists (Fig. 109).

FIGURE 109

Processing of sublist 1 requires approximately $\frac{1}{2}(n-3)$ compares, as does processing of sublist 2. In fact, processing of each superpass requires $\sigma(n)$ compares.

On the average, $\log_2 n$ superpasses are required to sort the list completely. Thus the quicksort requires an average of $\sigma(n\log_2 n)$ comparisons. This is the best performance we have found so far in a sort technique; recall that the linear methods of Chapter 7 all required $\sigma(n^2)$ comparisons.

In some cases, the quicksort requires more than $\log_2 n$ superpasses. In fact in the worst case, n superpasses are required. The worst case arises when the initial list is already sorted. Rather than tending to reduce by half the number of comparisons needed at each superpass, sorting an initially sorted list results in a reduction of merely one comparison at each superpass. The worst case behavior of $\sigma(n^2)$ is as bad as the linear sort algorithms' performances. However, it is possible to arrange that a quicksort never gets near its worst-case behavior. It is a very good sort.

THE HEAPSORT

The quicksort on the average provided improved performance over linear sort algorithms. In this section we consider another important nonlinear sort, the *heapsort*, which performs as well as the quicksort on the average *and* performs better than the quicksort in the worst cases. The heapsort exhibits better all-around performance than any other internal sort that we present; however it is rather complex to program. (Nothing is free!) A properly engineered quicksort is sometimes faster than a well-engineered heapsort and is somewhat less complex to program. It was developed in 1964 by J. W. J. Williams.

The heapsort is based upon use of a special type of binary tree (called a *heap*) to structure the sorting process. The branching structure of the tree keeps the number of comparisons required at $\sigma(n\log_2 n)$.

There are two phases to a heapsort:

1. Creation of the heap.
2. Processing of the heap.

In the first phase, the unsorted keys are placed into a binary tree in such a way that they form a heap. A *heap* of size n is a binary tree of n nodes that adheres to the following two constraints:

1. The binary tree is *almost complete*, i.e., there is an integer k such that:
    (a) every leaf of the tree is at level k or level $k + 1$, and
    (b) if a node has a right descendant at level $k + 1$, then that node also has a left descendant at level $k + 1$.
2. The keys in the nodes are arranged such that for each node i:

    $$K_i \leqslant K_j$$

    where node j is the father of node i.

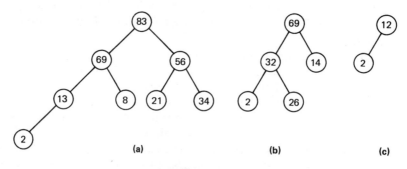

(a) (b) (c)

FIGURE 110(a)

The first constraint means that levels of the heap are filled left to right and that a node is not placed on a new level until the preceding level is full. The binary trees of Fig. 110(a) all qualify as heaps. Note that these trees do not qualify as binary search trees. Why?

The binary trees of Figure 110(b) are *not* heaps.

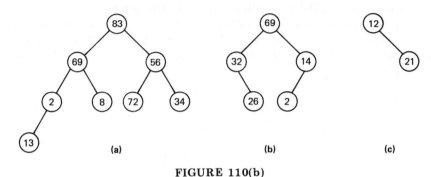

(a)   (b)   (c)

FIGURE 110(b)

The key-placement constraint is violated at nodes 2–13 and 56–72 in tree (a); the almost-complete constraint is violated on level 2 of tree (b); the key-placement constraint and the almost-complete constraint both are violated in tree (c).

Let us consider first the heap-creation phase. In this phase we pass sequentially through the unsorted keys, placing them into a heap. The size of the heap grows as it contains each new key. To create a heap of size i, the ith key (K_i) is placed into an existing heap of size $i-1$. The node first is positioned such that the almost-complete constraint is satisfied. Then the value of K_i is compared with the key value of the node's father. If K_i is greater, then the contents of that new node and the father node are interchanged. This comparison-interchange process is repeated until either the father's key value is not less than K_i or K_i is at the root of the tree. The tree will then qualify to be a heap of size i. More formally, in Pascal, to create a heap of size i by adding a key (here named *newkey*) to a heap (here globally known, named *key* and housed in an array) of size $i-1$ (where $i \geqslant 1$):

```
procedure crheapi (i, newkey:integer);
var father, temp, next : integer;
begin next := i;
      father := next div 2;
      key[next] := newkey;
      while (next <> 1 and key[father] <= key[next])
      do begin {interchange father and son}
             temp := key[father];
             key[father] := key[next];
             key[next] := temp;
```

```
                    {advance up tree}
                    next := father;
                    father := next div 2
          end;
    end;
```

This procedure is called for each addition to the heap.

Fig. 111 illustrates the building of a heap to contain the following list of unsorted keys: 6, 25, 7, 2, 14, 10, 9, 22, 3, 14. A dashed line in the figure indicates that the nodes on the ends of the edge have been interchanged.

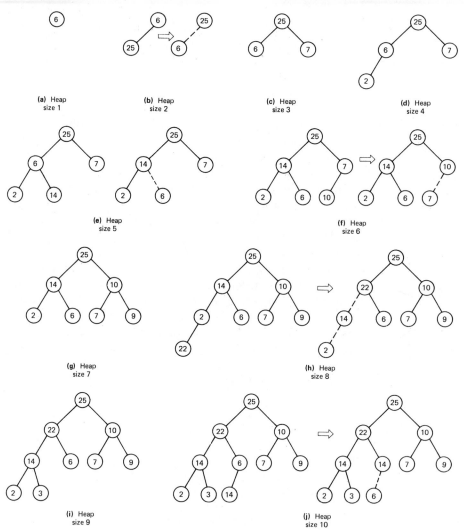

FIGURE 111

This heap would appear in an array as depicted in Fig. 112.

Subscript	1	2	3	4	5	6	7	8	9	10
Key	25	22	10	14	14	7	9	2	3	6

FIGURE 112

Note that node i is the father of nodes $2i$ and $2i + 1$. Thus, because the tree is a heap, $key(i) \leqslant key(i/2)$, where use of integer division is understood.

If the keys were initially in a different order in the unsorted list, then the resulting heap would be different. For example, the unsorted list $9, 14, 10, 22, 7, 25, 3, 14, 6, 2$ results in the heap shown in Fig. 113.

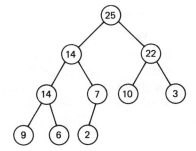

FIGURE 113

Recall that the objective of the heapsort is to generate a sorted list of keys. All we have at this point is a heap of keys. The processing phase of the heapsort traverses the heap in such a way that the sorted keys result. Note that the largest key in a heap is always on top. The processing phase is built upon this fact. After creating the heap, the top element is again removed, and so forth until the resulting heap is of size 0. More formally, a Pascal procedure to process a heap of size n follows. We take advantage of the fact that the heap is still housed in an array called *key* (resulting from use of our *crheapi* procedure); the largest key value is at the top of the heap: $key[1]$. We successively move that value to the end of the array ($key[n]$ the first time through the loop), then adjust the array to be a heap of size $n-1$. At the end, the keys in the array are in sorted order; $key[1]$ is the smallest value and $key[n]$ is the largest value.

```
procedure prheapn;
var father, son, last, waslastkey : integer;
for last := n downto 2
do begin {move root key down to last place}
        waslastkey := key[last];
        key[last] := key[1];
        {adjust tree to heap of size last-1}
        father := 1;
```

```
{find larger of root's sons}
if(last–1 >= 3) and (key[3] > key[2])
then son := 3
else son := 2;
{move keys upward until find place}
{for saved waslastkey}
while (son <= last–1 and key[son] > waslastkey)
do begin key[father] := key[son];
        father := son;
        son := father * 2;
        {find larger of father's sons}
        if(son+1 <= last–1) and (key[son+1] > key[son])
        then son := son+1;
end;
key[father] := waslastkey
end;
```

Fig. 114 illustrates processing of the heap built in Fig. 111. The doubly circled nodes are nodes that have been moved to their final positions in the array and are no longer part of the heap. A dashed line indicates that the nodes at the ends of the edge have been interchanged while adjusting the tree to be a heap again. After the n–1st (here 9th)

FIGURE 114

(f) Heap
size 4

(g) Heap
size 3

(h) Heap
size 2

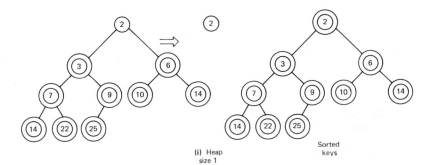

(i) Heap
size 1

Sorted
keys

FIGURE 114 *(Cont.)*

pass, the keys can be read sequentially (1 to n) from the array housing the heap and will be in properly sorted order.

As with the quicksort algorithm, analysis of the heapsort algorithm is rather straightforward. During the heap-creation phase, insertion of the ith key requires $\sigma(\log_2 i)$ comparisons and interchanges even in the worst case, where the keys arrive in already sorted order. Insertion of a key on the kth level can force comparison and interchange with a maximum of k other keys along the branch to the root of the heap. Similarly, during the heap-processing phase, treatment of a heap of size i requires $\sigma(\log_2 i)$ comparisons and interchanges even in the worst case. Movement can be made only along one of the heap's branches.

Thus on the average, the required number of comparisons and interchanges is:

$$\frac{1}{2} \sum_{i=2}^{n} \log_2 i \quad + \quad \frac{1}{2} \sum_{i=2}^{n} \log_2 i$$

which is $(n-1)\log_2 n$. In the worst case, the required number of comparisons and interchanges is:

$$\sum_{i=2}^{n} \log_2 i \quad + \quad \sum_{i=2}^{n} \log_2 i$$

which is $2(n-1)\log_2 n$. The worst case is not much worse than the average case. The heapsort therefore is *guaranteed* to be $\sigma(n\log_2 n)$. For large n, the complexity of the algorithm is outweighed by the sort's efficiency.

THE TOURNAMENT SORT

Another important tree-based sort is the *tournament sort*. This sort is sometimes called the *tree-selection sort* and is attributed to E. H. Friend (1956). The tournament sort process looks like the knock-out or elimination tournament trees typically used to organize sporting (especially tennis, ping-pong, squash) matches. Pair-wise competitions among players proceed until a final winner is established.

The tournament sort is used perhaps more frequently than any other internal sort. Many software vendors incorporate it in their file-sorting packages. We will discuss the workings of the tournament sort here, then consider its incorporation in file sorts in Chapter 18.

Consider again the unsorted list of keys that we have been using in examples: 6, 25, 7, 2, 14, 10, 9, 22, 3, 14, augmented by 8, 12, 1, 30, 13. For expository purposes, assume that space constraints limit us to having only four of these keys in memory at once. The tournament sort pairs these four into two matches (Fig. 115(a)).

```
6 ─┐
   ├─
25 ─┘

7 ─┐
   ├─
2 ─┘
```

FIGURE 115(a)

Assuming that we are performing an ascending sort, the winners of those matches are 6 and 2, which can then be paired for the finals (Fig. 115(b)).

```
6 ─┐6
25 ┘ ├─
7 ─┐2
2 ─┘
```

FIGURE 115(b)

2 wins and is the first key output from the sort (Fig. 115(c)).

```
6 ─┐6
25 ┘ 2 ══>2
7 ─┐2
2 ─┘
```

FIGURE 115(c)

The next pass of the tournament sort will identify the second key of the sorted list. 2 cannot participate in this second pass. We could just play with 7, who would win the first match by default, then would play against 6 (Fig. 115(d)).

```
6 ─┐6
25 ┘ 6 ══> 2, 6
7 ─┐7
* ─┘
```

FIGURE 115(d)

This would result in a pure tree-selection sort. Instead, however, let us bring another candidate into the tournament from our remaining un-sorted list: 14, 10, 9, 22, 3, 14. Then we can play the second pass of the tournament (Fig. 115(e)).

```
6 ─┐6
25 ┘ 6 ══> 2, 6
7 ─┐7
14 ┘
```

FIGURE 115(e)

This replacement policy will enable the sort to generate longer sorted strings than if we did not bring in new players. Our sort now more properly is named a *tree replacement-selection sort*.

The third pass then is shown in Figure 115(f),

$$
\begin{array}{c}
10 \\
24
\end{array}\bigg]10 \qquad
$$

$$
\begin{array}{c}
7 \\
14
\end{array}\bigg]7
$$

$\underline{\quad 7 \quad} \Longrightarrow 2, 6, 7$

FIGURE 115(f)

and the fourth pass is shown in Figure 115(g),

$$
\begin{array}{c}
10 \\
25
\end{array}\bigg]10
$$

$$
\begin{array}{c}
9 \\
14
\end{array}\bigg]9
$$

$\underline{\quad 9 \quad} \Longrightarrow 2, 6, 7, 9$

FIGURE 115(g)

and the fifth pass is shown in Fig. 115(h).

$$
\begin{array}{c}
10 \\
25
\end{array}\bigg]10
$$

$$
\begin{array}{c}
22 \\
14
\end{array}\bigg]14
$$

$\underline{\quad 10 \quad} \Longrightarrow 2, 6, 7, 9, 10$

FIGURE 115(h)

The sixth pass brings 3 into the tree (Fig. 115(i)).

$$
\begin{array}{c}
3 \\
25
\end{array}\bigg]
$$

$$
\begin{array}{c}
22 \\
14
\end{array}\bigg]14
$$

FIGURE 115(i)

If 3 is allowed to play, the sorted sequence of the output list will be broken. To prevent this, the tree replacement-selection sort invokes the following rule:

> If $Key_{new} < Key_{lastout}$
> then Key_{new} is placed into the tree but is temporarily disqualified.

We mark disqualified entrants by asterisks. Thus the sixth pass results in Fig. 115(j).

$$
\begin{array}{c}
*3 \\
25
\end{array}\bigg]25
$$

$$
\begin{array}{c}
22 \\
14
\end{array}\bigg]14
$$

$\underline{\quad 14 \quad} \Longrightarrow 2, 6, 7, 9, 10, 14$

FIGURE 115(j)

The next key of the unsorted list (14) is brought in, and can play since it is not less than 14 (Fig. 115(k)).

```
*3¬
25┘ ]25
        14  ==> 2, 6, 7, 9, 10, 14, 14          FIGURE 115(k)
22¬
14┘ ]14
```

Pass 8 brings in key value 8, which must be disqualified because it is less than 14, but the other entrants can play (Fig. 115(l)).

```
*3¬
25┘ ]25
        22  ==> 2, 6, 7, 9, 10, 14, 14, 22      FIGURE 115(l)
22¬
*8┘ ]22
```

Pass 9 results in Fig. 115(m).

```
*3¬
25┘ ]25
        25  ==> 2, 6, 7, 9, 10, 14, 14, 22, 25   FIGURE 115(m)
*12¬ ]*
*8┘
```

Pass 10 brings in 1 (Fig. 115(n)).

```
*3¬
*1┘ ┐
     ├──
*12¬ ┘                                          FIGURE 115(n)
*8┘
```

Now all entries are disqualified. Note that even though we allowed only four players into the tournament at any given time, the resultant sorted string contains nine keys! We now remove the disqualifications and start again. This time we will generate a *second* sorted string. Pass 10, then, is Fig. 115(o).

```
3¬
1┘ ]1      2, 6, 7, 9, 10, 14, 14, 22, 25;
        1  ==>  1                               FIGURE 115(o)
12¬
8┘ ]8
```

Pass 11 brings in 30 (Fig. 115(p)).

```
3¬
30┘ ]3      2, 6, 7, 9, 10, 14, 14, 22, 25;
        3  ==>  1, 3                             FIGURE 115(p)
12¬
8┘ ]8
```

Pass 12 is Fig. 115(q).

$$13 \rceil 13$$
$$30 \rfloor \quad \rceil 8 \implies \begin{array}{l} 2, 6, 7, 9, 10, 14, 14, 22, 25; \\ 1, 3, 8 \end{array}$$
$$12 \rceil 8$$
$$8 \rfloor$$

FIGURE 115(q)

Now the input list is empty, so we must enter placeholders into the tree and allow the tournament to be played to competition. Pass 13 results in Fig. 115(r).

$$13 \rceil 13$$
$$30 \rfloor \quad \rceil 12 \implies \begin{array}{l} 2, 6, 7, 9, 10, 14, 14, 22, 25; \\ 1, 3, 8, 12 \end{array}$$
$$12 \rceil 12$$
$$* \rfloor$$

FIGURE 115(r)

Passes 14 and 15 empty the tree.

This example has resulted in two sorted lists:

$$2, 6, 7, 9, 10, 14, 14, 22, 25;$$
$$1, 3, 8, 12, 13, 30$$

These two strings can now be merged in a straightforward manner to form a single sorted output string. The first elements of each string are compared and the one with the lower value is output and removed from further consideration. This simple *two-way merge* can be programmed as follows. Arrays *key1* and *key2* hold the initially sorted lists; array *merged* holds the resultant merged list. *n1* and *n2* are subscripts of the next element to be considered in *key1* and *key2* respectively. *size1* and *size2* are the number of elements in *key1* and *key2* respectively. *next* is the subscript showing the place for the next element in the merged list.

```
begin
        next := 1;
        n1 := 1;
        n2 := 1;
        while (n1 <= size1) and (n2 <= size2)
        do begin if (key1[n1] <= key2[n2])
                    then begin merged[next] := key1[n1];
                            n1 := n1 + 1
                        end;
                    else begin merged[next] := key2[n2];
                            n2 := n2 + 1
                        end;
                    next := next + 1
        end;
        while (n1 <= size1) {fill with remaining list 1}
        do begin merged[next] := key1[n1];
                n1 := n1 + 1;
```

```
                next := next + 1
        end;
        while (n2 <= size2) {fill with remaining list 2}
        do begin merged[next] := key2[n2];
                        n2 := n2 + 1;
                        next := next + 1
        end;
end;
```

The example was arranged such that two sorted lists conveniently resulted. In reality, many sorted lists may result. These can be merged by a sequence of two-way merges or by higher order merges, say three or four lists at a time.

How well does the tournament sort perform? Consider first the case in which the tournament tree is spacious enough to hold all n keys to be sorted. To identify the first winner,

$$\frac{n}{2} + \frac{n}{4} + \ldots + \frac{n}{2^k} =$$

comparisons must be made, where k is the number of levels in the tournament tree. $k = \log_2 n$. After this initial setup of the tree, k comparisons are required to adjust the tree and identify the next winner. Thus the number of comparisons required to process the entire tree is $\sigma(n\log_2 n)$. Note that only one string results when the entire field of players fits into the tournament tree.

Consider now the case in which the tournament tree can hold only p keys at any given time, $p << n$. Each pass through the tree now requires $\log_2 p$ comparisons to identify the next winner. Thus $n\log_2 p$ comparisons are required to generate the ordered sublists.

These sublists then must be merged. It can be shown that the expected length of each of the sorted lists resulting from the tournament sort with replacement of entries is $2*p$. (The interested reader should see Knuth's snowplow explanation of this fact in *The Art of Computer Programming, Vol. 3, Sorting and Searching*, from Addison-Wesley, 1973.) The n keys are thus allocated to $n/2p$ lists. Use of a two-way merge requires $\log_2 (n/2p)$ passes. For example, if $n = 256$ and $p = 8$, then the expected number of sublists is 16. Merging 16 lists, 2 at a time, requires $\log_2 16$, i.e., 4, passes (Fig. 116). Each pass requires n compares. Thus

$$n \log_2 (n/2p)$$

compares are required in the merge phase. Overall, then, on the average, the required number of comparisons is:

$$n \log_2 p + n \log_2 (n/2p)$$

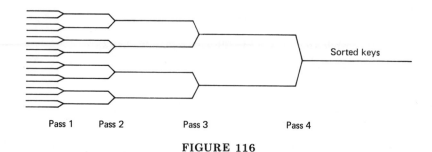

FIGURE 116

which is $\sigma(n \log_2 n)$ for $n >> p$. We will return to use of the tournament sort for very large n and relatively small p in the later chapter on file-sorting techniques.

SUMMARY

This chapter introduced several good techniques for searching and sorting. The *binary search* technique was discussed as a method of obtaining $\sigma(\log_2 n)$ search performance from a linear list. The prerequisite for applicability of the binary search technique is that the records in the list must be in sorted order by the search key value. The search proceeds by successive probes into the list; each probe eliminates one-half the remaining entries from further consideration. The binary search technique was presented in both recursive and iterative versions.

The *partition-exchange sort*, also known as *Hoare's quicksort*, was then presented as a method of obtaining good performance in a sort. During each comparison pass of the quicksort, keys are exchanged in such a way that when the pass completes, the list has been partitioned and the two sublists thereafter can be treated independently of each other. The quicksort requires an average of $\sigma(n\log_2 n)$ comparisons, but in the worst case requires $\sigma(n^2)$ comparisons.

The *heapsort* represents an improvement in performance over the quicksort; it guarantees $\sigma(n\log_2 n)$ comparisons, even in the worst case. The heapsort proceeds in two phases. In the first phase, the subject keys are structured into a heap, which is a special case of binary tree. In the second phase, the heap is processed and linearized in such a way that a sorted list of keys results.

The *tournament sort* (also known as *tree-selection sort*), and a variation, the *tree replacement-selection sort*, were presented as important techniques for sorting large collections of data. Keys are entered into a tournament tree and are compared in a pairwise manner to generate a sorted string. If the tree is not large enough to contain the entire collection of keys, then the sort generates several sorted strings.

The strings then must be merged to produce the final sorted list. With replacement-selection, the sort of p keys generates an expected sorted-string length of $2*p$. This property makes the tournament sort a popular selection for the internal phase of external file sorts. The tournament sort, like the other tree-oriented sorts, requires $\sigma(n\log_2 n)$ comparisons on the average.

For further details of sorting techniques, the reader should consult:

Knuth, D. E. *The Art of Computer Programming, Vol. 3., Sorting and Searching.* Reading, Mass.: Addison-Wesley Publishing Co., 1973.

Lorin, H. *Sorting and Sort Systems.* Reading, Mass.: Addison-Wesley Publishing Co., 1975.

Terms

binary search
$\sigma(n^2)$
$\sigma(n\log_2 n)$
partition-exchange sort

quicksort
tournament sort
tree-selection sort

Review Exercises

1. The text discussed the binary search technique for application to sorted linear lists. Develop and analyze a ternary search technique.

2. The text algorithms for the binary search assumed that the linear list was housed in an array with subscript range from 1 to n. Modify the algorithms to cope with subscript range a to b, where a and b need not be positive integers.

3. The text algorithms for the binary search assumed that the linear list was housed in an array. What are the relative advantages and disadvantages of applying the binary search technique to a linear list housed in a linked list?

4. Explain the procedural improvements that distinguish sorts that require $\sigma(n\log_2 n)$ operations from those that require $\sigma(n^2)$ operations.

5. Graph n^2 and $n\log_2 n$ (or n and $\log_2 n$) versus n and convince yourself of the extent of improvement achieved in nonlinear sorting.

6. Rewrite the algorithms given in this chapter for descending rather than ascending sorts.

7. Write a program to perform a tree-selection sort.

8. Write a program to perform a tree replacement-selection sort.

9. Write a program to perform the quicksort. Run it with a variety of sets of input data and compare the expected and worst-case performance.

10. Write a program to perform the heapsort. Run it with the same sets of input data used in exercise 9 and compare the expected and worst-case performance.

11. Develop a sort algorithm that guarantees $\sigma(n\log_3 n)$ performance. Characterize a sort algorithm that would guarantee $\sigma(n\log_k n)$ performance.

12. Are there any sort algorithms that produce $\sigma(\log_2 n^2)$ performance?

13. Develop guidelines for the effects of various relative values of n and p on tree replacement-selection sort performance. How should p be selected? What happens if $p = n$? What happens if p is nearly n? What happens if $p = 1$?

14. Consider a bidirectional linked list of data elements which has been implemented using pointer variables. When would you use a sequential search technique to find a particular element?

15. Analyze each of the sort algorithms presented in this chapter for stability. If a sort algorithm is not stable, how can it be modified to make it stable?

16. Read Knuth's excellent work on sorting and searching.

CHAPTER 11

M-Way Search Trees
and B-Trees

In this chapter we discuss two types of trees. Chapter 8 began our consideration of nonlinear data structures by introducing the binary tree as a special, nice case of the general data type tree. Chapter 9 covered a special case of binary tree—the binary search tree—and special cases of that special case—the AVL and BB trees. In this chapter we turn to the other direction and introduce a generalization of the binary search tree— the m-way search tree. In concept the m-way search tree is similar to the binary search tree; in topology the m-way search tree is a general tree, not a binary tree. A B-tree of order m is a relaxation of a completely balanced m-way search tree and is used instead of a completely balanced m-way search tree for the same reasons that an AVL or BB tree is used instead of a completely balanced binary search tree. B-trees are of outstanding importance in data management and file organization. Operations on B-trees are presented in this chapter; analysis of the performance of these operations shows why B-trees are used so widely.

BINARY SEARCH TREES AS INDEXES

Before introducing this new type of tree, let us reconsider the binary search tree which was discussed in Chapter 9. Recall that the nodes of a binary search tree are arranged in such a way that a search for a particular key value proceeds down one branch of the tree. The sought key value is compared with the key value of the tree's root: if it is less than the root value, the search proceeds down the left subtree; if it is greater than the root value, the search proceeds down the right subtree. The same logic is applied at each node encountered until the search is satisfied or it is determined that the sought key is not included in the tree.

To most applications, a key value does not stand alone. Rather the key value is associated with information fields to form a record. In general, storing these information fields in the binary search tree would make for a very large tree. In order to speed searches and to reduce the tree size, the information fields of records commonly are stored separate from the key values. These records are organized into files and are stored on secondary storage devices such as rotating disks. (We will discuss file organization techniques in detail later in this book.) The connection between a key value in the binary search tree and the corresponding record in the file is made by housing a pointer to the record with the key value. Thus the node structure for a binary search tree may be defined as follows in Pascal:

```
type nodeptr = ↑nodetype;
     recptr = ↑rectype;
     nodetype = record
                     key : integer;
                     infoptr : recptr;
                     left : nodeptr;
                     right : nodeptr
                end;
```

where *rectype* is defined appropriately for the application. The *key* field is defined here as integer data type; it could be of other types, of course.

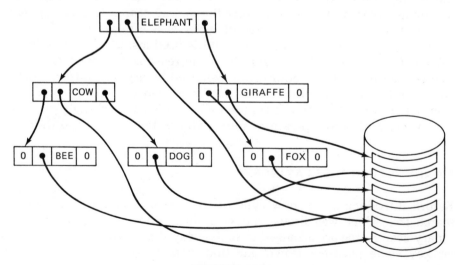

FIGURE 117

Fig. 117 shows the binary search tree of Fig. 104 with pointers included to the data records. At this time we will not concern ourselves with the actual location of those records on primary or secondary storage. Processing of this augmented binary search tree is the same as was presented in Chapter 9. When a search terminates successfully, the *infoptr* may be followed to find the data associated with the sought key.

This augmentation of the binary search tree to include pointers (i.e., addresses) out of the structure to data records qualifies the tree to be an index. An *index* is a collection of key value and address pairs; the primary purpose of an index is to facilitate access to a collection of records. An index is said to be a *dense index* if it contains a key value-address pair for each record in the collection. An index that is not dense is sometimes called a *sparse index*. There are many ways to organize an index; the augmented binary search tree is one approach.

If a binary search tree can be used as an index, then so can an AVL tree or a BB tree. As shown in Chapter 9, the maximum path length through an AVL tree is $o(\log_2 n)$. Thus use of an AVL tree to house a dense index to n records would result in a maximum search length of $o(\log_2 n)$ to locate the address of the sought record. Actually the maximum search length of an AVL tree is $1.40 \log_2 n$; the worst case to find a key when $n = 10$ then is about four comparisons through the tree.

DEFINITIONS: M-WAY SEARCH TREES

The performance of an index can be enhanced significantly by increasing the branching factor of the index tree. Rather than binary branching, m-way ($m > 2$) branching can be used. For expository purposes, we ignore for the moment pointers out of the structure to data records and consider only the internal structure of the tree. An m-*way search tree* is a tree in which each node has out-degree $< = m$. When an m-way search tree is not empty, it has the following properties.

1. Each node of the tree has the structure shown in Fig. 118.

FIGURE 118

where the $P_0, P_1, \ldots, P_n$ are pointers to the node's subtrees and the $K_0, \ldots, K_{n-1}$ are key values. The requirement that each node have out-degree $< =m$ forces $n < =m-1$.

2. The key values in a node are in ascending order:

$$K_i < K_{i+1}$$

for $i=0, \ldots n-2$.

3. All key values in nodes of the subtree pointed to by P_i are less than the key value K_i:

$$i=0, \ldots, n-1.$$

4. All key values in nodes of the subtree pointed to by P_n are greater than the key value K_{n-1}.

5. The subtrees pointed to by the P_i, $i=0, \ldots, n$ are also m-way search trees.

Note that the arrangement of key values in nodes is analogous to their arrangement in binary search trees. A five-way search tree has a maximum of five pointers out of each node, i.e., $n <= 4$. Some nodes of the tree may contain fewer than five pointers.

Fig. 119 illustrates a three-way search tree. Only the key values and the non-null subtree pointers are shown.

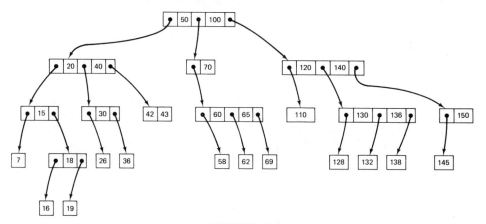

FIGURE 119

In the figure, leaf nodes have been depicted as containing just key values. Each internal node of the search tree has the structure depicted in Fig. 118, here with a maximum of three subtree pointers.

Each key-pointer pair (K_i, P_i) is in practice usually a triplet P_i, K_i, A_i where A_i is the address of the data record associated with key value K_i. Incorporating these addresses in Fig. 119 just would have confused the issue of the structure of the tree. Thus we can define the node type for an m-way search tree as follows in Pascal:

```
type nodeptr = ↑nodetype;
     recptr = ↑rectype;
     n1, keytype = integer;
     nodetype = record
                    n : integer
                 keyptrs : array [0. . n1] of record
                              ptr : nodeptr;
                              key : keytype;
                              addr : recptr
                           end;
                 keyptrn : nodeptr
              end;
```

Again the *key*'s type need not be *integer*; $n \leqslant m - 1$ and $n1 = n - 1$.

SEARCHING AN M-WAY SEARCH TREE

The process of searching for a key value in an *m*-way search tree is a straightforward extension of the process of searching for a key value in a binary search tree. A recursive version of the search algorithm follows. The variable *skey* contains the sought key value; *r* initially points to the root of the tree. The search tree is assumed to be global, with *var node: nodetype*.

```
procedure search(skey:keytype;var r:nodeptr,foundptr:recptr);
var i:0 . . n;
begin if (r=nil)
         then foundptr := nil;
         else begin i := 0;
                 while (i < n and skey > node.key[i])
                 do i := i + 1;
                 if (i=node.n and skey > node.key[n-1])
                 then search(skey,node.keyptrn,foundptr)
                 else if(i < n and skey=node.key[i])
                      then foundptr := node.addr[i]
                      else {found first node.key[i] > skey}
                           search(skey,node.ptr[i],foundptr);
              end;
      end;
```

The maximum search length is the height of the tree. In order to minimize this height for a tree containing *n* keys, the tree should be as bushy as possible. A three-way tree can provide shorter path lengths than can a two-way tree for the same set of keys. In general, the higher the order of branching of the tree, the shorter is the maximum search length. Each node visitation causes a selection from among a greater number of possible branches.

Consider an m-way tree with height h. The maximum number of nodes in this tree is:

$$\sum_{i=0}^{h-1} m^i$$

which is $\dfrac{m^h-1}{m-1}$. Each node carries a maximum of $m-1$ key values. Thus the maximum number of keys in the tree is m^h-1.

Turning the argument around, an m-way tree of n keys has a minimum height of

$$\lceil \log_m(n+1) \rceil.$$

The maximum search length of an optimal m-way tree of n keys, then, is $o(\log_m n)$. Setting $m=2$ gives the expected results for optimal binary search trees.

In order to have an m-way search tree of n keys have a maximum height of h, m must be at least $(n+1)^{1/h}$. For example, to ensure a maximum path length of 4 with 255 keys, the tree must have at least four-way branching; to ensure a maximum path length of 4 with 65,535 keys, the tree must have at least 16-way branching.

The extent of branching is not the only factor that determines the performance of an m-way search tree. As we discussed for binary search trees, performance can be improved by keeping the tree balanced. Note that the definition of an m-way search tree does not ensure that each interior node of the tree will have m non-null pointers to subtrees. The tree of Fig. 119 could exhibit improved search performance if it were balanced. As we discovered for binary search trees, keeping an m-way search tree completely balanced may not be worth the effort. Rather, it may be sufficient to constrain the extent to which we allow the tree to deviate from complete balance. Just as AVL trees enjoy more widely spread use than do their completely balanced binary search tree counterparts, so are almost-balanced B-trees more popular than completely balanced m-way search trees.

DEFINITIONS: B-TREES

The basic B-tree structure was discovered by R. Bayer and E. McCreight (1970) of Boeing Scientific Research Labs and has grown to become one of the most popular techniques for organizing an index structure. Many variations on the basic B-tree have been developed; we cover the basic structure here, then introduce some of the variations in the next chapter.

A *B-tree of order m* is an *m*-way search tree with the following properties:

1. Each node of the tree, except for the root and the leaves, has at least ⌈½*m*⌉ subtrees and no more than *m* subtrees.
2. The root of the tree has at least two subtrees, unless it is itself a leaf.
3. All leaves of the tree are on the same level.

The first constraint ensures that each node of the tree is at least half full. The second constraint forces the tree to branch early. The third constraint keeps the tree nearly balanced.

It should be noted that some authors use a different notation than we do. You may see a B-tree of order *m* defined as a *d*-way search tree in which each node bears a minimum of *m* keys and *m* + 1 pointers and a maximum of 2*m* keys and 2*m* + 1 pointers; here *d* = 2*m* + 1. We will *not* use this notation.

Fig. 120 illustrates a B-tree of order 3 that contains the keys of the three-way search tree of Fig. 119. Not shown for each node is an indicator of the number of non-null subtree pointers that it contains. The leaves need not have space for those pointers. B-trees of higher order are certainly more interesting but become difficult to draw. Each node of a B-tree of order *m* has the same structure as a node of an *m*-way search tree. We have again omitted here pointers containing the addresses of the records corresponding to each of the key values. Each node has been marked with a letter to facilitate our later references to this example tree.

The size of a B-tree of order *m* and its search path lengths may be larger than for the optimal *m*-way search tree for the same collection of keys. However, as we will see in the next section, maintaining a B-tree is significantly easier than maintaining an optimal *m*-way search tree. The reasons for using a B-tree of order *m* rather than an optimal *m*-way search tree are the same as the reasons for using an AVL (or BB) tree instead of a completely balanced binary search tree.

OPERATIONS ON B-TREES

The fundamental operations on a B-tree are direct search, sequential search, insertion and deletion of key values. In this section we consider each of these forms of manipulation and analyze the performance of B-trees under these types of activities.

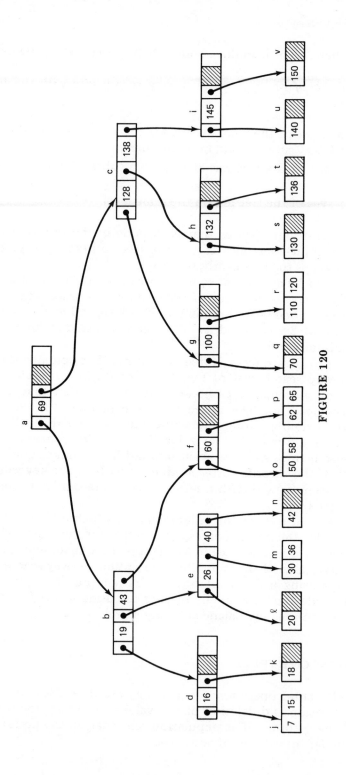

FIGURE 120

The search for a particular key value in a B-tree follows the same procedure as does the direct search of an m-way search tree. How well does a B-tree search perform? Consider first the question of the minimum number of keys in a B-tree of order m with height h. By definition, the root of a B-tree has at least two sons. Each of these nodes has at least $\lceil \frac{1}{2}m \rceil$ sons, and so forth down the tree to level $h-2$ (the leaves are on level $h-1$). Thus the tree must contain at least

$$1 + 2 + \sum_{i=3}^{h-2} 2*\lceil \tfrac{1}{2}m \rceil^{\,i-2}$$

interior nodes and at least $2*\lceil \frac{1}{2}m \rceil^{\,h-2}$ leaves. Each interior node except the root must contain at least $\lceil \frac{1}{2}m \rceil -1$ keys; the root and each leaf must contain at least 1 key. Thus the minimum number of keys in the tree is:

$$n \geqslant 1 + (2 + \sum_{i=3}^{h-2} 2*\lceil \tfrac{1}{2}m \rceil^{\,i-2})\,(\lceil \tfrac{1}{2}m \rceil -1) + 2\lceil \tfrac{1}{2}m \rceil^{\,h-2}$$

which reduces to:

$$n + 1 \geqslant 2*\lceil \tfrac{1}{2}m \rceil^{\,h-2}$$

That is, the maximum height of the tree is

$$h \leqslant 2 + \log_{\lceil \frac{1}{2}m \rceil} (\tfrac{n+1}{2}) \text{ for } m > 2$$

Recall that the leaves will all appear on a maximum level of $h-1$. Since the tree's height determines the maximum search length, we now know that the B-tree performs very well for direct searches. For $n = 2*10^7$ and $m = 200, h \leqslant 5$. For $n = 10^6$ and $m = 50, h \leqslant 6$.

Fig. 121 graphs the upper bound on height (h) versus the order of the tree (m) for $n = 2*10^7$.

A B-tree can also support sequential access to the key values it contains. The tree can be traversed sequentially by visiting the nodes in essentially in-order. Note that each internal node will be visited more than once since it contains several keys. The subtree associated with each key must be visited before the next key of the node is accessed. In fact, sequential access to the keys of a B-tree does not exhibit very good performance, especially when the memory requirements to trace the paths through the tree are considered. However, we will see later in this book that B-treelike structures have been processed sequentially in *many* data processing environments where both direct and sequential access to indexes have been required.

The insertion and deletion algorithms for B-trees are somewhat more interesting. Like operations on AVL and BB trees, operations on

FIGURE 121

B-trees must preserve the balanced character of the data structure. Recall that insertion or deletion in an AVL or BB tree may force rotation to keep the tree in balance. The algorithms for keeping a B-tree balanced are conceptually simpler than are those rather complex rotation algorithms.

Consider first insertions of several new keys—say 22, 41, 59, 57, 54, 33, 75, 124, 122, 123—into the B-tree of Fig. 120. The key value 22 should reside in node ℓ; that node has space enough for another key, so it simply is inserted. (Fig. 121(a))

$$\ell \qquad\qquad \ell$$
$$\boxed{20\ \ \ } + 22 \implies \boxed{20\ |\ 22}$$
FIGURE 121(a)

Similarly, key value 41, which should reside in node n, may be inserted there because there is space available (Fig. 121(b)).

$$n \qquad\qquad n$$
$$\boxed{42\ \ \ } + 41 \implies \boxed{41\ |\ 42}$$
FIGURE 121(b)

Note that the proper sequence of key values must be maintained; key value 42 is shifted right to make room for key value 41.

Key value 59 should reside in node o. However, node o already contains the maximum allowable number of key values for a B-tree of order 3. Whenever a key needs to be inserted in a node that is already full, a *split* occurs. The one node becomes two nodes; half of its keys go in one of the two nodes and half in the other. The remaining value is moved up to the parent node. The parent node also be must adjusted to include a pointer to the spawned node. Here, nodes f and o are both modified (Fig. 121(c)).

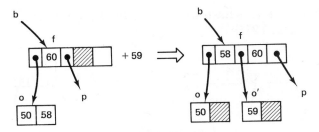

FIGURE 121(c)

Now, insertion of 57, the next key value, proceeds by simply placing 57 in node *o* (Fig. 121(d)).

FIGURE 121(d) [image of node o with 50, +57 ⟹ node o with 50 57]

Key value 54 also should be placed in node *o*, but node *o* is again full. The same splitting algorithm is applied (Fig. 121(e)).

[image of node o 50 57, +54 ⟹ node o 50, node o″ 57, +54 into the parent f]

FIGURE 121(e)

However, the parent node *f* is also full and cannot accommodate another key value and a pointer to node *o*″. The splitting algorithm is again applied, this time to node *f* (Fig. 121(f)).

FIGURE 121(f)

Again, the parent node *b* happens to be full and cannot accommodate another key value and a pointer to *f*'. The splitting procedure is now applied to node *b* (Fig. 121(g)).

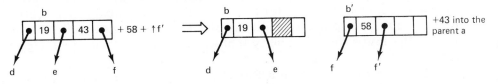

FIGURE 121(g)

The parent node *a* does have space available for another key value and a pointer to *b'* (Fig. 121(h)).

FIGURE 121(h)

Usually, especially with higher-order trees, a parent node has space available for another key value and pointer. In the worst case, the splitting procedure must be carried all the way up the tree to the root. The tree then increases in height by one level, lengthening the expected search length by one. Insertion of the next four keys in our example sequence—33, 75, 124, and 122—can be accommodated easily. Insertion of 123, however, causes the B-tree to grow one level in height. The resultant tree is shown in Fig. 122. You should work through these insertions to verify your understanding of node splitting. Note that the tree can now accommodate numerous insertions without node splitting, since each prior split opened space for insertions.

How frequently does node splitting occur? In the worst case, inserting a new node causes splitting to percolate up the entire tree, splitting $h-1$ nodes, where h is the tree's height before the insertion. However, the total number of splits that have occurred when the tree has p nodes is $p-2$. The first split adds two new nodes; all other splits produce one new node apiece. Each node has a minimum of $\lceil \frac{1}{2}m \rceil - 1$ keys, except the root, which must have at least one key. Thus a tree with p nodes contains at least

$$1 + (p-1)(\lceil \tfrac{1}{2}m \rceil - 1)$$

keys. The probability that a split is required upon insertion of a key value then is less than

$$\frac{p-2}{1 + (p-1)(\lceil \tfrac{1}{2}m \rceil - 1)} \qquad \frac{\text{(splits)}}{\text{keys}}$$

which is less than 1 split per $\lceil \frac{1}{2}m \rceil - 1$ key insertions (since $1/(p-2)$ approaches 0 for large p and $(p-1)/(p-2)$ is approximately 1). For $m = 10$, the split probability is .25; for $m = 100$, the split probability is .0204; for $m = 200$, the split probability is .0101. The higher the order of the B-tree, the lower the probability that key insertion will cause a node to split.

Deletion of a key from a B-tree is only slightly more complicated than is insertion. In order to keep the B-tree a B-tree, two nodes need

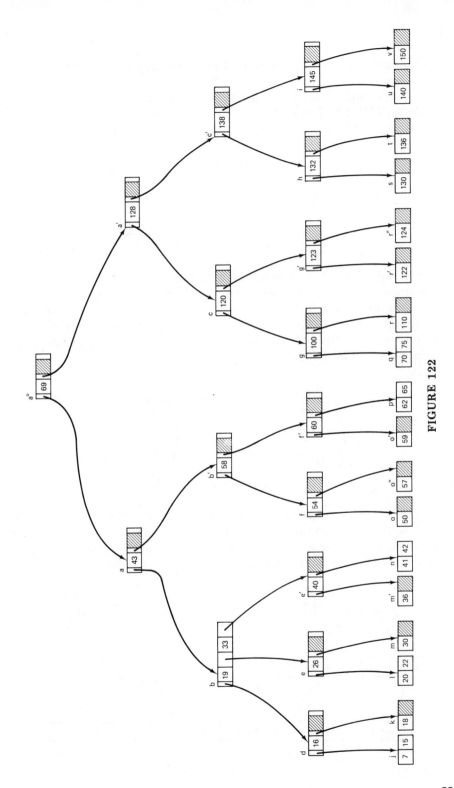

FIGURE 122

to be merged when one node would have fewer than the minimum required keys and pointers.

Consider deletion of the following sequence of keys from the B-tree of Fig. 122: 65, 7, 40, 16.

Removal of key value 65 from node *p* is easy (Fig. 123(a)).

$$\text{p} \qquad \qquad \text{p}$$
$$\boxed{62 \;|\; 65} \; -65 \implies \boxed{62 \;|\; \text{▨}} \qquad \textbf{FIGURE 123(a)}$$

Removal of key value 7 from node *j* is also easy (Fig. 123(b)).

$$\text{j} \qquad \qquad \text{j}$$
$$\boxed{7 \;|\; 15} \; -7 \implies \boxed{15 \;|\; \text{▨}} \qquad \textbf{FIGURE 123(b)}$$

Note that 15 has been shifted left to maintain proper key sequencing.

Removal of key value 40 leaves node *e'* with 2 pointers but no keys. Some key must be found to place in *e'* so that the minimum key requirement is met. A proper key value is the leftmost key of the subtree pointed to by the pointer after the deleted key; here that key value is 41 in node *n* (Fig. 123(c)).

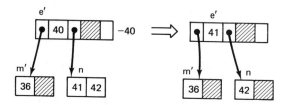

FIGURE 123(c)

Sometimes keys are distributed in such a way that nodes must be merged to maintain compliance with B-tree constraints. Deletion of 16 from node *d* gives us such a case. Not only are *d* and *e* merged, but *j* and *k* are also merged and ancestor node *b* is also affected (Fig. 123(d)).

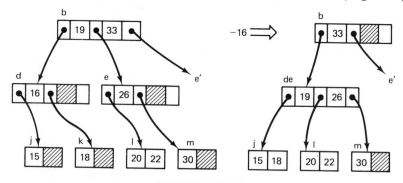

FIGURE 123(d)

If a merge percolates all the way to the highest level, then a new root is formed and the height of the B-tree is decreased by 1. Like node splitting, the probability of node merging decreases as the order of the B-tree increases.

Understanding of the insertion and deletion operations on B-trees will increase your comprehension of why B-trees are defined as they are. Splitting of a full node results in two nodes that both meet the requirement for a minimum number of keys and pointers. A subminimal and a minimally loaded node fit together nicely without violating the constraint on maximum number of keys and pointers when two nodes must be merged. The key arrangement makes it easy to find the prior or next key from any key in the tree. You should "play tree-manager" and perform various insertions and deletions yourself.

SUMMARY

This chapter began with a discussion of the use of binary search trees as indexes into larger collections of data. The performance of an index can be enhanced significantly by increasing the branching factor of an index tree. Rather than using binary branching, m-way ($m > 2$) branching can be used. This discussion motivated our introduction of the data type *m-way search tree*, which is a generalization of the binary search tree. In general, the higher the order of branching of a search tree, the shorter is the maximum search length. Each node visitation forces a selection from among a greater number of possible branches.

A special case of m-way search tree, the *B-tree of order m* was introduced as a data type that approximates a completely balanced m-way search tree. The basic operations on B-trees—direct search, sequential search, insertion, and deletion—were covered. The worst case direct search length in a B-tree of order m containing n keys was shown to be $\sigma(\log_{\lceil \frac{1}{2}m \rceil} \frac{n+1}{2})$. Although B-trees support sequential access to key values, they do not perform well in this capacity. Insertion and deletion algorithms require procedures to keep the B-tree in conformance with B-tree constraints. Insertion of a new key may require splitting of a node into two nodes. In the worst case, this splitting percolates all the way to the root of the tree, causing the tree to grow one level in height. The probability that a key insertion will cause a split in a B-tree of order m is less than 1 in $\lceil \frac{1}{2}m \rceil - 1$. Deletion of a key may require shifting of other key values within the tree and merging of nodes. If a merge percolates all the way to the tree's root, the height of the tree is decreased by one. As with node splitting, the probability of node merging decreases linearly as the order of the B-tree increases.

B-trees have been the subject of much interest, both to practitioners and researchers. They are the most widely used data structure for organizing indexes. We will encounter them several more times in this book in discussions of memory management and file processing. Numerous variations on the basic B-tree have been developed, and several of these are introduced in the next chapter.

For further details of B-trees, you are urged to peruse R. Bayer and C. McCreight's "Organization and maintenance of large ordered indexes," in *Acta Informatica*, Vol. 1, No. 3, 1972. Illustrative examples of B-tree insertion and deletion procedures are given in D. Comer's "The ubiquitous B-tree," in the *ACM Computing Surveys*, Vol. 11, No. 2, June 1979.

Terms

AVL tree
BB tree
binary search tree
B-tree

dense index
index
m-way search tree
sparse index

Review Exercises

1. What is the difference between a binary search tree and an *m*-way search tree?
2. A binary search tree is a two-way search tree. True or false?
3. An AVL tree is to a binary search tree as a _____ is to an *m*-way search tree. (Fill in the blank.)
4. A full node in a 16-way search tree contains how many key values? How many pointers?
5. A node in a 16-way search tree contains a minimum of how many key values? How many pointers?
6. What is the maximum number of nodes in a three-way tree with height 5? What is the maximum number of key values in this tree?
7. What is the maximum number of nodes in a four-way tree with height 5? What is the maximum number of key values in this tree? (Compare with exercise 6.)
8. What is the minimum height of a three-way tree with 242 key values? With 1023 key values?
9. What is the minimum height of a four-way tree with 242 key values? With 1023 key values? (Compare with exercise 8.)

10. A full node in a B-tree of order 16 contains how many key values? How many pointers? (Compare with exercise 4.)

11. A node in a B-tree of order 16 contains a minimum of how many key values? How many pointers? (Compare with exercise 5.)

12. What is the probability that a key insertion will cause a split in a B-tree of order 16?

13. What is the number of nodes that need to be visited in the worst case to find a key in a B-tree of order 3 with 242 keys? With 1023 keys?

14. What is the number of nodes that need to be visited in the worst case to find a key in a B-tree of order 16 with n keys?

15. Write an algorithm for traversing a B-tree of order m in in-order.

16. Perform a sequence of key insertions and deletions on the B-tree of Fig. 120.

17. Write a program that builds a B-tree of order 3 from an input sequence of key values.

18. Write a program to traverse a B-tree of order 3 in sequence by key value.

19. Write a program to locate a given key value in a B-tree of order 3.

20. Write a program to maintain a B-tree of order 3. Be able to accommodate key insertions and deletions.

CHAPTER 12

B*-Trees, B⁺-Trees, and Tries

This short chapter wraps up our discussion of the tree data structure. Two variations on B-trees—the B*-tree and the B⁺-tree—are introduced. These variants are used quite frequently, but many others have been proposed and appear in practice. Discussion of another type of m-way tree—the trie (pronounced trēe)—closes the chapter.

B*-TREES: SPECIAL B-TREES

The B*-tree data structure was identified by Knuth in his tome on searching and sorting (1973) as one of several possible variations on the basic B-tree. Recall that insertion and deletion activity in a B-tree may introduce overhead to keep the tree in conformance with B-tree constraints. Insertion of a new key value may cause a node to split into two nodes, each containing half of the original keys. This splitting activity may percolate all the way to the root of the tree, in which case the tree's height (and maximum search length) increases by 1. Deletion of a key may cause a node to have fewer than the minimum required number of keys. In this case keys need to be shifted around and/or two nodes may be merged. This overhead needed to keep a B-tree balanced is the price paid for the very good direct search performance that a B-tree provides.

One motivation for the multitude of B-tree variations that have been proposed has been to reduce the overhead required to accommodate insertions and deletions. The other primary motivation has been to improve the direct search performance.

A *B*-tree* is a B-tree in which each node is at least two-thirds full instead of at least half full. A basic idea of the B*-tree is to reduce the frequency of node splitting. When a node becomes full, rather than its being split, a redistribution scheme takes keys and pointers from the full node and places them into a brother node.

Consider, for example, the portion of a B-tree of order m shown in Fig. 124.

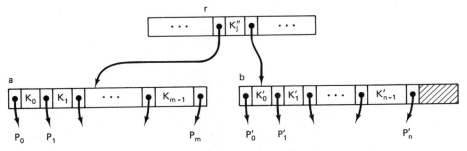

FIGURE 124

Assume that insertion of a key value into the tree causes node a to overflow with one too many key-pointer pairs. For the sake of argument, assume that the extra pair is K_m, P_{m+1}, where $K_m < K_j''$. This insertion can be accommodated by shifting key values from node a to node b through node r. Note that the separator key value in node r must be changed to reflect the rotation.

The keys may be redistributed in several ways. One approach is to place half the total number of keys, here $m + 1 + n$, in each node a and b, as shown in Fig. 125.

> where $c = \lfloor (m+1+n)/2 \rfloor$
> and key K_{c+1} is the middle key of the
> collection $K_0, K_1, \ldots K_{m-1}, K_m, K_j'', K_0', K_1', \ldots, K_{n-1}'$
> from nodes a, r, and b.

The free space from brother node b has been used to accommodate the overflow from node a. Moreover, that free space has been redistributed between nodes a and b such that each now has half of it.

Consider the situation shown in Fig. 126(a). Insertion of key value 24 into node a would cause overflow. However, the insertion could be accommodated by shifting key values from node a to node b through node r. The total number of keys involved is 7 (18, 20, 22, 24, 26, 33, 35). About half (i.e., $\lfloor 7/2 \rfloor$) of the keys (18, 20, 22) would be placed in node a; the middle key (24) would become the separator key in node r;

FIGURE 125

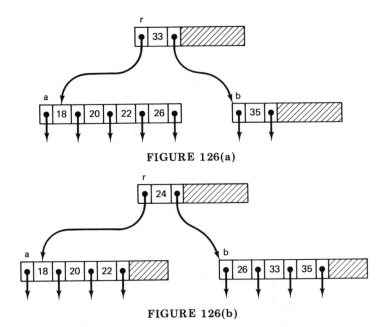

FIGURE 126(a)

FIGURE 126(b)

the remaining $\lfloor 7/2 \rfloor$ keys (26, 33, 35) would be placed in node b, as shown in Fig. 126(b). Free space from node b has been used to accommodate the overflow from node a. Moreover, the remaining free space has been redistributed between nodes a and b such that each now has half of it.

What if node b were also full and did not have free space to accommodate node a's overflow? In a B*-tree, *two* nodes are split to form *three* nodes, each of which is about two-thirds full. The total number of keys involved is $2m + 2$ (m from each a and b, 1 in r, 1 to be added). The resultant three nodes should contain each about $(2m)/3$ keys; two keys are placed into the parent node to act as separators. A diagram illustrating the result of the split is shown in Fig. 127.

$$\text{where } \alpha \ = \left\lfloor \frac{2m-2}{3} \right\rfloor$$

$$\text{and } \beta \ = \ \left\lfloor \frac{2(2m-2)}{3} \right\rfloor + 1$$

Returning to our example, consider the situation shown in Fig. 128(a). Now insertion of 24 cannot be accommodated by shifting key values from node a to node b, because node b is already full. Instead we split nodes a and b into three nodes, each of which is about two-thirds full. The total number of keys involved is 10. About one-third of the keys that are not separators are placed in each node a, a', and b as shown in Fig. 128(b).

where $\alpha = \left\lfloor \dfrac{2m-2}{3} \right\rfloor$

and $\beta = \left\lfloor \dfrac{2(2m-2)}{3} \right\rfloor + 1$

FIGURE 127

FIGURE 128(a)

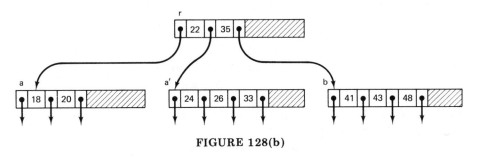

FIGURE 128(b)

As another example, consider a B*-tree of order $m = 90$. Assume that nodes a and b are both full. Say

> node a : key values $K_{100}, \ldots, K_{189}$
> node b : key values $K_{191}, \ldots, K_{280}$
> node r : key values $\ldots, K_{99}, K_{190}, K_{281} \ldots$

We wish to insert key value K_{189}' where $K_{189} < K_{189}' < K_{190}$. K_{189}' cannot fit in node a, and node b has no free space to share. A new node—call it node a'—is allocated and keys are shifted such that

> node a : key values $K_{100}, \ldots, K_{159}$
> node a' : key values $K_{161}, \ldots, K_{219}$
> node b : key values $K_{221}, \ldots, K_{280}$
> node r : key values $\ldots, K_{99}, K_{160}, K_{220}, K_{281}, \ldots$

Nodes a, a', and b each has free space for 29 key values. The new key K_{189}' resides in node a'.

B+-TREES: SPECIAL B-TREES

Another variation on the basic B-tree is the B+-tree. A B+-tree has two parts: the *index part* consists of the interior nodes; the *sequence set* is the leaves. The index part provides routing information for rapid direct access to the keys in the leaves.

The most frequent use of a B^+-tree is to index access to a collection of records. The key values in the B^+-tree's sequence set are the key values in the record collection; the key values in the B^+-tree's index part exist solely for internal purposes of directing access to the sequence set. Thus a key that appears in the index part will *also* appear in the sequence set if it corresponds to the key of a record in the collection. (Actually not all key values in the record collection need appear in the sequence set. We will see in a later chapter on indexed sequential file organization that a key value in a B^+-tree's sequence set may index a group of records in the data collection.)

Fig. 129 shows a B^+-tree that contains the same key values as does the basic B-tree of Fig. 120. Nodes a through i form the index part; nodes j through y form the sequence set. Examination of the B^+-tree in Fig. 129 reveals a new set of pointers: the leaves have been connected to form a linked list of the keys in sequential order. The linked sequence set is one of the most beautiful aspects of a B^+-tree; the keys can be accessed efficiently both directly and sequentially. Recall that our analysis in Chapter 11 of a basic B-tree for sequential access to key values revealed rather poor performance. The sequence set of a B^+-tree remedies the problem. Note that if there were record keys in the index part of the B^+-tree that did not appear in the sequence set, then linking of leaves would not form a sequential ordering of the record keys.

We have designed our B^+-tree such that pointer P_i in the index points to the subtree containing key values greater than those in the subtree pointed to by P_{i-1} and *less than or equal to* key value K_i. Sometimes B^+-trees are designed such that pointer P_i in the index points to the subtree containing key values greater than those in the subtree pointed to by P_{i-1} and *less than* key value K_i. The leaf containing key value K_i then is in the subtree pointed to by P_{i+1}.

Insertion of a new key value into a B^+-tree proceeds in almost the same way as insertion of a new key value into a basic B-tree. When a leaf node is split into two nodes, a copy of the low-order key value from the rightmost node is promoted to be the separator key value in the father node. The new node, of course, also must be inserted in the linked list of the sequence set.

Deletion of a key value from a B^+-tree is somewhat easier than if the tree were a basic B-tree. When a key value is deleted from a leaf, there is no need to delete that key value from the index of the tree. That key value still can direct searches to the proper leaves.

A direct search in a B^+-tree must terminate in a node of the sequence set. If there is a key in the index that matches the sought key, the preceding pointer is followed until eventually the correct leaf is reached. Not every key in the index part need also appear in the sequence set. A key may have been deleted from the sequence set when

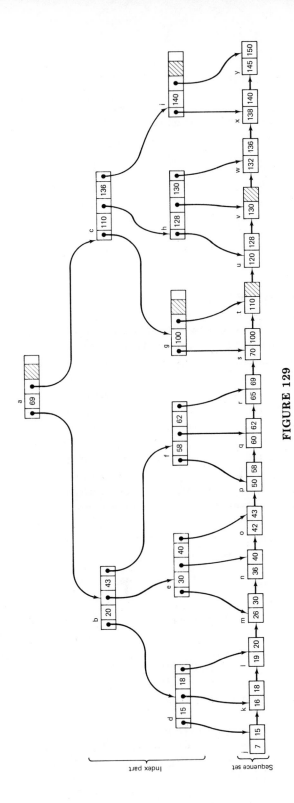

FIGURE 129

233

its corresponding record was deleted from the record collection, but the key may have been retained in the index part of the B^+-tree for purposes of guiding access to the sequence set.

A B^+-tree provides about as good performance for direct searching as does a basic B-tree of the same order. The maximum height of a B^+-tree of order m with n key values is $(\log \lceil \frac{1}{2}m \rceil \frac{n+1}{2})$.

If the B^+-tree is providing an index to a collection of data records that are stored elsewhere, each entry in the index is made of tree pointer/key value pairs. An actual address of a separate data record is found by searching the index, then finding the record's location from its entry in the sequence set.

TRIES: SPECIAL GENERAL TREES

To this point we have based our searches through tree structures on comparisons between key values. A trie is a data structure that uses instead the representations of key values as sequences of characters or digits to guide searches through the structure. The name *trie* was suggested by E. Fredkin (1960) because it is part of information re*trie*val.

A trie is an m-ary tree. It is *not* a search tree of order m; that is, the ordering of key values in the nodes does not conform to the rules of an m-way search tree (see Chapter 11). The order of a trie is determined by the radix used to represent key values. The radix of key values represented by digits is 10; the radix of key values represented by alphabetic characters is 26 (or 27 if the space is included). Each node of a trie of order m is essentially a one-dimensional array of m pointers. Each element in the array corresponds to one of the elements of the radix set. A node in a 10-ary trie is shown in Fig. 130.

FIGURE 130

Note that the node is composed entirely of pointers. The position of a pointer in the node determines the value to which it corresponds.

The height of a trie is determined by the length of the key field. For a node on the jth level of a 10-ary trie, P_i points to a subtree representing all key values whose jth digit is i. For example, P_4 on the sixth level of a 10-ary trie points to a subtree representing all key values whose sixth digit is 4.

A node in a trie used to represent alphabetic key values contains 26 pointers. For a node on the jth level of such a trie, P_i points to a subtree whose jth character is the ith letter of the alphabet. For example P_{10} on the third level of the trie points to a subtree containing all key values whose third character is J.

We will assume that the jth character is always determined from left to right. That is, the first character is the high-order digit in a numeric key value or the leading letter in an alphabetic key value. Certainly, a trie could be constructed with the character positions determined from right to left. Can you think of applications in which this alternative would be more advantageous?

Fig. 131 illustrates part of a trie for structuring a collection of 4-digit key values. This example trie represents the following collection of key values:

```
2302, 2303, 2305, 2306, 2307, 2308
2350, 2352, 2353, 2355, 2356, 2358, 2359
2581, 2582, 2584, 2585, 2586, 2588, 2589
2590, 2591, 2593, 2594, 2596, 2597, 2599
2900, 2901, 2903, 2904, 2905, 2906, 2907, 2908, 2909
32xx . . .
35xx . . .
52xx . . .
59xx . . .
7312, 7313, 7315, 7316
7390, 7391, 7393, 7395, 7397, 7399
7490, 7492, 7494, 7496, 7498
```

The non-null pointers in the leaves may be either (1) place-holders to indicate that the corresponding key values are valid and exist or (2) addresses of data records stored elsewhere that correspond to the represented key values.

Note that the basic trie shown in Fig. 131 does not include nodes that are full of null pointers. These empty nodes have the potential to exist and may be inserted into the tree when key value insertion makes them nonempty. The maximal structure of the tree is fixed by the radix of the key set and the length of the key field.

Not storing null nodes makes better use of memory when the distribution of key values is such that there are many null nodes. This very well may be the case, especially when the key range is sparsely used. For example, consider a company with 250 employees. Assume that the 9-digit social security number is used as the key field to identify employee payroll records. A basic trie built upon this key field would have nine levels and potentially space for 10^9 employee record pointers on the leaf level. Only 250 of these elements (.000025%) would be occupied.

As with a B+-tree, successful direct searches in a basic trie must terminate at leaf nodes. Thus the length of a successful search is determined by the height of the trie, which is determined by the length of

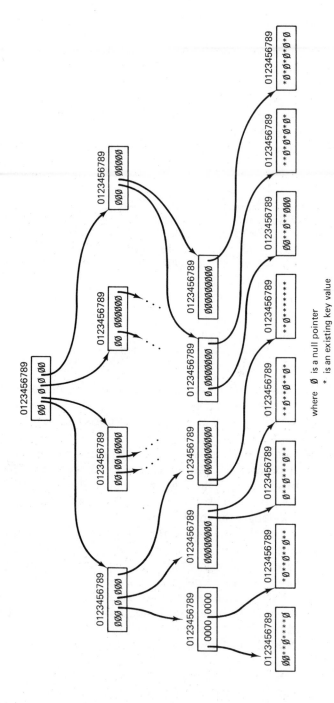

where Ø is a null pointer
      * is an existing key value

FIGURE 131

236

the key field. Recall that the length of a search in an m-way search tree is determined by the number of key values represented. In the trie of Fig. 131, a successful search requires visitation of four nodes regardless of whether there are three key values represented or 10^4.

On the other hand, an unsuccessful search terminates when it is determined that a sought key value does not reside in the structure. In a trie, an unsuccessful search may terminate on any level of the structure. For example, visitation of just the root node of the trie of Fig. 131 is enough to determine that there are no key values in the trie with high-order digit from the set $[0, 1, 4, 6, 8, 9]$. This good performance for unsuccessful searches is a major attractive feature for use of the trie in some applications.

It may help you to understand tries if you recognize another similarity between a trie and a B+-tree. Recall that a B+-tree has an index part and a sequence set of key values. Similarly, a trie has an index part (the interior nodes) and an information (or key value) part composed of the leaves.

Inserting a new key value in a trie is relatively easy. The correct leaf to represent the new value is located using a direct search. It may be that the correct leaf does not exist. In this case, nodes must be added properly to the index part of the structure to direct a search to the new leaf node. The correct element of that leaf is found and changed from non-null to a place-holder value or to the address of the related data record. Deletion of a key value requires the same location process and modification of the proper leaf element to have a null value. Note that there is no node splitting or merging, although nodes may need to be added when a new value appears the first time in a particular character position.

There are several variations possible on the basic trie. For example, the trie can be modified slightly to accommodate more efficiently a variable-length key field. Consider an alphabetic key field with values that are people's last names. Some of these names are very short, others are quite long. Building a 26-way trie to structure names of up to, say, 30 characters would mean that even searches for short names would require 30 node visitations. Assume that 80% of the names to be represented are no more than eight characters in length. The trie can be built with the following node structure. Each internal node can contain 27 elements; 26 are for the letters of the alphabet, and one (say ξ) is to represent key values that terminate at the represented length. Each name is represented as if its low-order character were ξ. For example, IGOR is represented as IGORξ. A name that terminates with a ξ on level j would be a name with j characters. For example, the name IGOR would be represented with an I on level 0, pointing to a G on level 1,

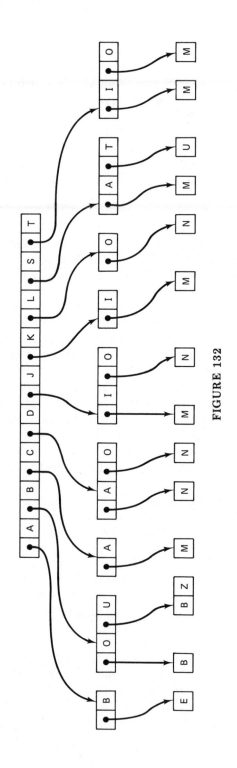

FIGURE 132

pointing to an O on level 2, pointing to an R on level 3, pointing to ξ on level 4.

The trie itself could be constructed with eight levels. Each leaf node could contain the 27 usual elements, plus pointers to (for example) binary search trees containing the remaining parts of the names with more than eight characters. Thus 80% of the searches would require a maximum of eight node visitations; 20% of the searches would travel completely through the trie and into a binary search tree.

Another alternative for improving the space requirements of a trie is to reduce node sizes by not making provision for all possible values of the radix in each node. Instead, only those values that are actually in use might be represented. Fig. 132 shows an example trie that uses this variation in storing a small set of three-letter boys' names. Each internal node of the trie contains both pointers and the radix value corresponding to each pointer; each leaf of the trie contains one or more radix values.

Prior knowledge of distributions of key values can be used to further reduce memory needs. For example, if the trie of Fig. 132 were used only to store names and not then provide an index to corresponding data records, we could take advantage of the fact that N and M appear frequently in leaves. How? Would the resultant structure still be a tree, according to the definition given in Chapter 8?

SUMMARY

This chapter introduced two variations on the B-tree and a general type of tree that appear frequently in practice. A *B*-tree* is a B-tree in which each node is at least two-thirds full instead of at least half full. This variation tends to make better use of memory and to decrease the maximum direct search length through the tree.

A *B+-tree* is a B-tree in which all key values reside in the leaf nodes. This constraint separates the B+-tree into two parts: the index part and the sequence set, which is composed of the leaves. A major benefit of a B+-tree results when the sequence set nodes are linked together. This connection allows the B+-tree to support rapid direct access to key values through the index part *and* rapid sequential access to key values through the linked sequence set.

A *trie* uses the representation of key values as sequences of characters or digits to guide searches. The order of the basic trie is determined by the radix used to represent key values. The height of the basic trie is determined by the length of the key field. The actual shape of a trie is determined by the distribution of key values; uniform distribution of key values results in a relatively balanced trie. The trie exhibits very good performance for unsuccessful direct searches. For applications in which unsuccessful search performance is important, the trie generally is a better structure to use than an m-way search tree or one of its variants. Many variations on the basic trie have been developed in attempts to improve its direct search performance for successful searches and its memory requirements.

For further details, the interested reader should consult:

Bayer, R., and E. McCreight. "Organization and maintenance of large ordered indexes," *Acta Informatica*, 1: 290–306, 1972.

Comer, D., and R. Sethi. "The complexity of trie index construction," *J. ACM*, 24(3): 428–440, July 1977.

Knuth, D. E. *The Art of Computer Programming, Vol. 3., Sorting and Searching.* Reading, Mass.: Addison-Wesley Publishing Co., 1973, pp. 471–505.

Terms

B-tree	m-way search tree
B*-tree	sequence set
B+-tree	trie
index	

Review Exercises

1. What is the difference between a B-tree and a B*-tree?
2. What is the difference between a B-tree and a B+-tree?
3. What is the difference between a B-tree and a trie?
4. What determines the shape of a B+-tree?
5. What determines the shape of a trie? When is a trie short and bushy? When is a trie tall and slender?
6. When would you want to balance a B+-tree?
7. When would you want to balance a trie?
8. When might you use a B-tree instead of a B+-tree?
9. When might you use a B+-tree instead of a B-tree?
10. When might you use a trie instead of a B+-tree?
11. Consider the following B+-tree:

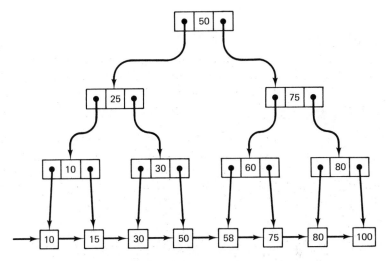

(a) What are the keys of records indexed by this B+-tree?
(b) Show the results of the following activities:
    delete key 30
    insert key 28
    insert key 26

12. What is the node structure of a trie used to represent the employee numbers 0001 to 9999, where 70% of the available numbers are used? How many levels does the trie have?

13. Draw a trie to represent all two-letter English words. What is the node structure? How many levels does the trie have?

14. Modify the trie from exercise 13 to represent all one- and two-letter English words. What is the node structure? How many levels does the trie have?

15. Draw a B+-tree that corresponds to the set of key values shown in the B-tree of Fig. 122.

16. Draw a trie to represent the set of key values shown in the B-tree of Fig. 122.

CHAPTER 13

Graphs

In this chapter we return to the data structure introduced in Chapter 8: *graphs*. We thus complete the cycle of nonlinear data structures that we began back in that chapter. Before discussing graphs in some detail, it is useful to review that cycle of development. As shown by the progression in Fig. 133, we first introduced the general data type graph, then constrained that data structure to give the definition of a general tree. We then further constrained general trees and began investigation of binary trees. These are clean data structures with which to work because of their predictable and consistent numbers of subtrees. By imposing constraints on the arrangement of data in a binary tree, we encountered two special cases: binary search trees and heaps. We investigated the virtues of balancing trees and identified two nice types of nearly balanced, binary search trees: AVL-trees and BB-trees. By generalizing binary search trees, we cultivated m-way search trees; we could instead have found these trees by constraining general trees. The B-tree and B*-tree were then introduced as special cases of the m-way search tree. In turn, the B+-trees are special cases of B-trees. We then again touched base with general trees as we discussed tries. In this chapter we are now back at the most general of the nonlinear data structures— the graph.

Graphs and related terminology were defined in Chapter 8. We will not repeat those definitions here, but instead start with a discussion of how graphs are represented in COBOL and Pascal. As with the other complex data structures that we have studied, the common programming languages do not have a built-in data type called "graph." Instead,

FIGURE 133

the data structure's characteristics are simulated by housing it in another
data type. There are three major approaches to representing graphs:
matrix representation, list representation, and multi-list representation.
After considering each of these, we delve into discussion of some of the
more common operations on graphs: graph traversal and path analysis.

ADJACENCY MATRIX REPRESENTATION

Consider a graph G with set of nodes V_G and set of edges E_G. Assume
the graph is of order N, for $N >= 1$. One approach to representing this
graph is to use an *adjacency matrix*, which is a N-by-N array A, where:

$$A(i,j) \quad = \begin{cases} 1 \text{ if and only if edge } (v_i, v_j) \text{ is in } E_G \\ 0 \text{ otherwise.} \end{cases}$$

If there is an edge connecting nodes i and j, then $A(i,j) = 1$.
    Fig. 134 shows an *undirected graph*.

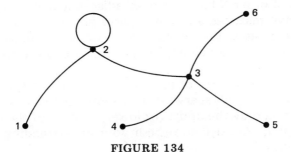

FIGURE 134

The adjacency matrix for this graph is:

i \ j	1	2	3	4	5	6
1	0	1	0	0	0	0
2	1	1	1	0	0	0
3	0	1	0	1	1	1
4	0	0	1	0	0	0
5	0	0	1	0	0	0
6	0	0	1	0	0	0

An edge of a *directed graph* has its source in one node and terminates in another node. By convention, edge (v_i, v_j) denotes direction from node v_i to node v_j. A directed graph is shown in Fig. 135.

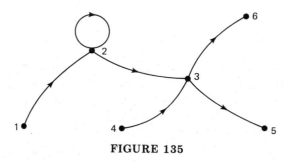

FIGURE 135

The adjacency matrix for this example is:

i \ j	1	2	3	4	5	6
1	0	1	0	0	0	0
2	0	1	1	0	0	0
3	0	0	0	0	1	1
4	0	0	1	0	0	0
5	0	0	0	0	0	0
6	0	0	0	0	0	0

A graph of order N has an N-by-N adjacency matrix. In many cases these adjacency matrices are quite sparse and can be stored as sparse arrays. In these cases, the matrix representation approach generally is not as suitable as the linked approaches that we will introduce later in this chapter.

The adjacency matrix of an undirected graph is symmetric. Thus even if the matrix is not sparse, storage requirements can be cut almost in half by storing only the upper (or lower) triangle of the matrix. Refer back to Chapters 2 and 6 to refresh your understanding of triangular and sparse arrays.

The following array definition can be used to declare a graph named *GRAPH* of order 24 in COBOL:

```
01  GRAPH.
    02  ROW OCCURS 24 TIMES.
        03  COL OCCURS 24 TIMES.
            04  EDGE PIC 9.
```

EDGE (I,J) then has value 1 if an edge exists between nodes *I* and *J* and has value 0 otherwise.

Another way to interpret an adjacency matrix is as a boolean data type. For example, in Pascal:

type graph : array [1 .. 24, 1 .. 24] of boolean;

Here *graph [i,j]* has value *true* if an edge exists between nodes *i* and *j* and has value *false* otherwise.

In fact, however, it is often convenient to be able to do arithmetic on an adjacency matrix. For example, the degree of node *i* in an undirected graph is:

$$\sum_{j=1}^{N} A(i,j).$$

The in-degree of node *i* in a directed graph is the column-sum of the matrix:

$$\sum_{k=1}^{N} A(k,i).$$

and the out-degree of node *i* is the row-sum of the matrix:

$$\sum_{k=1}^{N} A(i,k)$$

We will discuss other common results of manipulating the adjacency data later in the chapter. If the adjacency matrix is defined to be boolean, then these common manipulations are not quite so straightforward. Instead of summation, they require series of boolean operations (*and* and *or*).

There are many graph applications in which variations on the pure adjacency matrix representation are appropriate. Consider the graph shown in Fig. 136. This is an example of a graph with weighted edges. The nodes represent cities and the edges represent truck routes between cities. Each edge is labeled with the distance between the connected pair of cities. Rather than using a bit matrix to represent this trucking system, we instead might use matrix representation (Fig. 137).

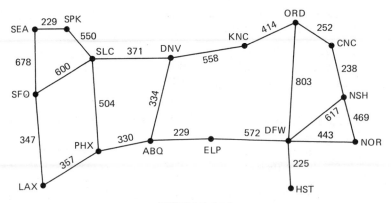

FIGURE 136

	1	2	3	4	5	6	7	8	9	10	11	12	13	14	15	16
1		0	0	334	229	0	0	0	0	0	0	330	0	0	0	0
2			0	0	0	0	0	0	238	0	252	0	0	0	0	0
3				0	572	225	0	0	617	443	803	0	0	0	0	0
4					0	0	558	0	0	0	0	0	0	0	371	0
5						0	0	0	0	0	0	0	0	0	0	0
6							0	0	0	0	0	0	0	0	0	0
7								0	0	0	414	0	0	0	0	0
8									0	0	0	357	0	347	0	0
9										469	0	0	0	0	0	0
10											0	0	0	0	0	0
11												0	0	0	0	0
12													0	0	504	0
13														678	0	229
14															600	0
15																550
16																

FIGURE 137

where node 1 = ABQ   6 = HST   11 = ORD   16 = SPK
        2 = CNC   7 = KNC   12 = PHX
        3 = DFW   8 = LAX   13 = SEA
        4 = DNV   9 = NSH   14 = SFO
        5 = ELP   10 = NOR   15 = SLC

Weighted edges are used frequently. In transportation applications, the weights commonly represent distances, as above. In flow applications, the weights commonly represent capacities. For example, the nodes on a graph might represent the gallon/minute capacity of a pipeline between the connected locations, or the bits/second capacity of a communications facility between the connected switching stations.

In other applications, the edge weights represent time. For instance, graphs can be used to represent networks of activities. Each edge represents a task or activity. The weight on the edge represents the amount of time required to complete the activity. Each node represents an event, the completion of the set of activities represented by the edges coming into the node. No activity on an out-edge can be started until all activities on in-edges to a node have completed. (Variations on the basic activity graph allow a completion event to be signaled by a subset of the incident activity edges.) We will consider activity graphs in more detail later in our discussion of critical path analysis.

LINKED REPRESENTATIONS

Representation of a graph using the adjacency matrix technique requires storage of edge information for each possible pair of nodes. For graphs of N nodes with few edges relative to the possible N^2 connections, a linked representation generally is more appropriate.

A new programmer on a project at the city's computer center discovered the hard way the benefits of selecting the appropriate representation for a data structure for the application. He was responsible for a COBOL program which was to be part of the transportation system. The program was to be used to keep track of traffic volumes on major city streets. The nodes on the graph were to represent intersections; the edges were to represent streets. Weights on the edges were to represent the traffic volumes. Each edge for a one-way street had only one weight; each edge for a two-way street carried two weights. Data were collected for 500 intersections. The programmer used an adjacency matrix to represent the traffic graph. Few of the intersections represented the confluence of more than four street segments. The vast majority of the adjacency matrix thus held zeroes; the program's storage requirements prevented it from fitting in the city computer's main memory. The programmer did not recognize the problem with the matrix representation, and instead spent many hours compacting the *PROCEDURE DIVISION* code. The program completion date passed (several times) and the code had never even been tested. Alas, the programmer left for greener pastures. An experienced programmer found the troublesome code on her desk, identified the gross storage requirements of the matrix, converted the program to use a linked representation, and completed the project.

The linked representations store information about only those edges that exist. As edges are added or deleted from the graph, the linked representation must be modified accordingly. There are two fundamental types of linked structures to represent graphs; one is called the node directory representation and the other one is called the multilist representation.

Node Directory Representation

The *node directory representation* includes two parts: a directory and a set of linked lists. There is one entry in the directory for each node of the graph. The directory entry for node *i* points to a linked list that represents the nodes that are connected to node *i*. Each record of the linked list has two fields: one is a node identifier; one is a link to the next element on the list. The directory represents nodes; the linked list represents edges.

A node directory representation of the undirected graph of Fig. 134 is given in Fig. 138.

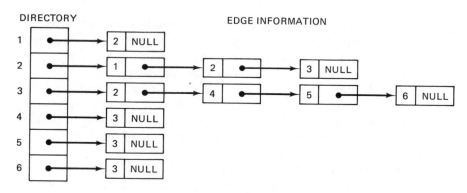

FIGURE 138

An undirected graph of order *N* with *E* edges requires *N* entries in the directory and $2*E$ linked list entries, except that each loop reduces the number of linked list entries by one. (Why?)

A node directory representation of the directed graph of Fig. 135 is given in Fig. 139.

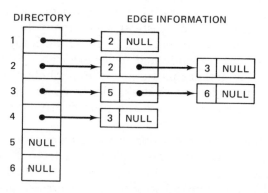

FIGURE 139

A directed graph of order *N* with *E* edges requires *N* entries in the directory and *E* linked list entries.

The linked list headed by the ith directory entry corresponds to the ith row of the adjacency matrix representation. The directory entries are ordered sequentially by node identifier. Although we also have ordered the linked list entries by node identifier, they could have appeared in any order since each entry bears its node identity.

A COBOL declaration of the node directory representation of an undirected graph of order 24 with a maximum of 100 edges is:

```
01  GRAPH.
    02  NODE OCCURS 24 TIMES
                PICTURE 9(3).
    02  EDGES.
        03  LIST-ENTRY OCCURS 200 TIMES.
            04  NODE-ID PICTURE 99.
            04  NEXT-ENTRY PICTURE 9(3).
```

Representation of a graph with weighted edges requires making provision in the data structure for storage of those weights. Fig. 140 shows a directed graph with weighted edges. This particular example is an activity graph: each node represents an event and each edge represents a task whose completion helps to trigger the next event, which is the start of other tasks. Each edge's weight is its required time.

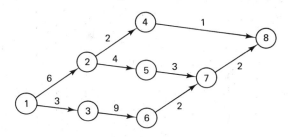

FIGURE 140

A node directory representation for this graph follows. The data structure for each edge entry is the identifier of the destination node, the weight of the edge, and a pointer to the next edge with the same source node (Fig. 141).

To determine the degree of a node in an undirected graph requires counting the number of entries on its linked list. The out-degree of a node in a directed graph also can be determined by counting the number of entries on its linked list.

Determining the in-degree of node i is more complex. Each of the linked lists must be accessed in order to detect whether or not node i appears as a destination node. To facilitate finding prior nodes and determining in-degrees, an auxiliary directory of edges coming into nodes may be maintained.

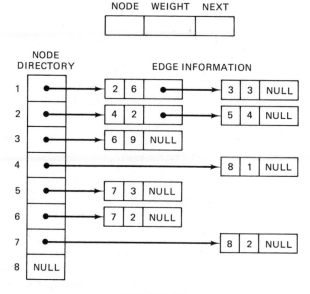

FIGURE 141

We will see that some types of graph analysis are easier with the adjacency matrix representation than with linked representation. However, if storage space were the only criterion for selection, then the linked representation generally would require less space, unless the graph were highly connected. If a graph has a highly volatile structure, then it may require less work to add or delete edges in the adjacency matrix representation than in the node directory representation. Changing a matrix entry generally is easier than is adding (deleting) another entry to a linked list.

Multi-list Representation

In the *multi-list representation* of graph structures, there are again two parts: a directory of node information and a set of linked lists of edge information. There is one entry in the node directory for each node of the graph. The directory entry for node i points to a linked adjacency list for node i. Each record of the linked list area appears on two adjacency lists: one for the node at each end of the represented edge. Using the data structure of Fig. 142 for each edge entry (v_i, v_j),

NODE 1		NODE 2	
ID	ADJ	ID	ADJ
V_i	$NEXT_1$	V_j	$NEXT_2$

FIGURE 142

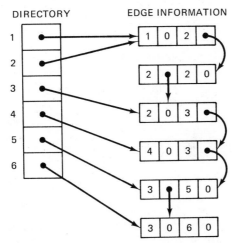

FIGURE 143

a multi-list representation for the example graph of Fig. 134 is Fig. 143. This is not the only multi-list representation for this graph. It is based on the set of edges {(1,2),(2,2),(2,3),(4,3),(3,5),(3,6)}. An alternative representation based upon the set of edges {(2,1),(2,2),(2,3),(3,4), (5,3),(3,6)} is shown in Fig. 144.

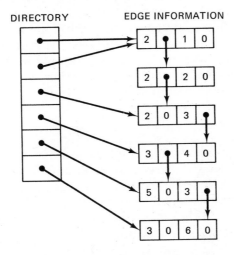

FIGURE 144

If the graph were directed, there would not be such flexibility in selecting identifiers for edges.

An edge weight can be stored with the other information recorded for the edge, just as was done in earlier examples of graph representations.

A Pascal declaration of a weighted graph of order 24 follows. Here we use pointer variables.

```
type nodeid = 0 .. 24;
     nodetype = ↑edgeinfo;
     edgeptr = ↑edgeinfo;
     edgeinfo = record node1 : nodeid;
                       node2 : nodeid;
                       adjlist1 : edgeptr;
                       adjlist2 : edgeptr;
                       weight : integer
               end;
     graph = array [1 .. 24] of nodetype;
```

GRAPH TRAVERSAL

We have already studied various techniques for traversing binary trees. The same need arises with graphs; in many applications it is necessary to visit all the nodes of a graph. The three tree traversal rules that we discussed were pre-order, in-order, and post-order. The two basic graph traversal techniques that we present are breadth-first and depth-first.

In graph traversal, as in tree traversal, it is necessary to take precautions to visit each node only once. In a tree there is only one path from the root to any other node; in a graph there may be several paths between any pair of nodes. To prevent visiting a node more than once, graph traversal algorithms generally *mark* each node as it is visited. A previously marked node cannot be revisited. Alternatively, a graph traversal algorithm may mark each edge as it is followed. A previously marked edge cannot be part of another path. "Mark bits" can be stored with the other node or edge information.

Breadth-first Traversal

In *breadth-first traversal* of a graph, one node is selected as the start position. It is visited and marked, then all unvisited nodes adjacent to that node are visited and marked in some sequential order. Finally, the unvisited nodes immediately adjacent to these nodes are visited and marked, and so forth, until the entire graph has been traversed.

Breadth-first traversal of the graph of Fig. 140 results in visiting the nodes in the following order: 1, 2, 3, 4, 5, 6, 7, 8. The sequence 1, 3, 2, 6, 5, 4, 7, 8 is also a valid breadth-first traversal visitation order.

The traversal algorithm uses a queue to store the nodes of each "level" of the graph as they are visited. These stored nodes are then treated one by one and their adjacent nodes are visited, and so forth until all nodes have been visited. This terminating condition is reached when the queue is empty. The *queuestruct* data type and the *insert* and *remove* procedures were defined in Chapter 5.

Assume that the global data typing used for the graph is:

```
type nodeid = 0 .. ordergraph;
     edgeptr = ↑edgeinfo;
     nodetype = record mark : 0 .. 1;
                       adjlist : edgeptr
                end;
     edgeinfo = record node : nodeid;
                       weight : integer;
                       next : edgeptr
                end;
     graphtype = array [1 .. ordergraph] of nodetype;
var graph : graphtype;
    firstnode : nodeid;
```

This is the node directory representation that was discussed earlier, with mark bits added to the node information.

The iterative procedure is programmed as follows in Pascal:

```
procedure breadth (firstnode:nodeid);
var : queuestruct;
    savenode : nodeid;
    adjptr : edgeptr;
begin {visit firstnode here}
     graph[firstnode].mark := 1;
     insert(firstnode);
     while g.f <> 0
     do begin remove (savenode);
              adjptr := graph[savenode].adjlist;
              {visit nodes adjacent to savenode}
              while adjptr <> nil
              do begin savenode := adjptr↑.node;
                       if (graph[savenode].mark = 0)
                       then begin insert(savenode);
                                  {visit savenode here}
                                  graph[savenode].mark := 1
                            end;
                       adjptr := adjptr↑.next
              end;
        end;
end;
```

This procedure could be invoked by a statement such as:

```
breadth(firstnode)
```

Depth-first Traversal

Whereas breadth-first traversal of a graph is analogous to level-by-level traversal of a tree, depth-first traversal of a graph is analogous to traversing a tree by following first a path from the root to a leaf, then another path from root to leaf, and so forth until all nodes have been visited.

Depth-first traversal of the graph of Fig. 140 results in visiting the nodes in the following order: 1, 2, 4, 8, 5, 7, 3, 6. A path is pursued until no unvisited nodes remain reachable; then the algorithm backs up to the last node that was visited that has an unvisited adjacent node. An equally valid sequence to result from depth-first traversal of the example graph is: 1, 3, 6, 7, 8, 2, 5, 4.

Breadth-first traversal was described easily using an iterative procedure; depth-first traversal lends itself well to recursive definition. Following is a recursive Pascal procedure to conduct a depth-first traversal of a graph represented by the node-directory structure declared in the preceding section.

```
procedure depth (var thisnode:nodeid);
var savenode : nodeid;
    adjptr : edgeptr;
begin {visit thisnode here}
        graph[thisnode].mark := 1;
        adjptr := graph[thisnode].adjlist;
        while adjptr <> nil
          do begin savenode := adjptr↑.node;
                   if (graph[savenode].mark = 0)
                   then depth(savenode);
                   adjptr := adjptr↑.next
              end;
end;
```

This procedure would be invoked by a statement such as:

    depth (firstnode);

Comparisons

The exercises at the end of this chapter suggest that you write breadth-first and depth-first traversal algorithms for graphs that are represented by multi-list structures and for graphs that are represented by adjacency matrices. Let us now compare the relative time requirements of these traversal types with the linked and nonlinked representations.

In the breadth-first traversal, each node of the graph enters the node queue only once. Thus the outer *while* loop is executed N times, where N is the order of the graph (*ordergraph*). If the graph is represented by a linked structure, then only those nodes that are adjacent to the node at the front of the queue are examined. Thus the inner *while* loop is executed a total of E times, where E is the number of edges in the graph. The traversal is then $o(N*E)$.

However, if the graph is represented by an adjacency matrix, then the inner *while* loop is executed once for each other node in the graph, since the entire row of the adjacency matrix must be examined. Thus the traversal is $o(N^2)$.

The same type of logic can be applied to show that depth-first traversal of a graph represented by a linked structure is $o(N*E)$, while breadth-first traversal of a graph represented by an adjacency matrix is $o(N^2)$.

How does one determine whether a depth-first or a breadth-first traversal should be conducted? As with selection of the appropriate tree traversal technique, the application of the graph is the determining factor. The discussion of depth-first and breadth-first generation of game trees in Chapter 8 carries over to "game graphs."

REACHABILITY AND SHORTEST PATHS

Graph analysis commonly involves following paths through the graph. There are many interesting problems in analysis of graph paths. We will consider just two in this section: reachability and shortest paths. Use of the adjacency matrix representation will facilitate the initial discussion.

In some problems edge weights are important. For example, determining the shortest path between a pair of cities in the graph of Fig. 137 uses the edge weights, which are distances. On the other hand, determining whether or not two nodes are connected need not consider edge weights. We initially assume that edge weights are all one.

An adjacency matrix represents node connections. Each nonzero entry represents an edge; it also represents a path of length 1 between nodes. Consider the adjacency matrix A for the directed graph of Fig. 140:

i \ j	1	2	3	4	5	6	7	8
1	0	1	1	0	0	0	0	0
2	0	0	0	1	1	0	0	0
3	0	0	0	0	0	1	0	0
4	0	0	0	0	0	0	0	1
5	0	0	0	0	0	0	1	0
6	0	0	0	0	0	0	1	0
7	0	0	0	0	0	0	0	1
8	0	0	0	0	0	0	0	0

Conventional matrix multiplication is used to find A^2. That is, the i,jth element of A^2 is the result of multiplying row i by column j of A:

$$A_{ij}^2 = \sum_{k=1}^{n} A_{ik} A_{kj}$$

$A_{ij}^2 = 1$ if there is a path of length 2 from node i to node j; $A_{ij}^2 = 0$ otherwise.

In general, the mth power of the binary adjacency matrix:

$$A_{ij}^m = \begin{cases} 1 \text{ if there is a path of length } m \text{ from node } i \text{ to node } j, \\ 0 \text{ otherwise.} \end{cases}$$

The problem of determining whether or not pairs of nodes are connected thus can be solved by finding:

$$\sum_{t=1}^{N} A^t$$

which results in a matrix called the *transitive closure of* A, commonly denoted A^+. Actually the summation need not be carried out N times, where N is the order of the graph, but rather only as many times as the length of the longest path. For the example of Fig. 140,

$$A^+ = \sum_{t=1}^{4} A^t$$

The transitive closure of A is also referred to as the *reachability matrix* of A.

In addition to determining if node j can be reached from node i, it is commonly of interest to find the shortest path from node i to node j. Development of the general algorithm is left as an exercise, but we do make two observations about shortest paths here. These points should help your development efforts. Refer to the graph of Fig. 136. Following is a table of the shortest paths from DNV to each other city, listed in the order in which a shortest-path algorithm detects them.

path	distance
DNV–ABQ	334
DNV–SLC	371
DNV–KNC	558
DNV–ABQ–ELP	334+229 = 563
DNV–ABQ–PHX	334+330 = 664
DNV–SLC–SPK	371+550 = 921
DLV–SLC–SFO	371+600 = 971
DNV–KNC–ORD	558+414 = 972

DNV-ABQ-PHX-LAX	$334+330+357 = 1021$
DNV-ABQ-ELP-DFW	$334+229+572 = 1135$
DNV-SLC-SPK-SEA	$371+550+229 = 1150$
DNV-KNC-ORD-CNC	$558+414+252 = 1224$
DNV-ABQ-ELP-DFW-HST	$334+229+572+225 = 1360$
DNV-KNC-ORD-CNC-NSH	$558+414+252+238 = 1462$
DNV-ABQ-ELP-DFW-NOR	$334+229+572+443 = 1578$

There are several possible paths between many of the pairs of cities. Note that:

1. The shortest paths are detected in nondecreasing order of their distances; i.e., the next destination node is the one with the minimum distance from the source node of all those nodes not yet selected.

2. The shortest path to that next destination node goes through nodes that have already been selected.

If the edge weights were to represent costs rather than distances, then the same algorithm could be used to detect cheapest paths. If the edge weights were to represent speeds (e.g., kilobits/second), then the algorithm could be modified easily to detect fastest paths.

CRITICAL PATHS

The graph of Fig. 140 represents an activity graph. Nearly all projects can be represented by such graphs. Quite good techniques have been developed to assist in the evaluation and analysis of activity graphs, e.g., the Critical Path Method (CPM), Performance Evaluation and Review Technique (PERT), and Resource Allocation and Multi-project Scheduling (RAMPS) techniques. Here we introduce only the basic aspects of activity graph analysis.

The graph structure of a project shows that several tasks can be executed in parallel. For example, tasks from events 2 and 3 can proceed concurrently in Fig. 140. Of interest to the management of the project is determining which events are critical to timely completion of the project. An event is *critical* if slippage of its scheduled completion time causes the completion of the entire project to be delayed. The shortest possible completion time for the project is the longest path through the graph. The longest path is called the *critical path*; the critical events lie along this path. The length of this path is called the *critical path time*, CPT.

One way to detect the critical path and to determine allowed slippage times for events not on the critical path is to find earliest and latest start times for the events. The *earliest start time* of event i, EST_i, is the earliest possible trigger time for the event. For the graph of Fig. 140:

event	EST
1	0
2	6
3	3
4	8
5	10
6	12
7	14
8	16

The EST_i is calculated from the longest path to node i from the start node. Note that tasks from both nodes 5 and 6 must complete before event 7 is triggered. More formally,

$$EST_i = \max_{j \in P(i)} \{EST_j + T(j,i)\}$$

where $P(i)$ is the set of immediate predecessors to node i
$\qquad$ $T(j,i)$ is the weight of the edge from node j to node i.

The *latest start time* of event i, LST_i, is the latest possible time that event i can be triggered with the graph completing in critical path time. The set of LST_i are calculated backwards from the last event. For the graph of Fig. 140:

event	LST
1	0
2	13
3	3
4	15
5	11
6	12
7	14
8	16

Formally,

$$LST_i = \min_{j \in S(i)} \{LST_j - T(i,j)\}$$

where $S(i)$ is the set of immediate successors to node i.

The difference between the LST_i and EST_i is the allowable slippage of event i.

event	LST-EST
1	0
2	7
3	0
4	7
5	1
6	0
7	0
8	0

The critical events thus are represented by nodes 1, 3, 6, 7, and 8, which are on the longest path of the graph. These are the events that need to be controlled in order for the project to complete on time. Note that if a noncritical event were to slip beyond its allowable window, then the critical path through the graph would be changed.

SPANNING TREES

Many applications call for the identification of the spanning tree for a connected graph. A *spanning tree T* is a tree that contains all the nodes of graph *G* and has no other nodes. Figs. 145 and 146 show two of the many spanning trees of the graph of Fig. 136. Can you construct others?

FIGURE 145

FIGURE 146

Of primary interest is the identification of a *minimal spanning tree* for a graph. The cost of a spanning tree is the sum of its edge weights. The cost of the spanning tree of Fig. 145 is 6845 miles; the cost of the spanning tree of Fig. 146 is 6567 miles. Neither of these happens to be the spanning tree of least possible cost.

One approach to finding minimal spanning trees is an algorithm developed by Kruskal. This algorithm considers inclusion of graph edges in order by increasing cost; an edge is included if it does not form a cycle. A cycle would mean that two paths exist between pairs of nodes. Applying Kruskal's algorithm to the graph of Fig. 136 proceeds as follows:

1. Lowest cost: DFW–HST (225)
2. Lowest cost: ABQ–ELP (229)
3. Lowest cost: SEA–SPK (229)
4. Lowest cost: CNC–NSH (238)
5. Lowest cost: ORD–CNC (252)

The developing minimal spanning tree now is as shown in Fig. 147(a).

FIGURE 147(a)

6. Lowest cost: PHX–ABQ (330)
7. Lowest cost: DNV–ABQ (334)
8. Lowest cost: SFO–LAX (347)
9. Lowest cost: LAX–PHX (357)
10. Lowest cost: KNC–ORD (414)

The minimal spanning tree now is as shown in Fig. 147(b).

11. Lowest cost: DFW–NOR (443)
12. Lowest cost: NSH–NOR (469)

FIGURE 147(b)

13. Lowest cost: PHX–SLC (504)
14. Lowest cost: SLC–SPK (550)
15. Lowest cost: DNV–KNC (558)

We have been very lucky in avoiding cycles! The minimal spanning tree
is shown in Fig. 147(c).

FIGURE 147(c)

In fact, we now have included all nodes and the minimal spanning tree
is complete, with cost of 5479.

   Assume for the moment that all nodes had *not* yet been included.
Consideration of the next lowest cost edge (ELP–DFW) would detect a
cycle. That edge would be rejected and the edge with the next lowest
cost would be considered, and so forth until all nodes were included.

   Minimal spanning trees thus are the least-cost way to connect the
nodes of the graph. Cost, of course, can be measured in terms of distance, time, money, and so forth, depending upon the edge weight units.

SUMMARY

In this chapter we first reviewed the cycle that we have followed in studying nonlinear data structures, then discussed graphs in some detail. Three fundamental techniques for representing graphs were covered: adjacency matrix representation and two forms of linked representation—node directory and multi-list. Use of an adjacency matrix tends to make graph analysis algorithms at least $o(N^2)$, while use of a linked representation tends to make graph analysis algorithms $o(N*E)$. Examples of declaring graphs in COBOL and Pascal were given.

Two basic graph traversal techniques were introduced: breadth-first and depth-first. These algorithms take precautions to visit each node only once by marking each node as it is visited or each edge as it is traversed. Breadth-first traversal generally is programmed as an iterative procedure, whereas depth-first traversal generally is programmed as a recursive procedure.

Several path analysis problems were discussed. Powers of a graph's adjacency matrix can be used to detect paths of a given length between node pairs and to determine if one node is reachable from another node. An example was used to illustrate the algorithm for detecting the shortest paths between one node and the other nodes. Critical path analysis was introduced, along with the concepts of earliest and latest start times. Finally, spanning trees and a technique (Kruskal's algorithm) for identifying a minimal spanning tree of a graph were introduced.

For more details of the data type graph, you are urged to consult the excellent book entitled *Flows in Networks* by L. Ford and D. Fulkerson, published by the Princeton University Press, 1962.

Terms

activity graph	in-order
adjacency matrix	latest start time
breadth-first	minimal spanning tree
critical path	out-degree
depth-first	post-order
directed graph	pre-order
earliest start time	reachability matrix
graph	spanning tree
in-degree	transitive closure

Review Exercises

1. Assume that a directed graph of order N is represented by an adjacency matrix, where *graph (i,j)* = 1 if an edge connects nodes i and j and is zero otherwise. What are the expressions for determining the following: (a) the in-degree of node i, (b) the out-degree of node i?

2. Draw a directed graph. What is its adjacency matrix? What is its reachability matrix? Represent the graph using a node-directory structure. Represent the graph using a multi-list structure. Traverse the graph using the breadth-first approach. Traverse the graph using the depth-first approach. What is the minimal spanning tree of the graph?

3. One linked representation of a graph maintains a directory of nodes and corresponding linked lists of edges. Develop an alternative linked representation which maintains a directory of edges and corresponding linked lists of nodes. Analyze the storage requirements of your representation and compare them with the requirements of the linked representation given in the chapter.

4. Write programs to do (a) a breadth-first traversal and (b) a depth-first traversal of a graph represented by a multi-list structure.

5. Write programs to do (a) a breadth-first traversal and (b) a depth-first traversal of a graph represented by an adjacency matrix.

6. Write a program to find the critical path of a weighted graph represented by (a) an adjacency matrix, (b) a node-directory structure, (c) a multi-list structure.

7. Develop an activity graph for your own activities for the next week or month. Find the critical path through the graph.

8. Write a program to generate the set of shortest paths from node i to all other nodes in a graph of order n. Assume that the graph is represented by (a) an adjacency matrix, (b) a node-directory structure, and (c) a multi-list structure.

CHAPTER 14

Introduction to File Organization and Management

Over two-thirds of the workers in our society are now producing services rather than making goods or farming. In a service-oriented economy like ours, one of the most important resources is information and, as we know, data are the bases of information. Much of these data are managed by computerized systems. In general, not all of the data being processed by a program can reside simultaneously in the computer's main memory. Instead, large collections of data commonly are stored on auxiliary memory devices. The various techniques that have been developed for structuring these collections of data are the topic of the rest of this book.

This part of the book assumes that you have a reasonable understanding of the data structures discussed in the first part, because those are the foundation for file and database organization techniques.

In the first part of this book we assumed that the entire data structure resided in main memory; generally the data structures were housed in arrays. When evaluating the performance of a program that accessed a data structure, we assumed that there was essentially equal time required to access any element of the structure given its address or a pointer to it. We now turn our concern to the organization and management of data structured on secondary storage devices such as magnetic tapes and disks. These collections of data commonly are referred to as *files*. The techniques required to manage files are different from the data organization techniques that are effective in main memory, although they build on those techniques. This introductory chapter is designed to give you an understanding of what files are, of their roles in information systems, and of the basic problems in their organization and management. Much of the material in this chapter may be review for you if you are acquainted with a production data processing environment or are already familiar with the basics of management information systems.

FILES

A *file* is a collection of logically related records. Recall (from Chapter 3) that a record is a structure of logically related fields, or elements, of information. Usually all of the record occurrences on a file are of a single format, although we will study some examples of files with multiple record formats. Generally the records on a file are stored together for some common purpose; for example, they support payroll processing or employee benefit record-keeping, or they contain inventory information or data gathered in a scientific experiment.

There are at least three good reasons for structuring a collection of data as a file. First, a collection of data may be stored as a file simply because it is too large to fit entirely in main memory. Second, it may be stored as a file because only a small portion of the collection is accessed by a program at any given time, making it unreasonable to store the entire collection in main memory simultaneously. Tape and disk files can be shelved in archives and later made accessible to the appropriate programs and users on demand. Third, even if the collection of data is quite small, it may be desirable to retain the data collection independently of the execution of any particular program.

There are five basic types of files, classified by the functions they perform in an information system:

1. Master file
2. Transaction file
3. Report file
4. Work file
5. Program file

A file only rarely has more than one of these functions. A *master file* represents a static view of some aspect of an organization's business at a point in time. For example, a manufacturing organization might have a payroll master file, a customer master file, a personnel master file, an inventory master file, a material requirements master file, and others. Depending upon how recently the contents of a master file were brought up to date and how much the pertinent status has changed since that time, the master file is a more or less accurate snapshot of some aspect of the "real world." A master file contains relatively permanent data or historical status data. A special type of master file is a dictionary file, which contains descriptions of data rather than the data themselves.

Changes that are going to be applied to a master file are collected on a *transaction file*. As we discuss later in this chapter, a transaction may contain data to add a new record or to remove or modify an existing record on a master file.

A *report file* contains data that are formatted for presentation to a user. The file may be spooled to a printer to produce a hard-copy report or may be displayed on a terminal screen.

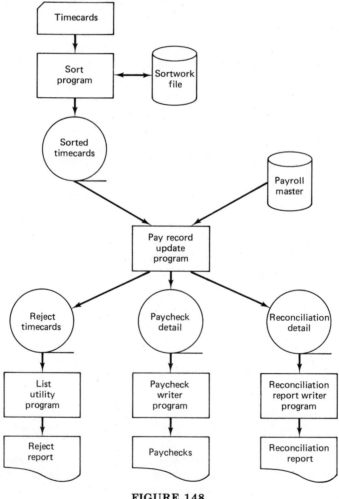

FIGURE 148

A *work file* is a temporary file in a system. It has neither the long-term character of a master file nor the input or output character of a transaction or report file. A work file is a means for passing data created by one program to another program for input. The use of work files is common in information systems.

A *program file* contains instructions for the processing of data which may be stored in other files or resident in main memory. The instructions may be written in a high-level language (e.g., COBOL, Pascal), an assembler language, machine language, or a job control language. The instructions may be in the form of source code or may be the result of compilation, linking, interpretation, or other processing.

Consider the example system flow diagram given in Fig. 148. This system is a rudimentary payroll system that eventually produces paychecks from employee timecard and payroll information. The following table lists the name of each file and its function in the information system. The actual execution of this system generally would involve the use of other files, containing for example, system audit data, diagnostics, user accounting data, executable program code, and job control instructions.

File	Function
timecards	transaction
sort program	program
sort-work file	work
sorted-timecards	transaction
payroll master	master
pay record update program	program
reject timecards	work
paycheck detail	work
reconciliation detail	work
list utility program	program
reject report	report
paycheck writer program	program
paychecks	report
reconciliation report writer program	program
reconciliation report	report

Another approach to classifying the use of a file in an information system is by the way that a program accesses the file. There are three possible modes of access to a file by a program:

1. Input
2. Output
3. Input/output

An *input* file is only read by a program. For example, a file of tax rates and tables would be an input file for a program that computes income taxes. A transaction file is generally an input file to an update program. A program file of source code is an input file to a compiler program.

An *output* file is only written to by a program; it is created by the program. For example, a report file may be the output of a program that updates a master file. A program file of object code is an output file from a compiler program.

An *input/output* file is both read from and written to during program execution. For example, the payroll master file might be used by the payroll program both as a source of data about employee pay rates and as a repository of month-to-date and year-to-date pay totals. An input/output file could be created by one phase of a program, then either modified or just read by another phase of the same program. A master file commonly is an input/output file, as are the work files of sort programs. The chapter on file sorting techniques will illustrate the extensive use of the temporary input/output files that are used as work files by sort programs.

The following table indicates the mode of access for the files in the system shown in Fig. 148.

program file	input file	output file	input/output file
1. sort	timecards	sorted timecards	sort-work file
2. pay record update	sorted timecards	reject timecards paycheck detail reconciliation detail	payroll master
3. paycheck writer	paycheck detail	paychecks	
4. reconciliation report writer	reconciliation detail	reconciliation report	
5. list utility	reject timecards	reject report	

Note again that a given file may have more than one function if it is used by more than one program. A common example of this is the output of a file by one program that is input to another.

FILE ORGANIZATIONS

The technique used to represent and store the records on a file is called the *file organization*. The four fundamental file organization techniques that we will discuss are the following:

1. Sequential
2. Relative
3. Indexed sequential
4. Multi-key

Precise definitions of each of these techniques will be presented in later chapters.

There are two basic ways that the file organization techniques differ. First, the organization determines the file's *record sequencing*, which is the physical ordering of the records on the external storage device. The records of a file are arranged physically either in *sorted* order by the value of some sort-key field, or in *random* order.

Second, the file organization determines the set of operations necessary to find records that have a particular value in some data field. This data field may or may not have duplicate values in the file; it can be a group or elementary item. Some file organization techniques provide rapid accessibility on a variety of data items; other techniques support direct access only on the value of a single item.

The organization most appropriate for a particular file is determined by the operational characteristics of the storage medium used and the nature of the operations to be performed on the data. The most important characteristic of a storage device that influences selection of a file organization technique (or, to turn the argument around, that influences selection of a storage device once the appropriate file organization technique has been determined) is whether the device allows *direct access* to particular record occurrences without accessing all physically prior record occurrences that are stored on the device, or allows only *sequential access* to record occurrences. Magnetic disks are examples of direct access storage devices (abbreviated DASD's); magnetic tapes are examples of sequential storage devices.

FILE OPERATIONS

The way that a file is going to be used in an information system is an important factor in determining how the file should be organized. Two major aspects of a file's use are its mode of use and the nature of the operations on the file.

A file can be accessed by a program that executes in *batch* mode or by a program that executes *interactively*. With batch mode access, transactions generally can be organized in such a way as to improve master file access, whereas with interactive access the transactions are processed as they arrive. With batch mode access, it is the performance of processing a *group* of transactions that is of interest, whereas with interactive access the performance of processing *each* transaction must be considered. Some file organizations are better suited to support interactive access than are others.

The fundamental operations that are performed on files are the following:

1. Creation
2. Update, including:
   record insertion
   record modification
   record deletion
3. Retrieval, including:
   inquiry
   report generation
4. Maintenance, including:
   restructuring
   reorganization

The initial *creation* of a file also is referred to as the *loading* of the file. The bulk of the work in transaction and master file creation involves data collection and validation. In some implementations, space is first allocated to the file, then the data are loaded into that skeleton. In other implementations, the file is constructed a record at a time. We will see examples of both approaches. In the majority of cases, data are loaded into a transaction or master file in batch mode, even if the file actually is built one record at a time. In other cases, data are loaded into a file interactively; however this mode of transaction or master file loading can be excessively time-consuming if large volumes of data are involved.

The contents of a master file represent a snapshot in time of the part of the real world that the master file is supposed to represent. For example, the payroll master file represents the present state of the company's payroll situation: month-to-date and year-to-date fields indicate appropriately accumulated figures for amounts paid, vacation taken, vacation due, etc., for each employee. Changing the contents of a master file to make it reflect a more current snapshot of the real world is known as *updating* of the file. These changes may include (1) the insertion of new record occurrences, e.g., adding a record for a newly hired employee, (2) the modification of existing record occurrences, e.g., changing the pay rate for an employee who has received a raise, and (3) the deletion of existing record occurrences, e.g., removing the record of an employee who has left the company. The updated file represents a more current picture of reality.

In some implementations, the records of a file can be modified in place, new records can be inserted in available free space, and records can be deleted to make space available for reuse. If a file is updated in place by a program, then the file usually is an input/output file for that program. Some implementations are more restrictive and a file cannot be updated in place. In these cases the old file is input to an update program and a new version of the file is output. The file is essentially recreated with current information. However, not all of the records need have been modified; some (maybe even most) of the records may have been copied directly from the old version to the updated version of the file. We will consider this situation further in the chapter on sequential file organization.

The access of a file for purposes of extracting meaningful information is called *retrieval*. There are two basic classes of file retrieval: inquiry and report generation. These two classes can be distinguished by the volume of data that they produce. An inquiry results in a relatively low-volume response, whereas a report may create many pages of output. However, some installations prefer to distinguish between inquiry and report generation by their modes of processing. If a retrieval is processed interactively, these installations would call the retrieval an inquiry. If a retrieval is processed in batch mode, the retrieval would be called report generation. This terminology tends to make report generation more of a planned, scheduled process and inquiry more of an *ad hoc*, spontaneous process. Both types of retrieval are required by most information systems.

An inquiry generally is formulated in a *query language*, which ideally is a natural-language-like structure that is easy for a "non-computer-expert" to learn and to use. A *query processor* is a program that translates the user's inquiries into instructions that are used directly for file access. Most installations that have query processors have acquired them from vendors rather than designing and implementing them in-house.

A file retrieval request can be comprehensive or selective. *Comprehensive* retrieval reports information from all the records on a file, whereas *selective* retrieval applies some qualification criteria to choose which records will supply information for output. Examples of selective retrieval requests formulated in a typical but fictitious query language are the following:

- FIND EMP-NAME OF EMP-PAY-RECORD WHERE
  EMP-NO = 12751
- FIND ALL EMP-NAME, EMP-NO OF EMP-PAY-RECORD
  WHERE EMP-DEPT-NAME = "MIS"
- FIND ALL EMP-NAME, EMP-NO OF EMP-PAY-RECORD
  WHERE 20,000 < EMP-SAL < 40,000

- FIND ALL EMP-NAME, EMP-AGE, EMP-PHONE OF
  EMP-PAY-RECORD WHERE EMP-AGE < 40 AND
  EMP-SEX = "M" AND EMP-SAL > 50,000
- COUNT EMP-PAY-RECORDS WHERE EMP-AGE < 40
- FIND AVERAGE EMP-SAL OF EMP-PAY-RECORD
  WHERE DEPT-NAME = "MIS"

In each case the *WHERE* clause gives the qualification criteria. Note that the last two queries apply the aggregate functions *COUNT* and *AVERAGE* to the qualifying set of records. Some file organizations are better suited to selective retrievals and others are more suited to comprehensive retrievals. We will study examples of both types.

Changes made to a file for purposes of improving the performance of programs that access them are known as *maintenance*. There are two basic classes of maintenance operations: restructuring and reorganization. *Restructuring* of a file implies that structural changes are made to the file within the context of the same file organization technique. For example, field widths could be changed, new fields could be added to records, more space might be allocated to the file, the index tree of the file might be balanced, or the records of the file might be resequenced, but the file organization method would remain the same. File *reorganization* implies change from one file organization to another.

The various file organizations differ in their maintenance requirements. These maintenance requirements are also very dependent upon the nature of activity on the file contents and how quickly that activity changes. Some implementations have file restructuring utilities that are automatically invoked by the operating system; others require that data processing personnel notice when file activity has changed sufficiently or program performance has degraded enough to warrant restructuring or reorganization of a file. Some implementations perform file maintenance on a routine basis. For example, a utility might be run weekly to collect free space from deleted records, to balance index trees, and to expand or contract space allocations.

In general, master files and program files are created, updated, retrieved from, and maintained. Work files are created, updated, and retrieved from, but are not maintained. Report files generally are not updated, retrieved from, or maintained. Transaction files are generally created and used for one-time processing.

PERFORMANCE CONSIDERATIONS

Data structures that are stored in main memory are evaluated in terms of the expected and maximum numbers of comparisons required to find a particular element. File structures are evaluated using different parameters.

When evaluating the performance of programs that access a data structure, it is usually assumed that essentially equal time is required to access any element of the structure given its address or a pointer to it, because the data structure resides entirely in main memory. A file, however, resides on secondary storage. Access to secondary storage is quite time-consuming relative to access to primary storage. The performance of a program that accesses a file is generally measured by the expected and maximum numbers of accesses to secondary storage required to perform a requested operation.

The factors that influence the selection of the appropriate file organization technique also relate to the performance of programs that access the resultant file. We have already introduced the importance of data usage on file performance. Not only is the nature of the operations important, but also the volume and frequency of transactions are significant. One important measure of master file usage is the *file activity ratio*, which we discuss in Chapter 16. Another important factor in file organization selection is the response time required for transactions and retrieval requests. Some organizations provide rapid access to individual records; others do not.

SUMMARY

Files form the cornerstones of many of our information systems. The logically related records that are collected to form a file are structured and stored on an auxiliary memory device. In order to provide effective support for an information system, a file must be structured and organized to meet the requirements of that system.

Files have various basic functions in information systems; a file may contain master data, transaction data, data that are formatted for reports, temporary working data, or program instructions. Files also can be classified by the manner in which a particular program accesses the contained data: input, output, or input/output.

The four fundamental file organization techniques that will be discussed in this text are the sequential, direct, indexed sequential, and multi-key organizations. These techniques differ in their sequencing of records and the accessibility of the records. Some organizations provide for direct access based upon data-item value; others support sequential access to series of records.

The selection of the appropriate organization for a file in an information system is important to the performance of that system. The fundamental factors that influence the selection process include the following:

1. Nature of operations to be performed

2. Characteristics of storage media to be used
3. Volume and frequency of transactions to be processed
4. Response time requirements

The remainder of this book is dedicated to giving an understanding of the fundamental file organization techniques and the trade-offs between them.

Terms

auxiliary memory	primary memory
batch mode	program file
direct access	query language
file	query processor
file activity ratio	record
file organization	relative file organization
indexed sequential file organization	report file
input file	report-writer package
input/output file	secondary storage
interactive mode	sequential file organization
master file	serial access
multi-key file organization	transaction file
output file	work file

Review Exercises

1. For what reasons might a collection of records be structured as a file on secondary storage rather than as a data structure in main memory?
2. Why do most computer systems support several file organization techniques?
3. What file organization techniques are supported by the various compilers available at your installation?
4. Who at your installation selects the type of organization that a file will have?
5. What, if any, general-purpose report-writer programs are available at your installation? What types of file organizations do the programs accommodate for their input files?
6. Obtain access to a system flowchart for a production system at your installation. Identify the master files, transaction files, report files, work files, and program files. Can you identify any additional types of files?

7. For several of the major programs of the system studied for question 6, identify the input files, output files, and input/output files. Complete the following table by filling in the names of files in each function–access mode classification. Are there any boxes with no entries? Which boxes would you expect to be empty and why?

	Input	Output	Input/Output
Master files			
Transaction files			
Report files			
Work Files			

8. How much of a programmer's time in your installation is expended in activities related to each of the following: file creation, file update, file retrieval, and file maintenance?

CHAPTER 15

File Storage Devices

With this chapter we momentarily leave our discussion of techniques for structuring and organizing data and discuss the characteristics of some of the devices that are used to store and retrieve data. We will first introduce the characteristics of storage devices in general, then focus on particular devices. Major emphasis is placed on magnetic tape and disk memories, because of their prevalence in today's world of information processing. Much of the material in this chapter will be review for readers who have a background in the basics of computer systems.

FUNDAMENTAL CHARACTERISTICS
OF FILE STORAGE DEVICES

A storage device is a storage medium and a mechanism for storing and retrieving data on that medium. The *storage medium* is the physical material that holds the data representation. There are two types of storage media: volatile and nonvolatile. The data representation on a volatile medium is erased when electrical power is turned off, whereas the data representation on a nonvolatile medium is retained even without power. The punched card is a familiar example of a nonvolatile storage medium. In fact, nearly all of the media that are of interest for long-term storage of files are nonvolatile.

The *access mechanism* of a storage device provides a means of reading or writing data representations onto the storage medium. Although termed a "mechanism," access generally is supported by a combination of electronic and mechanical techniques.

Nearly all computers have at least two types of storage devices that are used to hold representations of data: *primary memory* (or *main memory*) and *secondary memory* (or *auxiliary memory*).

Equal time is required to access any of the contents of primary memory. Access is extremely fast, the storage is relatively expensive, which brings us to the most basic trade-off to be considered in selection of storage devices: the faster the access that the device supports, the more expensive the device. The most common technology used today to implement main memory is semiconductor (occasionally and incorrectly called *core*) storage.

Secondary memory (or *auxiliary memory*) is accessible indirectly by instructions such as GET, PUT, READ, WRITE, etc. Instructions that cause access to data on secondary memory are called input/output, or simply I/O, instructions. A major operational distinction between primary and secondary memories is that access times on secondary memory are dependent on the location of the target record on the medium and the positioning of the access mechanism. The time to access one record stored on a disk may be quite different from the time required to access another record stored on the same device. The physical arrangement of data on a secondary storage medium can affect the performance of a program that accesses the data.

There are two basic classes of secondary storage devices: *serial-access* and *direct-access* devices. On a serial-access storage device, the time required to access record B after record A is a function of the space between their locations (addresses) on the device. It takes longer to access B after A if they are far apart than if they are closer together. By contrast, on a direct-access storage device, the time required to access record B after record A is not necessarily dependent on their relative locations. In some cases it may be faster to access a record that is farther on the device from the starting point than to access a relatively close record. As with serial-access devices, the physical arrangement of data on a direct-access device can affect the performance of a program that accesses the data.

In addition to the serial/direct nature and relative cost of storage devices, the choice of storage devices should include consideration of storage capacities, failure rates and reliability, maintenance requirements, interfacing needs, and various environmental factors.

MAGNETIC TAPE STORAGE

One of the most widely used devices for computer data storage is magnetic tape. Magnetic tape storage has roots in a voice recorder (called a Telegraphone) that was patented in 1898 by Denmark's Valdemar

Poulsen. This particular device apparently was never commercially built but served as a source of ideas for development of related voice-recording devices that were used widely in the 1930's. By the late 1940's magnetic tape storage was used with computers and the medium's utility for data storage was recognized. Substantial improvements in both the storage medium and tape access mechanisms have resulted in the highly reliable, low-cost, high-capacity tape devices that we use today. We can expect these improvements to continue to produce new generations of magnetic tape devices.

There is a variety of magnetic tape media available today; we will describe here a representative example of the most commonly used choices. The tape medium is a strip of thin (about 2 mils thick), flexible plastic called Mylar, with a coating of ferric-oxide film. The tape is generally 2400 feet long and ½ inch wide, although shorter and narrower tapes also are common, especially for use with microcomputers. The tape is kept on a reel, which is mounted on a *tape drive* (the access mechanism) for read/write access. A reel of tape is quite inexpensive; costs generally range from nine to forty dollars. Tape drives, however, may cost from $5,000 to $40,000, depending on their capabilities. A single tape drive can be used to access any number of tape reels, one at a time.

Magnetic tape is a serial-access storage device. We will discuss many characteristics of magnetic tape, but this serial-access nature is the most important. The records on the tape are stored in physically sequential order. The time required to access record B after record A is a function of how far apart they are on the tape. The best case is that record B would appear immediately following record A; the worst case is that record B would be at the other end of the tape. It is possible to read the records on a tape file in other-than-sequential order, but such access requires rewinds and advances and can be quite time-consuming. In nearly all cases, tape files are read sequentially; they are usually written sequentially. Once a tape file has been written, a record in the middle usually cannot be updated. We will see the limitations that this poses on file processing in Chapter 16 on sequential file organization. Some tape drives allow new records to be appended to the end of an existing tape file, but this is the only type of change allowed.

Data Representation and Density on Magnetic Tape

Data are recorded digitally on the tape medium as magnetized spots in the ferric-oxide film coating. Positive magnetization represents a 1-bit, while negative magnetization represents a 0-bit, or vice versa. These areas of magnetization are induced when the tape is moved (at a typical speed of 200 inches per second) past an appropriately charged coil in a tape drive's WRITE-head mechanism. The ferric-oxide film retains the resultant magnetization; thus the medium is nonvolatile. To read the recorded data, the tape is moved past a tape drive's READ-head mechanism. The magnetization induces current in the coil, and the represented data can be sensed.

The magnetized areas are not randomly located on the medium; rather they are arranged in tracks, which run parallel to the edge of the tape. Today there are usually nine tracks on a tape. Eight of them record data and the ninth records error-control bits. Fig. 149 diagrams a section of a tape; the bits of a single character appear essentially perpendicular to the edge of the tape.

Tape storage medium!

FIGURE 149

One important characteristic of a tape is the density at which data are recorded. Density is a function of both the tape medium and the drive used to record onto the medium. Some devices can accommodate multiple densities. Density is measured in units of bits per inch (bpi), which is equivalent to a measure of characters per inch. Today the most common densities are 800 bpi, 1600 bpi, and 6250 bpi.

Parity and Error Control on Magnetic Tape

In order to interpret correctly the data that are stored on a tape, the encoding scheme that was used when the data were written must be known. For example, the data might be represented in EBCDIC, or ASCII, or some other code. Additionally, the technique used to record error-control bits has to be known in order for that information to be used. One common technique for error control on magnetic tapes is *parity*. If data on a tape are recorded using *odd parity*, then there must be an odd (as opposed to even) number of 1-bits represented for each character. If the bits making up a character's binary representation already have an odd number of 1-bits, then the parity bit (in the ninth track of a 9-track tape) is a 0-bit; if there is an even number of 1-bits, then the parity bit for that character is a 1-bit, making the total number of 1-bits for that character's representation odd. Similarly, parity bits on a tape with *even parity* are recorded so that there is an even number of 1-bits represented for each character.

Parity bits are written when data on the tape are written, then are checked when the tape is read to verify that an error has not occurred. For example, a speck of dust or cigarette ash on the tape surface might interfere with the read head and cause a 0-bit to be sensed incorrectly as a 1-bit. A parity discrepancy can be used to detect the error. This simple technique of even/odd parity can detect single-bit (or 3-bit or 5-bit or 7-bit) errors in a character's representation, but can not detect 2-bit, 4-bit, 6-bit, or 8-bit errors. Furthermore, the technique does not indicate which of the bits is wrong.

When a parity error is detected, the read may be retried automatically, then if the error persists, the computer operator is notified. The error can be overridden or access to the file may be terminated. Some operating systems allow the person who sets up a program's job control specifications to request that parity errors be ignored for a tape. The result, of course, may be missing or incorrect interpretation of data on the tape. Such a request may be quite useful, however, for salvaging data from a "bad" tape.

Errors may appear on a magnetic tape because of dirt deposits, bends or wrinkles, areas where the ferric-oxide coating is missing, worn edges, stretched areas, too low a level of magnetization, errors in recording the data in the first place, and so on. A good quality tape generally can be read or written several thousand times before the medium deteriorates. This assumes however that the tape is kept in a dust-free, controlled-humidity environment. The faulty-write problem commonly is approached by positioning the read and write heads of the access mechanism so that the tape passes by the read head after passing by the write head. This configuration allows a read to be attempted immediately after a write, for a self-check on parity.

Blocking on a Magnetic Tape

Data are read from or written to a tape in groups of characters called *blocks*. A block is the smallest amount of data that can be transferred between secondary memory and primary memory in one access. A block may contain one or more records. A block is sometimes referred to as a *physical record*. In order to read or write data properly, the tape medium must be moving at a constant speed when it passes by the head mechanism. Because requests to read or write blocks do not arrive at a tape drive at a constant rate, there must be a gap (sometimes called an *interblock gap*) between each pair of blocks, forming a space to be passed over as the tape slows from read/write speed and as the tape accelerates to read/write speed. The medium is not strong enough to withstand the stress that it would sustain with instantaneous starts and stops. If you have seen a magnetic tape drive in operation, you may have noticed the jerky nature of the movement of the reel. Because the tape is not moving at a constant speed while the read/write head is positioned at a gap, a gap can not contain user data. Fig. 150 diagrams a section of tape, showing the gaps and the user records.

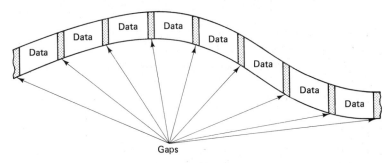

Gaps

FIGURE 150

Each gap typically is .75 inches long. The block size can significantly affect the amount of data that can be stored on a tape. Contrast, for example, the case of one 100-character record per block with the case of twenty 100-character records per block. Assume that the medium is 2400 feet in length and that data are recorded at a density of 6250 bpi. With one record per block, the tape can contain:

$$\frac{2400 \ \dfrac{ft}{tape} \ * \ \dfrac{12 \ in}{ft}}{1 \ \dfrac{rec}{block} \ * \ \dfrac{100 \ char}{\dfrac{rec}{\dfrac{6250 \ char}{in}}} \ + \ \dfrac{3 \ in}{4 \ gap} \ * \ \dfrac{1 \ gap}{block}} \ = \ 37,598 \ \frac{blocks}{tape}$$

which is 37,598 records, while with twenty records per block, the tape can contain:

$$\frac{2400 \ \dfrac{ft}{tape} \ * \ \dfrac{12 \ in}{ft}}{20 \ \dfrac{rec}{block} \ * \ \dfrac{100 \ char}{\dfrac{rec}{\dfrac{6250 \ char}{in}}} \ + \ \dfrac{3 \ in}{4 \ gap} \ * \ \dfrac{1 \ gap}{block}} \ = \ 26,916 \ \frac{blocks}{tape}$$

which is 538,320 records. In the first case, 98% of the tape is occupied by gaps; with twenty records per block, the gaps occupy 70% of the tape. Increasing the number of records per block (also known as the *blocking factor*) would improve further the utilization of the tape space.

Perhaps more important is the effect of the blocking factor on the time required to access the tape. Assume that the required tape speed for read/write access is 200 inches per second and that 0.15 second is required to stop and restart through a gap. The time required to access our example full tape with 1 record per block and a delay in each gap is:

$$\frac{37{,}598\frac{\text{blocks}}{\text{tape}}*.016\frac{\text{in}}{\text{block}}}{200\frac{\text{in}}{\text{sec}}}+37{,}598\frac{\text{blocks}}{\text{tape}}*\frac{.15\text{ sec}}{\text{gap}}*\frac{1\text{ gap}}{\text{block}}=5643\frac{\text{sec}}{\text{tape}}$$

which is 1.57 hours, whereas the time required to access the same collection of records with 20 records per block is:

$$\frac{1880\frac{\text{blocks}}{\text{tape}}*.32\frac{\text{in}}{\text{block}}}{200\frac{\text{in}}{\text{sec}}}+1880\frac{\text{blocks}}{\text{tape}}*\frac{.15\text{ sec}}{\text{gap}}*1\frac{\text{gap}}{\text{block}}=285\text{ sec}$$

which is 4.75 minutes. A program that accesses a file of data stored on a tape can execute no faster than that file can be accessed. Selection of the appropriate blocking factor of a tape file thus is significant to the performance of a program that accesses that file. The blocking factor used when a file is written must be known when that file is later read.

Why not just have one block include all of the records of the file? This approach certainly would minimize the number of blocks, thus also minimizing the number of gaps and the time required to access the file. The problem with this approach is that regardless of the block size, there must be space allocated in main memory to hold the contents of a block prior to writing the block onto the tape (for an output file) or prior to reading the block into a program (for an input file). This space in main memory is called a *buffer* and is shown in Fig. 151.

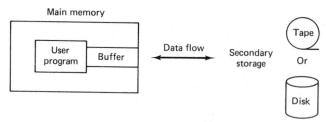

FIGURE 151

The size of a buffer for a file is the same as that file's block size. Main memory is relatively much more expensive than is tape storage. Furthermore, main memory is commonly a scarce resource, especially in smaller computer systems. Not only do the charging algorithms used in most computing facilities reflect the expense and scarcity of main memory, but in many cases tasks are prioritized by the amount of main memory they require to execute: small tasks generally get higher priority than do the large tasks.

When a program requests a record from a tape file with a blocking factor of one record per block, the tape is accessed, one block is moved into the buffer, and the record is available. The next read of the file causes the same sequence of events to occur. What happens when there is more than one record per block? A program still requests a read of *one* record at a time, but an entire block must be brought into the buffer at once. The I/O control system (which we discuss in more detail in Chapter 17) makes available to the program one record at a time, keeping track of which records have been released to the program. When the buffer is empty (i.e., when all records have been accessed by the program), the I/O control system initiates another access to the tape, another block is moved into the buffer, and the first record of the new block is made available to the program.

Charging algorithms in many computing facilities include the number of access requests to secondary storage in their calculations of costs. This is another reason why it may be beneficial to use a large blocking factor. Selection of the appropriate blocking factor for a tape file involves trade-offs between the time required to access the tape, the cost of main memory buffer space, and the number of accesses to secondary storage. We will discuss more details of the selection of blocking factor in the chapters on sequential file organization, I/O control systems, relative file organization, and indexed sequential file organization.

Tape Marks and Labels

Let us consider now several other characteristics of the tape medium. The beginning (after a leader section) and end (before a trailer section) of the tape reel are each marked by an aluminum, reflective strip that can be sensed by a photoelectric sensor in the tape drive. The tape mark at the beginning of the tape reel is known as the *load point*. When the tape reel is mounted on the drive, the tape is threaded through the access mechanism and positioned at the load point. Data can be written on the tape after this point, and up until the point where the other tape mark, which is known as the *end-of-tape mark*, is encountered. A primary function of the end-of-tape mark is to prevent the unthreading of the tape and consequent destruction of part of the reel.

A tape reel generally has an *external label*, which is a piece of adhesive affixed to the reel's plastic casing. This label bears a number and is used by the operator and tape librarian to identify the reel.

A tape may also have an *internal label*, which is recorded electronically on the tape. A tape with an internal label is said to be a *labeled tape*. Standards have been developed for formatting internal labels; some computer facilities instead use their own home-grown formats. An internal label contains information such as tape number (which is usually the same as the external number), retention period, password, creation date, and similar information. Some tapes also have trailer labels, which follow the user data.

It may be important to ensure that a program does not write on a tape file that already contains data, thus obliterating that data. To allow write access to a tape, a plastic ring can be inserted in the tape casing, thus activating the write head. The ring also can be removed easily by an operator should it be necessary to prevent writing to the tape.

Tape Usage

Magnetic tape has evolved to be an important medium for the storage of large master files, backup files, and archive-history files. The medium is portable and provides relatively low-cost storage for relatively large quantities of data. Its serial-access nature seriously impacts the design and processing of files stored on tape. In fact, the serial-access nature of the tape medium also has impacted many experienced programmers' and analysts' approaches to designing data systems; they have continued to impose unnecessarily the limitations of the tape medium on files stored on direct-access media.

Punched Cards

Punched cards were developed by Herman Hollerith (then 20 years old!) for data storage in the 1890 census and were inspired by techniques for the automation of weaving looms developed by a Frenchman named Jacquard. Several variations on the basic punched card have been developed, but the most popular continues to be the 80-column (i.e., 80-character), 3-1/4- by 7-3/8-inch card developed by Hollerith. It has been suggested that the dimensions of the card match those of an 1890 dollar bill, a size selected by Hollerith in an attempt to make his invention feel more familiar in people's hands.

The punched card has proven itself through the years. It is a permanent form of relatively cheap data storage. It is simple to verify that the intended data actually were recorded on the medium. It is easy to replace cards anywhere in a deck.

Despite these tangible benefits, the punched card is no longer used extensively. Magnetic media have usurped much of the role of punched cards in our information systems. There are several reasons for this demise. Reading and writing of punched cards are quite slow, primarily because of the mechanical nature of the operations. The fastest reading speed that can be expected from a card reader (without shuffling and spewing of cards) is approximately 1500 cards per minute; the fastest writing speed that can be expected from a card punch is about 500 cards per minute. Compare this with the example speeds used in our discussion of magnetic tapes. Storage of punched cards can become a severe problem. The data that can be stored on one 1600 bpi tape would occupy approximately 125,000 punched cards. One box containing 2000 cards occupies about 20 by 6 by 3½ inches of space. The 62.5 boxes that would be required to hold the contents of one magnetic tape would occupy about 73 feet of shelf space, probably in a room with reinforced flooring. Cards are heavy! They also are sensitive to changes in humidity and do not recover easily from bending, folding, or mutilation. Decks of cards are prone to being shuffled and inadvertently dropped. Furthermore, they are not an exceptionally cheap medium. A box of 2000 cards costs approximately $2. Thus the 62.5 boxes required to hold one magnetic tape's contents would cost about $125. Compare this with the price of a reel of tape.

Paper Tape

Punched paper tape is another relatively common form of serial-access storage medium. It has some of the same disadvantages that punched cards do: slow read and write processing, bulky storage requirements, and propensity to mutilation. Paper tape tends to be lighter than punched cards per unit of storage. Although obsolescent, it probably will continue to be used for many years, because of its prevalence as a medium for output from many types of scientific devices. For example, machines that measure physical characteristics of samples of rock, soil, air, or fuel commonly output data to punched paper tape, which then is input to a computer for analysis of the data. Paper tape provides a means for these specialized pieces of equipment to communicate with computer support.

MAGNETIC DISK STORAGE

A trend for several years now has been the increasing use of direct-access storage devices (DASD's). This trend has resulted both from improved economics of DASD's and the growing need to support interactive access to data. Magnetic disk storage is the most prevalent type of DASD. In this section we will discuss the characteristics of so-called "hard disks"; we will introduce "flexible disks" (known as floppy disks or floppies) in the next section.

The first DASD, the magnetic drum, was developed in the

mid-1950's as a means to increase a computer's memory capacity and to provide direct-access capability to that capacity. Although magnetic tapes had been used for computer data storage for only a few years, the limitations of that serial-access device were readily apparent.

The RAMAC (*Random Access*) was the first DASD made available to the computer industry. This magnetic disk unit, developed by International Business Machines, Inc., was physically much larger than today's DASD's. It stood several feet tall and had fifty fixed disk platters, each about two feet in diameter. Like today's magnetic disks, the platters rotated at a high rate of speed on a spindle. Access arms with read/write heads were positioned between the platters and performed retrieval and storage of data representations on the surfaces of the platters. Data were recorded in concentric tracks, much as they are today. The RAMAC's capacity was about 5 million characters.

Continuous development since the RAMAC's appearance in 1955 has resulted in much faster, higher capacity, smaller magnetic disk devices. DASD's are available today in a wide range of configurations that offer a choice of performance, capacity, and price to match the needs of various computer systems. Disks differ with respect to their number of recording surfaces, data transfer rates, read/write head movement times, access mechanism technologies, rotational delays, densities, and other features. We will describe here representative examples of the most commonly used devices. Development in DASD technologies will continue to produce improved devices.

Physical Characteristics of Magnetic Disks

The typical magnetic disk storage device is a *disk pack* composed of several stacked, rigid aluminum platters mounted on a spindle. Commonly there are eleven platters in a pack. Each platter is 14 inches in diameter (8 inches in mini-disks) and resembles a phonograph record; its surface is coated with a metal-oxide film that retains magnetization in much the same way that the film on a magnetic tape does. In contrast to the way information is recorded on a phonograph record, data are recorded on a disk platter in concentric *tracks* rather than in a spiral groove. The number of tracks on a platter is determined by the recording characteristics of the surface coating and the capabilities of the disk drive and access mechanism. Today's disks have from 200 to 800 tracks per surface. (The number of tracks on a platter is fixed.) There are twenty recording surfaces in a disk pack of eleven platters; both sides of each platter are used except for the topmost and bottommost surfaces, which are more susceptible to contamination than are the inside surfaces. Also the arms for those outside surfaces would access only half as much data.

For access, a disk pack is mounted on a disk drive, which includes a controller, access arms, read/write heads, and a mechanism for rotating the pack. Some drives are manufactured with built-in disk packs, which are *nonremovable*. A drive that can support any number of disks (one at a time) uses *removable* disk packs. Disk drives are commonly combined in banks of two, six, or eight, sometimes with an additional spare drive; the combination of drives is referred to as a *unit*.

A *disk controller* handles decoding of record addresses, including selection of the appropriate drive of a unit and decoding of the position of the requested data on the disk pack of that drive. The controller also manages buffer storage for the unit, handles error detection and correction, and controls read/write activities.

The platters of a mounted disk pack spin continuously at a speed of about 3600 revolutions per minute. Unlike magnetic tape devices, a rotating disk device does not stop between block accesses.

The read/write heads of the disk drive are mounted on access arms that are positioned between the platters of the device. The heads float on a cushion of air less than 1-millionth of an inch above the surface of the platter. The unfortunate case of having a read/write head actually come into contact with a platter surface is called a *head crash*. Such contact can damage the head and the recording surface rather severely and take the disk out of commission.

Data Representation and Addressing on a Magnetic Disk

The data on a disk are blocked in the same way as are the data on a magnetic tape. Recall that a block is the amount of data that is accessed in one request to the storage device. As was discussed for tape storage, data from a disk device are moved to a buffer in the main storage of the computer for access by a program. The selection of the proper block size for a disk file is somewhat more difficult than for a tape file. The direct-access capability of the disk device implies that records will not always be accessed sequentially. Increasing the block size will not always reduce the number of accesses to the DASD.

There are two basic techniques for addressing the data records that are stored on a disk: the cylinder method and the sector method. With the *cylinder method*, a record's address is its cylinder number, surface number, and record number. All the tracks of a given diameter on the disk pack form a cylinder (see Fig. 152). Thus a disk pack with 200 tracks per surface has 200 cylinders. The surface number part of a record's address determines on which surface of the cylinder the record is stored. If there are eleven platters, then the surface-numbers range from 0 to 19 (or 1 to 20). The record number part of an address determines where the record resides on the particular track designated

FIGURE 152

by the cylinder number, surface number. An index point can be sensed by the disk access mechanism at the start of each track.

With the *sector method*, each track of the pack is divided into sectors, as illustrated in Fig. 153.

FIGURE 153

Each sector is a storage area for a fixed number of characters. A record's address is simply its sector number. Given a sector number, the disk controller can determine which track should be accessed and where on the track the addressed record resides.

Each track on a platter has the same recording capacity, even though the tracks are of different diameters. The uniformity of capacity is achieved by appropriate adjustment of the density of data representation for each track's dimensions. A major benefit of this uniform-capacity approach is that files can be relocated on the disk without changing the number of sectors (or tracks or cylinders) allocated to the file. Some operating systems allow the person who sets up a program's job control language specifications to request the number of sectors (or tracks or cylinders) that are to be allocated to a file.

Movable-head Disk Access

There are several types of access mechanisms available today for magnetic disk storage devices. A *movable-head disk drive* has one read/write-head for each recording surface. A mechanical system is used to position the set of access arms such that the read/write head of the addressed surface is at the desired track. All of the access arms of the device move in unison, but only the head for the desired surface is activated. The head-positioning system requires a high degree of accuracy in order to locate the heads precisely over the closely spaced tracks. Environmental factors, including temperature variations and usage, can affect the accuracy of positioning; movable-head disk drives require periodic maintenance to keep the positioning servomechanisms within tolerance limits.

For access of a record that is stored on a disk pack, the following sequence of events must occur. The disk controller decodes the desired record's address and determines on which track of the device the record resides. The access arms are moved so that the read/write heads are positioned at the appropriate cylinder. The read/write head for the desired track is activated. The disk then must rotate until the desired record is located at the read/write head. The data then can be read and transferred across the channel to the requesting program in the computer.

This sequence of events has the following time components:

ACCESS TIME = SEEK TIME (move arms to cylinder)
+ HEAD-ACTIVATION TIME (select track)
+ ROTATIONAL DELAY (select record)
+ TRANSFER TIME.

Of these factors, *seek time* is the most significant because it involves the mechanical movement of the access arms. A typical disk drive requires an average of 60 ms to seek the desired cylinder. By contrast, head-activation time is essentially zero, since it is an electrical function. *Rotational delay* (sometimes called *latency*) times are determined by the speed of revolution of the disk platters. At 3600 revolutions per minute, the worst case rotational delay is 16.6 ms, when the desired record has just been passed over (Fig. 154(a)).

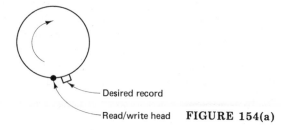

FIGURE 154(a)

The best case is when the read/write head is correctly positioned at the start. In the average case, rotational delay is 8.3 ms (Fig. 154(b)):

FIGURE 154(b)

Transfer time is determined by the speed of revolution and the amount of data to be transferred.

If records of a file stored on disk are to be accessed sequentially, then access times can be minimized by properly allocating disk space to the file. Assume the file requires ten tracks of space. Rather than allocating ten tracks on one surface to the file, space should be allocated to tracks of one cylinder, thereby minimizing the arm movement required to access the records.

Actually, minimizing seek time can be very difficult in a multi-user environment in which different users' accesses to the same disk can be interleaved. Also difficult to optimize are the usual cases in which the direct-access capabilities of the disk are used. It may be impossible to predict the order of access to records.

Fixed-head Disk Access

A *fixed-head disk drive* sharply reduces access times by virtually eliminating the major delay component of movable-head systems: seek time. A fixed-head disk drive has one read/write head for each track of each recording surface. The time components of access time then reduce to:

$$\text{ACCESS TIME} = \text{HEAD-ACTIVATION TIME} \\ + \text{ROTATIONAL DELAY} \\ + \text{TRANSFER TIME.}$$

In addition to the advantage of reduced access times, the mechanical simplicity of the fixed-head approach results in enhanced reliability over the movable-head approach. The mean time between failures is typically 1000 hours for a movable-head disk drive and 10,000 hours for a fixed-head disk drive. Fixed-head disk drives also tend to be easier to repair. The basic causes of disk failures are mechanical problems including head crashes, electronic malfunctions, and errors due to surface contamination.

The costs of the fixed-head approach are increased price and decreased capacity. The number of read/write heads causes the price of a fixed-head disk drive to exceed that of a movable-head disk drive. A drive to access disks with 200 tracks per surface has 200 times as many heads if the heads are fixed rather than movable. Disks for use with fixed-head drives tend to have slightly lower capacities than do disks for use with movable-head drives; they also have lower densities because of head spacing requirements.

Head-per-track Drives and Winchester Disks

One variation on the fixed-head disk drive is the *parallel head-per-track drive*, which can activate more than one head at the same time. Thus data can be read from multiple tracks in parallel. This type of device requires a controller that expects parallel streams of data. These drives are not used widely today, but they may come into greater use with the database machines of the mid- and late-1980's.

Another variation on the DASD's we have introduced is the *Winchester disk*. In a Winchester disk, the recording surfaces, access mechanism, and read/write heads are manufactured together in a sealed cartridge, which can be either removable (i.e., multiple packs can be used on a single drive) or nonremovable (i.e., it is manufactured as an integral part of the disk drive). These devices provide for very high storage densities. For example, the IBM 3350 records more than 3 million bits of data per square inch of disk surface. The increased densities result from the Winchester head configuration, which governs the flow of air around the head so that it floats very close to the disk surface.

The cost of direct-access storage has been decreasing steadily. Today, $1 can buy storage space for over 16,000 characters, whereas in 1964, $1 could buy storage space for about 300 characters. Each magnetic disk is substantially more expensive than is a magnetic tape, but each disk has much higher capacity, as well as direct-access capability. Much of the cost improvement in disk storage has been the result of technologies that have increased recording densities. One surface of a modern disk pack typically can store more data than could the entire RAMAC device with fifty 2-foot-diameter platters.

OTHER DIRECT-ACCESS STORAGE DEVICES

Flexible Disk Storage

One of the most important developments in DASD's has been flexible disk storage devices, now familiar as *floppy disks*, or just *floppies*. They are also called *diskettes*. The floppy was introduced in 1970 as a storage medium for a large IBM magnetic disk storage system. The flexible disks are now widely used as DASD's for microcomputers and minicomputers, as auxiliary memory for intelligent terminals, and as a storage medium for key-data entry devices.

The medium of a floppy disk is essentially the same as that of a magnetic tape: mylar coated with a magnetic oxide film. A floppy is thicker than magnetic tape and is cut as a disk. Diameters vary, but dimensions are typically 5¼ or 8 inches. The "typical" floppy has 77 concentric tracks, each with 26 sectors, each with a user-addressable space of 128 characters. A floppy's track density is about 48 tracks per inch, while a Winchester disk has a track density of about 1000 per inch. Recording density on a floppy is typically 3200 bpi. The user-addressable capacity of the storage surface is approximately 242K bytes. (Three of the tracks are usually reserved for system usage.) Some floppies have just one recording surface; others can have data recorded on both sides. The flexible disk is enclosed in a square plastic or paper envelope, much like a dust-jacket for a 45 rpm phonograph record.

For access, the disk-and-envelope medium is inserted into a slot in the drive, and the disk is held against a rotating spindle by a clamp. The material used as the interior surface of the envelope allows the disk to rotate inside the envelope while the envelope is held stationary. Typical rotation speed is 360 rpm. Pressure pads hold the read/write head in physical contact with the disk surface. This contact causes some wear of the surface, but many vendors guarantee their floppies for 2 million passes per track.

Floppies provide inexpensive, direct-access secondary storage capability. Their usage, especially with microcomputers, undoubtedly will continue to grow.

Mini-disk Cartridges

Another development in DASD's that is enjoying widespread use with microcomputers are the small "hard disks" known as *mini-disk cartridges*. These devices provide greater storage capacities (generally 2 million to 20 million characters) and better reliability than do the flexible disks; they can support higher recording densities because of their stable, hard surfaces. Of course, they are also more expensive than are floppies.

Several vendors now offer "mini-Wini's," which are applications of Winchester technology to small (typically 5-inch) disks. These devices have high densities, high reliability, and (because they are being produced in quantity) relatively low cost (about $3,000).

Mass Storage

Mass storage devices are used for extremely large volumes of data to which only relatively slow access times are required. For example, the storage capacity of the IBM 3850 ranges up to 236 billion bytes (236 gigabytes). Data are stored in cylindrical cartridges; each cartridge contains a 771-inch-long piece of 4-inch-wide magnetic tape which can hold about 50 megabytes. These cartridges are stored in banks of honeycomb-like cells. When data from a cartridge are requested, the cartridge is extracted from its cell and moved to a read/write device, and the contents of its tape are written to a hard disk. The requested data are then accessed from the disk and moved to main memory. Thus the disk acts as a staging area in the hierarchy of storage devices. Access times to data are about 8 to 13 seconds, including the time to extract the appropriate cartridge from its cell and to transfer the data to disk.

As demands for data storage explode, so will technologies for mass storage continue to develop. Mass storage devices may be especially effective for managing very large files and databases that need to be shared and accessed by several computers.

SUMMARY

There is quite a variety of file storage devices available, and rapid technological development keeps the field in a changing state. File storage devices can be characterized by the following parameters:

1. Serial-access versus direct-access
2. Usable storage capacity
3. Access time (average, maximum)

4. Data transfer rate
5. Interfacing requirements
6. Maintenance requirements
7. Environmental requirements
8. Reliability
9. Standardization
10. Price

The most widely used file storage devices today include magnetic tape storage and magnetic disk storage (movable-head, fixed-head, and flexible). The physical characteristics of these devices were discussed, as were characteristics of data representations on the media. Concepts of parity, blocking, and buffering were also introduced.

Terms

access mechanism
auxiliary memory
block
blocking factor
buffer
controller
cylinder
cylinder addressing
direct-access storage device (DASD)
disk drive
diskette
disk pack
end-of-tape mark
even parity
external label
fixed-head disk
floppy disk
head crash
interblock gap
internal label
labeled tape
latency

load point
magnetic disk storage
magnetic tape storage
main memory
mass storage
mini-disk
movable-head disk
nonvolatile storage
odd parity
parallel head-per-track drive
parity
physical record
primary memory
rotational delay
secondary storage
sector
sector addressing
seek time
serial-access device
storage medium
volatile storage
Winchester disk

Review Exercises

1. Consider a short section of tape that contains the following codes:

track 1:	1	1	1	1	1	1
	1	1	1	1	1	1
	0	0	0	0	1	1
.	1	0	1	0	0	0
.	0	0	1	1	0	1
.	1	0	0	0	0	0
	1	0	0	0	1	0
track 8:	1	1	1	1	1	0

   What does track 9 contain if the data are recorded using (a) even parity, (b) odd parity?

2. Why does a computer installation nearly always have a variety of storage devices available?

3. Consider a magnetic tape with 1600 bpi and three-quarter-inch interblock gaps. Assume that 80-byte records are to be stored on a 2400-foot tape. (a) How many records could be stored on the tape if a blocking factor of 5 records per block were used? (b) How many records could be stored on the tape if a blocking factor of 15 were used?

4. Assume that the transport speed for the tape of exercise 3 is 100 inch/sec when reading or writing and that it takes .005 seconds to start or stop the tape between blocks. (a) How long would it take to read the tape with a blocking factor of 5 records per block? (b) How long would it take to read the tape with a blocking factor of 15 records per block?

5. What is the difference between a fixed-head disk and a movable-head disk with respect to data access time?

6. Which of the following activities makes the greatest contribution to the access time of a block on a movable-head disk? (a) head activation, (b) cylinder selection, (c) rotational delay.

7. Which of the following activities makes the greatest contribution to the access time of a block on a fixed-head disk? (a) head activation, (b) cylinder selection, (c) rotational delay.

8. What types of storage devices are available at your installation? Which devices support serial access and which support direct access?

9. What are the relative advantages and disadvantages of each of the following: magnetic tape, punched cards, magnetic disk?

CHAPTER 16

Sequential File Organization

Sequentially organized files have been the workhorses of many data processing organizations for years. In this chapter we first discuss the characteristics of sequential files, then introduce the basic operations on sequential files: their creation, retrieval of their contents, and updating of their records. We also consider factors that affect the design of sequential files.

DEFINITIONS AND APPLICATIONS: SEQUENTIALLY ORGANIZED FILES

The most basic way to organize the collection of records that form a file is to use *sequential organization*. In a sequentially organized file, the records are written consecutively when the file is created and must be accessed consecutively when the file is later used for input (Fig. 155).

In many cases the records of a sequential file are ordered by the value of some field in each record. Such a file is said to be a *sorted* file; the field(s) whose value is used to determine the ordering is known as the *sort key*. If a file is sorted by the value of a field named KEY, ascending, then,

> record *I* precedes record *J*
> if and only if
> the value of KEY in record *I*

FIGURE 155

is less than or equal to
the value of KEY in record J.

A file may be sorted in ascending or descending order by a sort key comprised of one or more fields. In Chapter 18 we will discuss several techniques that are commonly used for sorting sequential files.

A sequentially organized file may be composed of records of several different types. Multiple record types would be grouped together to form a file if they had a common functional purpose and were closely related logically. For example, in an integrated personnel-payroll system, the employee file might contain two types of records.

PERSONNEL

REC TYPE	EMPNO	NAME	PHONE	ADDRESS	MARITAL STATUS	SEX	HOME LOC	MIL CODE	EDUC YR	DEG	SO
1											

(a)

and

PAYROLL

REC TYPE	EMPNO	FUND TYPE	ACCOUNT CODE	NO	BASE SALRATE	% TIME	RESP DEPT	DATE START	DATE CHANGE	...
2										

(b)

FIGURE 156

An employee may have one personnel record (Fig. 156(a)) and one or more payroll records (Fig. 156(b)), one for each account from which his or her salary is drawn. Note that the records on the file need not have the same format and need not be of the same size. However, there does need to be a way to determine the type of any given record occurrence. Here the first field of the record is used for that purpose. This example file might be sorted by EMPNO,RECTYPE.

An employee's records would be consecutive; the employee's personnel record would precede the related payroll records. The value of the RECTYPE field could be used by a program to determine the format of a particular record.

Variable length and/or format records are not supported directly by all file systems. It may be necessary in these systems to make the records appear to be nonvariable, e.g., by padding short records with trailing blanks to provide consistent record lengths.

Processing requirements determine the appropriate sort order for a sequential file. For example, the records of a sequential file used to generate the white pages of a telephone directory would be sorted by subscriber last name and first name, because that is the required ordering for the report.

There are some cases, however, when it *is* useful to have a telephone directory with records sorted by subscriber address, or by zip code, or type of business. For example, a telephone poll of opinions based on particular areas of a city or a follow-up campaign for census data might use such a directory. If the directory data are stored as a sequential file, they can be in only one sorted order. One sequential file of records cannot be in sorted order by last name, first name and *also* be in sorted order by address. To satisfy both of these sort requirements, there would have to be two sequential files. They would contain the same data but be sequenced differently.

Information systems that are built around sequential files tend to exhibit replication of record types across files that are in different sort orders. Usually not all of these files are retained; many are considered to be temporary and are deleted after they have been input to a following program or their contents have been printed. For example, a payroll system might generate a variety of reports; some would order the same pay data by employee social security number, some by source account code, some by check number, some by deposit account number, etc.

Because the records of a sequentially organized file must be accessed consecutively, sequential files are used more commonly in batch processing than in interactive processing. For example, a sequential file of customer data (names, addresses, credit ratings, and the like) could be accessed in batch mode to print mailing labels to advertise a special sale; each customer record would be accessed. A sequential file of employee payroll data could be accessed in batch mode to generate paychecks; nearly all employee records would have activity. Changes to employee benefit information could be gathered over a period (say a week or month), then batched together to update the employee file. Monthly processing (such as customer billings), quarterly processing (such as tax reporting), semiannual processing (such as inventory reporting), and annual processing are examples of types of applications in which transactions are collected and then applied as a batch to be processed together. Later in this chapter we will discuss more fully the processing of sequential files. Recall from Chapter 14 that the fundamental operations that are performed on files are creation, update, retrieval, and maintenance.

The major advantage of the sequential technique of organizing files is the ability to access the "next" record quickly. As long as the pattern of access to a sequential file matches the ordering of records on the file, access times are very good. However, if a program's patterns of access do not match the record ordering pattern, then performance of the program can be terrible.

Consider, for example, a sequential file of employee information sorted by EMPNO. Accessing employee records sequentially by EMPNO (or by requesting "next" through the entire file) matches the file organization. Accessing employee records by EMPNAME does not match the file organization, nor does accessing records in the order EMPNO = 12751, EMPNO = 98103, EMPNO = 54216. Actually, we have turned the design process around here. The pattern of access should be determined, *then* the file should be organized to suit that pattern, not vice versa.

STORAGE OF SEQUENTIALLY ORGANIZED FILES

A sequentially organized file can be stored on a serial-access storage medium (such as a deck of punched cards, a reel of magnetic tape, a roll of punched paper tape) or on a direct-access storage device (such as a floppy disk or a hard magnetic disk). In either case, the records of the file are accessed sequentially.

Some of the reasons that it may be desirable to store a sequential file on a DASD are the following:

1. The computer may be configured with fewer serial-access drives than are required for a particular application. For example, if three sequential files are used in a program, say an old master file, a transaction file, and an updated master file, and there are only two tape drives, then one of the files could be stored on disk.
2. The system may be configured such that certain types of files are always written on disk. For example, the printer controller may

expect that all files that are to be printed will be spooled* to disk. Thus if a report file is created by a program, it will be assigned to a disk device.

3. The characteristics of channel traffic and channel capacities in a system may make it advantageous to split files across devices. For example, a system might be configured with two tape drives on one channel and two disk drives on another channel. If large volumes of data are generated by a program for two sequential files, it can be advantageous to put them on separate channels (and here therefore on different types of devices) rather than to have them assigned to devices that share a channel.

In some installations it is the programmers' responsibility to assign files to devices. In other installations the system will supply a default assignment if the programmer does not select a device. In many systems the programmer assigns a file to a *type* of device (such as magnetic disk or magnetic tape) rather than to a *particular* device. For example, if a sequential file is being written on tape, the programmer may not know (or care) which specific reel of tape is used; it suffices that the reel number be known *after* the file is created, so that the file can be used as input to another program execution.

If a sequential file is used as input to a program and the programmer is specifying that file's device assignment, the device type must match the actual type of device on which the file is stored. A reel of magnetic tape cannot be mounted easily on a disk drive!

DECLARATION OF SEQUENTIAL FILES IN PROGRAMS

Nearly all programming languages provide the capability to declare sequentially organized files, and nearly all programming languages provide this capability differently. In this section we introduce the basic concepts required to be able to declare sequential files in COBOL and Pascal. For details of declaration requirements you should consult local language manuals and inquire about local installation standards and procedures.

Sequential Files in COBOL

The COBOL programmer provides file declaration information in both the *ENVIRONMENT DIVISION* and the *DATA DIVISION* of a program. The entries in the *ENVIRONMENT DIVISION* serve to iden-

---

Spooling is the use of buffers (here in the form of temporary files on disk) to reduce the effects of timing differences between the central processing unit and peripheral equipment (here the printer). See also Chapter 17.

tify the storage devices to be used for files; the entries in the *DATA DIVISION* describe the organization, physical characteristics, and format of records in files. Let us look first at pertinent *ENVIRONMENT DIVISION* entries.

File-oriented information is provided in the *INPUT-OUTPUT SECTION* of the *ENVIRONMENT DIVISION*. The *SELECT* clause of the *FILE-CONTROL* paragraph associates each file used in the program with a storage device. The format of the *SELECT* clause is*:

SELECT [OPTIONAL] filename ASSIGN TO [implementor-name] ...

[RESERVE integer $\begin{bmatrix} \text{AREAS} \\ \text{AREA} \end{bmatrix}$]

[ORGANIZATION is SEQUENTIAL]

[ACCESS MODE is SEQUENTIAL]

[FILE STATUS is data-name].

The *filename* is the name by which the file is known in this program. The *implementor-name* is the name of the device upon which the file resides. Depending upon the implementor (compiler vendor) and the computer installation, the implementor-name may refer to 1) a particular device (e.g., card reader #1, tape reel #9T4311, disk unit #DA2), 2) a class of devices (e.g., card reader, tape reel, disk unit), or 3) a logical device (e.g., PRSNMSTR, TRANS) which will be assigned to a physical device by commands external to the program. The third approach provides greatest flexibility, because device assignments can be changed without recompilation.

The *OPTIONAL* phrase indicates that this particular file need not necessarily be present when the program is executed. For example, a program might expect a variable number of transaction files.

The *RESERVE* phrase is used to specify the number of input-output areas (buffers) to be allocated to the file.

The *ORGANIZATION* and *ACCESS MODE* phrases specify the file organization technique and the manner in which records in a file are accessed, respectively. (A sequentially organized file can support only sequential access.) In most installations, both *ORGANIZATION* and *ACCESS* default to *SEQUENTIAL* unless otherwise specified.

The *FILE STATUS* phrase is used to declare a variable whose value will indicate the status of each I/O operation performed on the file, e.g., successful completion, permanent I/O error, at end-of-file.

Typical *SELECT* clauses for sequential files are:

SELECT TRANS-FILE	ASSIGN TO INPUT.
SELECT EXCP-RPT-FILE	ASSIGN TO OUTPUT.
SELECT MSTR-FILE	ASSIGN TO SYS024-UT-2400-S-MSTRIN.
SELECT SUM-RPT-FILE	ASSIGN TO SYS001-UR-1403-S.

*See the appendix for explanation of the syntax notation used here.

The *MULTIPLE FILE* clause of the *I-O-CONTROL* paragraph of the *INPUT-OUTPUT SECTION* is used to specify the location of files when more than one share the same physical reel of tape. The format of the clause is:

MULTIPLE FILE TAPE CONTAINS {file name-1
    [POSITION integer-1]}. . .

Only the files on the reel that are used in the program need to be specified. For example:

MULTIPLE FILE TAPE CONTAINS
    TRANS-WEST-DIV POSITION 1
    TRANS-EAST-DIV POSITION 4.

A program can have only one multiple-file tape open at any time.

File-oriented information is also provided in the *FILE SECTION* of the *DATA DIVISION*. Each file used in the program must have an associated *FD* (file description) entry. An *FD* contains clauses that give information about the physical structure, identification, and record names of a given file. The basic clauses have the following format:

FD filename
    [BLOCK CONTAINS [integer 1 TO]
                    integer 2 {RECORDS / CHARACTERS}]
    [RECORD CONTAINS [integer 3 TO]
                 integer 4 CHARACTERS]
    LABEL {RECORD IS / RECORDS ARE}   {STANDARD / OMITTED}
    [DATA {RECORD IS / RECORDS ARE}   [dataname 1] . . .].

The *filename* in the *FD* is the same as the *filename* in the *SELECT* clause for the file. The *BLOCK CONTAINS* and *RECORD CONTAINS* clauses indicate minimum and maximum block and record sizes on the file. The *LABEL RECORDS* clause is the only mandatory clause in an *FD*; it indicates the presence or absence of internal labels. The *DATA RECORDS* clause names the record type(s) to be found on this file. Other clauses are sometimes available to specify the character code set used externally to represent the file's data, to specify the logical page size for print/display files, to give a value to an item in the file's label record, and to name the reports in a report file.

One or more record description entries follow a file's *FD*. Each describes the format of a record type (see Chapter 3).

The following program excerpts illustrate a COBOL declaration of four sequential files: *RPT-FILE*, *TRANS-FILE*, *MSTR-FILE-IN*, and *MSTR-FILE-OUT*.

.
.
.

ENVIRONMENT DIVISION.
INPUT-OUTPUT SECTION.
FILE-CONTROL.
     SELECT RPT-FILE   ASSIGN TO OUTPUT.
     SELECT TRANS-FILE   ASSIGN TO TAPE1.
     SELECT MSTR-FILE-IN   ASSIGN TO TAPE3.
     SELECT MSTR-FILE-OUT   ASSIGN TO TAPE2.
I-O-CONTROL.
     MULTIPLE FILE TRANS-FILE POSITION 2.

. . .

DATA DIVISION.
FILE SECTION.
FD RPT-FILE
     LABEL RECORDS OMITTED.
01 RPT-REC   PICTURE X(132).
FD TRANS-FILE
     RECORD CONTAINS 13 TO 82 CHARACTERS
     LABEL RECORDS STANDARD
     DATA RECORDS TRANS-REC-ADD, TRANS-REC-DELETE.
01 TRANS-REC-ADD.
     02 TRANS-REC-CODE   PICTURE X.
     02 TRANS-REC-ADD-DETAIL   PICTURE X(81).
01 TRANS-REC-DELETE.
     02 TRANS-REC-CODE   PICTURE X.
     02 TRANS-REC-DELETE-DETAIL   PICTURE X(12).
FD MSTR-FILE-IN
     BLOCK CONTAINS 40 RECORDS
     LABEL RECORDS STANDARD.
01 MSTR-REC-IN   PICTURE X(87).
FD MSTR-FILE-OUT
     BLOCK CONTAINS 40 RECORDS
     LABEL RECORDS STANDARD.
01 MSTR-REC-OUT   PICTURE X(87).

. . .

Sequential Files in Pascal

The input/output facilities of the Pascal language have not been standardized. You will find considerable variation in file declaration requirements from compiler to compiler. We use a representative example of Pascal here, but be sure to verify the particular requirements of the Pascal compiler that you use.

The names of the files that are used in a Pascal program are given in its *program* statement. For example,

     program mstrupdt (outfil,trans,mstrin,mstrout);

Some compilers require that the names of files that are used as input be distinguished from the names of output files. For example,

> program mstrupdt (outfil,trans*,mstrin*,mstrout);

Files are assigned to storage devices by statements external to the Pascal program. However, use of some file names (such as *input* or *output*) may imply use of a particular storage device or class of storage devices.

The format of the records on a file is declared using either *type* or *var* statements, as discussed in Chapter 3. Each file (except *input* and *output* if they are system defaults) is declared of type *file*.

The following program excerpts illustrate a Pascal declaration of four sequential files: *outfil*, *trans*, *mstrin*, and *mstrout*.

```
program mstrupdt(outfil,trans,mstrin,mstrout);
type mstrrec = record
                empno : 1 .. 99999;
                empname : packed array [1 .. 25] of char;
                dept : packed array [1 .. 5] of char;
                . . .
              end;
     transrec = record
                  transcode : A,D;
                  detail : packed array [1 .. 81] of char
                end;
var outfil : text;
    trans : file of transrec;
    mstrin,mstrout : file of mstrrec;
```

In many cases the Pascal programmer cannot specify the same level of detail about the physical characteristics of a file as can a COBOL programmer. However, because the input/output facilities of a Pascal compiler are implementor-defined, the level of file specification capability given the programmer varies.

CREATION OF SEQUENTIAL FILES

The creation of a sequential file involves writing records in the desired sequence onto a storage medium. The creation of a sequential transaction file involves the tasks of collecting data, converting the data to a machine-readable form, editing the data, correcting rejected transactions, and sorting the edited data (Fig. 157).

Data entry devices include key-to-card, key-to-tape, key-to-disk, optical scanners, and devices that respond to voice input. The input process often includes a verification procedure to check that the data values

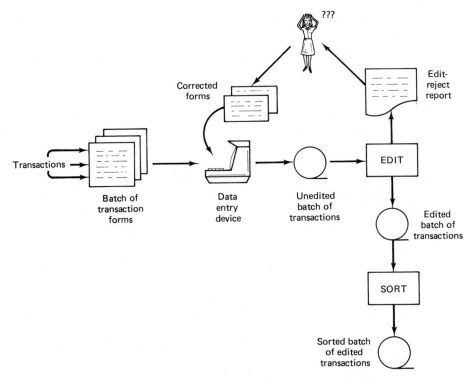

FIGURE 157

entered were actually the same as the data values written or marked on the transaction documents.

The edits performed on transaction data might include the following types of checks:

1. Proper ranges of values, e.g., hrs.-worked must be less than 60; sex must be M or F.
2. Presence of required fields, e.g., must have employee number.
3. Proper types of values, e.g., numeric in numeric field.
4. Accuracy of self-checking field-values, e.g., low-order digit of the sum of the first 8 digits of account-code must equal the 9th digit of account-code.
5. Presence of related fields, e.g., if transaction is of type add, then transaction fields empno, department, and start-date must not be blank.
6. Control totals, e.g., sum of dollar amounts for all transactions in batch must equal an input total.
7. Counts, e.g., count of transactions must equal an input count.

8. Hash totals, e.g., sum of employee-numbers for all transactions (a non-sensical quantity) must equal an input total.

These checks help to find incorrect transactions, incorrectly input but correct transactions, and cases where transactions were lost or re-input during the input process.

The edits might include also checks and changes that are not related directly to finding bad data. For example, the edit might:

9. Change leading blanks to zeros in numeric fields.
10. Change mnemonics or text to appropriate codes, e.g., change department value 'PERSONNEL' to 61; change 'STREET' to 'ST'.
11. Insert data values, e.g., for input-data.

Rejects of the edit process are not included in the output of the edit, but rather are brought to a human's attention, usually via a reject report. The incorrect transactions can then be located, corrected, and re-input, and, it is hoped, will emerge successfully from another pass through the edit. These newly edited transactions then can be merged with the originally correct, edited transactions and be input to a sort procedure to produce the sorted batch of edited transactions.

An attractive approach, which can avoid much of the delay incurred in manual correction of rejected transactions, is to use an intelligent data-entry device and to edit transactions when they are input (Fig. 158).

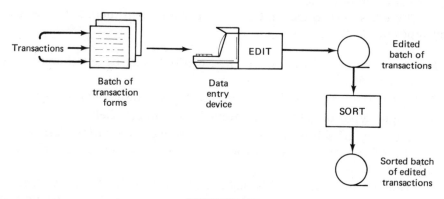

FIGURE 158

If the operator of the data-entry device cannot correct an error, the transaction will have to be corrected and re-input later.

Sorting of transactions is generally required in order to put them in the same sequence as the master file that they are destined to update. We will discuss the update of sequential files later in this chapter and the sorting of sequential files in Chapter 18.

Records are written on a sequential file using the following types of statements:

In COBOL:

> WRITE record-name [FROM identifier]
>
> where the record-name is defined in the file's FD and the optional identifier of the FROM clause is defined in WORKING-STORAGE.

In Pascal:

> writeln (filename, recordname);
> or write (filename, recordname);
>
> depending upon whether or not a new line is to be started after this one, where the filename appears in the program statement and the recordname variable contains the data to be written.

The records will appear on the file in the same order as they are written to the file.

The creation of a sequential master file may be done using the same procedure as discussed for creation of a sequential transaction file. Sometimes, however, a sequential master file is created by running an update process against an empty (or null) input master file. Each transaction is processed as an add (or insert) to this empty master. We will discuss this later.

The creation of a sequential work file involves writing the results of a program execution so that they can be input to another program. A difference between a work file and a master file is that a work file is temporary but a master file is retained for some period of time.

The creation of a sequential report file involves the tasks of gathering the data to be reported, formatting the data, and calculating appropriate summary information. The records on such a file are of several types:

1. *Header* records, including report headers, page headers, and group headers—identifying information.
2. *Detail* records—the "meat" of the report, generally arranged in columns.
3. *Footer* records, including group footers, page footers, and report footers—summary information.

Summary data are generally calculated in *control breaks*, which are changes in the value of some identified field. For example, the data records for a sales report might be in sorted order by REGION, DE-PARTMENT, SALESMAN-ID.

> REGION major,
> DEPARTMENT,
> SALESMAN-ID minor.

Control breaks might be specified upon change of SALESMAN-ID (giv-ing totals for each salesperson), upon change of DEPARTMENT (giving totals for all sales-people within each department), and upon change in REGION (giving totals for all departments within each region). Report totals might also appear.

Commonly the creation of a report file is done in a separate pro-gram from the routine that creates the data to be reported (Fig. 159).

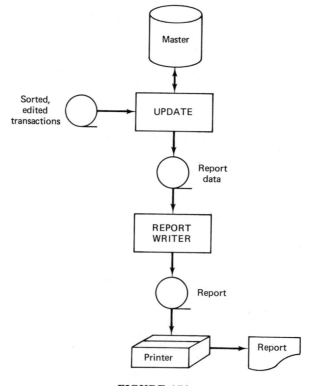

FIGURE 159

The processes of editing, sorting, and report writing may be imple-mented either as applications programs with code written specifically for the particular files and applications involved, or as more general-purpose utility routines. Very common utilities include software that can do the following:

1. Copy a sequential file from one storage medium to another, e.g., card to tape, card to disk, tape to disk, disk to tape, tape to print, disk to print.
2. Copy a sequential file to another sequential file on the same storage medium, e.g., tape to tape, disk to disk.
3. Perform simple edits on records, e.g., value type, sequence checking.
4. Perform simple reformatting of records, e.g., rearranging fields, simple calculations.
5. Sort a file on given fields, ascending or descending.
6. Merge multiple sorted files to form a single sorted file, based on the value of given fields, ascending or descending.
7. Prepare reports, including formatting and a variety of control-break summaries.

Nearly all installations use general-purpose file management utilities to offload some programming burden from their staffs.

Some programming languages include features that are designed to simplify the creation of report files. For example, the full syntax for the COBOL *WRITE* statement for sequential files is:

$$
\text{WRITE recordname } [\underline{\text{FROM}} \text{ identifier-1}]
$$

$$
\left[\left\{ \begin{array}{l} \underline{\text{BEFORE}} \\ \underline{\text{AFTER}} \end{array} \right\} \text{ADVANCING} \left\{ \begin{array}{l} \left\{ \begin{array}{l} \text{identifier-2} \\ \text{integer} \end{array} \right\} \left[\begin{array}{l} \text{LINE} \\ \text{LINES} \end{array} \right] \\ \left\{ \begin{array}{l} \text{mnemonic-name} \\ \underline{\text{PAGE}} \end{array} \right\} \end{array} \right\} \right]
$$

$$
\left[\text{AT} \left\{ \begin{array}{l} \underline{\text{END-OF-PAGE}} \\ \underline{\text{EOP}} \end{array} \right\} \text{ imperative-statement} \right]
$$

The programmer can thus control line spacing (single, double, triple . . .) and activities to be executed in conjunction with page ejection. The *FD* for a report file can include a specification of the number of lines per page so the programmer can control page ejection.

COBOL also includes a report-writer facility. The format of a report file is defined in an *RD* (report description) rather than in an *FD*. Features enable the declaration of control break levels and of various types of field editing and print formatting. Rather than using *WRITE* for records to these files, the programmer uses *GENERATE* statements. After being *OPEN*ed, the report file is readied using an *INITIATE* statement. The final control break is caused by a *TERMINATE* statement.

RETRIEVAL FROM SEQUENTIAL FILES

Records must be retrieved from a sequential file in consecutive order. The order in which records were written to the file when the file was created determines the order in which records can be retrieved from the file. In fact, it is really the other way around: the desired order of record retrieval should dictate the order in which records should be written.

Retrieval from a file can be classified as either report generation or inquiry, depending on the volume of output produced. Sequential files are very commonly accessed in report-generation mode. Because the records must be accessed consecutively, it is quite efficient to access every record on the file. Report generation from a sequential file is the same as creation of a sequential report file, where the input to the process is a sequential file, (for example, see Fig. 159).

Using the terminology that was introduced in the previous section, each record of the input file produces a detail line on the report. The basic logic flow of report generation is shown in Fig. 160.

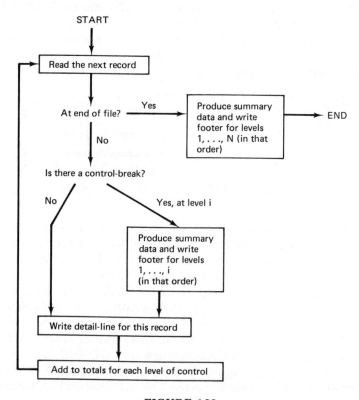

FIGURE 160

For example, control levels might be:

1. salesman-id
2. department
3. region

Here $N = 3$, unless there is an overall report footer defined, in which case $N = 4$. The logic would be somewhat different if multiple records were combined to form a single detail-line.

Records are read from a sequential file using the following types of statements:

In COBOL:

> READ filename INTO identifier
>   AT END imperative-statement.

> where the filename is defined in an FD, the optional INTO clause specifies an identifier in WORKING–STORAGE that will receive the contents of the record (which will also be received by any records defined with the file's FD), and the AT END clause is required to specify what is to happen when the input file is exhausted.

In Pascal:

> read (filename,recordname);
> or readln (filename,recordname);

> depending on the disposition of any "leftover" characters in the input record, where the filename appears in the program statement and the recordname variable will receive the data.

Inquiry from a sequential file is constrained by the consecutive-retrieval requirement of the file organization. (Many so-called inquiries are really report generators.) However, the following types of inquiries might be serviced satisfactorily by a sequential employee file, since each requires access to all the records of the file.

- What are the mean and standard deviation for employee salaries?
- How many employees are enrolled in each of our four medical-benefit plans?
- Which employee has the maximum number of years with the company?
- Which employee has the lowest ratio of salary to years of service with the company?

The *hit ratio* for an inquiry of a file is the number of records that must be accessed to respond to the inquiry divided by the number of records on the file. The lower the hit ratio, the more inappropriate is sequential organization; the higher the hit ratio, the more satisfactory is sequential organization.

UPDATE OF SEQUENTIAL FILES

A master file represents the static view of some aspect of an organization's business at a single time. However, most aspects of an organization's business are not static; rather, changes occur continuously: employees are hired and fired, product prices change, job assignments change, and so forth. In order for a master file to reflect accurately the state of an organization, these changes must be incorporated into the data on the master file; the master file must be updated.

Because we are discussing sequential files, we confine our attention now to batch updating. Transactions are collected and are periodically applied to update a master file. The frequency at which a master file should be updated depends on several factors, including the following:

- Rate of change of the data
- Size of the master file
- Urgency of need for current data on master file
- File activity ratio

The *file activity ratio* is the number of master file records affected by a batch of transactions divided by the number of records on the master file. The number of records affected does not necessarily equal the number of transactions in the batch; several transactions may affect a single master record. (Rarely does one transaction affect more than one master record. We postpone discussion of transactions such as "Give each employee a 7% raise" and require that a transaction specify only one master record.) In general, the greater the length of time between master file updates, the greater will be the file activity ratio.

Between updates, the average age of data on the master file increases. If the master file is accessed for retrieval between updates, then some of the reported data will no longer be current. The greater the need to have current data on the master file, the more frequently it should be updated.

However, the more frequently that the master file is updated, the higher is the processing cost, especially with a large file. Thus the fundamental trade-off: the more current the data, the higher the processing cost.

Interactive transaction processing of a sequential file can be very expensive. The records must be accessed sequentially; transactions applied interactively usually are not in the appropriate order for a sequential file update.

Additionally, most sequential files cannot be updated in place; rather they must be rewritten. Thus the general system flow diagram for update of a sequential file is as shown in Fig. 161. The old master and new master are two separate files. The lower the file activity ratio, the greater the number of records that are merely copied from the old file to the new one: expensive busy-work for the computer.

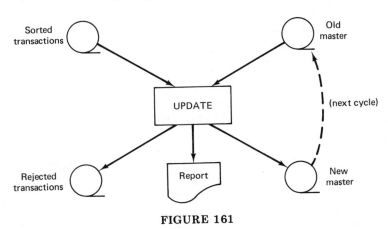

FIGURE 161

During the next cycle of updating, today's new master will be the old master file. These multiple versions of a master file are commonly known as *generation files*. The files have the same name; they differ only in their generation numbers. If today's old master were generation 1, then today's new master would be generation 2; the new master in the next cycle would be generation 3, and so forth. If absolute generation numbers like these are used then the actual generation number needs to be known in order for one to refer to a particular version of the file. Relative generation numbers can also be used. For example, if today's old master were relative generation 0, then today's new master would be relative generation +1, next cycle's new master would be +2 (relative to today's old master) or +1 (relative to today's new master), last cycle's old master would be -1 relative to today's old master or -2 relative to today's new master or -3 relative to the next cycle's new master, and so forth. Both conventions are used. In most systems, omission of an absolute or relative generation number results in a reference to the most current version of the file.

An organization might retain several generations of a file for purposes of facilitating recovery or for historic reporting needs.

There are three basic types of updates that can be applied to a master file:

1. Insert a new record.
2. Delete an existing record.
3. Modify an existing record.

Each transaction contains a code that indicates its type and the value of the key of the corresponding master record. If the transaction is an insertion, it generally specifies not only the key for the new master record, but also values for other fields in the new master; an example is given in Fig. 162.

TRANS -CODE	EMPNO	NAME	ADDRESS	DEPT	PHONE
I	12751	SMITH, IGOR	EASY STREET	TOY	

FIGURE 162

The transaction code and key value are required here; the other fields could be left blank (to be updated later). If the transaction were a deletion it commonly would be enough to specify just the key value of the corresponding master record. If the transaction were a modification, the key value and values of fields to be modified would be required. Usually those fields that are not to be changed are left blank. (Note that program logic must not interpret those blanks as "change to spaces.")

Changes to a master file result either from real changes (such as hiring or firing an employee or changing an office assignment) or as attempts to correct errors that have gotten into the file in previous runs. Commonly no real distinction in processing is made between these two types of transactions.

There are many kinds of errors that must be accounted for in a file update, including trying to

1. Insert a record that already exists.
2. Delete a record that does not exist.
3. Modify a record that does not exist.

The proper action to take when these errors occur is application-dependent, but errors should not be allowed to pollute the file. Generally an update program produces an error report that identifies each transaction that was not processed and the reason it was not processed.

The logic required to process a batch of transactions that update a sequential file is classic. The same basic logic is used over and over in many different programs. The idea is to merge the keys of the transaction records and the keys of master file records. We assume that the transaction file and the master file have matching sort orders. Consider first the case of only one transaction record per master file record. A flowchart of the logic is given in Fig. 163. We use *TRANS-KEY*, *OLD-MSTR-KEY*, and *NEW-MSTR-KEY* to refer to the key fields of records

FIGURE 163

on the transaction file, old master file, and new master file, respectively. The meat of the logic is comparing the next *TRANS-KEY* and the next *OLD-MSTR-KEY*. There are three possible cases. (1) The *TRANS-KEY* is lower. There can be no old master record that matches this transaction record. The transaction must be either an insertion or an error. Once the transaction is processed, another must be read from the transaction file to be matched with the pending old master record. (2) The *TRANS-KEY* is greater. There can be no transaction record that matches this old master record. The old master record must be copied directly to the new master file. Another record must be read from the old master file to be matched with the pending transaction. (3) The keys match. If the transaction is a *MODIFY*, the changes are made and a record is written on the new master. If the transaction is a *DELETE*, the old master record is ignored. Other transaction types are errors. In any case, the next transaction record must be read. If there was not an error (that is, if the old master record was processed), then a record must also be read from the old master file. It is likely that one file will be exhausted before the other; the records from the remaining one must be processed.

The logic is somewhat more complex when multiple transactions can affect a single old master record. In this case, a break in *TRANS-KEY* must occur (to indicate that all transactions for a given old master record have been handled) before writing (or not writing) the modified record to the new master file. With multiple transactions, it is usually important to apply them in the order in which they appear in the transaction file. However, in some applications, the programmer needs to table all the transactions with a given *TRANS-KEY* value, then apply them according to some rules of precedence established by the application, even though the transactions may have been entered in some other sequence. We leave specification of the multiple-transaction update logic as an interesting exercise.

DESIGN OF SEQUENTIAL FILES

Three main questions need to be addressed in designing a sequential file:

1. What is the layout of fields in the records?
2. What is the key field(s)?
3. What is the appropriate blocking factor?

The record layout problem is the same as the problem addressed in Chapter 3. Of main consideration now are the questions of activity to the fields and fixed-length versus variable-length records. Consider an application that needs a file of employee personnel information. Some information about employees may be used more frequently than other information about the same employees. If so, then it may be advantageous to split the employee data into two record types and to place them in separate files. For example, a primary employee personnel file might contain records of the format shown in Fig. 164.

EMPNO	DEPT	JOBCODE	PROJECT	HEALTH PLAN	COVERAGE CODE	INS. PLAN	HIRE DATE

FIGURE 164

A secondary employee personnel file might contain records of the format shown in Fig. 165.

EMPNO	GRAD. DATE	LAST DEGREE	SCHOOL	JOBCODE HISTORY	HOME TOWN	MOTHERS NAME	

FIGURE 165

Splitting the employee data into an active file and a relatively inactive file reduces the size of the active file and therefore reduces processing time on that file. The split does complicate processing procedures, however, since it must be possible to recognize when there is activity on the relatively inactive file.

Sometimes a sequential file is split into an active file and an inactive file by record occurrences rather than by field types. For example, an organization might have one file of mailing label information for its frequent customers and another file of the same type of information for customers who are contacted semiannually instead of weekly. Again, the activity ratio is a reasonable indicator of how active a file is.

Records can be fixed length, in which case all records have the same length, or they can be variable length, in which case some records are longer than others. Consider, for example, the following student record, declared in COBOL:

```
            01  STUDENT.
                02  MATRIC-NO          PIC 9(5).
                02  NAME.
                    03  LAST           PIC X(10).
                    03  INIT1          PIC X.
  assume            03  INIT2          PIC X.
   104          02  ADDRESS.
 characters         03  STREET         PIC X(25).
                    03  CITY           PIC X(10).
                    03  STATE          PIC X(2).
                    03  ZIP            PIC 9(5).
                    . . .
                02  NO-OF-COURSES      PIC 9(2).
                02  COURSE OCCURS 0 TO 50 TIMES
                            DEPENDING ON NO-OF-COURSES.
                    03  DEPT           PIC X(4).
   each             03  ID             PIC X(4).
    17              03  SEQUENCE-NO    PIC 9(5).
 characters         03  SEMESTER       PIC 9.
                    03  YR             PIC 9(2).
                    03  GRADE          PIC X.
```

This record type has minimum size of 104 characters and maximum size of 954 (104+50*17) characters. If the average student record contains data for 15 courses, then it would be rather wasteful to maintain space for the more unusual case of 50 courses for every student.

Variable-length records are stored with some control information that specifies the length of each individual record. This control information generally appears in a system-used field that precedes each record on the file. The programmer cannot access the control field but needs to account for its presence when specifying record lengths (but not in the record descriptions).

The appropriate field(s) to form the key of a sequential file are determined by the application requirements. If the file is a transaction file, then it should have the same key as does the master file that it updates. If the file is a report file, then the ordering of records is determined by the desired form of the output. If the file is a master file, then the key usually is some obvious identifier.

A third design consideration with sequential files is blocking. When a sequential file is stored on a serial-access storage device, it is generally desirable to make the blocks as large as possible. The limiting factors become main memory buffer space availability, operating system parameters (which may limit block size), and the local charging algorithm (which trades off main memory use and secondary storage accesses). The effects of blocking factors were discussed in Chapter 15 in the context of blocking tape files.

When a sequential file is stored on a direct-access storage device, it is generally desirable to make the block size as close as possible to the sector size (if sector addressing is used) or to the track size (if cylinder-track addressing is used), since an entire sector or track will be passed over to access anything on that sector or track anyway.

SUMMARY

A sequentially organized file is a collection of logically related records whose access sequence is determined by their ordering. The records must be written consecutively when the file is created, and they must be read consecutively when the file is later used for input. A sequential file operates in the same way as does a large queue: the first record is the first record written. Because the records must be accessed consecutively, sequentially organized files are used more commonly in batch processing than in interactive processing. The major advantage of sequential organization is the ability to quickly access the "next" record.

A sequentially organized file may be stored on either a serial-access or a direct-access storage medium. Some aspects of the declaration of a file appear in programs; other aspects are specified external to programs. The basic concepts required for declaring sequential files in COBOL and Pascal were covered and illustrated with examples.

The fundamental process of creating a sequential file was discussed and illustrated. The differences between creating transaction files, master files, and report files were introduced. Some programming languages, such as COBOL, have special features for the definition and creation of report files.

Retrieval from a sequential file is usually report generation but sometimes can be the result of inquiry. Examples of statements used to retrieve from sequential files in COBOL and Pascal programs were given. The concept of hit ratio was introduced.

The process of updating a sequential master file is important. The frequency at which a master file should be updated depends on several factors, including volatility of the data, size of the file, urgency of need for current data, and the file activity ratio. The concept of generation files was introduced, and absolute and relative generation numbers were discussed. The basic types of updates to a master file are insertion of new records, deletion of old records, and modification of existing records. The logic required to apply these updates was introduced.

Three fundamental aspects of designing sequential files are record design, key designation, and blocking factor selection.

Sequentially organized files have been used for a great many years;

they are simple and can be stored on inexpensive media. They are very suitable for applications that require only sequential access to the contained data. They are not suitable for applications that require direct access to only particular records of the collection. They do not provide adequate support for interactive applications. Nonetheless, they will continue to be important.

Terms

channel
file activity ratio
generation file
hit ratio

sequential file organization
sorted file
sort key
spooling

Review Exercises

1. Figs. 157 and 158 show a sort following the edit program. Why might this be preferable to sorting before editing?

2. An installation has two tape drives and one disk drive. An application program requires access to three sequential files: an old master file, a transaction file, and an updated master file. Which file should be stored on the disk?

3. Consider a miniscule master file containing 10 records. Assume that the following batch of transactions is to be processed:

Rec-Id	Trans-Type
111	2
111	1
96	3
400	1
96	1
111	2
400	3
342	3
96	2

What is the file activity ratio for this batch of transactions?

4. What factors should be considered when deciding how frequently a sequential master file should be updated?

5. What factors should be considered in determining how many generations of a file should be retained?

6. Describe a process for updating a sequential master file from a sequential file of transactions, where the two files do not have matching sort orders.

7. What is the typical retention period for sequential master files at your installation? How many generations of a sequential master file are retained?

8. Find out who designs record layouts for files at your installation. Determine whether or not any formal design guidelines are used in the design process.

9. Find out whether your installation has any files that are split into active and inactive portions. What is the criterion used for deciding when a record occurrence is inactive? How is a record from the inactive file reactivated?

10. Write a program to create a sequential file.

11. Write a program to print or display the contents of a sequential file.

12. Write a program to update a sequential file, creating a new version of the file. Accommodate record insertions, deletions, and modifications. Assume that there will be a maximum of one transaction applied to a master file record.

13. Do exercise 12 with the assumption that there may be up to five transactions per master file record. These transactions are to be processed in the order in which they are received.

14. Do exercise 12 with the assumption that there may be up to five transactions per master file record. Assume there are three types of modify transactions. Type 1 must be applied before type 2, which must be applied before type 3. *Do not assume* that transactions are always sorted by type.

15. Write the basic logic for report generation when two records are combined to form each detail line.

16. Write the basic logic for report generation when there are no detail lines but only summary (footer) lines.

17. Write the basic logic for a master file update in which multiple transaction records can affect a single old master record. Be sure to consider all possible conditions.

CHAPTER 17

Introduction
to I/O Control

The purpose of this chapter is to introduce the nature of input/output (I/O) control activities, which are of great importance in determining the cost of file operations. It is difficult to appreciate the extent of file management support that is provided by an operating system unless you understand the basic functions that an I/O control system performs.

We first discuss the basic requirements of an I/O control environment, then describe the fundamental concepts of I/O channels and channel programs. We discuss simple techniques of buffer management and relate I/O control activities to operations on files.

DEFINITIONS AND REQUIREMENTS: I/O CONTROL

Accessing (reading and writing) data on secondary storage devices requires a great deal of activity that is transparent to the application programmer. Programming languages enable programmers to define rather complex file organization techniques (like indexed sequential organization, which we will discuss in Chapter 20) with quite simple language statements. The supporting file management system converts those simple statements to the specified low-level I/O instructions. Similarly, a programmer's simple request to READ or WRITE a record on a file typically invokes a complex sequence of supporting device management operations. These details are generally hidden from the programmer. The programmer's job would be considerably more difficult if it involved contending with detailed I/O control operations.

An I/O control system has as its purpose exactly what its name implies: it provides support to the computer's users to enable them to access files without being concerned about details of storage characteristics and device timings. I/O control involves the file management and device management parts of an operating system; other parts of an operating system include a manager of main memory and a process manager and scheduler. Sometimes the part of an operating system that provides I/O control is called an I/O supervisor.

File access requires both file management support, which provides file organization techniques, and device management support, which provides access to physical storage devices. We will discuss some aspects of both types of support. In some operating systems a file manager and a device manager are distinguished from each other; in other systems they are combined to form a single I/O control function.

The responsibilities of an I/O control system are many and varied. Among the tasks that an I/O controller performs are the following:

1. Maintaining a directory of file identification and location information.
2. Establishing pathways for data flow between main memory and secondary storage devices.
3. Coordinating communication between the CPU and secondary storage devices and vice versa, including:
   (a) Handling the imbalance in speeds of the computer's CPU and of storage devices in such a way that the CPU does not spend an inordinate amount of time waiting idly for I/O operations to be completed.
   (b) Handling data in such a way that they can be held if the sender (CPU or secondary storage device) and the receiver (secondary storage device or CPU) are not ready at the same time.
4. Preparing files for input or output use.
5. Handling files when their input or output use has terminated.

We will consider each of these tasks and see how the tasks fit together in the remainder of this chapter.

FILE DIRECTORIES AND CONTROL INFORMATION

Before a file can be accessed by a program, the operating system must know on which secondary storage device the file resides. Nearly all operating systems use some sort of directory structure to manage the identification and location information about files.

Fig. 166 illustrates the basic concepts of a directory structure used to keep track of files in a typical file management system. The directory shown is for one unit (e.g., disk pack or tape reel) of secondary storage. The label includes identifying information, access control information, and a pointer to a table of contents, which contains a control block for each file on the unit. A control block contains information about the name of a file, its attributes (such as record length, block size, organization), and its boundaries on the storage medium. A control block points to the start of the corresponding file. Thus when a file is requested, the table of contents of the appropriate unit is consulted for information required to locate the file in storage.

FIGURE 166

Different file management systems use different structures for their file control blocks. A representative system constructs two tables to describe each file. The first contains information on file organization and processing mode, descriptions of record sizes and types, blocking sizes, error counts and flags, information used by I/O control system routines to determine file status and position, and the file's logical (external) name. It also contains a pointer to the file's second descriptive table, which is associated with a particular storage device and contains information about the physical characteristics and current status of the device. The device controller routines use this table to interface requests to the file and to monitor the status of I/O activities on the file. Control information in this system is split between the tables in an attempt to separate file-oriented and device-oriented descriptors. This modularization can improve the processing of I/O requests.

DEVICE CONTROL

I/O activities basically involve the movement of data between main memory and secondary storage devices or I/O devices such as line printers, terminals, and card reader/punches. While they may appear to be simple to programmers, I/O operations actually require detailed device control support. For example, assume that the file directory has already been consulted and the requested file's location on a secondary storage device or I/O device has been determined. In order to be able to write to that device or read from that device, the following tasks must first be accomplished: A pathway between main memory and the device must be established, and it must be determined that the necessary components of the pathway (including the target device) are available and ready for use. The I/O operation itself requires that appropriate signals be transmitted to the device to cause it to react correctly: disk arms may be moved and read/write heads activated; a cursor on a terminal screen may be positioned; a page eject command may be sent to a line printer. If errors occur during I/O activity, they must be handled. At the end of the I/O operation, the requestor must be notified that activities have terminated successfully or unsuccessfully, as the case may be.

In most computer systems the CPU is not burdened with handling these I/O-related tasks. Rather, responsibility for device control is delegated to I/O processors, which are also known as I/O *channels*. An I/O channel is itself a programmable processor; the programs that it executes are called *channel programs*. These programs specify the operations required for device accesses and control the data pathways. The operating system supplies standard routines that are used to drive the I/O channels.

Fig. 167 illustrates some of the components involved in I/O activity. The I/O channel is under the command of the operating system and

FIGURE 167

therefore the CPU. The I/O channel does not drive the storage devices directly. Rather, it interfaces with one or more device control units. This arrangement simplifies channel programs significantly, as it is a control unit's responsibility to interpret I/O signals appropriately for the particular types of devices under its control and to control the devices accordingly.

Before an I/O operation can begin, a path between main memory and the device must be established. If the channel, the control unit, or the addressed device is busy, then the pathway construction must wait. In order to avoid such waits, a computer system may have several channels and control units. Usually the devices managed by a particular control unit must be of the same type, for example all disk drives, or all tape drives, or all line printers.

There are several types of channels available. A *selector channel* can manage data flow between main memory and only one device at a time. Since channels are fast processors, selector channels are usually used only with high-speed I/O devices such as disks. Putting a slow-speed device such as a card reader on a selector channel would waste most of the channel's processing power.

A *multiplexor channel* can manage data flow between main memory and several devices. Multiplexor channels are more effective with slow-speed devices than are selector channels. With a multiplexor channel, several devices can be active simultaneously, but the channel must complete the channel program for one device before it starts the channel program for another. A channel program controls a single read or write to the device.

A *block multiplexor channel* further interleaves the management of data flow to multiple devices. A block multiplexor channel can execute one instruction of the channel program for one device, then can switch to perform an instruction of the channel program for another device. Each channel program may contain several instructions. The entire channel program for one device does not have to be completed before another is serviced.

The devices that require management in a computer can be classified into two types: *dedicated* devices, which are suitable for access by only one user at a time, and *shared* devices, which allow concurrent access by multiple users. A terminal is an example of a dedicated device, while a disk is an example of a shared device.

The I/O control activities for shared devices are more complex than they are for dedicated devices. Two of the important functions of I/O control for shared devices are space allocation and the granting of access rights. The latter activity may include ordering of requests to the shared device in an attempt to improve performance. For a shared disk, requests could be ordered to minimize arm-movement time.

A third type of device is a unit that users would like to share but that is really not suitable for concurrent use. For example, multiple programs might want to address the line printer concurrently, but the resultant output of interleaved lines from several sources would be quite useless. I/O control systems use *virtual* devices to address this type of need. A program that is using a virtual printer has the impression that it is writing lines to a printer, but in reality the lines are being written to a disk. When that output file is completed by the program, it is then queued and written in its entirety to the printer. Support of virtual I/O devices sometimes is called *spooling*, after *S*imultaneous *P*eripheral *O*peration *O*n-*L*ine. The purpose of a spooling system is to permit the apparent concurrent sharing of devices that are really only sequentially sharable. Nearly all multi-user computer systems support spooling. Non-virtual addressing of a printer would be prohibitively slow and inefficient.

CHANNEL MANAGEMENT

We have already introduced the notion that an I/O channel acts as an intermediary between the CPU-main memory and the control unit-storage devices. The CPU communicates with a channel via some simple commands. A representative channel would respond to instructions such as:

1. Test I/O, to determine whether or not the pathway to the addressed device is busy.
2. Start I/O, on a particular device.
3. Halt I/O, on a particular device.

A channel usually communicates with the CPU by use of interrupts. An interrupt would be issued when an error is detected, e.g., invalid CPU command, or when an I/O activity is completed. When an interrupt occurs, control branches to an interrupt-handler routine, which determines what caused the interrupt, performs appropriate actions, then returns control to the caller.

When a program requests a READ from a file, the following sequence of events occurs (see Fig. 168):

1. The program issues a READ, which interrupts the I/O controller.
2. The I/O controller builds a channel program in main memory.
3. The channel program is read and executed by the addressed channel.

FIGURE 168

4. Appropriate signals are transmitted to the addressed control unit.
5. These signals are interpreted by the control unit and used to control device operations to read the requested data.
6. The requested data flows from the device along the pathway to the file's buffer area in the program's main memory space.
7. An interrupt is issued by the channel to signal continuation of the program's execution.
8. Control returns to the program.

Note that the data are read into a buffer, which is an area of main memory that is reserved to hold data for this file. When the buffer is full, the program can begin to use the data.

An analogous sequence of events occurs when a program requests a WRITE to a file. Thus the expense of I/O accesses! These events must occur for *every* READ and WRITE command that is issued to a device.

The most commonly used technique to reduce the number of device accesses that a program must request is to block records such that multiple records are read/written in a single access to the device. If there are n records per block, then only every nth READ by the program causes an access to the device. Commonly, a program's READ command is translated to a GET instruction by the I/O control system. The channel program then converts the GET to a device READ if the buffer is empty, causing the buffer to be filled. The program's GET procures the next record from the buffer (Fig. 169).

The buffer provides the holding area required to interface relatively slow storage devices with the much faster CPU. It also provides the holding area that makes blocking of records feasible. Recall our discussion of blocking of records on tape in Chapter 15; now you should understand why large blocking factors can be so important to the performance of sequentially organized files. Every record on the file will be accessed, so

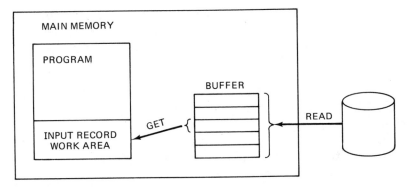

FIGURE 169

as many records as possible should be procured at once. The cost of a large block size is, of course, the cost of the additional main memory required.

BUFFER MANAGEMENT

We consider now several important but simple approaches to the management of file buffers. We will start with single buffering, then consider the management of multiple buffers.

Single Buffering

Fig. 170 shows the data structure of a buffer in a simple system in which there is one record per block and one buffer per file, and where the buffer is filled *on demand* from a program. The buffer structure includes a pointer to the starting address of the channel program for this file's current operation.

FIGURE 170

The basic structure of the channel program to fill this buffer is:

Wait for instruction READ from the program.
Issue start–I/O command to control unit.
Wait while buffer is being filled.
Issue interrupt to program so that it may start reading from the buffer.

A problem with this simple system is that the user program sits idle while waiting for the buffer to be filled. An alternative approach which removes some of this potential for a waiting CPU is to use *anticipatory buffering*. With anticipatory buffering, the I/O control system attempts to anticipate the program's need for data. It tries to keep the buffer always full, so that the data are already there when the program issues its READ instruction. The objective is to keep the program from having to wait.

Anticipatory buffering requires slight modification of the buffer's data structure to include a flag that indicates whether or not the buffer is full (Fig. 171). The channel keeps testing this flag. If the buffer becomes empty because the user program has read its contents, the flag is reset and the channel program initiates refill of the buffer. The basic structure of the channel program to fill a buffer with anticipatory buffering is shown in Fig. 171.

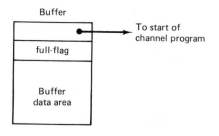

Buffer

To start of
channel program

full-flag

Buffer
data area

where   full-flag = 0 if the buffer is empty,
              = 1 if the buffer is full.

loop: if full-flag = 1 go to loop.
          issue start-I/O command to control unit.
          wait while buffer is being filled.
          full-flag: = 1.
          go to loop.

FIGURE 171

A complementary routine to empty the buffer into the program's record work area is also required.

Our buffer filling and emptying routines always come in pairs: one of the pair represents a producer and one a consumer. For an input file, the producer is the channel program and the consumer is the user program. For an output file, the producer is the user program and the consumer is the channel program.

The consumer routine that accompanies the above producer routine is:

wait: if full–flag = 0 go to wait.
          read the buffer contents into the
              record work area.
          full–flag := 0.
          go to wait.

Initially, *full–flag* = 0, causing the channel program to fill the buffer.

Let us now assume that a blocking factor of n records per block is being used. The producer/consumer routines must be changed to reflect the fact that only every n^{th} READ by the user program causes a device access. The buffer structure needs to be modified slightly to include a counter or pointer that keeps track of which record of the n records in the buffer should be next read into the user program's record work areas (Fig. 172).

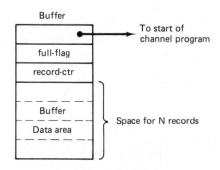

FIGURE 172

```
Buffer

                    •  ──────────→  To start of
                                     channel program

     full-flag

     record-ctr

─ ─ ─ ─ ─ ─ ─ ─        ⎫
     Buffer            ⎬  Space for N records
─ ─ ─ ─ ─ ─ ─ ─        ⎭
    Data area
─ ─ ─ ─ ─ ─ ─ ─

where   full-flag = 0 if the buffer is empty,
                    1 otherwise.
        record-ctr = 1, . . ., N
```

The producer routine is modified only slightly:

```
loop:    if full–flag = 1 go to loop.
         issue start–I/O command to control
             unit.
         wait while buffer is being filled.
         record–ctr := 1.
         full–flag := 1.
         go to loop.
```

The consumer routine is changed a bit more:

```
wait:    if full–flag = 0 go to wait.
         read record (record–ctr) into the
             record work area.
         record–ctr := record–ctr + 1.
         if record–ctr > n
             full–flag := 0.
         go to wait.
```

Initially, *full–flag* = 0. Note that the program's consumer routine is in the wait state between READs, but the program itself is executing other instructions. Does the program ever have to really wait because the buffer is empty? Yes—it waits for every n^{th} record. It is important to recognize that while the buffer is in the state of being emptied by a consumer, it cannot also be being filled by a producer.

Double Buffering

In order to reduce the probability of program waiting, double buffering is commonly used. Two buffer areas instead of just one are assigned to the file. The basic idea of double buffering is that while the consumer is emptying one of the buffers, the producer can be filling the other buffer. By the time the first buffer is emptied, the second one should be full. The consumer can then empty the second one while the producer fills the first one, and so forth.

The buffer structure for double buffering now includes a pointer to the next buffer (Fig. 173(a)). The presence of this pointer allows the producer and consumer routines to be quite general.

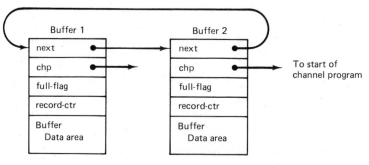

where   full-flag = 0 if the buffer is empty or is being filled,
              = 1 if the buffer is full or is being emptied;
       record-ctr = 1, . . ., N

FIGURE 173(a)

We now give the anticipatory producer and consumer routines for the case of n records per block. Two auxiliary pointers are required:

pfill, which points to the next buffer to be filled or being filled,
pempty, which points to the next buffer to be emptied or being emptied.

The producer fills the buffer that is pointed to by *pfill*, which initially should point to buffer 1. Initially the *full–flags* of both buffers should be 0, since they are both empty. For an input file, the channel is the producer and executes the following channel program.

    loop: if pfill↑ .full–flag = 1 go to loop.
          issue start–I/O command to control
             unit.
          wait while pfill↑ .buffer is being
             filled.

```
pfill↑.record-ctr := 1
pfill↑.full-flag := 1
pfill := pfill↑.next
go to loop.
```

The channel program loops at *loop* only when one buffer is full and the other, which *pfill* points to, contains a *record-ctr* value less than n, indicating that it is either full or being emptied but is not yet empty.

The consumer empties the buffer that is pointed to by *pempty*, which initially should point to buffer 1. For an input file, the user program is the consumer and executes the following input routine:

```
wait: if pempty↑.full-flag = 0 go to wait.
      read record (pempty↑.record-ctr) into the
          record work area.
      pempty↑.record-ctr := pempty↑.record-ctr + 1
      if pempty↑.record-ctr > n
        begin;
                    pempty↑.full-flag = 0
                    pempty := pempty↑.next
        end;
      go to wait.
```

This routine loops at *wait* only when one buffer is empty and the other, which *pempty* points to, contains a *record-ctr* value greater than n, indicating that it is either empty or being filled but is not yet full.

If the producer is filling the buffers at a faster rate than the consumer is emptying them, then the producer (the channel program for input files) will spend time looping at *loop*. It is more desirable to have the channel program loop than to have the user program wait. This unfortunate situation occurs if the consumer (the user program for input files) is emptying the buffers at a faster rate than the rate at which the producer is filling them. One approach to reducing this problem is to chain together more than two buffers for the file.

Figure 173(b) illustrates a three-buffer system. The situation that is illustrated is the following:

Buffer 1 is full.

Buffer 2 is being filled.

Buffer 3 is being emptied; the mth record in the buffer will be read into the record work area next.

The next buffer that will be emptied is buffer 1.

The next buffer that will be filled is buffer 3.

This approach assumes that if any buffer is empty, the producer can move to fill it. For example, if, after buffer 3 is filled in the above sit-

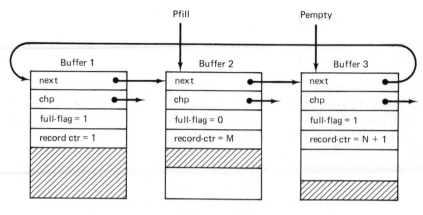

FIGURE 173(b)

uation, the consumer is still emptying buffer 1, then the producer should fill buffer 2; otherwise the consumer will have to wait.

If the producer consistently fills the buffers at a slower rate than the rate at which the consumer empties them, the consumer *will* have to wait. Multiple buffering can be effective in smoothing the results of uneven data requirements by the user program.

Thus the advantage of having more than one buffer is the potential to overlap the filling and emptying operations, thereby reducing wait time. The cost of multiple buffering is the slight increase in complexity and processing time of the producer and consumer routines and the increased main memory requirements.

OPENING AND CLOSING FILES

We have now considered a few aspects of I/O control in some detail. We have glimpsed the complexity of activity that occurs when a program issues a simple READ statement. (Description of activities ensuing from a WRITE is left as an exercise.) Let us now see what happens when a file is opened and when it is closed.

Before a program can access a file for input or output, that file must be opened. This processing may be initiated by an *OPEN* statement (required in COBOL) or in conjunction with the first *READ* or *WRITE* issued to the file. In either case, essentially the same activities result. These activities include the following:

- If necessary, a request is issued to an operator to mount the requested volume (e.g., tape reel or removable disk).
- The required channel program skeletons are constructed.

- Labels are checked if the file is opened for input; labels are written if the file is opened for output.
- The user's authorization to access the file is verified.
- The file's buffer area(s) are constructed and flags are properly initiated.
- If anticipatory buffering is in effect for an input file, then the first buffer is filled.
- The file's control block in the system's file directory is completed.

The information that is used to complete the file's control block can be extracted from several sources, including the program (using, for example, the *FILE-CONTROL* and *FILE SECTION* entries in COBOL), job control statements external to the program, and the file's labels (for an input file). Most systems impose priorities on these sources for purposes of resolving conflicts that arise should they contain contradictory descriptions for a file.

After a program has completed its use of a file, the file needs to be closed. This processing may be initiated by a *CLOSE* statement or by default at program termination. Closing a file prepares it for later use by another program execution. The activities involved in closing a file include the following:

- The buffer area(s) for an output file are emptied.
- The buffer area(s) and channel program spaces are released.
- End-of-file marks and trailer labels are written for an output file.
- The volume's disposition (e.g., rewind, dismount) is handled.

In a large program that uses several files, space requirements can be reduced by having files open only while they are active, rather than opening all files at the beginning of the program and postponing their closure until program termination.

SUMMARY

I/O control activities consume a significant portion of many computer systems' resources. File access requires both file management support and device management support. Nearly all operating systems use some sort of directory structure to manage the identification and location of information about files. This information describes both a file's organization and characteristics of the physical storage device upon which it resides.

Responsibility for device control is delegated to I/O processors, or

I/O channels. These programmable processors execute channel programs that instruct device control units to perform the operations required to fulfill a program's request to a file. Selector, multiplexor, and block multiplexor channels were introduced. The concepts of spooling and virtual devices were briefly discussed.

Understanding of the basic sequence of events that is required to perform a single device access shows the benefits of blocking records. Single and double buffering were introduced, and sample producer and consumer routines for buffer management were given.

Terms

anticipatory buffering	double buffering
block multiplexor channel	I/O control system
buffer	I/O supervisor
channel	multiplexor channel
channel program	selector channel
dedicated device	shared device
demand buffering	spooling
directory	virtual device

Review Questions

1. Is multiple buffering always anticipatory buffering?
2. Following are two incomplete buffer management routines.

Channel program	Application program
Loop: If flag=0 go to Loop.	Wait: If flag = <u>(b)</u>　　　Go to Wait.
Empty the buffer.	Counter := Counter + 1
Counter := 0	Move record work area into record
Flag := <u>(a)</u>	[counter]
Go to Loop.	If counter := <u>(c)</u>
	then flag := <u>(d)</u> 　.
	Go to Wait.

Assume that there are n records per block. Fill in the four blanks in the two routines.
(e) Does the application program have the file opened for input or for output?
(f) Explain the meanings of the possible values of flag.
(g) How many buffers are in use?

3. Why is anticipatory buffering important?

4. What benefits might there be in requiring a programmer to open a file explicitly rather than implicitly in the first access to the file?

5. What benefits might there be in closing a file explicitly rather than implicitly at the end of a run unit?

6. What arrangement of devices on channels is used at your installation?

7. Write the consumer and producer routines for double buffering for an output file. Who is the producer? Who is the consumer? Assume n records per block.

8. Obtain and try to decipher the listing for a channel program in use at your installation.

9. Find out what directory structure is used to manage files at your installation.

CHAPTER 18

Sorting and Merging Files

A common requirement of an information system is the ability to sort files. Transaction files must be ordered to support efficient updating of sequential master files; output data must be ordered to support proper formatting of sequential report files. Use of efficient sorting methods can be important to the overall performance of a computer installation and of an information system.

The sort methods that we discussed in Chapters 7 ($\sigma(N^2)$ techniques) and 10 ($\sigma(N\log_2 N)$ techniques) were internal sorting techniques. Each required that the complete collection of items to be sorted resides simultaneously in main memory. These methods are inappropriate for sorting large collections of records. Thus a variety of *file sorting*, or *external sorting* techniques have been developed; these techniques are the subject of this chapter.

INTRODUCTION TO FILE SORTING AND MERGING

Consider that a file of 2000 records must be sorted, and assume that only 1000 of these records will fit in the main memory at once. One approach to the problem would be to apply any internal sort method to sort separately two subsets of the file: records 1–1000 and records 1001–2000. (See Chapter 10 for a discussion of the relative performance characteristics of the better internal sorting methods.) The output from each application of the internal sort would be a sequentially organized file containing the sorted sublist. The two sorted sublists then could be merged (Fig. 174).

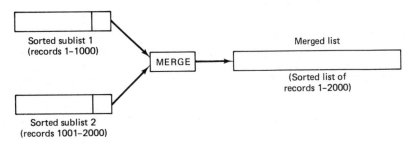

FIGURE 174

The merge here involves pairwise comparison of the "next" record key in each of the two sorted sublists. Whichever record has the lower key value (for an ascending sort) is the next record to be written to the merged file. The basic logic for the merge is given in Fig. 175, which should be compared with Fig. 163, which is the basic logic for updating a sequential file. Key1, key2, and keyM are used to refer to the record keys on sublist 1, sublist 2, and the resultant merged list, respectively. This logic relies upon having the incoming sublists in sorted order by the key that guides the merge. Note that the incoming lists need not be of the same length; when one list is depleted, the remainder of the other list is copied (in order) to the resultant merge file.

Nearly all of the file sorting techniques operate in essentially this way. The collection of records to be sorted is divided into a number of sublists, each of which is sorted by application of an internal sort method. Each sorted sublist is written as a sequential file. These sorted files are then merged to form the final sorted file. Thus file sorting techniques commonly are called *sort/merges*.

A file sort/merge has three phases:

1. Internal sort phase, which sorts the records into several runs distributed on two or more storage devices.
2. Merge phase, which combines the sorted subfiles into a single run.
3. Output phase, which copies the sorted file onto its final storage medium.

The file sort/merge techniques differ from each other in the following ways:

1. The internal sort method applied.
2. The amount of main memory space allocated to the internal sort.

FIGURE 175

3. The distribution of sorted sublists on secondary storage.
4. The number of sorted sublists that are merged together in one merge pass.

Given a file to be sorted, these parameters then determine the number of sorted sublists generated by the internal sort phase and the number of merge passes.

We evaluated internal sort methods by the number of comparisons each required to sort a collection of N keys. This is an inappropriate measure for the evaluation of file sort methods, because the CPU time required for key comparisons is negligible relative to the I/O time required to access secondary storage in reading and writing files. Thus file sort/merge techniques are compared by their relative frequencies of reference to secondary storage. One good measure of this frequency of reference is the number of passes over the data collection, that is, the number of times each record is involved in a merge.

In the examples used in the following sections, we will see that the following factors affect performance, as measured by the number of times records are read/written:

1. Starting the merge phase with sorted subfiles (or *runs*) that are as long as possible minimizes the number of runs that must be merged.
2. The greater the number of runs that are merged together at once, the fewer passes need to be made to merge the collection of runs.
3. Distributing runs on secondary storage for input to a merge pass may require I/O processing in addition to that actually required in performing the merge.

One of the most commonly used algorithms for the internal sort phase is the *tournament sort*. As we discussed in Chapter 10, the tournament sort tends to generate long runs relative to the amount of main memory that it uses. On the average, sorted runs of length $2P$ will result from a tournament sort that allows P keys to compete with each other. In the remainder of this chapter the actual algorithm used in the internal sort phase of a sort/merge will not be of interest; we will be concerned only with the merge phase.

There are many ways to handle the merge phase of a file sort/merge. In the following sections we consider several possible approaches:

- The natural merge
- The balanced merge
- The polyphase merge
- The cascade merge

NATURAL MERGES

A merge that handles two input files at once is called a two-way merge; a merge that handles M input files at once is called an M-way merge. M is referred to as the *degree* of the merge. An *M-way natural merge* is defined as a merge with M input files and just one output file.

Consider the problem of sorting a file of 6000 records. Fig. 176 illustrates several natural merges applied to this collection of data. The differences in performance that result as the number of sorted runs input to the merge phase and the degrees of the merges are varied are of

2-way merge: Assume 2 input files and 1 output file

(1) Distribute sorted runs onto 2 files (may be done in conjunction with internal sort phase)

(2) Merge pass 1:

(3) Distribute sorted runs from ③ onto 2 files

(4) Merge pass 2:

(5) Merge pass 3:

FIGURE 176(a)

importance. The storage medium depicted in the figures is tape; actually it could be a DASD or any serial storage device. We use "tape" here generically as a device that stores sequentially organized files. Note that between merges, the sorted runs generated by the prior pass must be redistributed from the one output file onto the appropriate number (M) of input files for the next pass.

The copying of data back and forth causes the I/O requirements of a natural sort/merge to be significant. The greater the number of initial runs and the lower the degree of the natural merge, the greater are the resultant I/O requirements.

3-way merge: Assume 3 input files and 1 output file

(1) Distribute sorted runs onto 3 files (may be done in conjunction with internal sort phase)

(2) Merge pass 1:

(3) Distribute sorted runs from (4) onto 3 files (here only 2 are used)

(4) Merge pass 2:

FIGURE 176(b)

BALANCED MERGES

The I/O requirements of a natural merge can be reduced by using a balanced merge. Nearly half the I/O activity of a natural merge is devoted to redistributing newly merged runs output from one pass onto multiple files for input to the next pass. (See Fig. 176 again.) A *balanced merge* avoids much of this copying of records back and forth by distributing the results of a merge pass directly onto the appropriate number of files for input to the next merge pass. By contrast, a natural merge distributes all its output merge runs onto a single file. An M-way natural merge uses $M + 1$ files, while an M-way balanced merge uses $2M$ files. In a balanced merge, the data are moved back and forth between an equal number of input and output files.

Consider for example a computer installation with four tape drives. The output sequences from the internal sort phase could be written onto two tapes. By alternating tapes, approximately half of the sorted runs would appear on each tape. The remaining two tape drives would

6000 records

Internal sort phase → 12 sorted subfiles @ 500 records

2-way merge: Assume 2 input files and 1 output file

(1) Distribute sorted runs onto 2 files (may be done in conjunction with internal sort phase)

(2) Merge pass 1:

| records 5001-5500; | records 4001-4500; | records 3001-3500; | records 2001-2500; | records 1001-1500; | records 1-500 | ① |
| records 5501-6000; | records 4501-5000; | records 3501-4000; | records 2501-3000; | records 1501-2000; | records 501-1000 | ② |

① records 1-500
② records 501-1000

→ Merge pass 1 →

③

records 1-1000; (Run 1)
records 1001-2000; (Run 2)
records 2001-3000; (Run 3)
records 3001-4000; (Run 4)
records 4001-5000; (Run 5)
records 5001-6000. (Run 6)

*Note that "Run 1 + 4" denotes the result of merging (not concatenating) Runs 1 and 4.

(3) Distribute sorted runs from ③ onto 2 files

(4) Merge pass 2:

Run 3; Run 2; Run 1 ①
Run 6; Run 5; Run 4 ③

→ Merge pass 2 →

② Run 1 + 4; *
Run 2 + 5;
Run 3 + 6;

(5) Distribute sorted runs from ② onto 2 files

(6) Merge pass 3:

Run 1 + 4 ①
Run 2 + 5 ②

→ Merge pass 3 →

③ Run 1 + 4 + 2 + 5;
(Run 3 + 6 is still on ②)

(7) Merge pass 4:

Run 1 + 4 + 2 + 5 ③
Run 3 + 6 ②

→ Merge pass 4 →

① Run 1 + 4 + 2 + 5 + 3 + 6 = sorted file.

Note that Record 1 is read and written 7 times

FIGURE 176(c)

344

6000 records

Internal sort phase → 12 sorted subfiles @ 500 records

3-way merge: Assume 3 input files and 1 output file

(1) Distribute sorted runs onto 3 files (may be done in conjunction with internal sort phase)

(2) Merge pass 1:

records 4501–5000; records 3001–3500; records 1501–2000; records 1–500 (1)

records 5001–5500; records 3501–4000; records 2001–2500; records 501–1000 (2)

records 5501–6000; records 4001–4500; records 2501–3000; records 1001–1500 (3)

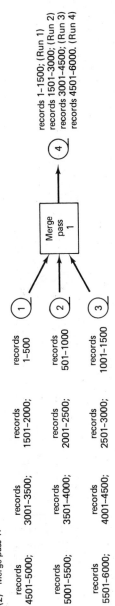

Merge pass 1 → (4)

records 1–1500: (Run 1)
records 1501–3000; (Run 2)
records 3001–4500; (Run 3)
records 4501–6000. (Run 4)

(3) Distribute sorted runs from (4) onto 3 files

(4) Merge pass 2:

Run 1 (1)
Run 2 (2)
Run 3 (4)

Merge pass 2 → (3) Run 1 + 2 + 3

(Run 4 is still on (4))

(5) Merge pass 3:

Run 1 + 2 + 3 (3)
Run 4 (4)

Merge pass 3 → (1) Run 1 + 2 + 3 + 4 = sorted file

Note that Record 1 is read and written 5 times.

FIGURE 176(d)

345

6000 records

Internal sort phase → 12 sorted subfiles @ 500 records

2-way balanced merge: Assume 4 files

(1) Distribute sorted runs onto 2 files (may be done in conjunction with internal sort phase)

(2) Merge pass 1:

records 5001-5500; records 4001-4500; records 3001-3500; records 2001-2500; records 1001-1500; records 1-500 ①

records 5501-6000; records 4501-5000; records 3501-4000; records 2501-3000; records 1501-2000; records 501-1000 ②

Merge pass 1

records 1-1000; (Run 1)
records 2001-3000; (Run 3)
records 4001-5000; (Run 5) ③

records 1001-2000; (Run 2)
records 3001-4000; (Run 4)
records 5001-6000. (Run 6) ④

(3) Merge pass 2:

Run 5; Run 3; Run 1 ③   Run 1 + 2; Run 5 + 6 ①
Run 6; Run 4; Run 2 ④   Run 3 + 4 ②

Merge pass 2

(4) Merge pass 3:

Run 1 + 2 ①
Run 3 + 4 ②

Merge pass 3

Run 1 + 2 + 3 + 4 ③
(Run 5 + 6 is still on ①)

(5) Merge pass 4:

Run 5 + 6 ①
Run 1 + 2 + 3 + 4 ③

Merge pass 4

Run 1 + 2 + 3 + 4 + 5 + 6 ②
= sorted file

Note that Record 1 is read and written 5 times.

FIGURE 177

be used to receive the results of the first merge pass. Initially, one run from each input tape is merged into a longer run and written on one output tape. The second run from each input tape then is merged into a longer run and written on the second output tape. The third runs are merged onto the first output tape, and so forth, alternating output tapes until the input tapes are exhausted. The two output tapes now become the input tapes for the second merge pass. (See Fig. 177 and compare with Fig. 176.)

During each merge pass, the total number of runs is divided by the degree of the merge, while each run is lengthened by a factor equal to the degree of the merge. In Fig. 177 the number of runs output from each merge pass is half the number of runs input to the pass. Each output run is approximately twice as long as each input run. If the internal sort phase results in R sorted subfiles to be merged, then an M-way balanced merge will require $\sigma(\log_M R)$ merge passes.

POLYPHASE MERGES

We have just seen that an M-way balanced merge technique uses $2M$ files. At any given time, runs are being read from M files and being written on one file. Thus $M-1$ files are always idle. Modification of the balanced merge approach can result in better file utilization. These "unbalanced" merges attempt to achieve a merge power greater than M by reading from more than M files at a time, using up to $2M-1$ input files and a single output file. One type of unbalanced merge is the *polyphase merge*, in which a constant number of input files is used. An M-way polyphase merge uses $2M-1$ input files. (We will discuss another type of unbalanced merge in the next section.)

The internal sort phase of an M-way polyphase merge must distribute its sorted runs onto $2M-1$ files in a manner that facilitates the later merge. Let us assume that the internal sort phase results in 17 sorted runs. As shown in Fig. 178, these runs should be distributed (for a two-way polyphase merge) onto three files such that file 1 contains 7 runs, file 2 contains 6 runs, and file 3 contains 4 runs. This distribution was determined by the sequence shown in Table 6. First one run is written on each file. Then in cycle 2 the number of runs on file 1 is written on files 2 and 3. In cycle 3 the number of runs on file 2 is written on files 1 and 3. And in cycle 4 the number of runs on file 3 is written on files 1 and 2. If there were more runs, then the number of runs on file 1 would be written on files 2 and 3, and so forth through the successive cycles.

Each pass then merges the runs from the input files until *one* of the input files is empty; the others still contain runs. That empty input

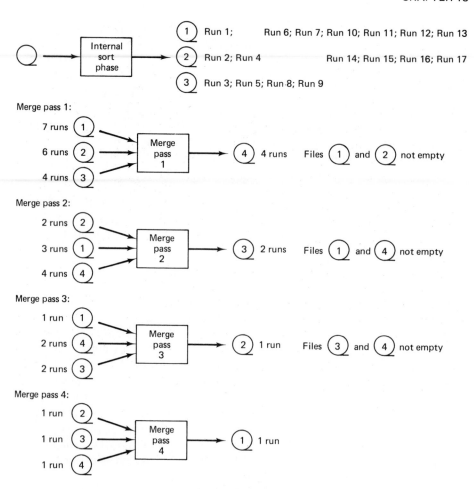

FIGURE 178

Table 6   # runs/file

file becomes the output file for the next merge pass. This approach reduces the amount of copying of records, because the next merge pass is still working with runs that were on the input files to the last pass. In fact, in this example, run 1 on file 1 is not copied to output until merge pass 3. Note that if this were a balanced merge, records of run 1 would have been copied five times (see Fig. 177).

The distribution of runs on the files during the merge passes is shown in Table 7.

Table 7 # runs/file

	start pass 1	end pass 1	end pass 2	end pass 3	end pass 4
File 1	7	3	1	0	1
2	6	2	0	1	0
3	4	0	2	1	0
4	0	4	2	1	0
total	17	9	5	3	1

Compare this table with Table 6, which shows the sequence of distributing runs during the internal sort phase. The similarity is more than coincidental! Actually, our initial assumption of 17 sorted runs was not accidental either; 17 happens to be a good number for this situation.

Padding the data collection with dummy records may be necessary to obtain the proper initial layout. For a given data collection, it is nearly impossible to determine exactly how many runs will result from the internal sort phase without actually doing the internal sort. The number of runs can be estimated if one knows the characteristics of the internal sort.

CASCADE MERGES

Another type of unbalanced merge that attempts to reduce the copying of records is called the *cascade merge*. A cascade merge of degree M uses $2M - 1$, then $2M - 2$, then $2M - 3, \ldots$, then two input files during the various phases of a merge pass. Like a polyphase merge, a cascade merge relies on a clever initial distribution of the runs by the internal sort phase.

Each merge pass begins with a merge from $2M - 1$ input files to one output file. When the first input file is emptied, it becomes the output file and the prior output file is set aside. Now $2M - 2$ input files are merged onto the new output file. As an input file is emptied, it becomes the output file and the prior output file is retired temporarily. Eventually all input files will be emptied. At the end of the merge pass, each record has been processed once.

Then the next merge pass starts. $2M - 1$ inputs are merged, then $2M - 2$, and so forth until the cycles of merge phases have been completed. A cascade merge of degree 2 for 17 initial runs, distributed as they were in Fig. 178, is shown in Fig. 179.

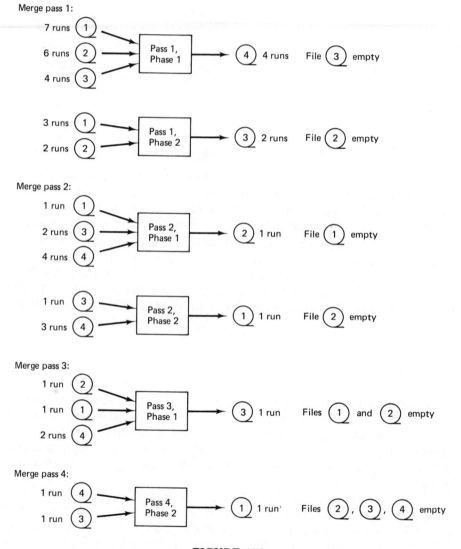

FIGURE 179

The cascade merge here achieves the same amount of run copying as did the polyphase merge, using the same number of files, but using a different method.

SORTING/MERGING USING UTILITIES

We have already stated that file sort/merging is a very common operation in information systems. Rather than reprogramming these sort/merges time after time, many installations make extensive use of acquired sort/merge packages (or utilities). The vendors of these packages are both independent software firms and hardware/software firms.

A sort/merge utility by definition provides general-purpose file sort/merge support. The details of the utilities vary from vendor to vendor, but in general they appear to be quite similar. Their capabilities generally are three:

1. Sort (one or more files)
2. Merge (two or more sorted files)
3. Sort and merge (two or more files)

The user of the sort/merge package must supply various directives to guide the process. These directives include the following types of specifications:

1. Names of files to be sorted/merged.
2. Identifications, locations, lengths, and data types of fields to be used as the sort/merge key.
3. Ordering (major to minor) of key fields.
4. Sequencing (ascending or descending) to be applied to each key field.
5. Collating sequence to be applied to each key field.
6. Name of the output file to contain the results of the sort/merge.

Additionally, some packages allow the user to specify other parameters, such as:

7. A user-defined collating sequence.
8. The algorithm to be used in the internal sort phase (e.g., tournament, heap).
9. The algorithm to be used in the merge phase (e.g., balanced, polyphase, cascade).

10. The action to be taken before/after using files (e.g., rewind, un-load).

11. Verification that input records to the merge phase are actually in correct sequence.

12. Period to be used to checkpoint/dump records for recovery purposes.

13. Estimated number of input records.

For example, use of a hypothetical but representative sort/merge might require the following stream of job control commands:

```
//SORTNOW    EXEC      SORTMRG
//SORTIN     DD        DSN=name of input file, . . . ,
//                         DISP=(OLD,KEEP)
//SORTOUT    DD        DSN=name of output file, . . . ,
//                         DISP=(NEW,KEEP)
//SYSIN      DD        *
    SORT FIELDS=(1,4,CH,A,20,10,CH,D),FILEZ=E2000
/*
```

Here the sort key is comprised of two fields: the major field starts in byte 1, for a length of 4 bytes, is character data, and is to be arranged in ascending order; the minor field starts in byte 20, for a length of 10 bytes, is character data, and is to be arranged in descending order. The input file contains an estimated 2000 records.

The following commands give another example of use of a sort/merge utility.

```
SORTMRG(inputfilename,outputfilename)

. . .
SORT,VAR=POLY
FILE,INPUT=name(CU),OUTPUT=name(R)
FIELD,DEPT(1,4,ASCII6),SALEDATE(20,10,ASCII6)
KEY,DEPT(A,ASCII6),SALEDATE(D,ASCII6)
```

Here the merge phase is to be a polyphase merge; the input file is to be closed and unloaded (CU) when the sort terminates; the output file is to be rewound(R). The sort keys are *DEPT* (major) in positions 1-4, of type ASCII6, and *SALEDATE* (minor) in positions 20-29, also of type ASCII6. Records are to be sorted in ascending *DEPT* order and descending *SALEDATE* order.

The availability of a sort/merge utility makes it a straightforward matter to specify a file sort. These sorts are also called *control card sorts*. As part of its output, a sort/merge utility usually lists the number of records that were input to the internal sort phase and the number of records that were written to the final output file. In most cases these figures should balance.

Some sort/merge packages have the provision that a user may specify "own-code" or "sort exit" procedures that are to be executed in the context of the sort/merge activities. These procedures usually are written in an assembler language and can be used to manipulate records at the following times:

1. After a record is read from the input file but before it enters the internal sort phase.
2. After a record leaves the internal sort phase but before it is written onto a file output from the internal sort phase.
3. When multiple records with matching values are encountered during the internal sort phase.
4. When multiple records with matching key values are encountered during the merge phase.

These procedures might eliminate records with certain characteristics (for example, DEPT-TYPE='ABOLISHED') from further consideration, or might select just one record when there are multiple records with matching key values, and so forth. In these cases the numbers of input and output records very well might not balance.

SORTING/MERGING IN PROGRAMS

Most file sorting/merging is conducted by use of utilities rather than through programming languages. However, COBOL does have a built-in feature that allows a sort/merge utility to be invoked from *within* a COBOL program.

The *SORT* verb creates a sorted file from one or more input files and has the following syntax:

$$\underline{SORT}\ \text{filename-1}\ \left\{ \text{ON} \left\{ \frac{\underline{ASCENDING}}{\underline{DESCENDING}} \right\} \text{KEY}\ \{\text{dataname1}\}\ldots \right\}\ldots$$

[COLLATING $\underline{SEQUENCE}$ IS alphabet-name]

$$\left\{ \begin{array}{l} \underline{INPUT}\ \underline{PROCEDURE}\ \text{IS section-name-1} \left[\left\{ \frac{\underline{THROUGH}}{\underline{THRU}} \right\} \text{section-name-2} \right] \\ \underline{USING}\ [\text{filename-2}]\ \ldots \end{array} \right\}$$

$$\left\{ \begin{array}{l} \underline{OUTPUT}\ \underline{PROCEDURE}\ \text{IS section-name-3} \left[\left\{ \frac{\underline{THROUGH}}{\underline{THRU}} \right\} \text{section-name-4} \right] \\ \underline{GIVING}\ [\text{filename-3}] \end{array} \right\}$$

The simplest form of the *SORT* verb for one input file is (for example):

```
SORT  SORTWORK  ON ASCENDING KEY DEPT
                      ON DESCENDING KEY SALE–DATE
          USING INPUTFILENAME
          GIVING OUTPUTFILENAME
```

SORTWORK here is a temporary file used during the sort/merge; it must be declared in an *SD* entry (as opposed to *FD* entry) in the *FILE SECTION* of the *DATA DIVISION*. The input and output files must both be sequentially organized.

The use of the *INPUT PROCEDURE* option allows the programmer to manipulate records prior to their release to the internal sort; use of the *OUTPUT PROCEDURE* option allows the programmer to manipulate records after their return from the sort but before they are written to the output file. These procedures are like the sort exits that were mentioned previously. Two examples of their use follow. Both procedures use the following *DATA DIVISION*:

```
DATA DIVISION.
FILE SECTION.
FD  IN–FILE LABEL RECORD IS STANDARD.
01  IN–REC.
        02  IN–DEPT              PIC X(4).
        02  FILLER               PIC X(15).
        02  IN–SALE–DATE         PIC X(10).
        02  DEPT–TYPE            PIC X(9).
        02  FILLER               PIC X(500).
FD  OUT–FILE LABEL RECORD IS STANDARD.
01  OUT–REC.
        02  OUT–DEPT             PIC X(4).
        02  FILLER               PIC X(15).
        02  OUT–SALE–DATE        PIC X(10).
        02  DEPT–TYPE            PIC X(9).
        02  FILLER               PIC X(500).
SD  SORT–FILE.
01  SORT–REC.
        02  DEPT                 PIC X(4).
        02  FILLER               PIC X(15).
        02  SALE–DATE            PIC X(10).
        02  DEPT–TYPE            PIC X(9).
        02  FILLER               PIC X(500).
```

The results of both examples are the same. This one uses an *INPUT PROCEDURE* to eliminate records: (Assume that a switch

```
01  EOF-IN-FILE-SW PIC X VALUE "N".
    88  EOF-IN-FILE VALUE "Y".
```

has been defined in *WORKING-STORAGE*.)

```
PROCEDURE DIVISION.
MAIN-LINE SECTION.

    . . .
    SORT SORT-FILE ON ASCENDING KEY DEPT
                   ON DESCENDING KEY SALE-DATE
    INPUT PROCEDURE IS READ-IN-REC
    GIVING OUT-FILE.

    . . .
READ-IN-REC SECTION.
DRIVER.
    OPEN INPUT IN-FILE.
    READ IN-FILE AT END MOVE "Y" TO EOF-IN-FILE-SW.
    PERFORM READ-REC UNTIL EOF-IN-FILE.
    CLOSE IN-FILE.
    EXIT.
READ-REC.
    IF DEPT-TYPE OF IN-REC NOT = "ABOLISHED"
    THEN MOVE IN-REC TO SORT-REC
        RELEASE SORT-REC.
    READ IN-FILE AT END MOVE "Y" TO EOF-IN-FILE.
```

This next example uses an *OUTPUT PROCEDURE* to eliminate records. Assume that a switch

```
01  EOF-SORT-FILE-SW       PIC X    VALUE "N".
    88  EOF-SORT-FILE       VALUE "Y".
```

has been defined in *WORKING-STORAGE*.

```
PROCEDURE DIVISION.
MAIN-LINE SECTION.

    . . .
    SORT SORT-FILE ON ASCENDING KEY DEPT
                   ON DESCENDING KEY SALE-DATE
    USING IN-FILE
    OUTPUT PROCEDURE IS WRITE-OUT-REC.

    . . .
WRITE-OUT-REC SECTION.
DRIVER.
    OPEN OUTPUT OUT-FILE.
    RETURN SORT-FILE RECORD
        AT END MOVE "Y" TO EOF-SORT-FILE-SW.
    PERFORM WRITE-REC UNTIL EOF-SORT-FILE.
```

```
        CLOSE OUT-FILE.
        EXIT.
    WRITE-REC.
        IF DEPT-TYPE OF SORT-REC NOT ="ABOLISHED"
        THEN MOVE SORT-REC TO OUT-REC
            WRITE OUT-REC.
        RETURN SORT-FILE RECORD
            AT END MOVE "Y" TO EOF-SORT-FILE-SW.
```

The first of these two examples would be the more efficient, since it reduces the number of records handled by the sort/merge.

The COBOL *MERGE* verb is used to merge already-sorted input files. The syntax is as follows:

$$\underline{\text{MERGE}} \text{ filename1} \left\{ \text{ON} \left\{ \frac{\text{ASCENDING}}{\text{DESCENDING}} \right\} \text{KEY \{dataname1\}} \dots \right\} \dots$$

[COLLATING $\underline{\text{SEQUENCE}}$ IS alphabet-name]

$\underline{\text{USING}}$ filename2 [filename3] ...

$$\left\{ \begin{array}{l} \underline{\text{OUTPUT}} \text{ PROCEDURE IS sectionname1} \left[\left\{ \frac{\text{THROUGH}}{\text{THRU}} \right\} \text{sectionname 2} \right] \\ \underline{\text{GIVING}} \text{ filename4} \end{array} \right\}$$

Note that no *INPUT PROCEDURE* can be specified and that at least two input files must be named.

SORT/MERGE PERFORMANCE

There are many factors that interact to determine how well a particular file sort/merge technique performs. With a given technique, performance is dependent upon:

1. The number of records to be sorted/merged.
2. The size of the records.
3. The number of storage devices used.
4. The distribution of those devices on available I/O channels.
5. The distribution of key values in the input file(s).

In most cases it takes about as long to sort 100,000 records, each with 10 characters, as to sort 10,000 records, each with 100 characters. It is the total volume of data rather than the volume of records which tends to be the more important factor. The actual key field size is usually an inconsequential factor. In fact, it is usually preferable to sort records with their keys rather than to sort detached keys and then later have to access and rearrange the records.

A practical factor which has not really entered the discussion of this chapter until now is the importance of being able to recover from a sort that terminates early and abnormally, because of either I/O errors or other system problems. One important axiom is never to destroy the files input to a sort/merge until the entire process has completed successfully.

In general, it is quite difficult to determine which merge pattern is the best one to use for a particular situation. The strategy employed in the initial allocation of sorted runs to files and the order in which they subsequently are merged also have significant impact on the performance of the file sort. In general, however, a natural merge performs worse than the other types of merges. A polyphase merge generally is better than a balanced merge when there are fewer than ten I/O-units available. A polyphase merge tends to be better than a cascade merge. There are other variations on "unbalanced" merging that perform better than the polyphase merge in particular situations, especially if there are more than ten I/O-units available.

SUMMARY

Nearly all techniques for file sorting use the following sequence of phases: (1) an internal sort phase that sorts the file into a number of sorted sublists (or runs) using an internal sort method; these runs are distributed to two or more files in some more or less clever manner; (2) a merge phase that combines the sorted runs into a single sorted run; and (3) an output phase that copies the sorted run to its final storage medium.

A tournament sort commonly is used for the internal sort phase because it tends to generate long runs relative to the amount of main memory that it uses.

There are many possible algorithms that can be used to implement the merge phase. An M-way natural merge uses M input files and one output file. Much of the consequent copying of records can be avoided by using a balanced merge. An M-way balanced merge uses M input files and M output files. At any given time, $M - 1$ of the output files are idle. Utilization can be improved by using an unbalanced merge, which attempts to achieve a merge power greater than M by reading from up to $2M - 1$ input files and using a single output file. An M-way polyphase merge uses a constant number of input files ($2M - 1$). By clever distribution of runs on those files, the output file can be recycled as an input file and the amount of record copying can be reduced significantly. A cascade merge of degree M uses $2M - 1$, then $2M - 2$, then $2M - 3, \ldots$, then 2 input files through the various phases of a merge pass; the output files are not recycled into the merge.

Many vendors provide software that implements one or more sort/ merge approaches. These packages, which fall into the category of utilities, can be invoked either by job control commands or from within COBOL programs by use of the *SORT* and *MERGE* verbs. The user supplies descriptions of the input and output files and of the keys to guide the sort/merge.

The most popular sort/merge technique is probably the polyphase merge used in conjunction with an internal tournament sort. For a particular situation, however, another technique may give better performance.

For more information about file sort/merge techniques, you should see Chapter 4 (External Sorting) of D. E. Knuth, *The Art of Computer Programming, Vol. 3, Sorting and Searching*, (Reading, Mass.: Addison-Wesley, 1973); Chapters 12 through 18 of H. Lorin, *Sorting and Sort Systems*, (Reading, Mass.: Addison-Wesley, 1975); and technical reference manuals for vendors' sort/merge utilities.

Terms

balanced merge	merge phase
cascade merge	natural merge
external sort	polyphase merge
file sort	run
internal sort phase	sort/merge
merge	tournament sort
merge degree	

Review Exercises

1. Why is a tournament sort usually a good type of sort to use for the internal sort phase of a file sort?

2. Why is the performance of an external sort usually evaluated by number of copies rather than by number of comparisons?

3. What kind of merge is used in the sort/merge utility available at your installation?

4. What kind of sort is used in the internal sort phase of the sort/merge utility available at your installation?

5. Compare the operation and performance of a balanced merge and an unbalanced merge.

6. Compare the operation and performance of a polyphase merge and a cascade merge.

7. Obtain a file of unsorted data. Sort the file in various ways, e.g., using the COBOL *SORT* verb, and using each of the merge-type options available in your local sort/merge utility. Compare the performance of the several methods.

8. Obtain a file of unsorted data. Sort the file in various ways, with each method allowing you either to extract or combine some records in addition to sorting the file—for example, using an *INPUT PROCEDURE* with the COBOL *SORT* verb, using an *OUTPUT PROCEDURE* with the COBOL *SORT* verb, and using data manipulation capabilities of the sort/merge utility. Compare the performance of the several methods.

CHAPTER 19

Relative File Organization

In this chapter we introduce another fundamental approach to organizing data on secondary storage: relative file organization. The organization method is first defined, then its utility in information systems is discussed. Many techniques have been developed for implementing the concept of relative file organization, and the most commonly applied methods are covered here. We then discuss the declaration and use of relative files in programs, including creation of relative files, retrieval from relative files, and update of relative files. The chapter closes with a review of some of the factors that should be considered in the design of a file with relative organization.

DEFINITIONS AND APPLICATIONS: RELATIVE FILES

An effective way to organize a collection of records when there is a need to access individual records directly is *relative file organization*. In a relative file, there is a predictable relationship between the key used to identify a particular record and that record's location on secondary storage. However, it is important to understand that the logical *ordering* of records need bear no relationship to their physical sequencing (Fig. 180). The records *do not* necessarily appear physically in sorted order by their key values.

How then is the Nth record found? When a relative file is established, the relationship that will be used to translate between key values

FIGURE 180

and physical addresses is designated. This relationship, call it R, is a mapping function

$$R \text{ (key value)} \longrightarrow \text{address}$$

from key values to addresses on secondary storage. When a record is to be written into a relative file, the mapping function R is used to translate the record's key value to an address, which indicates where the record is to be stored. When it is desirable to retrieve the record with a particular key value, the mapping function R is applied to that key value, translating it to the address on secondary storage where the record can be found. Thus the predictable relationship between record key values and record storage locations is used both when a record is stored and when it is retrieved.

Note that, in contrast to sequentially organized files, it is not necessary to access the records of a relative file in consecutive order. Rather, a particular record occurrence can be accessed directly. The direct-access character of relative file organization could not be taken advantage of if a relative file were stored on a serial-access medium such as magnetic tape. Therefore relative files are stored on DASD's.

It *is* possible to access the records of a relative file in physically consecutive order. However, it should be understood that the keys may not be in logical sequence. For example, serial access to the file depicted in Fig. 180 retrieves records in the order:

COW, ZEBRA, . . . , APE, EEL, DOG, . . . , CAT, BAT.

A relative file might be accessed serially when input to a file sort/merge.

A relative file of customer records might be accessed serially by a program that generates a mailing label for each customer but that does not care about the order in which those mailing labels are generated.

Because of their capability to support rapid access directly to particular records, relative files are used commonly in interactive processing. For example, consider an on-line banking system in which tellers have terminals and direct access to customer account data. A simple master file might have records of the format shown in Fig. 181(a).

CUSTOMER-ACCOUNT

ACCOUNT NUMBER	ACCOUNT TYPE	BALANCE	DATE-LAST -CREDIT	DATE-LAST -DEBIT

FIGURE 181(a)

Assume that the CUSTOMER-ACCOUNT file is a relative file, with key ACCOUNT-NUMBER. Teller inputs might be formatted into transactions with the format shown in Fig. 181(b).

TRANSACTION

ACCOUNT NUMBER	TRANS -TYPE	AMOUNT	DATE

FIGURE 181(b)

When a teller keys in a transaction, the specified ACCOUNT-NUMBER would be used to determine the location of the corresponding CUS-TOMER-ACCOUNT record on secondary storage. That record would be read and made available to the on-line transaction-processing program. If the TRANS-TYPE = 'I', the account's balance would be displayed to the teller. If the TRANS-TYPE = 'C' or 'D', the CUSTOMER-ACCOUNT record would be modified according to the AMOUNT and DATE information contained on the transaction, and the CUSTOMER-ACCOUNT record would be rewritten to the relative file, with the ACCOUNT-NUMBER again used to determine the record's location on that file.

First, note that it is not necessary to access master file records other than the target record. Compare this with the processing situation of a sequential master file! Second, note that records of the relative master file can be updated in place. Compare this with the way that a sequential master file is updated, by recreating the entire file.

Thus the major advantage of a relative file is the ability to access

individual records directly. A record can be retrieved, inserted, modified, or even deleted without affecting the other records on the file.
(Actually this last statement is a bit of a generalization. We will see
later that the insertion or deletion of a record may affect other records, but the effects are slight and quite localized.)

Let us now delve into the problems of implementing this concept
of relative file organization. There are three fundamental techniques
used by mapping functions R, where R (key value)———► address:

1. Direct mapping
2. Directory lookup
3. Calculation

DIRECT MAPPING TECHNIQUES FOR RELATIVE FILES

The simplest technique for translating a record key to a storage address
is direct mapping. Direct mapping is not widely used. We discuss it here
primarily because understanding of the disadvantages of the direct mapping techniques helps to build an understanding of the benefits of the
other techniques.

Absolute Addressing

One simple approach to implementing

R (key value)———► address

is to have

key value = address.

This mapping function is called *absolute addressing*. The key value supplied by a human or program user is the same as the record's actual address on secondary storage. When the record is first stored on the file,
the target location of the record ([cylinder-number, surface-number,
record-number] if cylinder addressing is used, or [sector-number,
record-number] if sector addressing is used) must be determined by the
user. When the record is later to be retrieved, its absolute location again
must be known and supplied by the user.

There are two advantages to this absolute addressing scheme:

1. The mapping function R is very simple.
2. Given a record's key value, no processing time is required to determine the record's location on secondary storage.

The disadvantages of the scheme nearly always outweigh the advantages:

1. Logical and physical considerations are not independent with absolute addressing; the user must know exactly how the records are stored physically.
2. Users generally do not supply the appropriate types of key values, e.g., use of the ACCOUNT–NUMBER key value in the earlier banking example. Use of ACCOUNT–NUMBER is a natural and logical way to identify CUSTOMER–ACCOUNT records; ACCOUNT–NUMBERs do not usually make reasonable physical storage addresses!
3. Absolute addresses are device-dependent. Should it be desirable to upgrade or change the device upon which the file resides, it is likely that key values would also need to be changed.
4. Absolute addresses are address-space-dependent. Should it be desirable to reorganize the relative file but to keep it on the same device, it is likely that key values would need to be changed. This reorganization might be for purposes of enlarging the address space, consolidating free space, collecting garbage space, or decreasing the address space.

Relative Addressing

Another simple approach to implementing

$$R \text{ (key value)} \longrightarrow \text{address}$$

which has essentially the same advantages as does direct addressing, but which removes some of the disadvantages of absolute addressing, is called *relative addressing*. Here

$$\text{key value} = \text{relative address.}$$

A relative address can be supplied to a channel program for translation to an absolute address.

The relative address of a record in a file is the record's ordinal number in the file. A file with space for N records has records with relative addresses from the set $\{1, 2, 3, \ldots, N-1, N\}$ (or $\{0, 1, 2, \ldots, N-2, N-1\}$). The Ith record has relative address I (or $I-1$).

The advantages of the relative addressing scheme are two:

1. The mapping function R is very simple.
2. Given a record's key value, essentially no processing time is required to determine the record's location on secondary storage.

Relative addresses are not nearly so device-dependent as are absolute addresses, thereby eliminating one of the disadvantages listed for absolute addressing. However, like absolute addresses, relative addresses are address-space-dependent.

Some types of natural key values are not well-suited for use as relative addresses. For example, although it could be converted to a numeric equivalent, employee name values are not good relative addresses; nor are many natural, numeric key values. For example, social security numbers are poor relative addresses. Why? Consider an organization with 2000 employees. The organization needs a relative file of employee data and wants to use social security numbers for the key. Such a relative file would have to be implemented with space allocated for 999,999,999 employees, since key values of employees could range from 1 to 999,999,999. The file will be 99.99998% empty. Even use of a 4-digit employee number would here result in a file that is 80% empty. The size of the file (i.e., the size of the file's address space) is determined by the range of possible values for the relative address, which with relative addressing is equivalent to the range of *possible* values for the key, *not* by the actual number of key values used.

One approach to this key-space problem is to identify or invent a key whose range of values is highly populated. For instance, in a relative file of part inventory data, a 4-digit part number might be a very good relative address, if the inventory contains, say 8200 types of parts. Of course, requests to access data about a particular part would have to be phrased in terms of the part's 4-digit part number, not in terms of its name or type or some other field value.

DIRECTORY LOOKUP TECHNIQUES FOR RELATIVE FILES

After direct mapping, the next most simple approach to implementing

$$R \text{ (key value)} \longrightarrow \text{address}$$

is *directory lookup*. This very commonly used approach takes advantage of the benefits of direct mapping while eliminating its disadvantages. It does, however, introduce a couple of new costs. We will see that this approach is quite similar to techniques used with indexed sequential files.

The basic idea of the directory lookup approach is to keep a table or directory of key value:address pairs (or key value:relative address pairs). In order to find a record on a relative file, one locates its key value in the directory and then the indicated address is used to find the record on storage.

In its simplest form, the directory is implemented as an array of key value:address records, as illustrated in Fig. 182(a).

DIRECTORY

KEY	ADDRESS
APE	I−1
BAT	N
CAT	N−1
⋮	
COW	1
DOG	I+1
EEL	I
⋮	
ZEBRA	2

RELATIVE FILE	Relative address
COW	1
ZEBRA	2
⋮	
APE	I−1
EEL	I
DOG	I+1
⋮	
CAT	N−1
BAT	N

FIGURE 182(a)

Here the directory entries are sorted by key value so that a binary rather than sequential search can be used to locate a target entry more rapidly. Note that the relative file entries are *not* in sorted order.

The directory alternatively could be organized as a binary search tree (see Fig. 182(b)), *m*-way search tree, or B-tree.

DIRECTORY

COW, 1

BAT, N → APE, I−1
BAT, N → CAT, N−1

EEL, I → DOG, I+1
EEL, I → ZEBRA, 2

RELATIVE FILE	Relative address
COW	1
ZEBRA	2
⋮	
APE	I−1
EEL	I
DOG	I+1
⋮	
CAT	N−1
BAT	N

FIGURE 182(b)

It is a fairly straightforward process to retrieve a record using the directory lookup scheme, but how are records stored in the relative file using this approach? One approach is to assign an address to every possible key value, making the directory initially complete. Addresses could be assigned using any of a variety of techniques, many of which we will introduce later in this chapter. The advantage of this approach is clear: it is easy to determine where a new record should be stored. The disadvantages usually outweigh the advantage. If the directory is initially full, then it really is not necessary to store the directory at all—as we will see in our discussions of address calculation techniques.

A more usual approach is to determine where there is free space for a record when it is time to store the record. Perhaps the record is placed as near to the top as possible, or as near to the record with a similar key value as possible, or at random. That new key value:address pair then would be added to the directory. If the directory is to be a sorted table (as shown in Fig. 182(a)), the new entry must be inserted in its proper position, with consequent movement of its successor entries. If the directory table is implemented as a sorted linked list, then insertion of the new entry is easier, but a binary search becomes impractical. If the directory is structured as a balanced binary search tree, then insertion of the new entry must include keeping the tree in balance. Directories are commonly implemented as B-trees, because of the need to insert and delete entries with relative ease and speed.

Thus the advantages of the directory lookup scheme to implement R (key value) $\longrightarrow$ address include the following:

1. A record's location can be determined with essentially no processing, once the key value is found in the directory.
2. Keys can be represented in intuitively understandable forms, since they are translated "internally" to addresses.
3. Logical-physical independence is achieved, because the key values are address-space-independent. If the relative file is reorganized, address entries in the directory must be changed, but the key values will not be affected.

The performance of the directory lookup scheme can be measured by the number of accesses to the directory that are required to find a desired key value. The technique used to implement the directory (e.g., unordered table versus B-tree) is an important determinant of search requirements. The organization of the directory is also an important determinant of the amount of processing required to maintain the directory.

We should note here that for very large relative files, the directory may also be large. In fact the directory usually is implemented as a separate file. If space permits, the entire directory file may be copied into main memory prior to execution of transactions that access the corresponding relative file. Commonly, space constraints do not permit this luxury.

ADDRESS CALCULATION TECHNIQUES FOR RELATIVE FILES

Another very common approach to implementing

$$R \text{ (key value)} \longrightarrow \text{address}$$

is to perform a calculation on the key value such that the result is a relative address. This technique can be used alone or in conjunction with the directory lookup scheme that was introduced in the last section.

The basic idea of address calculation is to apply a function that translates a relatively large domain of possible key values to a relatively small range of relative address values. Recall that one of the disadvantages of relative addressing is that space must be allocated to accommodate the entire range of key values, regardless of how many are actually used. Consider again the company with 2000 employees that wants to use social security numbers for the record access key of an employee file with relative organization. A desirable address calculation function for this example would map the domain of values (1 through 999,999, 999) onto approximately 2000 addresses.

One potential problem encountered in this process is that such a function may not be one-to-one; the calculated addresses may not all be unique. This situation, where

$$R(K_1) = R(K_2)$$
but
$$K_1 \neq K_2$$

is called a *collision*; two unequal keys have been calculated to have the same address. K_1 and K_2 here are called *synonyms*. Just as there are many possible address calculation techniques, there are a variety of collision resolution techniques. We will introduce the address calculation techniques in this section and discuss approaches to the collision resolution problem in the following section.

The concept of address calculation was first used to manage access to in-core symbol tables and later for addressing records in the early DASD's. A tremendous body of work since that time has contributed to the development of the many techniques for implementing the concept. Address calculation techniques are also referred to as:

- Scatter storage techniques
- Randomizing techniques
- Key-to-address transformation methods
- Direct addressing techniques
- Hash table methods
- Hashing

We will use the term *hashing* here, primarily because of its prevalence elsewhere. The calculation applied to a key value to obtain an address is called a *hash function*.

The primary advantages of using hashing to implement R (key value)⟶ address are:

1. Natural key values can be used, since they are translated "internally" to addresses.
2. Logical-physical independence is achieved, because the key values are address-space-independent. If the relative file is reorganized, the hash function may need to be changed, but the key values will not be affected.

The basic costs of using the hashing approach are:

1. The processing time required to apply the hash function.
2. The processing time and I/O accesses required to resolve collisions.

Thus a primary objective of a hash function is to generate relatively few collisions. A set of synonyms is sometimes called an *equivalence class*. A good hash function has small equivalence classes and few of them. Additionally, a good hash function is not too complex computationally.

Hashing can be used in conjunction with directory lookup, as shown in Fig. 183.

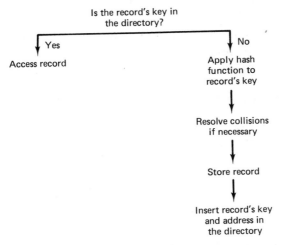

FIGURE 183

The benefits of avoiding recalculation and collision resolution for old records are paid for by the cost of storing and maintaining the directory. Also, depending upon directory organization and collision patterns, combining directory lookup and hashing together may yield longer search times than would hashing alone.

The performance of a hashing technique can be measured by its processing requirements and the I/O needed to store or retrieve a record. The performance of a particular hash function is dependent upon:

1. The distribution of key values that are actually in use.
2. The number of key values that are actually in use relative to the size of the address space.
3. The number of records that can be stored at a given address without causing a collision (for now we assume 1).
4. The collision resolution technique used.

Let us now discuss some of the most common hash functions:

- Division-remainder
- Mid-square
- Folding

We then will compare these approaches.

Division-Remainder Hashing

Some of the earliest investigations in hashing yielded a hash function known as the *division-remainder method*, or simply the division method. The basic idea of this approach is to divide a key value by an appropriate number, then to use the remainder of the division as the relative address for the record.

For example, let *div* be the divisor, *key* be the key, and *addr* be the resultant address.

In Pascal, the function R (key) $\longrightarrow$ addr would be implemented as:

        addr := key mod div;

and in COBOL:

                DIVIDE KEY BY DIV GIVING TEMP REMAINDER ADDR.

The remainder (and result of the *mod* function) is defined as the result of subtracting the product of the quotient and divisor from the dividend. That is,

                ADDR = KEY - DIV*TEMP.

In all cases here, ADDR should be declared to be an integer.

While the actual calculation of a relative address, given a key value and divisor, is straightforward, the choice of the *appropriate* divisor may not be quite so simple. There are several factors that should be considered in selecting the divisor. First, the range of values that result from the operation *key mod div* is 0 through *div*-1. Thus the value of *div* determines the size of the relative address space. If it is known that our relative file is going to contain at least *n* records, then we must, assuming that only one record can be stored at a given relative address, have *div* > *n*.

Second, the divisor should be selected such that the probability of collision is minimized. In fact, this is a difficult objective to achieve. We try to select a divisor that keeps the probability of collision relatively low, but we usually do not go to the effort of actually minimizing collisions. Investigations have shown that divisors that are even numbers tend to perform poorly, especially with the sets of key values that are predominantly odd.

Some research (e.g., W. Buchholz, "File organization and addressing," *IBM Systems Journal*, vol. 2, pp. 86–111, June 1963) has suggested that the divisor should be a prime number, thereby reducing skewed results. However, other work (e.g., V. Y. Lum, et al., "Key-to-address transform techniques: A fundamental performance study on large existing formatted files," *Communications of the ACM*, vol. 14, no. 4, pp. 228–239, April 1971) suggests that nonprime divisors work as well as prime divisors, as long as the nonprime divisors do not contain small prime numbers as factors. They suggest that selecting a number that does not contain any prime factor less than 20 is probably sufficient to ensure good performance.

It is not enough to pick a divisor that does not introduce skewed distribution of addresses. Additionally, it has been shown that regardless of how "good" the divisor is, when the address space of a relative file gets full enough, the probability of collision rises dramatically. Fullness of a relative file is measured by its *load factor*, which is defined as the ratio of the number of records in the file to the number of records that the file could hold if completely full:

$$\text{load factor} = \frac{\text{\# records in file}}{\text{max. \# of records file can contain}}$$

All hash functions begin to work quite poorly when the target file becomes almost full. As a general guideline, a load factor of 0.7 or 0.8 is about as great as can be tolerated with reasonable performance. When the file becomes greater than 70% or 80% full, it should be enlarged and reorganized. Thus, if it is known that our relative file is going to contain about *n* records, then the address space should have enough room for at least $1.25n$ records (for 80% loading).

For example, consider design of a relative file that will contain about 4000 records. The address space should accommodate at least

5000 records for 80% loading. A number that is approximately 5000 and that does not contain any prime factors less than 20 is 5003. Table 8 illustrates use of this divisor with a small set of key values.

Table 8

key value	relative address	
123456789	2762	
987654321	2086	
123456790	2763	
555555555	2424	
000000472	0473 ←	
100064183	4184	
200120472	0473	**collision**
200120473	0474	
117400000	4606	
027000400	3613	

Mid-square Hashing

In this hashing technique, the key is squared, then specified digits are extracted from the middle of the result to yield the relative address. If a relative address of n digits is desired, then digits are truncated at both ends of the squared key, leaving n digits from the middle. The same n digit positions must be extracted for each key. Table 9 illustrates use of the mid-square hashing technique for the same key values that were shown in Table 8. Digits in positions 7–10 (counting from the right) have been extracted to form a 4-digit relative address.

Table 9

key value	key squared	relative address
123456789	15241578750190521	8750
987654321	975461055789971041	5789
123456790	15241578997104100	8997
555555555	308641974691358025	4691
000000472	00000000000222784	0000 ←
100064183	10012860719457489	0719
200120472	40048203313502784	3313
200120473	40048203713743729	3713
117400000	13782760000000000	0000 **collision**
027000400	02430021600160000	1600

Note that in order to accommodate 4000 records, 4-digit relative addresses are required. The resultant address space has room for 10,000 records, giving a load factor of 0.4. Using the mid-square hashing function, the size of the resultant file is 10^n, where n is the number of digits extracted from the squared key values.

Hashing by Folding

In this hashing technique the key value is partitioned into a number of parts, each of which (except the last one) has the same number of digits as does the target relative address. These partitions are then folded over each other and summed. The result, with its highest order digit truncated, if necessary, is the relative address.

For example, consider the key value 123456789 and assume that the target relative address will have 4 digits. The key value is partitioned into 4-digit chunks:

| 1 | 2345 | 6789 |

then folded

| 1 | 2345 | 6789 |

to give

1
2345
9876

and summed to

13221.

The high-order digit is truncated, giving relative address 3221.

Table 10 shows the relative addresses that result when folding is applied to our set of example key values.

Table 10

key value	relative address
123456789	3221
987654321	8999
123456790	4321
555555555	6110
000000472	2740
100064183	4820
200120472	4752
200120473	5752
117400000	2740 **collision**
027000400	2740 **collision**

As was true with the mid-square method, the size of the relative address space is an integral power of 10.

Comparison of Hash Functions

There are many possible hash functions; we have introduced just three of them here. Thorough analysis of the performance of various hash functions has been reported in a series of papers, including the paper by Lum et al. that was referenced earlier, V. Y. Lum and P. S. T. Yuen, "Additional results on key-to-address transform techniques," *Communications of the ACM*, vol. 15, pp. 996–997, November 1972; V. Y. Lum, "General performance analysis of key-to-address transformation methods using an abstract file concept," *Communications of the ACM*, vol. 16, pp. 603–612, October 1973; and S. P. Ghosh, and V. Y. Lum, "An analysis of collisions when hashing by division," IBM Research Report RJ1218, May 1973. We summarize those results here.

Although another technique may perform better in particular situations, the division-remainder technique gives the best overall performance. No hash function *always* performs better than all others. The mid-square method can be applied to files with fairly low loading factors to give generally good performance, but sometimes it can generate poor performance with many collisions. The folding method may be the easiest technique to compute, especially if bit patterns rather than decimal values are used, but it produces quite erratic results, unless the key length is approximately the same as the address length.

If the distribution of key values is not known, then the division-remainder method is the preferred hashing technique. Thus, it is very commonly used. Like any other address calculation technique, it can be used in conjunction with a directory lookup scheme. (See Fig. 183 again.)

Note that hashing can be applied to non-numeric keys as well as to numeric keys. The collating sequence positions of the characters in a key value can be used as their "numeric" equivalents. Alternatively, the hash algorithm acts upon the binary representations of the characters.

The introduced hash functions all have addressed a fixed-size space. Increasing the size of a relative file created using one of these functions implies changing the hash function to address the larger space and reloading the new file. New hash techniques have been developed recently that allow the file to grow or shrink without forcing the relocation of old records. These schemes are known as dynamic hashing, extendible hashing, and virtual hashing. The allocated storage space is divided into buckets. When a record is to be inserted into a full bucket, it is split into two buckets among which the records are distributed. This approach should remind you of the technique used for space management in B-trees.

Dynamic hashing uses a binary-tree index structure to keep track of buckets and to guide access to records. *Extendible hashing* uses a tabular directory based on a degenerate trie structure to keep track of buckets and to guide access to records. *Virtual hashing* is a general name given to "any hashing which may dynamically change its hashing function" (W. Litwin, "Virtual hashing: A dynamically changing hashing," *Proc. 4th Conf. Very Large Databases*, W. Berlin, 1978, pp. 517–523). This term is quite broad and includes not only dynamic and extendible hashing but also techniques that do not use any indexes. For sources of further information about these approaches, you should consult the list of references in this chapter's summary section.

APPROACHES TO THE PROBLEM OF COLLISIONS

Because a hashing function maps a relatively large key-value space to a relatively small address space, there are certain to be collisions; more than one key value will be mapped to a single relative address.

Consider two key values K_1 and K_2, which are synonyms with hash function R. Assume that the equivalence class that contains K_1 and K_2 contains no other key values; that is, K_1 and K_2 have no other synonyms. If K_1 is stored in the file first and its address is $R(K_1)$, then K_1 is said to be stored at its *home address*.

There are two basic approaches to deciding where K_2 should be located: (1) *open addressing*, in which some address other than the home address is found for K_2 in the relative file, and (2) *separate overflow*, in which some address is found for K_2 outside of the primary area of the relative file in a special overflow area that is used only for storage of records that cannot be located at their home addresses.

Numerous techniques have been developed to handle collisions. We now consider two of the most common approaches:

- Linear probing, which is an open addressing technique
- Double hashing, which can be applied as either an open addressing or separate overflow technique

We will compare the performance of these techniques, then introduce two methods of improving behavior:

- Synonym chaining
- Bucket addressing

Linear Probing

One way to find a location for a record when it cannot be stored at its home address is to use *linear probing*, which is a process of searching sequentially from the home address to find the next empty location.

This technique is also referred to as the *consecutive spill* method. In order to implement linear probing, it must be possible to determine whether or not an address is empty. This may be done by setting a flag in each location as it is filled. The basic logic of storing a record by hashing with the linear probe technique is shown in Fig. 184(a).

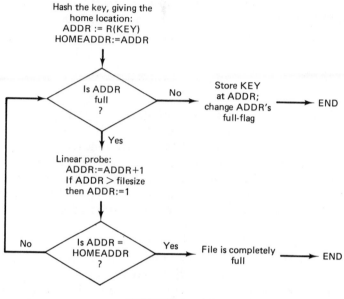

FIGURE 184(a)

Note first that linear probing can be used in conjunction with any hash technique. Note also that the application of linear probing must be done in such a way that ADDR does not fall off the end of the file. Rather than quitting when the bound of the address space is met, we cycle back to the beginning of the space and probe from there. It then becomes necessary to be able to detect when the home address (here HOMEADDR) has been encountered again, in which case the file is completely full and there is no room for KEY.

If linear probing is used to resolve collisions when records are stored, it must also be used when records are retrieved, unless a directory lookup scheme is used in conjunction with hashing. The basic logic for retrieving a record by hashing with linear probing is shown in Fig. 184(b). The key values of records encountered at the home address and at addresses reached by linear probe must be compared with the sought KEY value to determine whether or not the target record has been located. Many probes may be required to determine that the target record is not in the file or to find the target record if it was stored far from its HOMEADDR. A more efficient method for handling synonyms will be introduced in the section on synonym chaining.

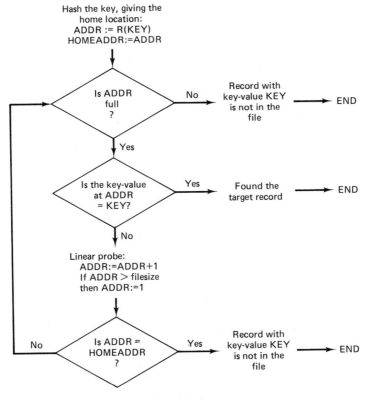

FIGURE 184(b)

Deletion of records makes things more difficult. Why? How would you modify the logic of Fig. 184 to accommodate deleted records?

Double Hashing

Another approach to finding a location for a record when it cannot be stored at its home address is to use *double hashing*, which applies a second hash function to the result of the first hash. The target address space of the rehash may be either the relative file itself or a separate overflow relative file. In the first case, where all records appear in a single file, the open addressing method is in use. In the second case, where only one record from each equivalence class appears in the primary file and synonyms appear in an overflow file, the separate overflow method is in use. In either case, some method for resolution is needed if collisions occur during the second hash.

The advantage of the separate overflow method is that it avoids the situation, which can occur in the open addressing method, whereby a record that is not stored in its home location displaces another record which later hashes to that home location. Actually this problem can be avoided with open addressing simply by moving the offending foreign record to another location (by probing or rehashing or. . .) and storing the new record at the now-empty home address. If directory lookup is being used with hashing, the directory must be updated to reflect the changed address of the moved record.

The cost of the separate overflow method is the overhead of maintaining a separate file. The relative file really is implemented as two files: a primary area and an overflow area. Both have relative organization.

Comparison of Linear Probing and Double Hashing

Linear probing and double hashing result in different distributions of synonyms in a relative file. Let us consider first the case of a file with a low load factor, say less than 0.5. Linear probing tends to cluster synonyms, while double hashing tends to disperse synonyms more widely across the address space.

For example, consider a small relative file with 224 records and a load factor of 0.7. Our data show an average of 1.31 probes per record required with linear probing and 1.20 probes per record required with double hashing. Thus both are about the same. However, the average distance that a displaced record is from its home location is 3.1 slots with linear probing and 122.1 slots with double hashing. In a paged environment, the clustering effects of linear probing may be quite desirable.

However, the clustering effects of linear probing can also be a disadvantage. For example, consider a very small file of 9 records in an address space for 19 records. Assume that records have been inserted in slots 2, 3, 5, 6, 12, 13, 14, 15, and 17, as shown in Fig. 185.

0	1	2	3	4	5	6	7	8	9	10	11	12	13	14	15	16	17	18
		X	X		X	X						X	X	X	X		X	

FIGURE 185

The next record to be added to the file will go into one of the ten available spaces. However, there is not a 10% likelihood that the record will go into any one of the slots. For example, address 16 will be the location of the new record if it hashes to address 12, 13, 14, 15, or 16. Address 8 will be the location of the new record only if it hashes to address 8. The probabilities of each address receiving the next record are given in Table 11, which assumes that the hash function yields a uniform distribution of addresses. The result of this clustering effect is that long searches tend to get even longer. With even moderate file load factors,

Table 11

Address	0	1	2	3	4	5	6	7	8	9
Probability of receiving next record	.05	.05	0	0	.16	0	0	.16	.05	.05

Address	10	11	12	13	14	15	16	17	18
Probability of receiving next record	.05	.05	0	0	0	0	.26	0	.11

there is relatively high probability that a new record will extend a cluster rather than start a cluster.

Double hashing tends to perform about as well as does linear probing for small load factors (less than 0.5), but does somewhat better than linear probing for larger load factors. At loading greater than 80%, linear probing generally results in terrible performance, while double hashing is quite tolerable for successful searches but not so good for unsuccessful searches.

Synonym Chaining

One good way to improve the performance of a relative file that uses address calculation without an auxiliary directory to guide retrievals is to chain together synonyms. Maintaining a linked list of records with the same home address does not reduce the number of collisions, but it *does* reduce the access times to retrieve records that are not at their home locations. Synonym chaining can be used with any collision resolution technique. Fig. 186(a) and (b) illustrate chaining of synonyms

(a) Linear probing with separate chaining.
Equivalence sets are (2), (3), (5, 6), (12, 14), (13, 15) and (17)

(b) Double hashing with separate chaining.
Equivalence sets are (2, 6), (3, 15), (5), (12, 17), (13), and (14)

FIGURE 186

when linear probing and double hashing, respectively, have been used to resolve collisions.

When a record is to be retrieved from the file, the basic logic illustrated in Fig. 187 is applied. Note that only synonyms of the target key are accessed. Without synonym chaining, nonsynonyms can also be accessed in pursuit of the target record. Note that this logic requires that a record not be displaced from its home location by a previously stored nonsynonym. If it were, then the linked list followed would not contain synonyms of the target record, and the target record would never be found.

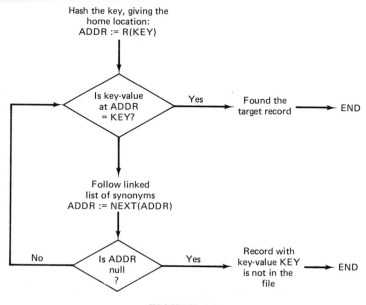

FIGURE 187

Deletion of records also is handled gracefully by the chained synonym approach. When a record is deleted, it simply is removed from its linked list. Recall that the deletion of records without synonym chaining can be a problem: either the vacated space must be marked so as not to be confused with a never-filled space, which would cause synonym searches to terminate prematurely, or synonyms have to be moved around to fill the vacated space.

Synonym chaining can be used whether the open addressing method is used or the separate overflow method is used. That is, the linked list beginning at a home address may have its next node either in the same file or in a separate file.

Synonym chaining nearly always works better than does collision resolution without synonym chaining, unless a directory lookup scheme is used to keep track of where records are actually stored. Synonym chaining and directory lookup both keep the number of accesses required to find records small, even with heavily loaded files.

Bucket Addressing

Another approach to handling the problem of collisions is to hash to blocks (or buckets) of space that can accommodate multiple record occurrences, rather than hashing to individual record slots. For example, consider a relative address space of 0 to M, and a bucket size of B records. The address space thus can contain $B(M+1)$ records. If the file contains N records, then its load factor is

$$\frac{N}{B(M+1)}.$$

B records can all hash to the same relative address without causing a problematic collision.

When a bucket does overflow, some new location must be found for the offending record. The approaches to the bucket overflow problem are basically the same as the approaches taken to handle collisions with record-slot addressing. If open addressing is used, available space is sought either in the next bucket (i.e., with linear probing) or in some other bucket (i.e., with double hashing). If the separate overflow area technique is used, the new record is placed in a specially designated set of buckets that are reserved for overflow usage. Each primary bucket generally would have a pointer to a chain of the records in the overflow area that should have been stored in the primary bucket but that ended up in overflow buckets instead. One overflow bucket could accommodate records that had hashed to several different primary buckets.

The records stored in a bucket may be managed in one of two ways: (1) They can be inserted in order by their arrival at the bucket. (2) They can be maintained in sorted order by their key values. The basic trade-off is ease of insertion versus ease of retrieval. When a record is retrieved from a relative file that uses bucket addressing, with bucket overflow handled by linear probing, the basic logic shown in Fig. 188 is followed.

When a record is retrieved from a relative file that uses bucket addressing, with bucket overflows placed in an overflow area and synonym chaining within the overflow buckets, the logic shown in Fig. 189 is followed.

Just as the records in the primary bucket area may be kept ordered by key value (*within* a bucket), so may the records on a synonym chain be maintained in order by key value. If so, adding a record to a full primary bucket may cause a record from that bucket to be moved into the overflow area, while the inserted record is stored in the primary area.

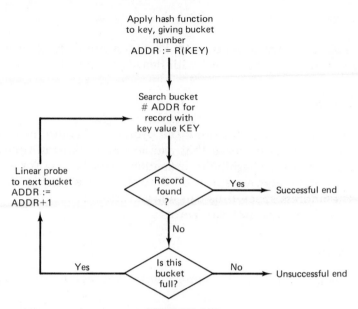

Apply hash function
to key, giving bucket
number
ADDR := R(KEY)

Search bucket
ADDR for
record with
key value KEY

Record
found
?

Yes → Successful end

No

Linear probe
to next bucket
ADDR :=
ADDR+1

Is this
bucket
full?

Yes

No → Unsuccessful end

FIGURE 188

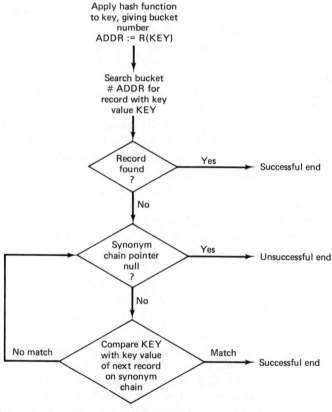

Apply hash function
to key, giving bucket
number
ADDR := R(KEY)

Search bucket
ADDR for
record with key
value KEY

Record
found
?

Yes → Successful end

No

Synonym
chain pointer
null
?

Yes → Unsuccessful end

No

Compare KEY
with key value
of next record
on synonym
chain

No match

Match → Successful end

FIGURE 189

The use of bucket addressing is very common. The size of a bucket may be determined by the size of a track or of a sector on a DASD or by the system's natural page size. Bucket size generally should be the same as block size for the file. This match allows the search for a record in its home bucket to be conducted with just one access to secondary storage. Access to the next bucket or to an overflow bucket would require a second I/O access.

One important advantage of using buckets that can hold multiple records is that variable-length records can be accommodated. With bucket addressing and variable-length records, the process of finding available space in a bucket for a new record becomes more complex than just searching sequentially for the first open slot. The space found must be large enough to accommodate the new record. Commonly space is managed in such a situation by maintaining a linked list of holes in the bucket. Holes may be dispersed among actual records because of deletions. The hole chain is searched when free space is requested. Recall the discussion in Chapter 6 of the linked AVAIL stack of holes used when a linked list was housed in an array. It is convenient to order the list of holes of a bucket by increasing size. The search for a hole results in the selection of the hole whose size most closely meets (or exceeds) the required amount of space.

Fig. 190 illustrates a bucket that contains a chain of holes. The bucket header includes information about where its smallest hole starts and how large its largest hole is. When a new record hashes to this

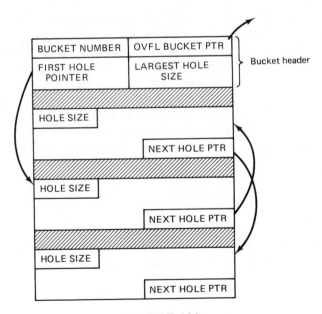

FIGURE 190

bucket, the search for free space can proceed directly to the next bucket, or to an overflow bucket if this home bucket does not have an adequately large hole. Otherwise the hole chain is searched. In the diagram, the hashed areas denote space where records are stored; the blank areas are holes.

When a hole is used to store a record, there may not be an exact fit. Leftover space can be returned in the form of a new (smaller) hole to an appropriate position in the hole chain.

When a record is deleted, its freed space should be added as a hole to the hole chain. If this freed space is contiguous to previously existing holes, the spaces can be combined to make one larger hole. A few large holes are more desirable than many small holes, because the probability of having to route a new record out of its home bucket is higher with smaller maximum hole sizes.

When variable-length records and bucket addressing are used, it is usually the record manager system rather than the programmer who is responsible for bucket space management.

THE USE OF RELATIVE FILES IN PROGRAMS

Relative files are used so commonly that many programming languages support their declaration, creation, retrieval, and update. Pascal is a notable exception, although some Pascal compilers do support language extensions for relative files.

In COBOL, FORTRAN, and PL/I, the programmer supplies to the system a record's relative address when the record is stored and when it is retrieved. It is the programmer's responsibility to perform the key-to-address transformation; this mapping is not done automatically by the system. Additionally the programmer must resolve any collisions that may occur. Thus the access methods that support relative files declared in these languages are quite efficient. They have very little overhead and do little processing. They are given relative addresses and convert these to absolute addresses for record access. The access methods do not do the hashing, directory lookups, or collision resolutions.

When a relative file is declared in a program, the information that is required includes the following:

- Filename
- Specification of physical device upon which the file resides.
- Organization relative (as opposed to sequential or other possibilities)

- Identification of the variable that contains relative addresses for records
- Record formats

along with other possible information about label records, and so forth. The techniques used to determine relative addresses and to resolve collisions are defined in the procedural code.

A relative file may be created in either sequential or direct-access mode. When it is created sequentially, the records are written in consecutive order. Sequential creation of a relative file is commonly used in conjunction with a directory lookup scheme. If an address calculation technique is used to map keys to addresses, sequential creation is nearly impossible, unless the records have been stored in an auxiliary table to be dumped sequentially to the file.

When hashing is used, a relative file more commonly is created in direct-access mode. In some implementations, a skeleton file of dummy records is created first, then records are inserted in some random order.

Similarly, records can be retrieved from a relative file in either sequential or direct-access mode. Sequential access retrieves the records in physically consecutive order, which may not be in key-sequence order. Many compilers support direct positioning of a relative file at a point (based on relative address) and sequential read access from that point.

More commonly, a relative file is accessed in direct mode. The key identifying a record to a user is translated by an application program into a relative address. The program then reads the record at that address. If there is no record at that location, then the target record does not exist. If there is a record at that location, the program then checks to determine if it has the desired key value. If so, the record is delivered to the user. If not, then the sought record is not at its home address and the application program applies its collision-handling technique to find the desired record. It either finds the record or determines that the record does not exist.

Update of a relative file nearly always is done in direct mode. Records of a relative file can be updated in place. The program uses a direct-retrieval algorithm to locate the desired record, makes specified modifications, then rewrites the record. In some languages (such as COBOL and PL/I) rewrite (modify) of an existing record is distinguished from write (insert) of a new record. In other languages (such as FORTRAN) the two actions use the same verb.

When a program interacts with a relative file, it must continually check for unexpected conditions. Examples of the types of conditions that can signal errors are listed below.

1. Sequential read
   - at end-of-file
2. Direct read
   - no record exists at the specified relative address
   - specified relative address out-of-bounds for the file
3. Sequential write
   - space limits exceeded on device
4. Direct write
   - record already exists at the specified address (i.e., collision)
   - specified relative address out-of-bounds for the file
5. Direct rewrite
   - no record exists at the specified address
   - specified relative address out-of-bounds for the file.

Once a record is delivered on a read, the program needs to verify that it has the desired user-key value. If not, the collision resolution technique used on the file must be applied to locate the desired synonym.

In the following sections we introduce the basic concepts required to declare and use relative files in COBOL programs. Other languages that support relative file organization use basically the same types of procedures for file creation and manipulation and ask the programmer to specify essentially the same information to define the file. For details of requirements, you should consult local language manuals and inquire about local installation standards and procedures. File I/O is commonly nonstandard.

RELATIVE FILES IN COBOL

As for sequential files, declaration information for relative files is supplied in both the *ENVIRONMENT DIVISION* and the *DATA DIVISION* of a COBOL program. The format of the *SELECT* clause of the *FILE–CONTROL* paragraph of the *INPUT–OUTPUT SECTION* of the *ENVIRONMENT DIVISION* for a relative file is:

SELECT filename ASSIGN TO {implementor-name}. . .

[RESERVE integer $\begin{bmatrix} \text{AREAS} \\ \text{AREA} \end{bmatrix}$]

ORGANIZATION IS RELATIVE

ACCESS MODE IS $\left\{ \begin{array}{l} \text{SEQUENTIAL [RELATIVE KEY IS} \\ \quad\quad\quad\quad\quad \text{dataname1]} \\ \begin{Bmatrix} \text{RANDOM} \\ \text{DYNAMIC} \end{Bmatrix} \quad \text{RELATIVE KEY IS} \\ \quad\quad\quad\quad\quad \text{dataname1} \end{array} \right\}$

[FILE STATUS IS dataname2].

The *filename* is the name by which the file is known in this program. The *implementor-name* is the name of the device(s) upon which the file resides. (See Chapter 16 for more details of this clause, the *RESERVE* clause, and the *FILE STATUS* clause.)

The *ORGANIZATION IS RELATIVE* clause is required in the declaration of a relative file. If this clause were omitted, the file would default to having sequential organization.

The *ACCESS MODE* clause specifies the manner in which records in the file are going to be accessed. The field identified by *dataname1* in the *RELATIVE KEY* phrase is the name of the field that contains the record's relative address, which in COBOL must be an integer *greater* than 0. Thus if the division-remainder hash method were used, 1 would be added to the resultant remainder. For example:

> DIVIDE USER-KEY BY DIV GIVING TEMP REMAINDER ADDR
> ADD 1 TO ADDR

where *ADDR* is the specified *RELATIVE KEY* field. This variable (*dataname1*) does not appear within the file's records or in the file's record description entries.

SEQUENTIAL access is the default. Sequential access of a relative file means that records will be accessed (read/written) in order by ascending relative addresses. *RANDOM* access means that records will be accessed by value of *dataname1*, which will contain relative addresses. *DYNAMIC* access means that records will be accessed sometimes in *SEQUENTIAL* mode and sometimes in *RANDOM* mode by the program.

Each relative file used in a program must have an associated *FD* (file description) entry. An *FD* contains clauses that give information about block size, record size, label records, and data records in the file. The entry is essentially the same for relative files as for sequential files.

File Creation

When a relative file is created in COBOL, it must be open for *OUTPUT* or *I-O*. Records then are written to the file either sequentially or not sequentially, using the *WRITE* verb.

If the file has *ACCESS MODE SEQUENTIAL*, then the following verb form is used:

> WRITE recordname [FROM identifier]

The order in which records are written is the same as their resultant physical order. If a *RELATIVE KEY* phrase is specified for the file in its *FILE CONTROL* entry, the associated data item will be given the value of the record's relative address in the file. These relative addresses might be loaded into a directory for later use in accessing the file by a directory-lookup scheme. Note that if the records are supplied to the file in some meaningful order, say sequentially by user-key value, then that ordering will be mirrored in the records' positions on physical storage. In order to retrieve by user-key value while avoiding sequential search, it must be possible to translate the user-key value to the corresponding relative address, which is where the directory-lookup scheme becomes useful.

If the file has *ACCESS MODE RANDOM*, then the following verb form is used:

> WRITE recordname [FROM identifier]
> INVALID KEY imperative-statement.

At the time that the *WRITE* for a record is executed, the data item specified in the *RELATIVE KEY* phrase for the file (in its *SELECT* clause) must contain the relative address for the record. If the *INVALID KEY* condition is raised, then a record with specified relative key value already exists in the file, i.e., COLLISION. The program would then apply its collision-resolution technique and try to write again. An example of the basic logic for this process follows:

```
   . . .
   SELECT EMP-MSTR ASSIGN TO DISK
        ORGANIZATION IS RELATIVE
        ACCESS IS RANDOM
             RELATIVE KEY IS REL-ADDR.
   . . .
   FD   EMP-MSTR
        LABEL RECORD IS STANDARD.
   01   EMP-REC.
        02   EMP-NO            PIC 9(8).
        02   FILLER            PIC X(316).
   . . .
   WORKING-STORAGE SECTION.
   01   FLAGS.
        02   COLLISION-FLAG    PIC X.
             88   NO-COLLISION    VALUE 'N'.
             88   COLLISION       VALUE 'Y'.
   . . .
   DRIVER.
        OPEN OUTPUT EMP-MSTR.
        ACCEPT EMP-REC.
        PERFORM PROCESS-EMP-REC UNTIL EMP-NO = ZEROS.
        CLOSE EMP-MSTR.
        STOP RUN.
   PROCESS-EMP-REC.
        PERFORM HASH-ON-EMP-NO.
        MOVE 'N' TO COLLISION-FLAG.
```

```
          WRITE EMP-REC
                INVALID KEY MOVE 'Y' TO COLLISION-FLAG.
          PERFORM RESOLVE-COLLISION UNTIL NO-COLLISION.

          . . .
          ACCEPT EMP-REC.
      RESOLVE-COLLISION.
          ADD 1 TO REL-ADDR.
          MOVE 'N' TO COLLISION-FLAG.
          WRITE EMP-REC
                INVALID KEY MOVE 'Y' TO COLLISION-FLAG.
      HASH-ON-EMP-NO.
          . . .
```

This example uses simple linear probing to resolve collisions. Note that foreign records may displace other records from their home addresses, and synonyms are not chained.

Record Retrieval

When records are retrieved from a COBOL relative file, the file must be open for *INPUT*, or for *I–O* if records are going to be both read and written. Records can be retrieved from the file either sequentially or not sequentially, using the *READ* verb. Sequential access may be positioned by the *START* verb.

If the file has *ACCESS MODE IS SEQUENTIAL*, then the following verb form is used:

> <u>READ</u> filename RECORD [<u>INTO</u> identifier]
>   AT <u>END</u> imperative-statement.

A loop through this statement will access the records in order by physical location. As with a sequential *WRITE* of a relative file, the associated *RELATIVE KEY* data item will be given the value of a record's relative address in the file as it is read. The *AT END* condition is raised when the end-of-file is encountered.

The *START* verb can be used to position subsequent sequential reads. The format of the *START* verb is:

$$\underline{\text{START}} \text{ filename } \left[\text{KEY IS} \left\{ \begin{array}{l} \underline{\text{EQUAL}} \text{ TO} \\ = \\ \underline{\text{GREATER}} \text{ THAN} \\ > \\ \underline{\text{NOT}} \underline{\text{ LESS}} \text{ THAN} \\ \underline{\text{NOT}} < \end{array} \right\} \text{ dataname} \right]$$

[<u>INVALID</u> KEY imperative-statement].

Positioning is done such that the relative address (of the next record to be accessed by a *READ*) bears the specified relationship to the

RELATIVE KEY data item for the file (given in its *FILE CONTROL* entry). The *dataname* specified in a *START* statement must be the same as the name of the *RELATIVE KEY* data item for the file. If the *KEY* phrase of the *START* verb is omitted, = is assumed. The *IN-VALID KEY* condition is raised if:

1. There is no record with this relative address (for =).
2. There is no record in any position higher than the one specified by the key (for >).
3. There is no record in the position specified by the key or in any higher position (for *NOT* <).

If the file has *ACCESS MODE IS RANDOM*, then the following verb form is used for retrieval:

> READ filename RECORD [INTO identifier]
>   INVALID KEY imperative-statement.

This statement causes read of the record whose relative address is contained in the data item named in the *RELATIVE KEY* clause for the file. If there is no record at this address, then the *INVALID KEY* condition is raised. If the file was created using a hashing technique, the program would need to verify that the retrieved record is the actual target record and not one of its synonyms. An example of the basic logic for this process follows, where the same *ENVIRONMENT* and *DATA DIVISION* entries are used as in the preceding program segment, with the addition of flag

```
02  FOUND-FLAG        PIC X.
    88  LOOKING        VALUE 'L'.
    88  FOUND          VALUE 'Y'.
    88  NOT-FOUND      VALUE 'N'.

DRIVER.
        OPEN INPUT EMP-MSTR.
        ACCEPT EMP-NO-TARGET.
        PERFORM FIND-EMP-REC UNTIL
            EMP-NO-TARGET = ZEROS.
        CLOSE EMP-MSTR.
        STOP RUN.
FIND-EMP-REC.
        PERFORM HASH-ON-EMP-NO-TARGET.
        MOVE 'L' TO FOUND-FLAG.
        READ EMP-REC
            INVALID KEY MOVE 'N' TO FOUND-FLAG.
        PERFORM CHECK-REC UNTIL NOT-FOUND OR FOUND.
```

```
        IF NOT-FOUND
            DISPLAY 'EMP' EMP-NO-TARGET 'NOT IN FILE'
        ELSE DISPLAY EMP-REC.
        ACCEPT EMP-NO-TARGET.
    CHECK-REC.
        IF EMP-NO = EMP-NO-TARGET
            MOVE 'Y' TO FOUND-FLAG
        ELSE ADD 1 TO REL-ADDR
            READ EMP-REC
                INVALID KEY MOVE 'N' TO FOUND-FLAG.
    HASH-ON-EMP-NO-TARGET.
        . . .
```

Again note that simple linear probing without synonym chaining is used.

If a relative file has *ACCESS MODE IS DYNAMIC*, then both sequential and direct (random) retrieval are supported.

File Update

When a COBOL relative file is updated, it must be open for *I-O*. New records then can be added using the *WRITE* verb; old records can be removed using the *DELETE* verb; records can be modified using the *REWRITE* verb.

If the file has *ACCESS MODE IS SEQUENTIAL*, then *WRITE* cannot be used. Records will be accessed in consecutive order. The sequential form of the *DELETE* verb is:

<u>DELETE</u> filename RECORD

Execution of the *DELETE* must have been preceded by a successful *READ* for the file. The record that was read is deleted.

The sequential form of the *REWRITE* verb is:

<u>REWRITE</u> recordname [<u>FROM</u> identifier]

As for the *DELETE*, execution of a sequential *REWRITE* must be preceded by a successful *READ*. The record that was read is replaced by the *REWRITE*.

If the file has *ACCESS MODE IS RANDOM*, then records can be accessed in any order. The random form of the *DELETE* is:

<u>DELETE</u> filename RECORD
     <u>INVALID</u> KEY imperative-statement.

The record identified by the *RELATIVE KEY* data item for the file is deleted. The *INVALID KEY* condition is raised if there is no record at the specified address.

The random form of the *REWRITE* is:

REWRITE recordname [FROM identifier]
        INVALID KEY imperative-statement.

The record identified by the *RELATIVE KEY* data item for the file is replaced. The *INVALID KEY* condition is raised if there is no record at the specified address. Note that neither the random *REWRITE* nor the random *DELETE* requires the target record to have been read previously.

Sequential and random update of a relative file can be intermingled in one program if the file has *ACCESS MODE DYNAMIC*.

DESIGN OF RELATIVE FILES

The primary questions that need to be addressed in designing a relative file include the following:

1. What is the layout of fields in the records?
2. What is the key field(s) used to identify record occurrences?
3. What is an appropriate key-to-address mapping function?
4. What is the appropriate bucket size?
5. What is an appropriate collision resolution method?
6. What are the capabilities provided by the relative file facility of the programming language to be used?

As was discussed in the section on design of sequential files, the record layout problem is the same as the problem addressed in Chapter 3. Fixed-length records can be accommodated by relative files with bucket size = 1. The presence of variable-length records implies that buckets that can accommodate multiple records must be used.

The appropriate field(s) to form the user key of a relative file is determined by the application. Use of a relative file rather than a sequential file implies that there is a need to access individual records directly. The field whose value is specified by a user to identify individual records should be the key field. If multiple, different key fields seem appropriate, then one of the file organizations that will be introduced in Chapter 21 may be more appropriate than relative organization.

The appropriate key-to-address mapping function is determined by the following factors:

1. Characteristics of the user-key field, e.g., if non-numeric, then a direct mapping technique is inappropriate.

2. Density of population of the range of values of the user-key field. If it is sparse, then a calculation technique can be used to reduce the size of the address space.

3. Expected increase in size of the file, which affects the selection of address calculation method. File load factors greater than 0.8 tend to result in poor performance.

4. Need for rapid accessibility, which may be facilitated by a directory lookup scheme. Records can be stored using a calculation technique, then accessed later via a directory without having to recalculate addresses and deal with collisions.

5. Distribution of user-key values, which can be used (if known) to optimize an address calculation technique.

Appropriate bucket size is determined by characteristics of the DASD to be used (e.g., bucket size = track size), by the size of records to be stored, by whether or not variable-length records need to be accommodated, by installation standards, and by characteristics of user-key value and the key-to-address mapping function. Use of buckets that are large enough to hold more than one record can significantly reduce the effects of collisions.

The appropriate collision resolution method is determined by:

1. The probability and patterns of collision.
2. The desirability of clustering synonyms physically.
3. The desirability of avoiding clusters of synonyms.
4. Bucket size.

If a directory lookup scheme is not being used for retrievals from a hashed file, then synonyms should nearly always be chained.

The capabilities of the programming language to be used also affect the design of the relative file. Many vendors supply nonstandard file organization techniques that implement relative files in a variety of ways. For example, one of the nonstandard COBOL compilers at our location offers four distinct types of "relative" file organization: *RELATIVE, DIRECT, STANDARD,* and *ACTUAL KEY*.

SUMMARY

In a relative file organization there is a predictable relationship between the key used by a user (human or program) to identify a particular record and that record's location on secondary storage. The physical ordering of records need bear no logical relationship to their ordering by key value. The major advantage of relative organization is the ability to access quickly an individual record by its key value without accessing other records.

The fundamental techniques for determining a record's location on secondary storage, given its user-key value, were discussed. These techniques include direct mapping (absolute and relative addressing), directory lookup, and address calculation (division-remainder, mid-square, and folding). When address calculation is used, it becomes necessary to be able to resolve collisions which occur when multiple records hash to one address. Techniques to handle collisions include linear probing, double hashing, synonym chaining, and bucket addressing. The relative performance of these methods was compared.

A relative file must be stored on a direct-access device. The file can be created either sequentially by writing the records in their desired physical order, or directly by supplying individual records without regard to their resultant physical order. The file can be accessed either sequentially (in physically consecutive order) or by direct specification of particular records' key values. The file can be updated in place; new records can be written, old records can be deleted, and existing records can be replaced without access to unaffected records on the file. The basic concepts required for declaring and using a relative file in COBOL were introduced. The same types of procedures are used for creating and accessing relative files in other programming languages. Finally, several aspects of the design of relative files were reviewed.

Relative files are used extensively. They generally require little system overhead and they provide for rapid access to individual record occurrences. They are the fundamental method of supporting many interactive applications.

The reader who is interested in further details should see the following references.

Buchholz, W. "File organization and addressing," *IBM Systems Journal*, vol. 2. pp. 86–111, June 1963.

Fagin, R., et al. "Extendible hashing: A fast access method for dynamic files," *ACM Trans. on Database Syst.*, 4(3): 315–344, September 1979.

Ghosh, S. P., and V. Y. Lum. "An analysis of collisions when hashing by division," IBM Research Rpt. RJ1218, May 1973.

Guibas, L. U. "The analysis of hashing techniques that exhibit k-ary clustering," *J. ACM*, 25(4): 544–555, October 1978.

Knott, G. D. "Hashing functions," *Computer J.*, 18(3): 265–278, August 1975.

Litwin, W. "Virtual hashing: A dynamically changing hashing," *Proc. 4th Conf. Very Large Data Bases*, W. Berlin, September 1978, pp. 517–523.

Lum, V. Y. "General performance analysis of key-to-address transformation methods using an abstract file concept," *Communications ACM*, 16(10): 603–612, October 1973.

——, et al. "Key-to-address transform techniques," *Communications ACM*, 14(4): 228–239, April 1971.

——, and P. S. T. Yuen. "Additional results on key-to-address transform techniques," *Communications ACM*, 15(11): 996–997, November 1972.

Maurer, W. D., and T. G. Lewis. "Hash table methods," *ACM Computing Surveys* 7(1): 5–20, March 1975.

Scholl, M. "New file organizations based on dynamic hashing," *ACM Trans. on Database Syst.*, 6(1): 194–211, March 1981.

Terms

absolute addressing	hashing
bucket addressing	home address
collision	linear probing
collision resolution technique	load factor
directory lookup addressing	open addressing
division-remainder hashing	relative addressing
double hashing	relative file organization
dynamic hashing	separate overflow addressing
equivalence class	synonym chaining
extendible hashing	synonyms
hash function	virtual hashing

Review Exercises

1. Compare the relative advantages and disadvantages of absolute addressing and relative addressing.

2. Discuss several alternative techniques for implementing a directory to be used for lookup of addresses into a relative file. Compare the techniques.

3. Compare the relative advantages and disadvantages of direct addressing, directory lookup, and address calculation (hashing). Consider both retrieval of records and storage of new records.

4. On what factors is the performance of a hash function dependent?

5. How is the performance of a hash function evaluated?

6. Compare the operations involved in the division-remainder, mid-square, and folding hash functions.

7. In the absence of information about the distribution of key values, which type of hash function in general performs the best?

8. At what load factor should a relative file generally be enlarged and reorganized?

9. Why does use of synonym chaining require that a record not be displaced from its home address by a record that is not its synonym?

10. Explain the clustering effect exhibited when linear probing is used.

11. What is the primary purpose of each of the following: (a) hash function, (b) linear probing, (c) double hashing, (d) synonym chaining?

12. Explain at least two techniques for handling bucket overflow.

13. Why can a bucket size > 1 record allow variable-length records to be accommodated?

14. How is free space managed when a bucket can hold multiple records? Consider both record insertion and deletion.

15. Discuss the differences in free-space management when a bucket can contain variable-length records instead of just fixed-length records.

16. Learn about virtual hashing techniques. Compare their performance with that of static hashing methods.

17. Modify the retrieval logic of Fig. 184(b) to accommodate possibly deleted records.

18. Write an algorithm to delete a record from the file created using the logic of Fig. 184(a).

19. Obtain a listing of a production program that creates or maintains a relative file from your installation. Determine how addresses are determined and how collisions are resolved.

20. Write a program that creates a relative file using division-remainder hashing and linear probing. Write another version of the program that additionally chains synonyms. Compare the performance of the two program versions with record insertion and retrieval activity.

21. Modify your program versions to accommodate deletion activity. How are you handling deletions? Compare the performance of the two program versions.

CHAPTER 20

Indexed Sequential File Organization

In this chapter we introduce the third major approach to organizing data on secondary storage: indexed sequential file organization. The organization method is first defined, then its utility in information systems is discussed. Two approaches to implementing the concept of indexed sequential organization are covered. We then discuss the declaration and use of indexed sequential files in programs. The chapter closes with a review of some of the factors that should be considered in the design of a file with indexed sequential organization.

DEFINITIONS AND APPLICATIONS:
INDEXED SEQUENTIAL FILES

An effective way to organize a collection of records when there is the need both to access the records sequentially by some key value and also to access the records individually by that same key is *indexed sequential file organization*. An indexed sequential file provides the combination of access types that are supported by a sequential file and a relative file.

One way to think of the structure of an indexed sequential file is as an index with pointers to a sequential data file (Fig. 191). In the pictured example, the index has been structured as a binary search tree. The index is used to service a request for access to a particular record; the sequential data file is used to support sequential access to the entire collection of records.

INDEX

	Position	SEQUENTIAL DATA FILE
	1	APE
	2	BAT
	3	CAT
	4	COW
	5	DOG
	6	EEL
	:	:
	N	ZEBRA

FIGURE 191

You are already familiar with this approach to structuring a collection of information to facilitate both sequential and direct access. For example, consider a dictionary: the thumb tabs provide an index into the sequentially organized collection of words. In order to find a particular word, say "syzygy," you usually do not scan the dictionary sequentially. Rather, you select the appropriate thumb tab, S, the first letter of the word, and use that tab to direct your search into the approximate location of the word in the data collection. Again, you probably would not proceed with a sequential search from the beginning of the S's to find your target word, "syzygy." Instead, you would use the column headings on each page which indicate the first and last elements on that page. Once you have located the proper page, your search might proceed sequentially to find the sought word.

It is important to note from the dictionary example that:

> the key that is used to sequentialize entries is the same as the key that is used to search directly for an individual entry.

The thumb tab and column-heading index structure does not work *unless* this point is true.

There are several approaches to structuring both the index and the sequential data portions of an indexed sequential file. We will discuss the most commonly applied techniques later in this chapter.

Because of its capability to support both sequential and direct access, indexed sequential organization is used frequently to support files that are used for both batch and interactive processing. For example, consider a credit card billing system with an indexed sequential master file of customer account information. An appropriate key for the file would be the account number of each record. The file could be accessed in batch mode, monthly, to generate customer invoices and to build summary reports of account activity. Each account record would be accessed once in this processing. The bills and the detail lines on the summary report would appear in account number sequence.

The credit card management agency wants to use the master file of account information also to support interactive inquiry of the current credit status of any account. When a customer makes a purchase, the master file will be consulted to determine the credit limit and then to update the remaining credit amount. This kind of processing could not be supported well by sequential access to the customer account file. Rather, the need to access an individual account, given its account number, dictates use of the index of the indexed sequential file organization.

Another example of an application that calls for support by an indexed sequential file is a class records system. Processing requirements for this system include the following:

1. List the names and addresses of all students.
2. Compute the average age of the students.
3. Compute the mean and standard deviation for students' grade point averages.
4. Compute the total number of credit hours for classes in which the students are presently enrolled.
5. Change the classification of a particular student from "probational" to "regular."
6. Display the grade record for a particular student.
7. Insert a record for a new student.
8. Delete the record for a particular student who has withdrawn from the school.

Some of these requirements call for sequential accessibility of the student file; others call for direct accessibility to particular records of the file. The combination of requirements can be satisfied by using indexed sequential file organization. The key for the file would be the student identifier.

IMPLEMENTATIONS OF THE
INDEXED SEQUENTIAL FILE ORGANIZATION

There are two basic approaches to implementing the concept of indexed sequential file organization:

1. Block indexes and data (dynamic)
2. Prime and overflow data areas (static)

We will consider each in the following two sections. Both approaches use an index part and a data part, each residing in a separate file. One of the reasons to separate the index part and the data part into two files is that they are implemented with different internal organizations. Each must reside on a direct-access storage device.

Block Indexes and Data

With this approach, both the index file and the data file are organized into blocks. The index file has a tree structure; the data file has a sequential structure with free space distributed among the populated records. Fig. 192 depicts an indexed sequential file of animal information.

This example as shown contains N data blocks and three levels of index. Each entry in the index is of the form < lowest key value, pointer>, where the pointer is to another block in which the key value is the lowest key value that appears. Each level of index block points to all of the blocks that form the next-lower level of the index, except for the lowest-level index blocks, which point to the data blocks.

When a request for access to a particular record, say the one with key value BAT, is received, the highest level of index (here block 3-1) is searched first. In this example, the pointer from AARDVARK is followed to index block 2-1. The appropriate pointer out of that box is the one found with AARDVARK and leads to index block 1-1. The pointer followed out of that box is the one found with BABOON and leads to data block 2. The data block is then searched for the record with the target key, BAT, and the record is made available.

A request to access the data in sequential order is serviced by accessing the data blocks in sequential order. For reasons that we will discuss shortly, it may be the case that data blocks that are logically consecutive are not actually physically consecutive. In this case the data blocks must be linked together in logical sequence, thus the chaining of the data blocks in Fig. 192.

Let us now consider a series of requests to insert new animal records in our indexed sequential file. Assume that each data block in the file has space adequate to hold five records and that each index block has space adequate to hold four < key value, pointer> pairs. These parameters would have been supplied to the system's data management support routines when the animal file was created. If insertions and deletions to file contents are expected, then both index and data blocks are created with some amount of free space, which is commonly called *padding* and is shown by the slashed areas in Fig. 192.

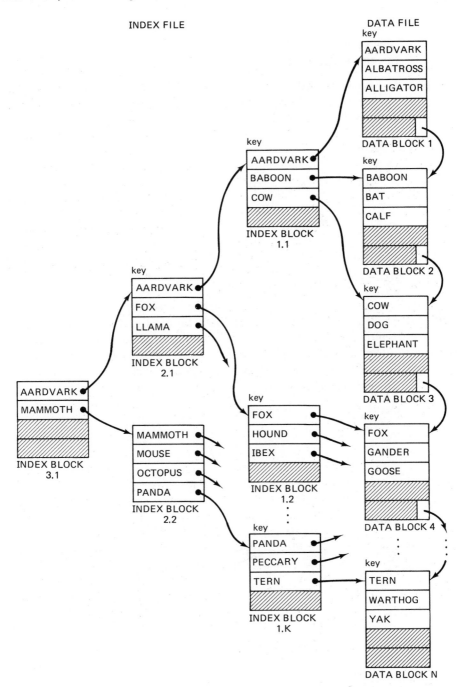

FIGURE 192

The requests:

> INSERT APE
> INSERT AIREDALE

are easy to service. Only data block 1 is affected, and it results in the contents shown in Fig. 193(a). Note that the entries in the block must be kept in ascending sequential order.

key

| AARDVARK |
| AIREDALE |
| ALBATROSS |
| ALLIGATOR |
| APE |

DATA BLOCK 1   **FIGURE 193(a)**

The request

> INSERT ARMADILLO

is a bit more difficult to handle. Search of the index structure reveals that ARMADILLO should reside in data block 1, but that block is already full. This condition necessitates a split of data block 1, with accompanying modification of index block 1-1, as shown in Fig. 193(b). Half of the contents of data block 1 remain there; the other half are moved to the newly created block : "data block 1A."

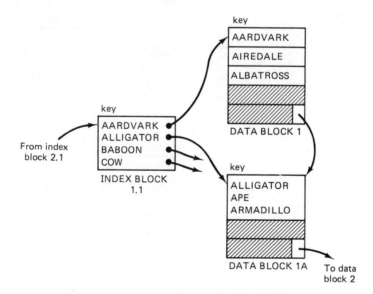

FIGURE 193(b)

The requests

INSERT CAT
INSERT BEAR
INSERT BOBCAT

fill data block 2, then cause it to split, forming data blocks 2 and 2A
(Fig. 193(c)). Index block 1-1 is already full and cannot accommodate
a pointer to block 2A, so it also must split, with the change percolating
up to index level 2.

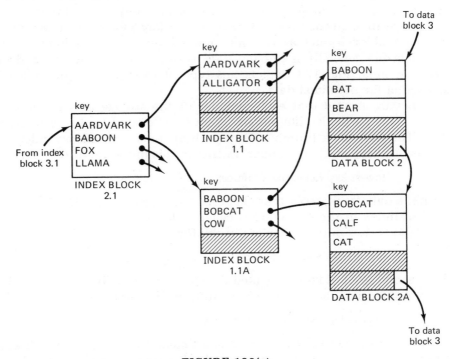

FIGURE 193(c)

When the index block at the highest level (here level 3) becomes
full, then splits, a new level is added to the index tree. All direct searches
would then require four index block accesses and one data block access.

This activity should be reminiscent of our discussion of B^+-trees in
Chapter 12. The leaf nodes of the B^+-tree are the data blocks; the nonleaf nodes of the B^+-tree are the index blocks.

This dynamic approach to implementing indexed sequential files is
common. For example, it is used with the Digital Equipment Company
(DEC) TOPS-10 operating system, with the Control Data Corporation
(CDC) NOS–BE and KRONOS operating systems, and with International

Business Machine's (IBM's) key-sequenced VSAM files. In VSAM terminology, a data block is referred to as a *control interval*. When the records in a control interval are stored in ascending order by a given key
(as they are in an indexed sequential file), the records are said to be in a
key-sequenced data set.

Prime and Overflow Data Areas

Another approach to implementing the indexed sequential file concept is to base the index structure more on the physical characteristics
of storage than on the logical distribution of key values. The index may
have several levels, such as a cylinder-index level and a track-index level.
The data file generally is implemented as two files: a prime area and an
overflow area. Fig. 194 depicts this type of structure for the indexed
sequential file of animal data.

Let us assume that each cylinder of the storage device has four
tracks. This particular file has six cylinders allocated to the prime data
area. The first track (number 0) of each cylinder contains an index to
the record keys on that cylinder. Entries in this index are of the form:

lowest key value, track number.

Within a data track, records are kept in sequence by key value. The first
level of index in the index file is called a *master index*. As is shown in
Fig. 194, entries in this index are of the form:

highest key value, pointer.

The second level of index is called the *cylinder index*. It contains pointers into the prime data file and has entries of the form:

highest key value, cylinder number.

When a request for access to a particular record, say one with key
value BAT, is received, the master index is searched first. Because BAT
precedes LYNX, the pointer from LYNX is followed into the cylinder
index. Because BAT precedes ELEPHANT, the pointer from ELEPHANT
is followed to track 0 of cylinder 1. Because BAT follows BABOON and
precedes COW, the pointer from BABOON is followed to track 2, which
is searched sequentially until BAT is found and made available or is
determined not to exist.

A request to access the data in sequential order is serviced by accessing the cylinders and tracks of the prime data file in sequence.

Let us now examine the handling of updates to an indexed sequential file that is implemented in this manner. Assume that each track of
the prime data file has space adequate to hold five records. (If insertions
and deletions to the file are expected, then it would be created with

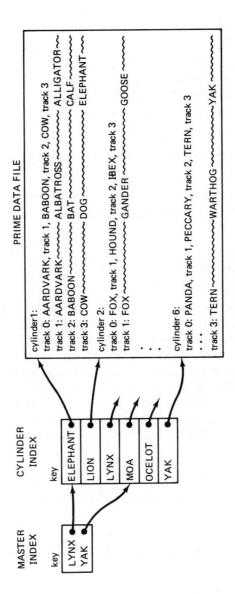

FIGURE 194

padding.) In our example, the prime data area was created with 40% free space (as was also the case for the structure of Fig. 192).

The requests

INSERT APE
INSERT AIREDALE

are easy to service. Only data track 1 of cylinder 1 is affected and it results in the contents shown in Fig. 195(a). Note that the entries in the track must be kept in ascending sequential order.

---

cylinder 1
track 0: no change
track 1: AARDVARK ~~~ AIREDALE ~~~ ALBATROSS ~~ ALLIGATOR ~~~ APE ~~~
track 2: no change
track 3: no change

FIGURE 195(a)

The request

INSERT ARMADILLO

is a bit more difficult to handle. Search of the index structure reveals that ARMADILLO should reside in track 1 of cylinder 1, but that track is full. This condition necessitates use of the overflow data area. This overflow area is in a separate file from the prime data area but is pointed to by entries in the prime data area. Fig. 195(b) shows the result of adding ARMADILLO. Because ARMADILLO belongs after the five existing entries of track 1 of cylinder 1, it must be placed in the overflow data area. The track index for cylinder 1 must be modified to show that there is now a record in the overflow area that logically should reside at the end of track one; thus the addition of the entry < ARMADILLO, ovfl-ptr>,

---

cylinder 1:
track 0: AARDVARK, track 1, ARMADILLO, ovfl-ptr, BABOON, track 2, COW, track 3
track 1: ⎫
track 2: ⎬ no change from Fig. 195 (a)
track 3: ⎭

OVERFLOW DATA FILE

cylinder 1:
track 1: ARMADILLO ~~~~~~

FIGURE 195(b)

where ovfl-ptr is the <cylinder, track, record> number of the corresponding record.

The requests

> INSERT CAT
> INSERT BEAR
> INSERT BOBCAT

fill track 2 of cylinder 1 of the prime data area, then cause use of the overflow area (Fig. 195(c)). Note that CAT is moved to the overflow area because not only must the entries in a prime track be in sequence, but also those entries must precede any overflow entries from that track.

PRIME DATA FILE

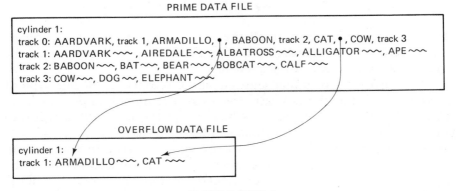

FIGURE 195(c)

Now service the request

> INSERT ANT.

Search of the index structure reveals that ANT should reside in track 1 of cylinder 1. Again, the proper ordering of keys in the prime area must be maintained, so ANT is placed in track 1 of cylinder 1 and APE is bumped to the overflow area (Fig. 195(d)). Track 1 now has more than one entry in the overflow area. In order to be able to access the records sequentially, and, in fact, in order to be able to find a record with direct access, the overflow from a track must be chained together in proper sequence. Thus the format of records in the overflow area is:

> key value, rest of record, pointer to next overflow
> record for this track

Note that a given track of the overflow area may contain records that represent several prime tracks and that the overflow chain for a particular prime track may span multiple overflow tracks. The file can be defined with either one overflow area per cylinder or a combined overflow

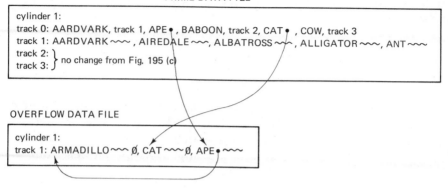

FIGURE 195(d)

area containing records from all the prime cylinders. Entries are made in the overflow area in order by time of insertion. The linked lists in the overflow area show the key sequencing.

The processes of direct and sequential retrieval from this type of indexed sequential file actually are somewhat more complex than we discussed earlier in this section. When a request for a particular record is received, the master and cylinder indexes are used to locate the correct cylinder in the prime data area for the target record. The index in track 0 of that cylinder then is searched. The pointer accompanying the key in the track index that is the largest key value not greater than the sought key value is followed. If that pointer is to a track in the prime area, the keys of records on that track are compared in sequence with the target key value. On the other hand, if the pointer is to a record in the overflow area, the linked list of records pointed to is searched. These records will be linked in ascending key value order but may be located physically anywhere in the overflow area.

A request to access the data in sequential order is serviced by accessing the next prime track, then following its overflow chain, and so forth until the prime and overflow areas have been exhausted.

It is easy to see that with many record insertions, long overflow chains could result. A direct access to a record that resides in the prime area generally requires four I/O-device accesses: two for the index file, one to the track-0 index, and one to the appropriate prime track. A direct access to a record that resides in the overflow area could require as many as $3+K$ I/O-device accesses: two for the index file, one to the track-0 index, and K to the overflow area, where the target record is K^{th} on the overflow chain. Access to each record on the overflow linked list could require a distinct I/O-device access.

Indexed sequential files that are implemented with prime and overflow data areas are susceptible to degradation of performance over a period of insertion activity. While the dynamic implementation discussed in the last section is self-reorganizing, indexed sequential files implemented as discussed in this section are static and require periodic and explicit reorganization. Usually the old indexed sequential file is read sequentially, then written sequentially to a new indexed sequential file with an expanded prime data area.

Deletions in this type of indexed file may be handled in two ways. With dynamic deletion, the subject record is physically removed from the file. If it resided in the overflow area, the linked list in which it participated is adjusted to compensate for its removal. If it was the first entry in the linked list, the track-0 entry for the chain is modified to contain the key of the next entry in the linked list and to point to its location. On the other hand, if it resided in the prime data area, the remaining entries in the prime area are "shifted left," one record from the track's overflow chain is brought into the prime area, and the track-0 entry for the chain is modified appropriately.

The other alternative to handling deletion is to mark the subject record as "deleted," but not actually to remove it. Retrievals skip over "deleted" records. A "garbage collection" routine could be processed at intervals to perform the tasks indicated above. An advantage of this approach is that the garbage-collection process need not be paid for with every single deletion. A disadvantage is that the space allocated to "deleted" (but not yet collected) records may not be available for re-use. Searches may extend into the overflow area because of "deleted" records in the prime area, and chains in the overflow area may include "deleted" records.

The static prime and overflow areas approach to implementing indexed sequential files was developed before the dynamic block index and data approach introduced in the prior section. It was widely used with IBM's ISAM files but is being replaced by the other approach.

INDEXED SEQUENTIAL FILES IN COBOL

Declaration information for indexed sequential files is supplied in both the *ENVIRONMENT DIVISION* and the *DATA DIVISION* of a COBOL program. The format of the *SELECT* clause of the *FILE–CONTROL* paragraph of the *INPUT–OUTPUT SECTION* of the *ENVIRONMENT DIVISION* for an indexed sequential file is:

SELECT filename ASSIGN TO {implementor-name}. . .

$$\left[\underline{RESERVE} \text{ integer } [\begin{array}{c} AREA \\ AREA \end{array}] \right]$$

ORGANIZATION IS INDEXED

$$\left[\underline{\text{ACCESS}} \text{ MODE IS } \left\{ \begin{array}{l} \underline{\text{SEQUENTIAL}} \\ \underline{\text{RANDOM}} \\ \underline{\text{DYNAMIC}} \end{array} \right\} \right]$$

<u>RECORD</u> KEY IS dataname-1

[FILE <u>STATUS</u> IS dataname-2]

The *filename* is the name by which the file is known in this program. The *implementor-name* is the name of the device upon which this file resides. Some implementations require specification of two devices here: one for the index and one for the data.

The optional *RESERVE* and *FILE STATUS* clauses have the same meanings that they have for sequential and relative files.

The *ORGANIZATION IS INDEXED* phrase is required for indexed sequential files. If this phrase were omitted, the file would default to having sequential organization.

The *ACCESS MODE* phrase specifies the manner in which records in the file are going to be accessed: sequentially, directly, or both. The *RECORD KEY* phrase specifies that *dataname-1* contains the key for sequencing and indexing records of the file. This is the key that provides access paths to the file's records. All values of this key field must be unique in the file. The key field must appear as part of the record description in the file's *FD*; the key field therefore must be contained within the record. It must be defined to be alphanumeric.

ACCESS MODE IS SEQUENTIAL means that records will be accessed (read/written) in order by ascending key value. *RANDOM* access means that the value of the key field will be used to identify a particular record to be read, written, deleted or modified. *DYNAMIC* access means that records will be accessed sometimes in *SEQUENTIAL* mode and sometimes in *RANDOM* mode by the program.

Each indexed sequential file used in a program must have an associated file description (*FD*) entry. An *FD* contains clauses that give information about block size, record size, label records, and data records in the file. The entry is essentially the same for indexed sequential files as for relative files; however the *RECORD KEY* must be included as a field in the file's record description(s), while the *RELATIVE KEY* for a relative file does not appear in its record description.

Some nonstandard COBOL compilers that implement the block index and data approach also allow the programmer to specify the sizes of index and data blocks, the percent of padding to leave in index and data blocks when the file is created, and the maximum number of levels that the index tree is allowed to attain.

Other programming languages that support indexed sequential files ask the programmer to specify these same kinds of information to describe the structure of the file.

File Creation

When an indexed sequential file is created in COBOL, it must be open for *OUTPUT*. In implementations based on the prime and overflow data areas approach, records must be written in sequential order by ascending *RECORD KEY* value. In some implementations based on the block index and data approach, this restriction may also be enforced. If it is not, it still is nearly always more efficient to create the file in ascending order. Thus we assume that the file is created with *ACCESS MODE IS SEQUENTIAL*.

The following form of the *WRITE* verb is used to store a new record on the file:

> WRITE recordname [<u>FROM</u> identifier]
> <u>INVALID</u> KEY imperative-stmt.

Prior to execution of the *WRITE* for a record, that record's *RECORD KEY* data item must have been given its appropriate value. The *INVALID KEY* condition is raised if the record's *RECORD KEY* value is not greater than that of the previously written record.

The data management system takes responsibility for correctly building the file's index structure; the programmer's job is made simple.

Some COBOL compilers do not support the creation of indexed sequential files. In these cases, the programmer uses a system utility supplied for this purpose. Typically, such a utility first asks the programmer a number of questions, such as:

What is
- the maximum data record size?
- the data type of the key field?
- the location of the key field in a record?
- the number of records per block in the file to be used as input in creating the indexed sequential file?
- the desired number of records per data block in the indexed sequential file?
- the desired padding in the data blocks?
- the desired number of entries per index block in the indexed sequential file?
- the desired padding in the index blocks?
- the maximum number of data records that the indexed sequential file should be able to contain?
- the name of the indexed sequential file?
- the device to be used for storage of the indexed sequential file?

These utilities generally read a sequential file of sorted records as input and create the index and data parts of the corresponding indexed sequential file. This file can then be input to a COBOL program for retrieval or update processing.

Record Retrieval

When records are retrieved from a COBOL indexed sequential file, the file must be open for *INPUT* (or for *I/O* if records are going to also be written). Records can be retrieved from the file either sequentially or not sequentially, using the *READ* verb. Sequential access may be positioned by the *START* verb.

If the file has *ACCESS MODE IS SEQUENTIAL*, then the following verb form is used:

> <u>READ</u> filename RECORD [<u>INTO</u> identifier]
>   AT <u>END</u> imperative-statement.

A loop through this statement will access the records in ascending order of the *RECORD KEY* field value. The *AT END* condition is raised when the end-of-file is encountered.

The *START* verb can be used to position subsequent sequential reads. The syntax and semantics of this *START* are essentially the same as for use with relative files. The verb does have, however, additional functionality when used with indexed sequential files. The data name specified in a *START* statement need not be the entire *RECORD KEY* data item but can be a leftmost field subordinate to this data item. This facility allows the programmer to specify a partial key match, also known as a *generic key*.

For example, consider an indexed sequential *COURSE-FILE* file declared with *RECORD KEY COURSE-ID*, where *COURSE-ID* is defined in the file's record description as:

```
02  COURSE-ID.
    03  DEPT        PIC X(3).
    03  NUM         PIC X(3).
    03  EXT         PIC X.
```

The statements:

```
MOVE 'MIS' TO DEPT OF COURSE-ID.
START COURSE-FILE KEY = DEPT
      INVALID KEY ~~~.
READ COURSE-FILE RECORD INTO WS-CLASS-REC
      AT END ~~~.
```

would cause the first record for courses in the 'MIS' department to be read. Subsequent sequential reads would access the rest of the records whose *RECORD KEY* fields started with 'MIS' and then would start on the "next" department.

If the indexed sequential file has *ACCESS MODE IS RANDOM*, then the following verb form is used for retrieval:

> READ filename RECORD [INTO identifier]
> INVALID KEY imperative-statement.

Prior to execution of the *READ*, the key value for the desired record must have been moved to the file's *RECORD KEY* data item. The record with that value for its *RECORD KEY* is the record that is retrieved. If there is no such record, then the *INVALID KEY* condition is raised.

If an indexed sequential file has *ACCESS MODE IS DYNAMIC*, then both sequential and direct (random) retrieval are supported.

File Update

When a COBOL indexed sequential file is updated, it must be open for *I-O*. New records can be added using the *WRITE* verb; old records can be removed using the *DELETE* verb; existing records can be modified using the *REWRITE* verb.

If the file has *ACCESS MODE IS SEQUENTIAL*, records must be accessed in sequential order of ascending *RECORD KEY* value. The *START* verb can be used to position sequential access. New records are written using the form of the *WRITE* verb introduced earlier. The sequential form of the *DELETE* verb is the same as for a relative file:

> DELETE filename RECORD.

Execution of the *DELETE* must have been preceded by a successful sequential *READ* for the file. The record that was read is deleted.

The sequential form of the *REWRITE* verb is:

> REWRITE recordname [FROM identifier]
> INVALID KEY imperative-statement.

As for the *DELETE*, execution of a sequential *REWRITE* must be preceded by a successful *READ*. The record that was read is the one that is replaced. The *INVALID KEY* condition is raised if the value of the *RECORD KEY* data item in the replacement record does not match the value of the *RECORD KEY* data item in the last record read from the file. That is, the key value cannot be changed between the execution of the *READ* and of the *REWRITE*.

If the file has *ACCESS MODE IS RANDOM*, then records can be accessed in any order. The random form of the *WRITE* verb is:

> WRITE record-name [FROM identifier]
> INVALID KEY imperative-statement.

Prior to the execution of the *WRITE* for a record, that record's *REC-ORD KEY* data item must have been given its appropriate value. The *INVALID KEY* condition is raised if there already is a record in the file with that *RECORD KEY* value.

The random form of the *DELETE* verb is:

<u>DELETE</u> filename RECORD
    <u>INVALID</u> KEY imperative-statement.

Prior to execution of the *DELETE* for a record, the *RECORD KEY* data item must have been given an appropriate value. The record with that *RECORD KEY* value is deleted. The *INVALID KEY* condition is raised if there is no record on the file with that *RECORD KEY* value.

The random form of the *REWRITE* verb is:

<u>REWRITE</u> recordname [<u>FROM</u> identifier]
    <u>INVALID</u> KEY imperative-statement.

Prior to the execution of the *REWRITE* for a record, the *RECORD KEY* data item must have been given an appropriate value. The record with that *RECORD KEY* value is replaced. The *INVALID KEY* condition is raised if there is no record on the file with that *RECORD KEY* value.

As with other operations, sequential and random update of an indexed sequential file can be intermingled in one program if the file has *ACCESS MODE IS DYNAMIC*.

Other languages that support indexed sequential files provide the same kinds of facilities for record insertion, access, modification, and deletion. In all cases, the function must be specified, the key value of the target record must be given (for direct access), and the action to be taken if an exceptional condition arises must be identified.

DESIGN OF INDEXED SEQUENTIAL FILES

The primary questions that need to be addressed in designing an indexed sequential file include the following:

1. What is the layout of fields in the record?
2. What is the key field(s) used to identify record occurrences?
3. How extensive are record insertions expected to be?
4. What approach is used locally to implement the indexed sequential construct?

As discussed with the other file organization techniques, the record layout problem is the same as the problem addressed in Chapter 3. Both fixed- and variable-length records can be accommodated by many indexed sequential implementations.

The appropriate field(s) to form the key for an indexed sequential file is determined by the application. The significant restriction of indexed sequential organization is that whatever field forms the key for sequential access of the file must also be the key for indexed access of the file. If this is not the case and different keys seem appropriate for sequential and indexed access, then one of the file organizations introduced in Chapter 21 is more appropriate than is indexed sequential organization.

The extent of expected insertions to the file determines how much free space should be allocated in the file when it is initially loaded. A rough guideline is to leave 40% padding.

Depending upon the approach used to implement the indexed sequential file, other design decisions must be made. Local data management manuals commonly give implementation-dependent guidance on determining parameters such as the following:

1. Block index and data approach:
   (a) data block size
   (b) index block size
   (c) number of index levels initially
   (d) maximum number of index levels
2. Prime and overflow areas approach:
   (a) index area size
   (b) levels of index
   (c) prime area size
   (d) overflow area size
   (e) record blocking in the prime area

These parameters are determined by the system's natural block size, the current and expected number of data records, and the usage of the file. The need for rapid direct retrieval implies use of a bushy index; the need for rapid sequential retrieval implies larger data blocks or larger prime data area and blocking factor. The more often data or index blocks must be split, the more expensive is update overhead. In general, the block index and data approach provides better performance in all ways: direct and sequential retrieval as well as update.

SUMMARY

An indexed sequential file supports both sequential access by key value and direct access to a particular record given its key value. This type of file organization is implemented by building an index on top of a sequential data file that resides on a direct-access storage device.

One good implementation approach is to use block indexes and data. This structure is very similar to a B$^+$-tree. Another implementation approach uses prime and overflow data areas and is based more on the physical characteristics of storage. These two approaches differ primarily in their treatment of overflow conditions. When a data or index block in the first approach overflows, it is split. When a data track in the second approach overflows, records are placed into a separate overflow area and chained together to maintain logical key sequence order.

The basic concepts required for using an indexed sequential file in COBOL were introduced. Compilers that support indexed sequential files interface with extensive data management facilities that shield the programmer from the details of implementing and maintaining indexed sequential files in storage. Finally, several aspects of the design of indexed sequential files were reviewed.

Indexed sequential files are used extensively when there is the need for both sequential and direct access to records in a file. If only sequential access is needed, sequential file organization generally is cheaper and can utilize tape storage devices. If only direct access is needed, then relative file organization incurs less system overhead since access by logical key sequence order need not be supported.

For further information about the indexed sequential file organization, the reader should consult the following references.

Keehn, D. G., and J. O. Lacy. "VSAM data set design parameters," *IBM Syst. J.*, vol. 3, pp. 186–212, 1974.

Larson, P. A. "Analysis of index-sequential files with overflow chaining," *ACM Trans. on Database Syst.*, 6(4): 671–680, December 1981.

Mullin, J. K. "An improved index sequential access method using hashed overflow," *Communications ACM*, 15(5): 301–307, 1972.

Nakamura, T., and T. Mizoguchi. "An analysis of storage utilization in block split data structuring schemes," *Proc. 4th Intl. Conf. on Very Large Databases*, W. Berlin, 1978, pp. 489–495.

Terms

B$^+$-tree	key-sequenced data set
control interval	master index
cylinder index	overflow data area
generic key	padding
indexed sequential file organization	prime data area

Review Exercises

1. A public utility company has a computerized billing system. Each month meter readings for each customer are fed into the computer. Each month two reports are output from the billing system. One report consists of a billing statement for each customer, showing the date and dollar amount due, meter readings and usage, customer's name, address, and ID number, previous balance due, and taxes. The second report is used internally and shows all of the billing information for each customer for the month. There are two basic files used by the billing system: (1) meter reading data file, and (2) customer data file (name, address, ID number, balance due).
   (a) What should the organization of each file be?
   (b) What should the key of the records on each file be?

2. A retail outfit has a computerized inventory control system. At the end of each day an inventory clerk informs the computer via a terminal of the number of units of each product sold during the day. Such reporting of daily sales by product provides constant inventory updating for each product. When the inventory of any particular item reaches a specified low point, new goods are ordered to replenish the stock. The outputs that are generated by the inventory control system are the following: (1) current inventory after the clerk inputs the desired information for a product on the terminal, (2) a summary report of the day-by-day inventory for each product, generated weekly, and (3) order forms containing supplier's name and address, date, number of units ordered, product number, and unit cost, generated when the reorder point of product is reached.
   (a) What should the organization of the product file be?
   (b) What should the key of the records on the file be?

3. A large restaurant chain maintains records of quantities of the various menu selections that are purchased by its patrons in order to better plan its purchasing of component foods. At each restaurant, information from the meal check is keyed at the time of customer checkout into a data terminal and recorded on a tape cassette. The tape cassettes from all the restaurant outlets are mailed each morning to a central site where they are batched and input to an analysis system.
   (a) What should be the organization of the file generated at each restaurant outlet?
   (b) What should be the key or identifier of each record on the file?

4. A large hospital has a computerized patient record system. Each nursing station has a terminal with display and key capability. When a patient is admitted, a record containing personal information and medical history is created. The patients' doctors record treatment information as the needs are diagnosed. Nurses access the information that the doctors have stored in the patient's records to determine medication dosages, dietary restrictions, etc. and they also update the records with temperature, pulse, blood pressure, etc., statistics which the doctors later access to brief themselves on patient progress.
   (a) What should be the organization of the patient file?
   (b) What should be the key or identifier of each record on the file?

5. (a) Which of the processing requirements in the class records system (described in this chapter) call for sequential accessibility of the student file?
   (b) Which call for direct accessibility to particular records of the file?

6. Why is a B^+-tree a better structure than is a B-tree for implementation of an indexed sequential file?

7. Describe the sequence of actions required to access an indexed sequential file sequentially. Describe the sequence of actions required to access a given record directly in an indexed sequential file. Describe the sequence of actions required to insert a record in an indexed sequential file. Describe the sequence of actions required to delete a record from an indexed sequential file. What type of implementation are you using in these descriptions?

8. The prime-and-overflow-data-area approach is being replaced by the block-index-and-data approach to implementing indexed sequential files. What are the relative advantages and disadvantages of the two approaches?

9. Obtain a listing from your installation of a program that accesses an indexed sequential file. Study the way the file is described and the series of actions taken by the programmer.

10. Propose another method for implementing an indexed sequential file and compare it with the block-index-and-data and the prime-and-overflow-data-areas approaches.

11. Write a program that implements the block-index-and-data approach to providing indexed sequential access to data. Be able to handle insertion of new records, deletion of old records, and retrieval of records. Be able to split and merge blocks.

12. Build an indexed sequential file using the language/utility facilities available at your installation. Access the file sequentially and using the index. Insert and delete records.

13. Build several versions of an indexed sequential file using the language/utility facilities available at your installation. Vary design parameters, e.g., block size, padding, index structure, and compare the performance of the resultant files for sequential and direct access and for update activity.

CHAPTER 21

Multi-key File
Organization

In this chapter we will introduce a family of file organization techniques that allow records to be accessed by more than one key field. Until this point, we have considered only single-key file organizations: sequential by a given key, relative giving direct access by a key, and indexed sequential giving both direct and sequential access by a key (Fig. 196). Now we broaden our horizons to include those file organizations that enable a single data file to support multiple access paths, each by a different key. These file organization techniques are at the heart of database implementations, which we will introduce in the next chapter.

There are numerous techniques that have been used to implement multi-key files. Most of the approaches are based on building indexes to provide direct access by key value. We will discuss two fundamental techniques for providing the linkage between an index and the file of data records:

- Inversion
- Multi-list organization

Many programming language compilers do not provide built-in capabilities to support multi-key files. Rather, a data processing group generally acquires an external software package that handles data management tasks for these types of files or writes its own data management system. Language compilers may then interface directly with this file support, or they may generate CALLs to this support. Here, we will

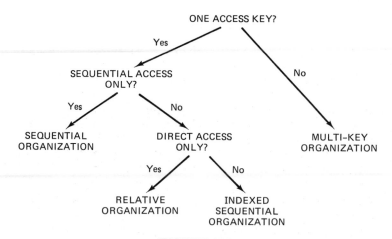

FIGURE 196

introduce the alternate-key indexed sequential facility of COBOL, which provides support for multi-key files.

The chapter closes with a review of the basic trade-offs that should be considered in the design of a multi-key file.

DEFINITIONS AND APPLICATIONS: MULTI-KEY FILES

Many interactive information systems require the support of multi-key files. Consider a banking system in which there are several types of users: tellers, loan officers, branch managers, bank officers, account holders, and so forth. All have the need to access the same data, say records of the format shown in Fig. 197.

ACCOUNT

ID	NAME		GROUP-CODE		SOCNO	BALANCE	OVERDRAW LIMIT
	LAST	FIRST	BRANCH	TYPE			

FIGURE 197

The various types of users need to access these records in different ways. A teller might identify an account record by its ID value. A loan officer might need to access all account records with a given value for OVER-DRAW-LIMIT, or all account records for a given value of SOCNO. A branch manager might access records by the BRANCH and TYPE group code. A bank officer might want periodic reports of all accounts data, sorted by ID. An account holder (customer) might be able to access his or her own record by giving the appropriate ID value or a combination of NAME, SOCNO, and TYPE code.

One approach to being able to support all of these types of access is to have several different files, each organized to serve one type of request. For this banking example, there might be one indexed sequential account file with key ID (to serve tellers, bank officers, and account holders), one sequential account file with records ordered by OVER-DRAW–LIMIT (to serve loan officers), one account file with relative organization and user-key SOCNO (to serve loan officers), one sequential account file with records ordered by GROUP–CODE (to serve branch managers), and one relative account file with user-key NAME, SOCNO, and TYPE code (to serve account holders). We have just identified five files, all containing the same data records! The five files differ only in their organizations, and thus in the access paths they provide.

Replicating data across files is not a desirable solution to the problem of providing multiple access paths through that data. One obvious difficulty with this approach is the resultant storage space requirements. However, a more serious difficulty with this approach is keeping updates to the replicated data records synchronized. The multi-key file is a classical and often successful solution to the multiple-path retrieval problem; it uses indexes rather than data replication.

Whenever multiple copies of data exist, there is the potential for discrepancies. Assume that you have three calendars. You keep one at home by the telephone, one in your briefcase, and one at work. What is the probability that those three calendars show the same record of appointments and obligations? The likely situation is that you will post some updates to one copy but forget to enter them in the other copies. Even if you are quite conscientious about updating all three copies, there must be some lag between the times that the updates actually appear in the three locations. The same difficulty arises in updating data that appear in multiple files.

The result of incomplete and asynchronous updates is loss of data integrity. If a loan officer queries one file and finds that account #123456 has an overdraw limit of $250, then queries another file and finds that the same account has an overdraw limit of $1000, he or she should question the validity of the data.

Another approach to being able to support several different types of access to a collection of data records is to have *one* data file with multiple access paths through the data records provided by a multi-key file organization technique. Now there is only one copy of any data record to be updated, and the update synchronization problem caused by record duplication is avoided.

The concept of multiple-key access generally is implemented by building multiple indexes to provide different access paths to the data records. There may also be multiple linked lists through the data records. We have seen already that an index can be structured in several ways, for example as a table, a binary search tree, or a B-tree. The most appropriate method of implementing a particular multi-key file is dependent upon the actual uses to be made of the data and the types of multi-key file support that the data processing group has available.

INVERTED FILE ORGANIZATION

One fundamental approach to providing the linkage between an index and the file of data records is called *inversion*. A key's *inversion index* contains all of the values that the key presently has in the data file and pointers to all of the data records that have the corresponding value. The data file is said to be *inverted* on that key.

A simple inversion index is structured as a table. For example, inverting the example ACCOUNT-FILE on SOCNO results in the inversion index shown in Fig. 198. This figure refers to the data records shown in Fig. 199 which will be used throughout the chapter.

SOCNO	ADDRESS
001234123	6
123456789	5
213823456	14
299167305	16
399042131	4
411625331	13
412631467	7
426135447	20
445062681	17
459463001	1
513014265	8
612305116	9
626311660	18
692122222	12
713214622	3
798392289	15
821346211	2
912346789	19
923146154	11
987654321	10

FIGURE 198

This particular inversion index has sorted entries, which facilitates searching for a particular key value. Overhead is incurred when a record is added to the file, because the inversion index also must be updated. Not all inversion indexes are maintained in sorted order.

Fig. 198 may bring to mind the index structures that we discussed in the context of relative files (see Fig. 182). At that time we referred to an index as a directory. Either term is correct. One difference between the example of Fig. 182 and the example of Fig. 198 is that the data records in the first example are not in key-sequence order, because they are organized as a relative file, whereas the data records in the second example are ordered by ID value. In either case, the ordering of the key values in the index need not match the ordering of the corresponding records in the data file.

A glance at Fig. 182(b) suggests that an inversion index need not be structured as a table but could be structured as a tree, which would provide shorter search times but would be somewhat more complex to manage.

An inversion index can be built on top of a relative file or on top of an indexed sequential file. An inversion index on key SOCNO for a relative file with user-key ID would provide a file that would support direct access by either ID or SOCNO. An inversion index on key SOCNO for an indexed sequential file with key ID would provide a file that would support direct access by either ID or SOCNO and would support sequential access by ID. A sorted SOCNO inversion index could be used to access records in order by SOCNO but would probably be expensive to use.

If one key field is used to determine the storage structure of the data file, it is called the file's *primary key*. Any other access keys are called *secondary keys*.

From a purist's point of view, use of the term *inversion* implies that the indexed data values have been taken out of the data records and reside only in the corresponding inversion index. The data records shown in Fig. 199 thus would not include a SOCNO field. A *completely inverted* file has an inversion index for every data field. If the corresponding values have been removed from the data records, the logical result is that a completely inverted file need have no data records! If a file is not completely inverted but has at least one inversion index, it is said to be a *partially inverted* file.

While taking an inversion key's values out of the data records conserves space, it can make processing more difficult. For example, the request: What is the SOCNO for the account with ID = '335812'? would require the following steps:

- Determine the address of the record with ID = '335812' in the data file (the technique used depends on how the file is organized).

Record Address	NAME ID	LAST	FIRST	GROUP-CODE BRANCH	TYPE	SOCNO	BALANCE	OVERDRAW LIMIT
1	111111	ADAMS	JOHN	DT	001	459463001	100.50	0.
2	112131	SMITH	IVAN	NW	001	821346211	2311.20	100.
3	198121	MORALES	JOSE	DT	002	713214622	-191.87	200.
4	201431	SMITH	ELOISE	DT	001	399042131	3142.93	100.
5	208432	JONES	JANE	NW	001	123456789	95.26	0.
6	291821	MORGAN	BILL	NW	002	001234123	146.92	0.
7	300123	ADAMS	MYRTLE	NE	002	412631467	3000.00	100.
8	310103	MATTHERS	ELMER	DT	001	513014265	243.63	0.
9	324196	BONES	IGOR	EA	001	612305116	0.02	0.
10	335812	BRILLO	JOSE	DT	002	987654321	88.72	0.
11	386132	MARTIN	JANE	WE	002	923146154	-89.98	100.
12	387122	KINKO	BOB	WE	002	692122222	10.95	0.
13	415631	SMITH	ELLIE	NE	001	411625331	426.86	100.
14	486212	GRANG	TED	DT	002	213823456	893.92	100.
15	511211	ULMER	OLIVER	NW	001	798392289	2814.12	250.
16	534216	GREEN	ED	EA	001	299167305	296.12	250.
17	535218	BROWN	JOE	EA	001	445062681	2814.12	250.
18	641230	WHITE	JANE	DT	002	626311660	-98.14	100.
19	686116	BLACK	JANIS	DT	001	912346789	3216.16	100.
20	696123	MAUVE	MABEL	NE	002	426135447	95.93	25.

FIGURE 199

- Search the SOCNO inversion index for the entry with that address. (Note that the SOCNO value is *not* in the data record.)

A sequential search of the SOCNO inversion index could be required, because inversion indexes usually are structured by their inversion key values, not by data record addresses.

An attractive variation on the inversion index structure is to use indirect addressing, as illustrated for our example file in Fig. 200. Rather than accompanying each SOCNO value with the address of the corresponding data record, index entries are in the form of < secondary key, primary key> pairs. This approach allows the data file to be reorganized and restructured physically without forcing changes to the index files. The trade-off is that extra work is required to actually find the data record with a given secondary-key value, since the corresponding primary-key value must be translated to the data record's address.

SOCNO	ID
001234123	291821
123456789	208432
213823456	486212
299167305	534216
399042131	201431
411625331	415631
412631467	300123
426135447	696123
445062681	535218
459463001	111111
513014265	310103
612305116	324196
626311660	641230
692122222	387122
713214622	198121
798392289	511211
821346211	112131
912346789	686116
923146154	386132
987654321	335812

FIGURE 200

In our example, SOCNO values are unique; each entry in the SOCNO inversion index has one corresponding data record. Inversion can also be used with keys that do not have unique values. Fig. 201 shows a tabular index for the GROUP–CODE key. As with the SOCNO index, the following index design questions are raised:

- Should key value entries be ordered?

- How should the index itself be structured?
- Should direct or indirect addressing be used?

GROUP-CODE BRANCH TYPE		ID
DT	001	111111, 201431, 310103, 686116
DT	002	198121, 335812, 486212, 641230
EA	001	324196, 534216, 535218
NE	001	415631
NE	002	300123, 696123
NW	001	112131, 208432, 511211
NW	002	291821
WE	002	386132, 387122

FIGURE 201

When a secondary key can have duplicate values, its inversion index must be able to cope with variable numbers of pointers for each key value. There are several alternatives:

- Manage variable-length index entries.
- For each value, allocate space to accommodate the maximum number of entries for any value and manage fixed-length index entries.
- Make one entry in the index for each <secondary key, primary key> pair; thus if key value x appears in 12 data records, there will be 12 index entries for value x.

With any of these approaches, the question arises of how to order the primary-key entries for a given key value. In Fig. 201, entries for a key value are ordered by ascending ID value. Ordering the primary-key entries can make record retrieval faster but incurs overhead when updating records.

One attractive feature of an inverted file is that some types of queries can be answered without accessing the data file. For example, the following requests can be processed just using the inversion indexes of Figs. 200 and 201.

1. Is there an account for SOCNO = '414556233'?
2. How many accounts are there with GROUP–CODE = 'EA001'?
3. How many accounts are there at BRANCH = 'NE'?
4. How many different types of accounts are there at BRANCH = 'NE'?
5. Does BRANCH = 'WE' have any TYPE = '001' accounts?
6. List the ID values for accounts in GROUP–CODE = 'DT002'.
7. List the ID values for accounts of TYPE = '002'.

8. Does ID = '696123' have an account of TYPE = '002'?
9. Does SOCNO = '426135447' have an account of TYPE = '002'?

The inversion approach to providing multi-key access is quite popular. It is used as the basis for physical database structures in several commercially available database management systems, including Intel's System-2000 and Software AG's Adabas. These systems are designed to provide rapid retrieval to data records via as many inversion keys as the designer cares to identify. They have user-friendly, natural-language-like query languages to assist the user in formulating inquiries.

MULTI-LIST FILE IMPLEMENTATION

The other basic approach to providing the linkage between an index and the file of data records is called *multi-list organization*.

Like an inverted file, a multi-list file maintains an index for each secondary key. There is one entry in the secondary key's index for each value that the secondary key presently has in the data file. The multi-list organization differs from inversion in that while the entry in the inversion index for a key value has a pointer to *each* data record with that key value, the entry in the multi-list index for a key value has just one pointer to the *first* data record with that key value. That data record contains a pointer to the *next* data record with that key value, and so forth. Thus there is a linked list of data records for each value of the secondary key. Multi-list chains usually are bi-directional and occasionally are circular to improve update performance.

Figures 202(a) and (b) illustrate the multi-list indexes for secondary keys GROUP–CODE and OVERDRAW–LIMIT respectively in our example file. Fig. 202(c) shows the corresponding data file. Note that while inversion did not affect the data file, use of the multi-list organization does. Each record must have space for the pointers that implement the secondary-key accessibility.

GROUP–CODE BRANCH TYPE		ID
DT	001	111111
DT	002	198121
EA	001	324196
NE	001	415631
NE	002	300123
NW	001	112131
NW	002	291821
WE	002	386132

FIGURE 202(a)

OVERDRAW LIMIT	ID
0.	111111
100.	112131
200.	198121
250.	511211

FIGURE 202(b)

The same types of design decisions must be addressed as were required with inversion:

- Should key value entries be ordered?
- How should the index itself be structured?
- Should direct or indirect addressing be used?
- Should data record entries for a given key value be ordered?

Here we have ordered key values, used tabular index structures with indirect addressing, and have linked data records by ascending ID value.

Note the result of building a multi-list structure to implement a secondary key that has unique values! If there are N data records, there will be N value entries in the index, each of which points to a linked list of length one. (See Fig. 198.) The index is the same as had the secondary key been implemented using inversion.

One attractive characteristic of the multi-list approach is that index entries can be fixed-length. Each value has associated with it just one pointer.

The multi-list approach provides the same type of secondary-key accessibility as does the inversion approach, but processing of the two types of files differs. For example, to respond to the requests:

2. How many accounts are there with GROUP–CODE = 'EA001'?
3. How many accounts are there at BRANCH = 'NE'?
6. List the ID values for accounts in GROUP–CODE = 'DT002'.
7. List the ID values for accounts of TYPE = '002'.
8. Does ID = '696123' have an account of TYPE = '002'?

the data records themselves must be accessed. (These queries could be answered by index access only in the example inverted file.) In order to be able to answer some types of "counting-queries" (such as 2 and 3), each value entry in the multi-list index may have stored with it not just a pointer to the first record with that key value, but also the length of

Record Address	ID	NAME LAST	FIRST	GROUP-CODE BRANCH	TYPE	NEXT	SOCNO	BALANCE	OVERDRAW LIMIT	NEXT
1	111111	ADAMS	JOHN	DT	001	201431	459463001	100.50	0.	208432
2	112131	SMITH	IVAN	NW	001	208432	821346211	2311.20	100.	201431
3	198121	MORALES	JOSE	DT	002	335812	713214622	-191.87	200.	0.
4	201431	SMITH	ELOISE	DT	001	310103	399042131	3142.93	100.	300123
5	208432	JONES	JANE	NW	001	511211	123456789	95.26	0.	291821
6	291821	MORGAN	BILL	NW	002	0	001234123	146.92	0.	310103
7	300123	ADAMS	MYRTLE	NE	002	696123	412631467	3000.00	100.	386132
8	310103	MATTHERS	ELMER	DT	001	686116	513014265	243.63	0.	324196
9	324196	BONES	IGOR	EA	001	534216	612305116	0.02	0.	335812
10	335812	BRILLO	JOSE	DT	002	486212	987654321	88.72	0.	387122
11	386132	MARTIN	JANE	WE	002	387122	923146154	-89.98	100.	415631
12	387122	KINKO	BOB	WE	002	0	692122222	10.95	0.	0.
13	415631	SMITH	ELLIE	NE	001	0	411625331	426.86	100.	486212
14	486212	CRANG	TED	DT	002	641230	213823456	893.92	100.	641230
15	511211	ULMER	OLIVER	NW	001	0	798392289	2814.12	250.	534216
16	534216	GREEN	ED	EA	001	535218	299167305	296.12	250.	535218
17	535218	BROWN	JOE	EA	001	0	445062681	2814.12	250.	696123
18	641230	WHITE	JANE	DT	002	0	626311660	-98.14	100.	686116
19	686116	BLACK	JANIS	DT	001	0	912346789	3216.16	100.	0.
20	696123	MAUVE	MABEL	NE	002	0	426135447	95.93	250.	0.

FIGURE 202(c)

the entry's linked list of records. Figs. 203(a) and (b) show this variation for the GROUP–CODE and OVERDRAW–LIMIT indexes.

GROUP–CODE BRANCH TYPE		ID	LENGTH
DT	001	111111	4
DT	002	198121	4
EA	001	324196	3
NE	001	415631	1
NE	002	300123	2
NW	001	112131	3
NW	002	291821	1
WE	002	386132	2

FIGURE 203(a)

OVERDRAW LIMIT	ID	LENGTH
0.	111111	7
100.	112131	8
200.	198121	1
250.	511211	4

FIGURE 203(b)

This length information is also useful for identifying the best access paths for some types of requests. For example, there are three potential access paths that could be used to respond to the request:

List the IDs of accounts of GROUP–CODE = 'EA001'
with OVERDRAW–LIMIT = 100.

The data file could be searched sequentially, the GROUP–CODE index could be used, or the OVERDRAW–LIMIT index could be used. Which of these is the best choice? Sequential search requires access to 20 data records, use of the GROUP–CODE index means access to 3 data records, and use of the OVERDRAW–LIMIT index means access to 8 data records. GROUP–CODE is the most desirable option. For each of the accessed records with GROUP–CODE = 'EA001', it is necessary only to check the value of the OVERDRAW–LIMIT field.

Two variations on the basic multi-list structure are the controlled-length multi-list and the cellular multi-list structures. In a *controlled-length multi-list* file, a maximum length is imposed upon the linked lists of data records. If a secondary-key value is possessed by more data records than that length allows, then the key value would appear more than once in the index and there would be more than one linked list of data records with that value.

In a *cellular multi-list* file, the list structures are determined in part by the characteristics of storage. For example, a cell could be defined as a cylinder, as a track, or as a page. A linked list is not allowed to cross cell boundaries. If there are records in three cylinders that have the same secondary-key value, then there would be three index entries and three linked lists for that value. This multi-list variation can be useful in reducing disk arm-movement requirements and I/O accesses.

The multi-list approach to implementing multi-key access is used quite extensively. It is the basis for physical database structures in most of the commercially available database management systems, including the CODASYL family of systems, Cincom's TOTAL, and IBM's IMS.

ALTERNATE-KEY INDEXED SEQUENTIAL FILES

COBOL provides multi-key file support by building upon the indexed sequential file organization that we discussed in Chapter 20. In addition to the index and sequential data files used to implement the already-discussed indexed sequential concept, another index is maintained (by the data management system, not by the programmer) for each defined secondary key.

Consider an example which is a subset of the banking application introduced earlier. We will use this example throughout the chapter. Assume that we need to be able to access account records in the following ways:

- Sequential by ascending ID value
- Direct by ID value
- Direct by SOCNO value
- Direct by GROUP–CODE value.

For expository purposes, assume that a person can have only one account, that is, SOCNO and ID values both will be unique. The first two requirements alone would suggest use of an indexed sequential file with key ID. The other two requirements suggest building additional index structures for access to the data file. COBOL calls such a multi-key file an alternate-key indexed sequential file.

File Declaration in COBOL

The *SELECT* clause for an alternate-key indexed sequential file is the same as for an ordinary *INDEXED* file, with the addition of one or more *ALTERNATE RECORD KEY* phrases. Each data item specified by an *ALTERNATE RECORD KEY* phrase becomes a secondary key for the file. For our example, the following *SELECT* clause would be appropriate:

```
SELECT ACCOUNT-FILE   ASSIGN TO DISK
       ORGANIZATION IS   INDEXED
       ACCESS MODE IS SEQUENTIAL or RANDOM or DYNAMIC
       RECORD KEY IS ID
       ALTERNATE RECORD KEY IS SOCNO
       ALTERNATE RECORD KEY IS GROUP-CODE
            WITH DUPLICATES.
```

The *WITH DUPLICATES* phrase on the second *ALTERNATE RECORD KEY* entry indicates that *GROUP-CODE* values need not be unique. The absence of this phrase on the first *ALTERNATE RECORD KEY* entry indicates that the *SOCNO* values must be unique. Recall that primary key values (here values of *ID*) must be unique in an *INDEXED* file.

The proper *ACCESS MODE* phrase for a file in a program is determined by the way that the program accesses the file by its primary key, not by secondary key values. *ACCESS MODE SEQUENTIAL* means that records are accessed by ascending value of the primary key. Sequential access by a secondary key implies use of *ACCESS MODE RANDOM*, since that access order probably does not match primary-key order.

Just as the primary key must be an alphanumeric field that appears in the record description for the file, so must any secondary key be alphanumeric and appear in the file's record description. The primary record key and alternate record keys are referred to collectively as *record keys*.

File Manipulation

The creation of an alternate-key indexed sequential file proceeds in the same way as does the creation of an indexed sequential file without secondary keys. If the file is created with *ACCESS MODE SEQUENTIAL*, then records must be written in order by ascending value of the primary key. The "system" builds not only the index for the primary key, but also an index for each secondary key. Either inversion or multi-list organization can be used to tie indexes to the data file.

Retrieval of records from an alternate-key indexed sequential file may be relative to the primary key or any secondary key. Unless otherwise specified, sequential retrieval is relative to the primary key, as discussed in Chapter 20. Sequential retrieval by an alternate key must be preceded by a *START* statement. The format of the *START* verb is:

$$\text{START filename } \left[\underline{\text{KEY}} \text{ IS } \begin{Bmatrix} \text{EQUAL TO} \\ = \\ \text{GREATER THAN} \\ > \\ \underline{\text{NOT}} \text{ LESS THAN} \\ \underline{\text{NOT}} < \end{Bmatrix} \text{dataname} \right]$$

INVALID KEY imperative-statement.

If the *KEY* phrase is omitted, then the *START* positions the file relative to the primary key's value. Otherwise, *dataname* must be either a record key (primary or alternate) or a component of a record key, sharing its left boundary in storage (see our earlier discussion of generic keys).

Following are several examples of COBOL code for sequential retrieval by alternate record key for the *ACCOUNT-FILE*. The first section of code retrieves the records of the account file in order by ascending *SOCNO* value. There should be no duplicates.

```
MOVE ZERO TO SOCNO.
START ACCOUNT-FILE
    KEY GREATER THAN SOCNO
    INVALID KEY . . . .
READ ACCOUNT-FILE RECORD INTO WS-ACCOUNT-REC
    AT END MOVE 'Y' TO EOF-ACCOUNT-FILE-SW.
PERFORM PROCESS-NEXT
UNTIL EOF-ACCOUNT-FILE.
    . . .
PROCESS-NEXT.
    . . .
    READ ACCOUNT-FILE RECORD INTO WS-ACCOUNT-REC
        AT END MOVE 'Y' TO EOF-ACCOUNT-FILE-SW.
```

The next section of code retrieves the records for accounts in the 'DT' branch, in order by ascending *TYPE* values (since alternate key *GROUP-CODE* is composed of *BRANCH* and *TYPE*). There may be more than one record with *BRANCH* = 'DT' and a given *TYPE* value; these "duplicates" are retrieved in the order in which they were written to the file initially.

```
MOVE 'DT' TO BRANCH OF GROUP-CODE.
START ACCOUNT-FILE
    KEY EQUAL TO BRANCH OF GROUP-CODE
    INVALID KEY. . . .
READ ACCOUNT-FILE RECORD INTO WS-ACCOUNT-REC
    AT END MOVE 'Y' TO EOF-ACCOUNT-FILE-SW.
PERFORM PROCESS-NEXT
    UNTIL EOF-ACCOUNT-FILE
        OR BRANCH OF GROUP-CODE NOT = 'DT'.
```

```
    . . .
PROCESS-NEXT.
    . . .
```

> READ ACCOUNT-FILE RECORD INTO WS-ACCOUNT-REC
> AT END MOVE 'Y' TO EOF-ACCOUNT-FILE-SW.

The *INVALID KEY* condition is raised on the *START* if there are no records with *BRANCH* = 'DT'. The looping through the account records has two stopping conditions: reaching end-of-file and encountering the next *BRANCH* value after 'DT'. Without the second condition, the sequential read would continue until the file were exhausted. A sequential read based on an alternate key does not recognize breaks in the key's value.

The key of reference for retrieval can be changed from one record key to another by use of a *START* (specifying the desired record key), by a *WRITE*, or by a command that specifies random (i.e., direct) access to records of the file.

The random form of the *READ* verb for alternate-key access is:

> <u>READ</u> filename RECORD [<u>INTO</u> identifier]
>   [KEY IS dataname]
>   <u>INVALID</u> KEY imperative-statement.

If the *KEY* phrase is omitted, the *READ* is relative to the primary key for the file. If the *KEY* phrase is included, then *dataname* must be a record key for the file.

To access the account record for the customer whose *SOCNO* value is '123456789', the following statement is used:

> MOVE '123456789' TO SOCNO.
> READ ACCOUNT-FILE RECORD INTO WS-ACCOUNT-REC
>   KEY IS SOCNO
>   INVALID KEY DISPLAY 'NO RECORD FOR SOCNO
>   123456789'.

To retrieve the records for accounts in the 'DT' branch, in order by ascending *TYPE* values, starting with *TYPE* = '001', the following section of code could be used:

> MOVE 'DT001' TO GROUP-CODE.
> READ ACCOUNT-FILE RECORD INTO WS-ACCOUNT-REC
>   KEY IS GROUP-CODE
>   INVALID KEY. . . .
> PERFORM PROCESS-NEXT
>   UNTIL EOF-ACCOUNT-FILE
>   OR BRANCH OF GROUP-CODE NOT = 'DT'.

```
    . . .
PROCESS-NEXT.
    . . .
```

READ ACCOUNT-FILE RECORD INTO WS-ACCOUNT-REC
AT END MOVE 'Y' TO EOF-ACCOUNT-FILE-SW.

Compare this section of code with that given earlier (two examples previous) to retrieve records for accounts in the 'DT' branch, in order by ascending *TYPE* values. There the *START* was used with generic key *BRANCH*; here the entire alternate-key value is specified.

Thus random retrievals can be used to access data by any record-key value. The name of the record key in use is given in the *READ*'s *KEY* phrase. Subsequent sequential *READ*s proceed from that position according to the same record key, until changed by a *START*, a random *READ*, or other random-access verb action on the file.

The update of an alternate-key indexed sequential file is governed by the primary record key. The *INVALID KEY* condition is raised on a *WRITE* or *REWRITE* if the insertion or replacement would violate a constraint on duplicates.

COMPARISONS AND TRADE-OFFS

Both inverted files and multi-list files have:

- An index for each secondary key.
- An index entry for each distinct value of the secondary key.

In either file organization:

- The index may be tabular or tree-structured.
- The entries in an index may or may not be sorted.
- The pointers to data records may be direct or indirect.

The indexes differ in that:

- An entry in an inversion index has a pointer to each data record with that value.
- An entry in a multi-list index has a pointer to the first data record with that value.

Thus an inversion index may have variable-length entries whereas a multi-list index has fixed-length entries. In either organization:

- The data record pointers for a key value may or may not appear in some sorted order.
- Keeping entries in sorted order introduces overhead.

The data record file:

- Is not affected by having an inversion index built on top of it.
- Must contain the linked lists of records with identical secondary key values in the multi-list structure.

Some of the implications of these differences are the following:

- Index management is easier in the multi-list approach because entries are fixed in length.
- The inverted file approach tends to exhibit better inquiry performance. Many types of queries can be answered by accessing inversion indexes without necessitating access to data records, thereby reducing I/O-access requirements.
- Inversion of a file can be transparent to a programmer who accesses that file but does not use the inversion indexes, while a multi-list structure affects the file's record layout. The multi-list pointers can be made transparent to a programmer if the data manager does not make them available for programmer use and stores them at the end of each record.

Additionally, the multi-list structure has proven useful in linking together occurrences of different record types, thereby providing access paths based upon logical relationships. It is also possible to provide multiple sort orders through a single data collection, by linking the records together in order by various keys.

FILE DESIGN SUMMARY

We have now discussed the basic approaches to structuring collections of records so that the files can support our information systems' requirements. File design is a complex problem, in part because there are so many parameters that can be considered. (Fig. 204)

FIGURE 204

Data characteristics include:

- Record length
- Record format: fixed or variable
- Maximum record length
- Primary key and its value distribution
- Secondary keys and their value distributions
- Average number of records with given secondary key value
- Logical structure of data

Usage characteristics include:

- Frequency of query
- Frequency of update
- Growth expected
- Volatility of data values
- Batch versus interactive access
- Random versus sequential access
- Record orderings needed
- Response time required
- Variety of types of transactions
- Priorities of requirements

Storage characteristics include:

- Type of storage devices available
- Block sizes
- Average random access times
- Average sequential access times
- Cost of I/O access
- Main memory availability for buffers
- Cost of storage
- Available file organization methods
- Available access methods

The performance of a particular file design can be judged on the basis of factors such as:

- Expected and worst case response times
- Expected and worst case update times

- I/O-access requirements
- Storage space requirements
- Complexity of required support
- Maintenance requirements
- Availability of required support

Of course, the relative importance of each of these factors is application-dependent.

Terms

alternate key
alternate-key indexed sequential
binary search tree
B-tree
cellular multi-list file
completely inverted file
controlled-length multi-list file
direct addressing
indirect addressing

inversion index
inverted-file organization
multi-key file organization
multi-list file organization
partially inverted file
primary key
record key
secondary key

Review Exercises

1. Discuss the trade-offs that should be considered in designing an inversion index for a multi-key file.
2. Discuss the trade-offs that should be considered in designing an index for a multi-list file.
3. Why do most implementations of the alternate-key indexed sequential structure use an inverted approach rather than a multi-list approach?
4. Describe the kinds of requests that can be serviced by the index alone in an inverted file.
5. In some multi-list files, each index entry includes the length of the corresponding linked list. What kinds of requests would benefit by having this information available?
6. Discuss the advantages and disadvantages of giving the application programmer the responsibility for designing the files used in his or her programs, versus having another person bear the responsibility.
7. Discuss the relative advantages and disadvantages of using an inverted approach

and of using a multi-list approach to provide access to a file via a secondary key that may appear a variable number of times in each record of the file. Which approach would you use in this situation?

8. Find out what procedures and guidelines are followed in designing files at your installation.

9. Who has the responsibility for designing files at your installation?

10. Write a program to implement a multi-key file. Build several versions of the file, using different design parameters in each. Document the variations and compare the performance of the several versions.

11. Write a program that builds a multi-key file using inversion. Maintain your own inversion indexes. Write another program that builds a multi-key file using multi-lists. Maintain your own indexes and linked lists. Compare the performance of the resultant files with various types of activity, including record retrieval, insertion, and deletion.

CHAPTER 22

Introduction to Database Management

We have now spent a great deal of time and effort studying techniques for structuring collections of data, yet we have just begun to scratch the surface of the subject of data management. In this chapter we introduce the idea of database management, which builds upon the concepts of data structuring and file organization. Our final objective in this book is to understand how the principles that we have discussed in Chapters 1 through 21 relate to the world of database management.

DEFINITIONS AND REQUIREMENTS: DATABASES

A file-oriented data processing system is one in which data files are designed to support the processing requirements of application programs. Figure 205(a) depicts such an orientation. Each application program, represented by a box, "owns" its own files, and files are controlled by particular programs.

Very commonly, the data that are required to support one program are also required by another program. Sometimes both programs expect the same format and organization, but sometimes they do not. The result is replication of data across multiple files, for use by different programs.

As we discussed at the beginning of Chapter 21, data duplication is not attractive. It causes update inconsistency problems and it wastes storage space. Additionally, the file-oriented approach can make it diffi-

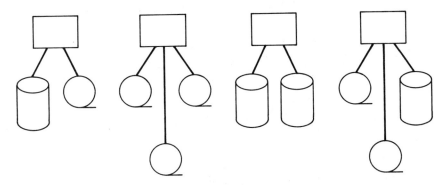

FIGURE 205(a)

cult to correlate and integrate data *across* application programs. Consider a vice-president's request for a "graph that correlates salespersons' salaries versus their revenue-generated-to-date figures." Presumably salespersons' salaries are stored in a payroll master file, and revenue data are buried in an accounts-receivable master file. Although the data exist, it may be quite a difficult task to overcome data format, coding, and organization incompatibilities to be able to respond to the user's request.

The ability of information systems to respond effectively to requests that cross traditional file and applications boundaries is becoming increasingly important. Top levels of management are demanding computer support for their decision-making activities. Everyone is becoming more and more aware of the potential power of computers and information systems.

One approach to avoiding the problems of update inconsistencies and integration difficulties encountered with the file orientation is to adopt a database orientation. Rather than structuring data files around each program's needs, the database orientation designs the data resource to meet *evolving* application requirements.

A *database* is a collection of logically related data that supports shared access by multiple users and is protected and managed to retain its value over time. Whereas a file contains data about one type of entity (say personnel, orders, customers, sales), a database contains data about multiple types of entities *and* information about how the entities are logically related to each other. The data are integrated, and there are multiple-access paths provided through the data.

One of the important tools for implementing the database orientation is a *database management system*, or *DBMS*, which acts as an interface between applications programs and the data that they process (Fig. 205(b)).

The DBMS shields applications programmers and users from details of physical database structuring and organization. More specifically, a DBMS provides facilities for:

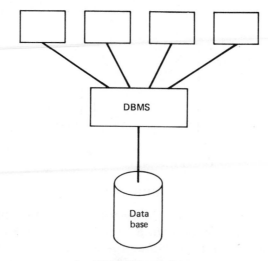

FIGURE 205(b)

- *Defining*, *representing*, and *storing* data so that they can be accessed later.
- *Organizing* data so that they can be selectively and efficiently accessed.
- *Interfacing* users with the data resource in manners that effectively support the users' decision-making environments.
- *Protecting* the data, including security, recovery, shared access control, and integrity protection mechanisms.

The DBMS maintains a stored description of the database structure and its contents; an application programmer need not recode these descriptions. The DBMS manages the internal implementation of the data; an application programmer need not maintain indexes and access paths. The DBMS provides appropriate interface facilities for users: natural, easy-to-learn query languages and report writers for noncomputer users and procedural languages for programmers. The DBMS provides access control, backup, concurrency, and data integrity protection; the application programmer need not build this functionality into each new program constructed.

Most of today's DBMS functions are implemented in software. In the future these functions will increasingly be provided in hardware or firmware (micro-code). Most of today's DBMS products work quite closely with and rely on operating system support. In the future, standalone DBMS's will appear. Some DBMS functions will also be incorporated directly into operating systems.

The market for DBMS products is well-established. Nearly every major operating system vendor offers a DBMS that is compatible with its operating system. Additionally, a number of software houses have developed and are marketing DBMS's.

DATABASE VIEWS

One of the basic tenets of the database approach is that there are several different ways of viewing data and that these views can be depicted as occurring at different levels (Fig. 206). *End-users* view data in terms of high-level entities, e.g., people, vehicles, warehouses, employment, orders. Formalization of the end-users' views results in the *external* database level. This level represents data in terms of entities, attributes of entities, and relationships among entities. A relationship (e.g., employment, which relates departments and people) may itself be an entity. The collection and integration of external views in an enterprise is the *conceptual* view. The *internal* level is the data structure and access path view of the database. The internal level may be expressed in terms of records and files, with pointers, linked lists, B-trees, indexes, and so forth. The *physical* database level is the memory manager's view of the database, represented in terms of pages, relative addresses, buckets, and so forth.

End-Users

External ⎫ Logical Views
Conceptual ⎭

Internal ⎫ Implementation
Physical ⎭   Views

FIGURE 206

Multiple levels of view are useful because different types of users need different types of database support. The levels provide for view integration while supporting view separation.

Database systems should be implemented in such a way that data independence is achieved. *Data independence* refers to separation of concerns of the various levels such that changes can be made to a lower-level view without causing a change at a higher level. For example, changing the amount of physical space allocated to the database should not cause changes to applications programs or users who access the database; changing an index from being implemented as an array to having a B-tree structure also should not cause changes to applications programs or users who access the database.

Achieving data independence is important to preserving the resiliency of the data resource. Data independence allows physical and internal implementation details to be changed to fine-tune the database's performance to match evolving requirements without forcing changes to users' and programmers' data views. Separation of logical and implementation concerns is of great importance in DBMS's, because one of the objectives of a DBMS is to protect the value of the data resource.

The data structures and file organization methods that we have discussed in this book are all techniques that are used to implement databases at the internal and physical levels. They are the techniques that provide access paths to the data. The primary difference between the internal processing of a file organization and of a database organization is that a database structure commonly requires access paths between multiple record types, while a file organization supplies access paths to a single record type.

LOGICAL DATABASE MODELS

We now briefly introduce three of the major approaches to formalizing the end-users' views of a database to form logical views. Here we will not distinguish between external and conceptual views, leaving that discussion to more advanced study.

The frameworks that are used to describe databases at the logical levels are called *models*. These models represent the subject database in terms of entities, attributes of entities, and relationships among entities. In some frameworks an attribute and/or a relationship can also be an entity.

The three logical database models that we briefly introduce here are:

1. The entity-relationship model
2. The relational model
3. The CODASYL model

Again, details of each are left to a more advanced text. Only the basic concepts are outlined here.

The Entity-Relationship Model

The entity-relationship model provides a graphical depiction of entities and relationships among entities. Three symbols are used (Fig. 207). Fig. 208(a) illustrates an *entity-relationship diagram* for a small database of student information. There are three types of entities:

- STUDENT

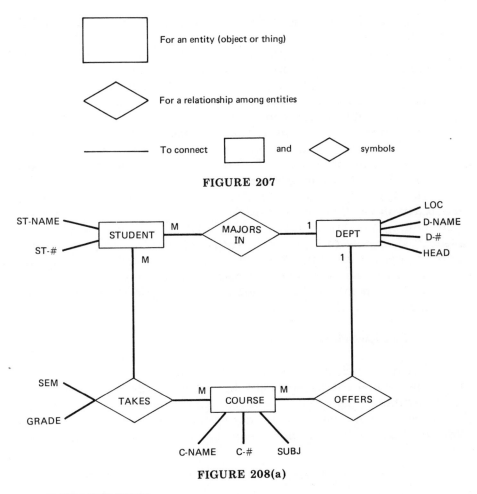

FIGURE 207

FIGURE 208(a)

- DEPARTMENT
- COURSE

Each of these entities has descriptors or attributes, which are shown on labeled lines outside the boxes. These are three types of relationships shown:

- MAJORS-IN, which relates STUDENT and DEPARTMENT
- TAKES, which relates STUDENT and COURSE
- OFFERS, which relates DEPARTMENT and COURSE

A relationship may have attributes. In this example, the TAKES relationship has attributes SEMESTER and GRADE, which indicate when a student took a particular course and what grade was earned.

Each relationship also bears an indication of how many entities are related. The MAJORS-IN relationship is STUDENT (M:1) DEPART-MENT; that is, a given student is associated with one department, but a department may have many (M) associated students. Such a relationship is said to be a *one-to-many* relationship. Another one-to-many relationship is OFFERS: a given course is offered by one department, but a given department can offer many courses.

The TAKES relationship is *many-to-many*; that is, a given student can take many courses and a given course can be taken by many students. Each pair of STUDENT–COURSE occurrences has associated SEMESTER and GRADE attributes.

This type of logical database model is far from the level of implementation detail that we discussed in the rest of this book! We have said nothing here about how an entity-relationship model would be implemented or how to translate an entity-relationship diagram to a supporting physical structure. The utility of a logical model is to formalize the *inherent* semantic meaning of data; it should be kept separate from eventual implementation of the internal and physical structures of the database.

The Relational Model

The relational model uses two-dimensional tables to depict entities. The columns of a relational table represent the corresponding entity's attributes. The rows represent actual values of those attributes. Relationships between entities occur when entities share attributes. Fig. 208(b) illustrates a *relational model* for the student information database.

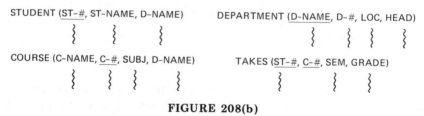

STUDENT (<u>ST-#</u>, ST-NAME, D-NAME) DEPARTMENT (<u>D-NAME</u>, D-#, LOC, HEAD)

COURSE (C-NAME, <u>C-#</u>, SUBJ, D-NAME) TAKES (<u>ST-#</u>, <u>C-#</u>, SEM, GRADE)

FIGURE 208(b)

There are four relations (tables):

- STUDENT
- DEPARTMENT
- COURSE
- TAKES

Each relation has one or more underscored attributes which comprise its *key*. The value of the key uniquely identifies rows in the relation's table. The relationship between students and departments is shown by the presence of the D-NAME attribute in the STUDENT relation. Each ST-# has one associated D-NAME; thus the one-to-manyness of the relationship. Similarly, the relationship between courses and departments is shown by the presence of the D-NAME attribute in the COURSE relation. Each C-# has one associated D-NAME.

The relationship between students and courses is shown by the TAKES relation. Both ST-# and C-# values are required to form the key; thus the many-to-many relationship between the entity identified by ST-# (student) and the entity identified by C-# (course).

The relational model includes operators for manipulation of relations. These operators allow rows of a table to be selected on the basis of their attribute values, columns of a table to be projected on the basis of attribute names, and rows of two tables to be joined on the basis of attribute values. There are several other relational operators, and numerous languages have been developed for interfacing with relational databases.

Again note that nothing has been said here about how relations are implemented, because such details are not the concern of a logical model.

The CODASYL Model

Another major model for structuring a logical database is the Conference on Data Systems Languages (CODASYL) model as specified in the Journal of Development of the CODASYL Data Definition Language Committee (DDLC). The model uses record types (depicted by boxes) to represent entities, data items to represent attributes, and sets (depicted by arrows) to represent relationships among entities. A *set* is a one-to-many relationship between an owner record type and a member record type. Fig. 208(c) gives a CODASYL model diagram for our example student database.

Here there are four record types:

- DEPARTMENT
- STUDENT
- COURSE
- TAKES

and four set types:

- MAJORS   owner: DEPARTMENT, member: STUDENT

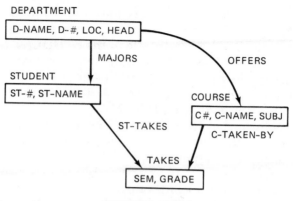

FIGURE 208(c)

- OFFERS   owner: DEPARTMENT, member: COURSE
- ST–TAKES   owner: STUDENT, member: TAKES
- C–TAKEN–BY   owner: COURSE, member: TAKES

MAJORS and OFFERS are one-to-many relationships between DE-
PARTMENT and STUDENT or COURSE respectively. The many-to-
many relationship between students and courses is shown by the combination of the ST–TAKES and C–TAKEN–BY sets. Those two sets
form a *confluent hierarchy*, because they share one base member record
type.

We have again omitted many details and nuances of the logical
model *and* we have said nothing about how such a logical structure
might be implemented at the internal and physical levels. The logical
model provides a design tool for understanding the inherent meaning of
a data resource. The logical model is then mapped to an internal structure and physical structure for implementation. Discussion of logical
models is an important part of most database texts.

DATABASE IMPLEMENTATION SUPPORT

The logical database models that we have just introduced can be translated to internal and physical structures that use linked lists, stacks, B^+-
trees, directories, hashing, and so forth. All of the material discussed
until this chapter is relevant to the implementation of databases. The
material on multi-key file organization is especially applicable, since the
multi-key structures build multiple access paths through the data, thus
supporting multiple users' access requirements.

We leave further discussion of database implementation support
to a more advanced text.

DATABASE MANAGEMENT SYSTEMS

The basic components of a DBMS are illustrated in Fig. 209. Not all commercially available DBMS's have this structure, but the processes shown are typical of database support tasks that must be accounted for.

The *description manager* maintains information that describes the logical and implementation structures of the database. Both types of description are needed, because user requests are phrased in terms of the logical views, yet the database is physically accessed according to the way it is implemented in storage.

The *interface-languages manager* provides support for the variety of languages that can be used to access the database. The languages commonly include a report writer, an interactive user-friendly nonprocedural language, and a procedural access facility. The latter may be embedded in a language such as COBOL, Fortran, PL/I, or Pascal.

The *access manager* provides the support required to actually access the physical database. It also provides protection against problems caused by concurrent access and by system failures. For instance, it may maintain backup database copies and journals of changes to the database.

The *communications manager* interfaces the rest of the DBMS to the interactive, outside world. It may provide screen formatting functions and manages messages that are to be presented to users at terminals.

The *database controller* is the heart of the DBMS. It coordinates

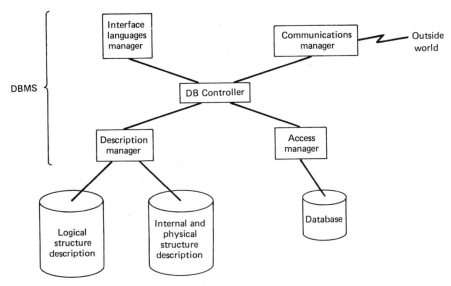

FIGURE 209

the activities of the other modules and ensures that the proper sequence of events occurs in response to user requests.

A DBMS is a complex set of software modules. However, your present understanding of the principles of data management and file processing should enable you to tackle the logical-level and implementation details of database systems.

Terms

access manager
CODASYL model
communications manager
conceptual database view
confluent hierarchy
database
database controller
database management system (DBMS)
data independence
description manager

entity-relationship model (ERM)
external database view
interface-languages manager
internal database view
many-to-many relationship
model
one-to-many relationship
physical database view
relational model
set

Review Exercises

1. Briefly describe the differences between a conventional file and a database.
2. What are the benefits of achieving data independence? Are there any costs? If so, what are they?
3. Why does use of the COBOL relative or indexed sequential file facilities not achieve data independence?
4. What DBMS packages are available for use at your installation?
5. Talk to a programmer who has worked both with a DBMS and without one. Find out what the differences are from the programmer's point of view.
6. Look through the current issue of *Datamation, Computerworld, MIS Week,* or some other data processing business publication. Identify all the DBMS products advertised or mentioned and their vendors.
7. Look through classified advertisements for data processing personnel. Identify the positions that are available for people with database knowledge and experience.
8. Take a course or read a book about database management.

Glossary

ABSOLUTE ADDRESSING. A technique for mapping records to storage where the key value is the record's actual address on secondary storage. Compare with *relative addressing*.

ACCESS MANAGER. The component of a DBMS that provides support to access the physical database.

ACCESS MECHANISM. The means for reading and/or writing data representations from and/or onto a storage medium.

ACTIVITY GRAPH. A graph representing the precedence required and parallelism possible among a set of activities or tasks; commonly the nodes of the graph represent activities and the edges represent precedence requirements.

ACYCLIC GRAPH. A graph that has no cycles. See *cycle*.

ADJACENCY MATRIX. A matrix used to represent the structure of a graph; $A(i,j) = 1$ if and only if edge (v_i, v_j) is in the set of edges for the graph, and 0 otherwise, where v_i and v_j are nodes of the graph.

ALMOST-COMPLETE BINARY TREE. A binary tree with K ($K \geqslant 2$) levels, where levels 0 through $K - 2$ are full and level $K - 1$ is being filled left to right.

ALPHABET. A set of elementary symbols, which in combination form the words of a vocabulary.

ALTERNATE KEY. See *secondary key*.

ALTERNATE-KEY INDEXED SEQUENTIAL. A COBOL multi-key file organization which builds secondary-key indexes upon an indexed sequential file.

ANTICIPATORY BUFFERING. A buffer management technique whereby data are read into a buffer before they are actually requested by a program. Compare with *demand buffering*.

ARC. See *edge*.

ARRAY. Finite, ordered set of homogeneous elements; a two-dimensional array is commonly referred to as a table.

ASCII. (American Standard Code for Information Interchange). A 7-bit character-encoding scheme developed as a standard for data transmission and now widely used for data representation in volatile and nonvolatile storage.

AUXILIARY MEMORY. See *secondary storage device*.

AVL TREE. A height-balanced binary tree; for each node R_i of the tree, the height of the left subtree of R_i and the height of the right subtree of R_i differ by at most 1.

BALANCED MERGE. A merge technique that uses an equal number of input devices and output devices.

BATCH MODE. The processing of transactions accumulated over a period of time. Compare with *interactive mode*.

BB TREE. See *bounded-balance tree*.

BINARY SEARCH. A search technique that is applied to a list of ordered keys. At each step of the search the list is partitioned into two equal parts, with the selection of the appropriate partition to probe in the next step made on the basis of relative key values.

BINARY SEARCH TREE. A binary tree where for each node R_i, all names of nodes in the left subtree of R_i precede the name labeling R_i, and the name labeling R_i precedes all names of nodes in the right subtree of R_i. A special case of m-way search tree, where $m = 2$.

BINARY TREE. A tree where the maximum out-degree of each node is 2, and leftness and rightness are imposed upon the subtrees of each node.

BIT STRING. A finite sequence of symbols derived from the alphabet $\{0,1\}$.

BLOCK. A collection of contiguous records recorded as a unit; sometimes called a *physical record*.

BLOCK MULTIPLEXOR CHANNEL. A channel that can execute one instruction of the channel program for one device, then can switch to perform an instruction of another device's channel program. Compare with *selector channel* and *multiplexor channel*.

BLOCKING FACTOR. Number of records per block, also sometimes number of characters per block.

BOOLEAN DATA TYPE. A primitive data type with value taken from the set $\{true, false\}$ and with fundamental operators: *not*, *and*, and *or*.

BOOLEAN OPERATOR. An operator with one or more operands of data type boolean; the fundamental boolean operators are defined by Table 2 in the text.

BOUNDED-BALANCE TREE (BB tree). A binary tree in which a designer-selected bound value (β) constrains the difference between the number of nodes in any node's left subtree and its right subtree, for $0 < \beta \leq \frac{1}{2}$.

BREADTH-FIRST. A method of graph traversal in which one node is selected as the starting point, it is visited, then all nodes adjacent to that node are visited, then nodes adjacent to those nodes are visited, and so on until the entire graph has been traversed. Compare with *depth-first*.

B*-TREE. A special case of B-tree in which each node is at least two-thirds full instead of at least one-half full.

B$^+$-TREE. A tree resembling a B-tree but in which there is a linked list connecting the leaf nodes. When a B$^+$-tree is used as an index, indexed key values appear in the leaf nodes; the interior nodes provide relatively direct access to the leaf nodes.

B-TREE OF ORDER m. A special case of m-way search tree in which each nonroot and nonleaf node have between $\lceil \frac{1}{2}m \rceil$ and m subtrees, the root has either zero or at least two subtrees, and all leaf nodes are on the same level.

BUBBLE SORT. An internal sort in which each key floats up to its proper position through a series of pairwise comparisons and exchanges with adjacent key values; requires $\sigma(N^2)$ comparisons to sort N key values.

BUCKET ADDRESSING. A technique for managing records on storage where a record's key value is mapped to an area of space (bucket) that can hold multiple records.

BUFFER. An area of storage reserved for use in performing input/output operations, into which data are read and from which data are written; used to compensate for a difference in the rate of flow of data between devices.

CASCADE MERGE. A merge technique that uses a decreasing number of input devices at each phase of a pass, temporarily retiring intermediate output files to be input at the start of the next pass.

CELLULAR MULTI-LIST FILE. A multi-list file in which no linked list crosses a boundary between physical cell areas (e.g., a cell may be a disk cylinder).

CHANNEL. A device that connects the processing unit and main memory with the I/O control units.

CHANNEL PROGRAM. The instructions that are executed by a channel to access devices and control data pathways.

CHARACTER DATA TYPE. A primitive data type with value taken from an alphabet; the basic element of the string data type.

CIRCULARLY LINKED LIST. A linked list in which the last node points to the first node or the header node of the list.

CODASYL MODEL. A framework proposed by a committee of the Conference on Data Systems Languages for describing the logical structure of databases in terms of record and set types.

COLLISION. Situation occurring when two unequal key values map to the same address.

COLLISION RESOLUTION TECHNIQUE. A technique applied to determine an alternative address for a key value when a collision occurs.

COMMUNICATIONS MANAGER. The component of a system that interfaces the DBMS to the outside, interactive world.

COMPLEMENT REPRESENTATION. An approach used to represent integer values, where a non-negative integer X is represented in its true form (i.e., X) and a negative integer $-X$ is represented in its complement form (i.e., $R - X$) for some complementation constant R. The complement representations of all integers are non-negative. Compare to *sign-and-magnitude representation*.

COMPLETE BINARY TREE. A binary tree that contains the maximum number of nodes possible for its height.

COMPLETELY INVERTED FILE. A file structure which includes an inversion index for every field of the records. Compare with *partially inverted file*.

CONCATENATION. An operator with two string operands, producing a string result. If $S =$ '$a_1 a_2 \ldots a_N$' and $S^0 =$ '$b_1 b_2 \ldots b_M$', then CONCAT (S, S^0) is '$a_1 a_2 \ldots a_N b_1 b_2 \ldots b_M$'.

CONCEPTUAL DATABASE VIEW. An enterprise view of a logical database.

CONFLUENT HIERARCHY. Two or more hierarchies that share a single base.

CONNECTED GRAPH. A graph that cannot be partitioned into two graphs without removing at least one edge.

CONTROL INTERVAL. A data block in an IBM VSAM (indexed sequential) file.

CONTROLLED-LENGTH MULTI-LIST FILE. A multi-list file in which no linked list exceeds a specified length.

CONTROLLER. A device that controls input/output operations at one or more devices.

CRITICAL PATH. The longest path in an activity graph.

CROSS-SECTION. A subset of an array, obtained by holding one (or more) of the subscripts at a constant value while varying the remaining subscripts through their entire ranges of values.

CYCLE. A path in a graph where both (1) no edge appears more than once in the sequence of edges, and (2) the initial node of the path is the same as the terminal node of the path.

CYLINDER. In a disk pack, the set of all tracks with the same distance from the axis about which the disk pack rotates; the tracks of a cylinder can be accessed without repositioning the access mechanism.

CYLINDER ADDRESSING. A technique for addressing the data records on a disk, where a record's address is its cylinder number, surface number, and record number. Compare with *sector addressing*.

CYLINDER INDEX. In an indexed sequential file, an index to the key values stored on each cylinder allocated to the file.

DATABASE. A collection of logically related data that supports shared access by multiple users and is protected and managed to retain its value over time.

DATABASE CONTROLLER. The central component of a DBMS; it coordinates the activities of the other components and ensures that the proper sequence of events occurs in response to user requests.

DATABASE MANAGEMENT SYSTEM (DBMS). An interface between programs and data, with responsibility for defining, representing, storing, organizing, and protecting data, as well as for interfacing users with the database.

DATA INDEPENDENCE. Immunity of users and applications to changes in data storage structures and access mechanisms, achieved by separating logical and physical concerns.

DEDICATED DEVICE. A device that is suitable for access by only one user at a time. Compare with *shared device*.

DEMAND BUFFERING. A buffer management technique whereby data are read into a buffer only when they are actually requested by a program. Compare with *anticipatory buffering*.

DENSE INDEX. An index that contains all the key values of the data collection being indexed. Compare with *sparse index*.

DEPTH-FIRST. A method of graph traversal in which one node is selected as the starting point, it is visited, then all nodes on one path leading from that node are visited, then all nodes on another path leading from the start node are visited, and so on until the entire graph has been traversed. Compare with *breadth-first*.

DESCRIPTION MANAGER. The component of a DBMS that maintains information describing the logical and implementation structures of the databases.

DIRECT ACCESS. The ability to access any of a collection of records without necessitating access to physically preceding records. Compare with *serial access*.

DIRECT-ACCESS STORAGE DEVICE (DASD). A storage device that supports direct access. Commonly refers to magnetic disk storage.

DIRECT ADDRESSING. Addressing or indexing that maps a record's key value directly to a corresponding relative or absolute address. Compare with *indirect addressing*.

DIRECTED GRAPH. A graph in which directionality is assigned to the edges; an edge has its source in one node and terminates in another node; each node then has both an in-degree and an out-degree.

DIRECTORY. (a) See *index* (b).
(b) A structure used to manage identification and location information about files or records.

DIRECTORY LOOKUP ADDRESSING. A technique for managing access to records whereby an index is used as an intermediary between key values and record addresses.

DISK DRIVE. A mechanism for moving a disk pack or single magnetic disk and for controlling its movements.

DISKETTE. A thin, flexible magnetic disk and a semirigid protective jacket in which the disk is permanently enclosed. Also called *floppy disk*.

DISK PACK. An assembly of magnetic disks.

DIVISION-REMAINDER HASHING. An address-calculation technique whereby the key value is divided by an appropriate number and the remainder is used as the record's relative address.

DOUBLE BUFFERING. A buffer management technique whereby two buffers are allocated to accommodate the input/output activity for a file.

DOUBLE HASHING. A collision resolution technique whereby a second hash function is applied to the key value. Compare with *linear probing*.

DOUBLY LINKED LIST. A linked list in which each node points to both the next node and the prior node in the list; a doubly linked list is not necessarily circular.

DYNAMIC HASHING. A virtual hashing technique that uses a binary tree index structure to keep track of buckets and to guide access to records. Compare with *extendible hashing*.

EARLIEST START TIME. The earliest possible trigger time for a node in an activity graph. Compare with *latest start time*.

EBCDIC (Extended Binary Coded Decimal Interchange Code). An 8-bit character encoding scheme widely used for both data storage and data transmission purposes.

EDGE. An elementary component of a graph, providing a connection between two nodes; depicted by a line. Also called *arc*.

ELEMENTARY ITEM. A field that is not decomposable to component fields.

END-OF-TAPE MARK. A mark on a magnetic tape used to indicate the end of the area where recording is permissible.

ENTITY-RELATIONSHIP MODEL (ERM). A framework for describing the logical structure of databases in terms of entities, relationships, and attributes.

EQUIVALENCE CLASS. A set of key values that are synonyms.

EVEN PARITY. A technique in which an extra bit is appended to the representation of each character and is set such that the number of 1-bits for the character is even. Compare with *odd parity*.

EXCHANGE SELECTION SORT. A variation on a straight selection sort in which the selected key value is moved to its final position by being exchanged with the key initially occupying that position; sorts in place; requires $\sigma(N^2)$ comparisons to sort N key values.

EXCHANGE SORT. One of a family of internal sort algorithms in which pairs of key values are compared and exchanged if they are not in the proper relative positions.

EXTENDIBLE HASHING. A virtual hashing technique that uses a tabular directory based on a degenerate trie structure to keep track of buckets and to guide access to records. Compare with *dynamic hashing*.

EXTERNAL DATABASE VIEW. An application or end-user's view of a logical database.

EXTERNAL LABEL. A label affixed to the exterior of a storage medium, used to identify the medium to humans.

EXTERNAL SORT. A method for arranging a collection of keys into a specified order, where the collection resides on an auxiliary storage device. Also called a *file sort*. Compare with *internal sort*.

FIELD. A specified area of a record used to represent a particular category of information.

FIELD ACTIVITY RATIO. The ratio of the number of records with activity during the period to the total number of records on the file.

FILE. A collection of logically related record occurrences that are treated as a unit; commonly stored on a secondary storage device.

FILE ORGANIZATION. The technique used to represent and store the records on a file.

FILE SORT. See *external sort*.

FIRST-IN-FIRST-OUT (FIFO). A method of linear list management in which the first element into the list will be the first element taken out of the list; defines the mode of operation of a queue. Compare with *last-in-first-out*.

FIXED-HEAD DISK. A disk in which there is one read/write head per track; the access mechanism never has to be moved. Compare with *movable-head disk*.

FLOPPY DISK. See *diskette*.

FOREST. A collection of rooted trees.

GENERATION FILE. One of multiple versions of a file created during successive cycles of processing.

GENERIC KEY. The leading portion of a key field.

GRAPH. A collection of nodes and edges, where each edge connects a pair of nodes.

GRAPH ORDER. The number of nodes in a graph.

GROUP ITEM. A field that is decomposable into component elementary and/or group items.

HASH FUNCTION. Calculation applied to a key value to obtain an address.

HASHING. An address calculation technique. Also known as *hash table method*, *direct addressing technique*, *key-to-address transformation method*, *randomizing technique*, *scatter storage technique*.

HEAD CRASH. Situation occurring when a read/write head comes into contact with the recording surface of a disk.

HEIGHT-BALANCED TREE. See *AVL tree*.

HIT RATIO. The percentage of records accessed by a given request or set of requests.

HOME ADDRESS. The address to which a key value hashes.

IN-DEGREE. The number of edges directed into a node in a directed graph. Compare with *out-degree*.

INDEX. (a) See *subscript*.
　　　　(b) A collection of key value, address pairs, used to facilitate access to a collection of records.

INDEXED SEQUENTIAL FILE ORGANIZATION. A file organization technique that supports both sequential and direct access to records by a key field.

INDIRECT ADDRESSING. Addressing or indexing that maps a key value to an intermediary value which is then mapped (sometimes via indexing) to a record's relative or absolute address. Compare with *direct addressing*.

INFIX NOTATION. A method of representing an arithmetic expression whereby a binary operator appears between its operands. Compare with *postfix* and *prefix notations*.

IN-ORDER TRAVERSAL. A method of visiting all the nodes of a binary tree, where the left subtree is first traversed in in-order, then the root is visited, then the right subtree is traversed in in-order. Compare with *pre-order* and *post-order traversals*.

INPUT FILE. A file that is read, but not written, by a program. Compare with *output file* and *input/output file*.

INPUT/OUTPUT FILE. A file that is both read from and written to by a program. Compare with *input file* and *output file*.

INSERTION SORT. One of a family of internal sort algorithms in which the next logically sequential key in the unsorted list is selected and then inserted into its proper relative position in a growing sorted list.

INTEGER DATA TYPE. A member of the following set of numbers:

$$\{\ldots, -(n+1), -n, \ldots, -2, -1, 0, 1, 2, \ldots, n, n+1, \ldots\}$$

INTERACTIVE MODE. The processing of transactions as they occur. Compare with *batch mode*.

INTERBLOCK GAP. The space between two consecutive blocks on a storage medium.

INTERFACE-LANGUAGES MANAGER. The component of a DBMS that provides support for the variety of languages that can be used to access a database.

INTERNAL DATABASE VIEW. The data structure and access path view of a physical database.

INTERNAL LABEL. A record of identifying information recorded with a file on a storage medium.

INTERNAL SORT. A method for arranging a collection of keys into a specified order, where the collection resides entirely in main memory. Compare with *external sort*.

INTERNAL SORT PHASE. In an external sort, the phase in which an internal sort technique is used to sort records into several runs and to distribute those runs onto two or more storage devices.

INVERSION INDEX. An index containing all the values that a primary or secondary key has in the data file and (direct or indirect) pointers to all of the data records that have the corresponding values.

INVERTED FILE ORGANIZATION. A multi-key file organization technique that uses inversion indices.

I/O CONTROL SYSTEM. A group of routines that provide support to programs, enabling them to access files without being concerned about details of physical storage characteristics and device timings.

I/O SUPERVISOR. The part of an operating system that provides input/output (I/O) control.

ITERATIVE PROCEDURE. A procedure that repeatedly executes a series of steps but that does not invoke itself; compare with *recursive* procedure.

KEY. (a) The identifying field of a record.
(b) The field whose value is used to place a collection of records into a sorted ordering.

KEY-SEQUENCED DATA SET. IBM VSAM term for the data records in an indexed sequential file; a control interval containing records in ascending order by a given key.

LABELED TAPE. A tape that includes an internal label.

LAST-IN-FIRST-OUT (LIFO). A method of linear list management in which the element most recently added to the list will be the next element to be taken out of the list; defines the mode of operation of a stack; compare with *first-in-first-out*.

LATENCY. See *rotational delay*.

LATEST START TIME. The latest possible trigger time for a node in an activity graph, where the entire graph will complete in its shortest possible time. Compare with *earliest start time*.

LEAF NODE. A node of a tree or graph with out-degree zero.

LEFT THREAD. A link from a node in a binary tree to its predecessor node in a traversal ordering. Compare with *right thread*.

LINEAR LIST. A general data structure comprised of an ordered set of elements; for each element there is a single "next" element; compare with *tree*.

LINEAR PROBING. A collision resolution technique in which a search for an empty location proceeds serially from the record's home address. Compare with *double hashing*.

LINEAR SEARCH. A technique applied to find the record of a collection with a particular key value; views the collection as a linear list and starts at the beginning of the linear list, sequentially comparing each record's key value with the sought key value until the target record is found or the end of the list is reached; requires $o(N)$ comparisons to search a collection of N key values. Also known as a *sequential search*.

LINKED LIST. A data structure in which the ordering of elements is indicated by the use of direct or indirect pointers rather than by physical sequentiality.

LOAD FACTOR. The percentage of the space allocated to a file that is actually in use holding records.

LOAD POINT. The beginning of the permissible recording area on a reel of magnetic tape.

LOOP. An edge that connects a node in a graph to itself.

LOWER BOUND. The minimum value that a subscript may validly have; compare with *upper bound*.

MAGNETIC DISK STORAGE. A direct-access storage device in which data are recorded by magnetic means on the surfaces of one or more flat, rotating disks.

MAGNETIC TAPE STORAGE. A serial-access storage device in which data are recorded by magnetic means on the surface of a tape that moves longitudinally.

MAIN MEMORY. See *primary storage device*.

MANY-TO-MANY RELATIONSHIP. A data relationship in which many occurrences of an entity type are related to many occurrences of another entity type. Compare with *one-to-many relationship*.

MASS STORAGE. Very large-capacity storage device.

MASTER FILE. A file that contains relatively permanent data; represents a view of some aspect of an organization's business at a point in time.

MASTER INDEX. In an indexed sequential file, an index to the key values indexed by each cylinder index for the file.

MERGE. The combination of records in two or more files that are both in the same sorted order to form one file that is also in that sorted order.

MERGE DEGREE. The number of files input to a merge.

MERGE PHASE. In an external sort, the phase in which the sorted runs are combined to form a single sorted run.

MINI-DISK. A disk storage device with a relatively small (typically 5-inch) diameter.

MINIMAL SPANNING TREE. A minimum cost spanning tree for a graph. See *spanning tree*.

MODEL. A framework used to formally describe something.

MOVABLE-HEAD DISK. A disk in which there is one read/write head per recording surface; the access mechanism must be moved from cylinder to cylinder. Compare with *fixed-head disk*.

MULTIGRAPH. A graph that is not simple. The graph has at least one loop or there is at least one pair of nodes n_i and n_j such that there are two or more edges connecting the pair.

MULTI-KEY FILE ORGANIZATION. A file organization technique that supports direct access to records by two or more key fields.

MULTI-LIST FILE ORGANIZATION. A multi-key file organization technique that maintains an index for each key. The index contains all values that the key has in the data file and a pointer to a linked list of data records with that key value.

MULTIPLEXOR CHANNEL. A channel on which several devices can be active simultaneously, but which must complete execution of the channel program for one device before starting another device's channel program. Compare with *selector channel* and *block multiplexor channel*.

M-WAY SEARCH TREE. A tree in which each node has out-degree $< = M$, each node is composed of a set of pointers and key values, and the key values are arranged in a specific manner that facilitates searches through the pointer structures. See *binary search tree* for a special case.

NATURAL MERGE. A merge technique that uses one output device and a constant number of input devices.

NODE. An elementary component of a graph or tree; depicted by a point. Also called *vertex*.

NONVOLATILE STORAGE. A storage device whose contents are not lost when power is removed. Compare with *volatile storage*.

NULL. The value given to a pointer variable that is empty, i.e., that points nowhere; also called *nil* in Pascal.

$\sigma(N)$. "on the order of N"—approximately N.

$\sigma(N^2)$. "on the order of N^2"—approximately N squared.

$\sigma(N\log_2 N)$. "on the order of $(N\log_2 N)$"—approximately N times the log base 2 of N.

ODD PARITY. An error-control technique in which an extra bit is appended to the representation of each character and is set such that the number of 1-bits for the character is odd. Compare with *even parity*.

ONE-TO-MANY RELATIONSHIP. A data relationship in which many occurrences of an entity type are related to one occurrence of another entity type. Compare with *many-to-many relationship*.

OPEN ADDRESSING. An approach to collision resolution whereby synonyms are all stored in the file's primary address space. Compare with *separate-overflow addressing*.

OUT-DEGREE. The number of edges coming out of a node in a directed graph. Compare with *in-degree*.

OUTPUT FILE. A file that is written, but not read, by a program. Compare with *input file* and *input/output file*.

OVERFLOW DATA AREA. An auxiliary file that contains records that do not fit in the prime data area.

PACKED-DECIMAL REPRESENTATION. A scheme for storing numeric data values, where two digits occupy 8 bits; compare with an *unpacked representation*, whereby the two digits would occupy 16 bits.

PACKED STRING REPRESENTATION. A scheme for storing string data values, whereby each of the successive codes for the characters of a string are placed in successive words of storage, with as many of the characters as possible in any given word. Compare with *unpacked string representation*.

PADDING. (a) Space inserted into a record for purposes of ensuring the correct alignment of fields on appropriate word boundaries. Also called *slack bytes*.

(b) Allocated space intentionally left empty when a file is created, for purposes of accommodating future additions to the file.

PARALLEL HEAD-PER-TRACK DRIVE. A fixed-head disk drive in which one head on each of the surfaces can be active simultaneously.

PARITY. An error-control technique by which one redundant bit is appended to the representation of each character. See *odd parity* and *even parity*.

PARTIALLY INVERTED FILE. A file structure including an inversion index on one or more, but not all, fields of the records. Compare with *completely inverted file*.

PARTITION-EXCHANGE SORT. An exchange sort. At each step of the sort the list is partitioned into two parts such that the key values in one partition are all less than a particular key value and key values in the other partition are all greater than that particular key value; the partitions are then treated independently in following steps of the sort. Also called *quicksort*.

PATH. A sequence of one or more edges that connects two nodes in a graph.

PATH LENGTH. The number of edges in a path.

PHYSICAL DATABASE VIEW. The memory manager's view of a database, in terms of pages, relative addresses, buckets, and so forth.

PHYSICAL RECORD. See *block*.

POINTER VARIABLE. A variable whose value must be an address or null.

POLYPHASE MERGE. A merge technique that uses a constant number of input devices and recycles each output device as an input device in the next phase of a pass.

POP. To remove an element from a stack; see also *last-in-first-out*. Compare with *push*.

POSTFIX NOTATION. A method of representing an arithmetic expression whereby a binary operator appears after its operands. Compare with *infix notation* and *prefix notation*.

POST-ORDER TRAVERSAL. A method of visiting all the nodes of a binary tree whereby the left subtree is first traversed in post-order, then the right subtree is traversed in post-order, then the root is visited. Compare with *in-order* and *pre-order traversals*.

PREFIX NOTATION. A method of representing an arithmetic expression whereby a binary operator appears before its operands. Compare with *infix* and *postfix notations*.

PRE-ORDER TRAVERSAL. A method of visiting all the nodes of a binary tree whereby the root is visited first, then the left subtree is traversed in pre-order, then the right subtree is traversed in pre-order. Compare with *in-order* and *post-order traversals*.

PRIMARY KEY. The main key field of a multi-key file. In an alternate-key indexed sequential file, the field for which direct and sequential access are supported.

PRIMARY STORAGE DEVICE. A storage device with the property that the time required to access the contents of one location is the same as the time required to access the contents of any other location of the memory. Also called *main memory*. Compare with *secondary storage device*.

PRIME DATA AREA. The main space allocated to a file.

PROGRAM FILE. A file that contains instructions for processing.

PUSH. To add an element to a stack; see also *last-in-first-out*. Compare with *pop*.

QUERY LANGUAGE. An end-user-oriented language for retrieving selected data from a file or database.

QUERY PROCESSOR. Software that translates a user's requests (phrased in a query language) into instructions that can be used directly for file or database access.

QUEUE. A linear list in which elements are added only to the rear of the list and are removed only from the front of the list; see also *first-in-first-out*.

QUEUEING THEORY. A formal analytic body of knowledge about the behavior of systems that involve queues.

QUICKSORT. See *partition-exchange sort*.

RANGE. (a) Of an array: the number of elements in the array.
(b) Of a subscript: the set of values that the subscript may validly have.

REACHABILITY MATRIX. A matrix used to represent the paths that exist between each pair of nodes in a graph; $R(i,j) = 1$ if and only if there is a path between nodes v_i and v_j in the graph. See also *transitive closure*.

RECORD. (a) A finite, ordered collection of possibly heterogeneous elements (fields) that are treated as a unit. Also called a *structure*.
(b) A collection of logically related fields treated as a unit.

RECORD KEY. A primary or secondary key.

RECURSIVE PROCEDURE. A procedure in which each step makes use of the results of earlier steps, generally by invoking execution of some part of itself; compare with *iterative procedure*.

RELATIONAL MODEL. A framework for describing the logical structure of a database in terms of tables.

RELATIVE ADDRESSING. A technique for mapping records to storage whereby a key value is mapped to the record's ordinal position in the file. Compare with *absolute addressing*.

RELATIVE FILE ORGANIZATION. A file organization technique that supports access directly to records by a key field.

REPORT FILE. A file containing data that are formatted for presentation to an end-user.

REPORT-WRITER PACKAGE. A software product that translates a user-oriented request for a report into instructions that are used directly for file access.

RIGHT THREAD. A link from a node in a binary tree to its successor node in a traversal ordering. Compare with *left thread*.

ROOTED TREE. A tree in which one node (called the root) is distinguished from the other nodes.

ROTATION. A type of restructuring applied to a tree to return it to a state of balance.

ROTATIONAL DISPLAY. The time required for an addressed block to appear under the read/write head of a rotating disk.

RUN. A sorted sequence.

SEARCH ARGUMENT. The value of the key of a record that is being sought.

SEARCHING. The process of trying to find the record or records that meet a given criterion.

SECONDARY KEY. In a multi-key file, any key field except the primary key.

SECONDARY STORAGE DEVICE. A storage device with the property that the time required to access the contents of one location may be different from the time required to access the contents of another location on the same device; generally slower and cheaper per bit than a primary storage device. Also called *auxiliary memory*.

SECTOR. That part of a track on a disk that can be accessed by the read/write heads in the course of a predetermined rotational displacement of the particular device.

SECTOR ADDRESSING. A technique for addressing the data records on a disk, whereby a record's address is its sector number, record number. Compare with *cylinder addressing*.

SEEK TIME. The time required for the read/write heads of a disk to be positioned at the appropriate cylinder.

SELECTOR CHANNEL. A channel that can manage data flow between main memory and only one device at a time.

SEPARATE-OVERFLOW ADDRESSING. An approach to collision resolution whereby all records that cannot be stored at their home addresses are stored in a separate file from the file's primary address space. Compare with *open addressing*.

SEQUENCE SET. The leaves of a B^+-tree.

SEQUENTIAL FILE ORGANIZATION. A file organization technique that supports serial access to records.

SEQUENTIAL SEARCH. See *linear search*.

SERIAL ACCESS. Access in physically consecutive order. Compare with *direct access*.

SERIAL-ACCESS DEVICE. A storage device that supports serial access. Compare with *direct-access storage device*.

SET. In the CODASYL database model, a construct that represents a one-to-many relationship between two record types.

SHARED DEVICE. A device that supports concurrent access by multiple users.

SIGN-AND-MAGNITUDE REPRESENTATION. A human-oriented approach for representation of numeric values, where a number is represented by a sign (+ or −) and a string of digits that represent its absolute value (i.e., its magnitude). Compare with *complement representation*.

SIMPLE GRAPH. A graph that has no loops and in which no pair of nodes is connected by more than one edge. Compare with *multigraph*.

SIMULATION. The use of programming techniques to represent certain features of the behavior of a physical or abstract system.

SLACK BYTES. See *padding* (a).

SORTED FILE. A file in which the records are ordered logically by value of a sort key.

SORTING. The process of arranging a collection of keys (and records) into a specified order.

SORT KEY. A field (elementary or group item) whose value is used to order records of a collection.

SORT/MERGE. See *external sort*.

SPANNING TREE. A tree that contains all the nodes of a graph and no other nodes; its branches are a subset of the graph's edges.

SPARSE ARRAY. An array with a relatively high density of elements with value zero.

SPARSE INDEX. An index that contains a proper subset of the key values of the data collection being indexed. Compare with *dense index*.

SPOOLING. The use of buffers on auxiliary memory to reduce the effects of timing differences between the central processing unit and peripheral equipment, commonly line printers.

STABLE SORT. A sort in which the original ordering of records with equal keys is preserved in the sorted ordering of those records.

STACK. A linear list in which elements are added to and removed from only the top of the list; see also *last-in-first-out*.

STORAGE MEDIUM. Physical material that holds data representations.

STRICTLY TRIANGULAR ARRAY. An upper-triangular array or a lower-triangular array in which the elements on the diagonal all have value zero.

STRING. A finite sequence of symbols taken from an alphabet.

STRING LENGTH. The number of symbols (i.e., characters) in a string; length is a fundamental attribute of a string.

STRUCTURE. See *record* (a).

SUBSCRIPT. A value that designates the ordinal position of an element in an array. Also called an *index* (a).

SYNONYM CHAINING. An approach to collision resolution in which access to synonyms is facilitated by maintaining a linked list of the records in an equivalence class.

SYNONYMS. Two or more unequal key values that hash to the same home address. See also *equivalence class*.

SYNTAX. Grammar; rules for the formation of the allowable strings of a vocabulary.

THREADED TREE. A tree that includes a linked list of the nodes according to a tree traversal ordering.

TOURNAMENT SORT. An internal sort; a repeated selection sort in which each sublist consists of no more than two keys; the sublists are organized into a binary tree for purposes of determining the elements in the next subject sublist. Also called *tree-selection sort*.

TRANSACTION FILE. A file of activity records to be processed against a master file.

TRANSITIVE CLOSURE. The sum of all powers of a graph's adjacency matrix; see also *reachability matrix*.

TRANSPOSE. Of a two-dimensional array: the array obtained by reversing the subscript positions. The transpose of an N-by-M array is an M-by-N array.

TREE. An acyclic, simple, connected graph.

TREE HEIGHT. One plus the number of the highest level on which the tree has non-null nodes, where the root is on level zero.

TREE-SELECTION SORT. See *tournament sort*.

TREE TRAVERSAL. A method for visiting all the nodes of a tree, whereby each node is visited once and only once. See also *in-order*, *post-order*, and *pre-order* traversals.

TREE WEIGHT. The number of leaf nodes in a tree.

TRIANGULAR ARRAY. An array in which all elements either above or below the diagonal have value zero.

TRIE. A general tree structure in which the node structure is based on the radix of the key values and searches through the tree are based upon representations of key values as sequences of characters rather than as key values themselves.

UNPACKED STRING REPRESENTATION. A scheme for storing string data values, whereby each of the successive codes for the characters of the string are placed in successive words of storage, with one character per word. Compare with *packed string representation*.

UPPER BOUND. The maximum value that a subscript may validly have; compare with *lower bound*.

VECTOR. A one-dimensional array.

VERTEX. See *node*.

VIRTUAL DEVICE. A device that does not physically exist.

VIRTUAL HASHING. Any hashing technique that may dynamically change its hash function.

VOCABULARY. The set of all possible strings that can be obtained from an alphabet. The vocabulary that is derived from alphabet A is denoted A^* (contains the null string) or A^+ (all strings have length greater than zero).

VOLATILE STORAGE. A storage device whose contents are lost when power is removed. Compare with *nonvolatile storage*.

WEIGHT-BALANCED TREE. A binary tree in which the balanced state is determined by the number of nodes in the left and the right subtrees of each node. Compare with *height-balanced tree*.

WINCHESTER DISK. A form of magnetic disk storage in which the recording surfaces, access mechanism, and read/write heads are manufactured together and packaged in a sealed cartridge.

WORK FILE. A temporary file.

Answers to Selected Review Exercises

1. Measurement, collection, transcription, validation, organization, storage, aggregation, update, retrieval, protection

Most expensive: collection and transcription, because this is where human labor commonly is used extensively

2. 1, 10, 2, –6, 0, and so forth

3. True, false

4. (a) False, (b) false, (c) true, (d) true, (e) true, (f) true, (g) false, (h) false, (i) true, (j) true, (i) false

5. (a) 5, (b) 6, (c) 'MAGICPIE', (d) 'EEL', (e) 'MAGPIE', (f) 'MAG WHEEL', (g) 'PIE', (h) 'PIE', (i) 'PILE', (j) 'MIC', (k) 'EELPIE'

6. –7 = 100, –6 = 1001, –5 = 1010, –4 = 1011, –3 = 1100, –2 = 1101, –1 = 1110, +0 = 0000, +1 = 0001, +2 = 0010, +3 = 0011, +4 = 0100, +5 = 0101, +6 = 0110, +7 = 0111

7. (a) 21, (b) 201

8. (a) 32 (R = 2^5), (b) 256 (R = 2^8)

9. N

10. N

11. (a) +16, –15, (b) +128, –127, (c) 2^{N-1}, $-(2^{N-2}-1)$

12. (a) +15, –15, (b) +127, –127, (c) $2^{N-1}-1$, $-(2^{N-1}-1)$

19. MAGPIEPIEMAGENTA ; MAGPIEMAGENTA ; MAGPIEξPIEξMAGENTAξ

PTR1S PTR2S PTR3S   PTR1S PTR2S PTR3S   PTR1S PTR2S PTR3S

20. Overlaying strings conserves storage but can greatly complicate processing when the values of string variables are changed.

21. Packing strings conserves storage but complicates processing when the values of string variables are modified.

22. (A) and (B) both allow overlaying of strings; (C) does not. (C) requires a smaller table than does (A) or (B). (A) and (B) both require some processing to find the end of a string.

Chapter 2.

1. 70

3. $(B-A+1)*(D-C+1)$

4. $N; 3(N+1)$

5. 16

6. (a) 1911; (b) 8578

7. $B+318*S$

9. (a) $(B-A+1)*(D-C+1)*(F-E+1)$, (b) correct answer depends upon the order of linearization of the three dimensions.

10. 3

11. 1200

Chapter 3.

1. The elements of an array must be of the same type, while the elements of a record can be of different types. Yes. Yes.

2. To be able to refer to and manipulate the component fields.

3. The first program apparently has no need to refer to the component fields of phoneno while the second program does.

4. FORTRAN does not have a facility for explicit declaration of record structures; these are important in file processing, which is ubiquitous in business data processing.

5. The COBOL SYNC feature insulates the programmer somewhat from physical implementation details, thereby improving program maintainability. However, other programming languages (such as Pascal, PL/I) do not have a SYNC feature, making brute-force padding or no padding the only alternatives. Padding improves execution times but increases space requirements. Padding increases program development times.

Chapter 4.

2. (a) Error condition; (b) i; (c) undefined or null; (d) i; (e) 0

3. (a) True; (b) false; (c) error condition

4. i

5. S

12. (a) $AB*CD+\text{-}EF\text{—}FHI\uparrow/+$; (b) $BC*CDF\uparrow/+G+$; (c) $AB\uparrow C*D\text{-}EF/GH+/+$

Chapter 5.

2. Rear, front

3. So that the storage space can be utilized more fully

4. No

5. Draw a picture, carefully label the queue slots, and hand-simulate the algorithm.

6. When slots are numbered starting at 0

7. The test is determined by the way that you establish and manage the pointers.

Chapter 6.

1. FIRST = 2
   AVAIL = 3

	INFO	NEXT
1	PEACH	0
2	APPLE	4
3		0
4	CHERRY	5
5	GRAPE	1

2. FIRST = 4
   AVAIL = 7

	DATA	NEXT
1	G	3
2	D	5
3	J	0
4	B	2
5	E	6
6	F	1
7		8
8		9
9		0

3. FIRST = 8
   AVAIL = 0

	DATA	NEXT
1	G	3
2	D	5
3	J	9
4	B	7
5	E	6
6	F	1
7	C	2
8	A	4
9	Z	0

6. *P*

11. At least 2

Chapter 7.

2. (a) .. 01; (b) 3.45; (c) key(*i*)   prob(*i*)   (d) 2.35

key(*i*)	prob(*i*)
12	.32
2	.26
10	.21
4	.15
8	.05

6. If it does not, space is required for $2*n$ entries instead of n.

Chapter 8.

1. Yes;

2. No

6. No, by definition of equivalence.

7. 2^I

8. 2^I for $I < K-1$ and a maximum of 2^I for $I = K-1$

9. Impossible;   ; 4; 10

10. Nodes in a binary tree have a fixed number of subtrees, whereas nodes in a general tree may have widely varying numbers of subtrees.

11. (a) A B D G L P E H M Q I C F J K N O; (b) P L G D Q M H I E B J N O K F C A; (c) P L G D B H Q M E I A C J F N K O

12. True

13.

14.

15.

16.

/*+ABC−DE; AB+C*DE−/; A+B*C/D−E

17.

18.

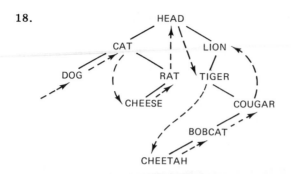

20. LEFT RIGHT INFO IN-ORDER THREAD POST-ORDER THREAD

21. No; usually only one traversal order is appropriate for the type of data stored in the tree.

Chapter 9.

1. Keep inserting the "middle" name next.

3. In-order

5. Balanced tree: left and right subtrees have equal *numbers* of nodes; height-balanced tree: left and right subtrees have nearly equal maximum path lengths.

Chapter 10.

3. There are no advantages to applying the binary search technique to a linked list of data.

4. The $\sigma(n \log_2 n)$ sorts repeatedly reduce (by approximately one-half) the number of keys remaining to be compared with each other, while the $\sigma(n_2)$ sorts do not repeatedly partition the keys into sublists.

14. See answer to question 4.

Chapter 11.

1. Binary search tree allows a maximum of two-way branching; m-way search tree allows a maximum of m-way branching.

2. True

3. B-tree

4. 15 key values; 16 pointers to subtrees, 15 pointers to records (1 per key value) if the tree is an index

5. 1 key value; 1 pointer to a subtree if the node is not a leaf, 1 pointer to a record if the tree is an index

6. 121 nodes; 242 key values

7. 512 nodes; 1023 key values

8. $\lceil \log_3 242 \rceil = 5; \lceil \log_3 1023 \rceil = 7$

9. $\lceil \log_4 242 \rceil = 4; \lceil \log_4 1023 \rceil = 5$

10. 15 key values; 16 pointers to subtrees, 15 pointers to records (1 per key value) if the tree is an index

11. 7 key values; 8 pointers to subtrees if the node is not a leaf, 7 pointers to records (1 per key value) if the tree is an index

12. 0.143

13. See answer to question 8

14. $\sigma(\log_8 \dfrac{n+1}{2})$

Chapter 12.

1. A B*-tree is a B-tree in which each node is at least two-thirds full instead of at least half full. The insertion and deletion algorithms differ.

2. In a B^+-tree the leaves are linked together to form a sequence set; interior nodes exist only for purposes of indexing the sequence set (not to index into data records). The insertion and deletion algorithms differ slightly.

3. Search through a B-tree is based on key values, while search through a trie is based on representations of key values.

4. The order of the tree (How many ways of branching?)

5. The distribution of key values

6. A B^+-tree is by definition in balance

7. A trie cannot be balanced without control of the key–value distribution.

8. When sequential access to the key values is never required

9. When both sequential and direct access to the key values are required

10. When rapid unsuccessful searches are important

11. (a) 10, 15, 30, 50, 58, 75, 80, 100

12. Ten pointers per node; four levels

Chapter 13.

1. (a) sum $graph(j,i)$ varying j from 1 to N; (b) sum $graph(i,j)$ varying j from 1 to N.

Chapter 14.

1. size, selective access requirements, data independence

2. A variety of file structuring requirements must be satisfied.

Chapter 15.

1. (a) 011010; (b) 100101

2. Users have a variety of storage needs; higher-cost devices tend to be faster than lower-cost devices; some devices support only serial access while others support direct access.

3. (a) 144,000 records; (b) 288,000 records

4. (a) 360 seconds; (b) 336 seconds

5. Seek time (arm movement time) is zero for a fixed-head disk, which has one head per track and therefore always has an access head positioned at the requested track. Seek time is greater than zero for a movable-head disk.

6. *b*

7. *c*

Chapter 16.

1. To eliminate erroneous records as early as possible in the process; to reduce the sort volume

2. Processing control might be simplified if the transaction file were stored on disk; thus the master files would always be on tape. This run's updated master is next run's old master.

3. 40%

4. High rate of data change, high file activity ratio, and high urgency for current data suggest frequent file update. Large size suggests infrequent update. Frequent update increases processing costs but improves data quality.

5. Probability of need to access old data for recovery purposes and historic reporting requirements should be considered

6. Sort the transaction file first!

Chapter 17.

1. Yes

2. (a) 0; (b) 1; (c) n; (d) 1; (e) output; (f) flag = 0 if the buffer is empty, = 1 otherwise; (g) 1

3. Anticipatory buffering can reduce program wait times caused by I/O requests.

4. Code generated by the compiler for a READ does not have to check if this is the first READ.

5. Buffer space allocated to the file may be freed prior to run-unit termination.

Chapter 18.

1. Tournament sort generates long runs relative to the amount of main memory space that it uses.

2. Number of copies reflects I/O requirements, while number of comparisons reflects CPU requirements. In most file sorting environments, I/O activity is "more expensive" than is CPU activity.

Chapter 19.

7. Division-remainder

8. 75% to 80%

11. (a) to calculate an address for a record with a given key value; (b) to resolve a collision; (c) to resolve a collision; (d) to improve access times to synonyms

Chapter 20.

1. (a) Both sequential; (b) customer ID number or name

2. (a) Relative (the weekly summary report could be generated from a sequential file derived from sorting the relative file) or indexed sequential; (b) product number

3. (a) Sequential (it's stored on a tape cassette); (b) records will be on the file sequentially by time of customer checkout; each record would include the keys of the pertinent menu selections.

4. (a) Relative; (b) patient identifier

5. (a) (a) – (d); (b) (e) – (h)

6. Sequential access to the keys of a B-tree is much slower than is sequential access to the keys of a B^+-tree, since the latter are linked in sequential order by definition.

APPENDIX:

Meta-language for COBOL

The following notation is used in the description of the syntax of COBOL-language statements:

Required reserved words are upper-case and underscored, e.g. READ

Optional reserved words are upper-case, e.g., RECORD

Programmer-supplied data-names are lower-case, e.g. filename

Optional phrases are enclosed in square-brackets, e.g.

[AT END imperative-statement]

Select at least one alternative of phrase choices that are given in curly braces, e.g.

SORT filename ON $\left\{ \begin{array}{l} \underline{ASCENDING} \\ \underline{DESCENDING} \end{array} \right\}$ KEY dataname1 [,dataname2]. . .

Repeat the phrase preceded by ellipses (. . .) zero or more times (e.g. see above).

Index

N

O

P